Sentences, Paragraphs, and Beyond

With Integrated Readings

Sixth Edition

Lee Brandon

Mt. San Antonio College

Kelly Brandon

Santa Ana College

WADSWORTH
CENGAGE Learning·

Australia · Brazil · Japan · Korea · Mexico · Singapore · Spain · United Kingdom · United States

WADSWORTH
CENGAGE Learning™

To Sharon

*Sentences, Paragraphs, and Beyond with
Integrated Readings, Sixth Edition*
Lee Brandon, Kelly Brandon

Senior Publisher: Lyn Uhl

Director of Developmental English:
Annie Todd

Development Editor: Karen Mauk

Associate Editor: Janine Tangney

Editorial Assistant: Melanie Opacki

Media Editor: Emily Ryan

Senior Marketing Manager: Kirsten Stoller

Marketing Coordinator: Ryan Ahern

Marketing Communications Manager:
Martha Pfeiffer

Senior Content Project Manager:
Margaret Park Bridges

Art Director: Jill Ort

Print Buyer: Sue Spencer

Senior Rights Acquisition Account Manager,
Text: Katie Huha

Text Permissions Editor:
Mary Dalton-Hoffman

Production Service: Books By Design, Inc.

Text Designer: Books By Design, Inc.

Photo Manager: John Hill

Cover Designer: Jill Ort

Cover Image: © Steve Chorney

Compositor: S4Carlisle Publishing Services

For product information and technology assistance, contact us at
**Cengage Learning Customer & Sales Support,
1-800-354-9706**

For permission to use material from this text or product, submit all requests online at **www.cengage.com/permissions**.
Further permissions questions can be e-mailed to
permissionrequest@cengage.com.

Library of Congress Control Number: 2009928731

Student Edition:
ISBN-13: 978-0-495-80213-6
ISBN-10: 0-495-80213-1

Wadsworth
20 Channel Center Street
Boston, MA 02210
USA

Cengage Learning is a leading provider of customized learning solutions with office locations around the globe, including Singapore, the United Kingdom, Australia, Mexico, Brazil, and Japan. Locate your local office at **international.cengage.com/region**

Cengage Learning products are represented in Canada by Nelson Education, Ltd.

For your course and learning solutions, visit **www.cengage.com**.

Purchase any of our products at your local college store or at our preferred online store **www.ichapters.com**.

Printed in the United States of America
1 2 3 4 5 6 7   13 12 11 10 09

Contents

Part IV WRITING PARAGRAPHS AND ESSAYS: INSTRUCTION, WITH INTEGRATED READING SELECTIONS 303

WRITER'S GUIDELINES   332

Chapter 19   Exemplification: Using Examples   335

 WRITER'S GUIDELINES   357

Chapter 20   Analysis by Division: Examining the Parts   359

WRITER'S GUIDELINES   387

Chapter 21   Process Analysis: Writing About Doing   388

WRITER'S GUIDELINES   436

Chapter 23   Comparison and Contrast: Showing Similarities and Differences   438

WRITER'S GUIDELINES   459

Chapter 24   Argument: Writing to Persuade   461

Thematic Contents

Preface

In this, the sixth edition of *Sentences, Paragraphs, and Beyond*, the surf writer, gallantly perched on a pencil, once more celebrates the "flow of writing." Like waves at a beach, writing is cyclical, moving forward and backward and forward again. The surf writer will always be searching for the "perfect wave," meaning the best possible expression. The recursive movement of writing and rewriting is the essence of good writing. Instruction in this book—comprehensive, flexible, relevant, and stimulating—is predicated on that systematic, relentless revision.

The Parts of a Flexible, Comprehensive Package of Instruction, Enhanced with Optional Reading-Based Writing

Written especially for English writing courses one or two levels below freshman composition, *Sentences, Paragraphs, and Beyond*, Sixth Edition, contains highly accessible writing instruction that will enable students to learn chiefly by the contemplation of good examples and by practice of established techniques. Each of twelve chapters on sentence writing offers writing along with exercises and begins and ends with attention to the microtheme, a brief self-administered writing activity that gauges skills before and after learning. Moreover, the Writing Process Worksheet, the Self-Evaluation Chart, annotated student demonstrations, and abundant topics and detailed prompts (reading-based, general, cross-curricular, and career-related) will support and guide the inexperienced writer from the foundation to the edifice of effective writing. While students master and polish their basic writing skills, other specific features, such as plentiful third-person exemplary reading selections and reading-based writing assignments, will help them transition into advanced courses where objective writing and writing about reading material are customary.

Here is a layout of the particulars.

Part I Reading Leading to Writing

- Reading techniques: underlining, annotating, outlining, taking notes
- Reading-based writing: summary, reaction, two-part response
- Giving credit for ideas and quotations: basic documentation
- Demonstrations, exercises, assignments

Part II   Writing Sentences

- Microthemes for before and after each chapter instruction; a self-administered diagnosis
- Sentence elements
- Sentence patterns
- Sentence combining
- Sentence rhetoric
- Diction
- Punctuation
- Spelling and phrasing
- ESL instruction

Part III   Using the Writing Process

- Stages of writing: exploring, organizing, writing
- Revising and editing
- Paragraphs and essays
- Demonstrations, exercises, assignments

Part IV   Connecting Reading and Writing: Instruction, with Integrated Readings

- Forms of discourse: descriptive narration, exemplification, analysis by division, process analysis, cause and effect, comparison and contrast, argument; with recognition that a single form often provides structure for paragraphs and essays but almost never occurs without the presence of other forms
- Forms of discourse adapted for career-related writing, with instruction and examples for the more career-minded students; for example, descriptive narration as incident report, analysis by division as vocational quest, process analysis as workplace process (how-to-do-it), comparison and contrast as face-off evaluation, and argument as business proposal
- Chapters 18 through 24 with identical formats: functional cartoon, writing instruction, an exercise in finding patterns in photos, two exercises in practicing patterns, model paragraphs and essays by student and professional writers, a student example of writing in stages, a student example of reading-based writing, a student example of career-related writing (in five chapters), writing prompts and topics (reading-based, general, cross-curricular, career-related), and a chapter summary

READING-BASED WRITING FOR DEVELOPMENTAL ENGLISH

Along with thorough instruction in basic writing skills and the writing process, Brandon books offer another dimension: reading-based writing. As a natural progression of linking reading and writing, reading-based writing moves students beyond the personal narratives to more analytical expression as they write about what they read. Reading-based writing provides substance for compositions and promotes critical thinking. Students engaged in reading-based writing will be able to transition more smoothly through developmental English and into freshman English composition, and to function better in courses across the curriculum.

READING-BASED WRITING DEFINED

The typical reading-based writing assignments in *Sentences, Paragraphs, and Beyond* require students to read a source, write an analytical reply, and give credit to the originator(s) for borrowed words and ideas. Credit can be noted formally (MLA **with 2009 Update** style in the Brandon books) or informally, depending on the instructor's preference. Specific assignments in reading-based writing are the summary, the reaction (paragraph or essay), and the two-part response (with separated summary and reaction used to teach students the difference between the two). Although the reaction can, and often does, include personal experience and reflect individual perspectives, analytical and interpretive discussion should be at the center of the writing. The reaction can also incorporate summary to convey a broad aspect of the text, but summary is never the main concern of the reaction.

READING-BASED WRITING IN THE SYLLABUS

Depending on their objectives and student needs, instructors assigning reading-based writing will determine the extent of its use: (1) beginning with personal experience assignments and phasing in reading-based writing during the course; (2) interspersing reading-based writing assignments with other writing assignments; (3) working with the summary, the reaction (a critique), and the two-part response as one of several units of instruction; or (4) using reading-based writing throughout the semester. Many instructors have found that a summary works well as a diagnostic writing test at the beginning of the semester, and an in-class reading-based essay, with a brief outline annotated with a few quotes brought to class, works well for the final exam. Annotated student examples of the three different kinds of reading-based writing appear throughout Brandon books.

Some Brandon Time-Tested Techniques

For the Student Companion Site, go to www.cengage .com/devenglish/brandon/ spb6e.

- The Writing Process Worksheet is available for students to print out from the Student Companion Site. Instructors can customize it on the Instructor Companion Site and print it out or post it online for students. This worksheet (page 6) guides students through the recursive stages of writing from Exploring to Organizing to Writing, with emphasis on rewriting.
- Each of Chapters 18 through 24 includes a student paragraph and a student essay, one of which is presented with all stages of writing in the Writing Process Worksheet form, explicitly answering the familiar student question: "How does a student like me do this assignment?"
- The six major parts of revision are represented by the acronym **CLUESS**: **C**oherence, **L**anguage, **U**nity, **E**mphasis, **S**upport, and **S**entences. Inexperienced writers can easily latch onto that memory device and use it as a checklist for revision.
- Another acronym—**COPS**: **C**apitalization, **O**missions, **P**unctuation, and **S**pelling—provides a similar aid for editing.
- As students move through the course, they can track their progress and become more self-sufficient by using the Self-Evaluation Chart on the inside front cover.
- Another feature that directs students toward text is "Finding Patterns in Photos," which immediately follows the writing instruction in each of

Chapters 18 through 24. Written for either individual or group work, this exercise provides students with an opportunity to sharpen their critical-thinking skills as they match chapter patterns with photo content and is especially good for spirited group discussions and follow-up writing assignments.

Other Features in *Sentences, Paragraphs, and Beyond,* Sixth Edition

- For the more career-minded or career-engaged students, instruction with examples of patterns of writing used at the workplace: incident report, vocational quest, workplace process (how-to-do-it), face-off evaluation, business proposal
- A focusing device for critical reading called "Mindset: Lock It In"
- The Microtheme, a brief self-administered writing activity to gauge learning of specific skills, in Chapters 2 through 12
- An alternative Thematic Contents for readings
- Nineteen readings new to this edition
- Forty-six readings with cultural and gender balance
- A restaurant review as a model form of analysis by division
- Seven cartoons that amuse while demonstrating patterns of thought
- More writing topics than any other textbook on the market, including an abundance of reading-based writing topics phrased as prompts, and additional writing topics and prompts grouped as general, cross-curricular, and career-related
- An ESL unit in the text and extensive online practice exercises available to be assigned selectively by the instructor from comprehensive ESL instruction on *WriteSpace*
- Full-color design

INSTRUCTIONAL SUPPORT

The Annotated Instructor's Edition (AIE) contains immediate answers and teaching tips for exercises and activities.

The Instructor's Guide is now located on the Instructor Companion Site at www .cengage.com/devenglish/brandon/spb6e. You can either download the material for photocopying or obtain a hard-copy text booklet by contacting Cengage Learning, Higher Education, at 800-354-9706.

The Instructor's Guide on the Instructor Companion Site includes the following:

- Tips for new instructors on ways to use the text
- Sample syllabi (one annotated, the other direct), with suggestions for adaptations for different pedagogies and course lengths
- List of readings that are especially effective for reading-based writing
- Reproducible sentence-writing quizzes from the chapters on sentence writing
- Reproducible quizzes on longer readings
- Instructions for ordering a printed quiz booklet from Cengage Learning, Higher Education, ideal for photocopying
- Suggestions for effective and time-saving approaches to instruction
- PowerPoint slides that can be downloaded and used to enhance classroom instruction
- Suggestions for ESL instruction
- Suggestions for teaching basic writers
- The Student's Answer Key

Answers to about half of the handbook exercises are now on the Instructor Companion Site. The instructor can make these answers available to students by printing them out or by posting them on the instructor's school web page. Instructors who do not post or distribute answers will now have almost twice as much uncorrected sentence writing exercise material for class discussion as was in the first through the fifth editions.

WEBSITE RESOURCES FOR STUDENTS

Sentences, Paragraphs, and Beyond, Sixth Edition, offers students additional opportunities to explore writing through the Student Companion Website at www .cengage.com/devenglish/brandon/spb6e. Features include the following

- A printable copy of the Writing Process Worksheet
- Interactive quizzes in sentence writing
- Interactive quizzes in the writing process
- Interactive quizzes in writing with patterns
- Interactive quizzes in reading-based writing
- A brief guide to APA style
- Additional instruction in writing letters of recommendation and résumés
- Instructions in taking tests

WriteSpace is a flexible, interactive, and customizable program that assesses students of English at all skill levels. *WriteSpace* motivates and assists students with varying skill levels by providing tutorial support. *WriteSpace* includes (1) diagnostic skills assessments in writing and grammar skills with test results linked to individualized concept reviews and study paths for self-remediation, helping motivate and prepare students for coursework; (2) *Exercises and Writing Modules* (tutorials) that give students additional practice beyond the classroom; (3) *Associated Press Interactives & NewsNow* that allow you to incorporate current events, critical thinking, and visual literacy into your course; (4) *Plagiarism Prevention Zone* that helps you keep plagiarism problems to a minimum; (5) *Online Tutoring*; (6) an *Online Handbook;* and (7) a *Gradebook.*

Acknowledgments

We are profoundly indebted to the many instructors who have reviewed *Sentences, Paragraphs, and Beyond* and helped it grow and remain fresh and innovative over the years. Here are a few of those thoughtful and imaginative reviewers: Kathryn Beckwith, Arizona State University; John Bell, New York City Technical College; Christena T. Biggs, DePauw University; Wendy Bishop, Florida State University; Marilyn Black, Middlesex Community College; Betty Bluman, Community College of Allegheny; Curtis Bobbit, University of Great Falls; Marlene Bosanko, Tacoma Community College; Elizabeth Breen, Pierce College; Deborah Burson-Smith, Southern University–A&M; Elizabeth Clark, Red Rocks Community College, Lakewood; Janet Cutshall, Sussex County Community College; Sarah Dangelantonio, Franklin Pierce University; Scott Earle, Tacoma Community College; Eddye Gallagher, Tarrant County Junior College; Nicole Greene, University of Southwestern Louisiana; Jacob Haeberle, Idaho State University; Roslyn J. Harper, Trident Technical College; Carolyn G. Hartnett, College of the Mainland; Bradley S.

Hayden, Western Michigan University; Grady Hinton Jr., St. Louis Community College, Forest Park; Wayne P. Hubert, Chaffey Community College; Anna Jo Johnson, Community College of Western Kentucky University; James C. McDonald, University of Southwestern Louisiana; Tracy A. Peyton, Pensacola Junior College; Margie Lee Pigg, Martin Methodist College; James Rice, Quinsigamond Community College; Atheme Sallee, Forsyth Technical Community College; Susan Schiller, University of California–Davis; Ann Shackleford, Bacone College; Ken Tangvik, Roxbury Community College; and David White, Walters State Community College. Thanks also to the English departments at Mt. San Antonio College and Santa Ana College.

We also deeply appreciate the expert, dedicated work of freelance editors Karen Mauk, Mary Dalton-Hoffman, Robin Hogan, and Nancy Benjamin, and our colleagues at Cengage Learning: Annie Todd, Kirsten Stoller, Margaret Bridges, Rick Nicotera, Martha Pfeiffer, Katie Huha, Janine Tangney, and Melanie Opacki.

We are especially grateful to our family members for their cheerful, inspiring support: Sharon, Erin, Michael, Kathy, Shane, Lauren, Jarrett, Matthew, Jessica, and Deborah.

Lee Brandon and Kelly Brandon

Student Overview

The Flow of Writing: Icon and Theme

You will see this icon frequently in *Sentences, Paragraphs, and Beyond*:

Follow the line from top left over the waves, then down and around to the pencil with the little surf writer getting ready to hang ten.

Like the surf writer, you follow that pattern in writing, the pattern of the tide near the shore. In flowing cycles, the tide advances and withdraws, then regroups and proceeds again. The tide does not merely rush forward at one time and be done with it. Writing also has a repetitive, rhythmic flow. You do not just write your message and walk away. Instead, you write—and, for revision and editing—back up, and rewrite, following that pattern until you are through. In writing, the back-and-forth movement is called *recursive*. It is the essence of the writing process.

In the coming pages, the icon will identify features that enable your own flow of writing and remind you of the importance of rewriting.

Sentences, Paragraphs, and Beyond shows how to proceed from fragmented ideas to effective expression by blending instruction, examples, and practice. Like the surf writer going back again and again in quest of that perfect wave, you as a writer will go back again and again looking for that best possible composition.

Writing effectively is not as difficult as you may think. You can learn to be a good writer if you practice effective techniques. The operative words are the last three: "practice effective techniques." A good piece of written material includes clear organization, solid content, and good use of language skills. You should have something to say, present it in appropriate order, and write correctly. All of those points will be covered in the four main parts of this book: Connecting Reading with Writing, Writing Sentences, Using the Writing Process, and Writing Paragraphs and Essays: Instruction with Integrated Reading Selections.

Part I: Connecting Reading with Writing

Much of your college writing will be related to what you read. Reading is a principal way of learning, and writing is a principal way of using learned information, especially in college. If you do not get the reading right, you will not get the writing right. If you cannot read well, your learning will be restricted, and if you cannot write well, you may not be able to show others what you really know and receive deserved credit. This part links techniques of effective reading and effective writing. Expect to sharpen your skills in reading comprehension as you study how to underline, annotate, outline, and take notes. Then link that comprehension to written expression by composing outlines, summaries, evaluations, and reactions.

Part II: Writing Sentences

The second part, Writing Sentences, concentrates on effectiveness. Beginning with the simplest aspects of sentences, namely parts of speech, the text moves to the larger word units of clauses and sentences, with their numerous patterns. It shows you the difference between complete sentences and incomplete sentences, between sound and unsound arrangements of words, and between correct and incorrect punctuation. While giving you the opportunity to experiment and develop your own style, it leads you through the problem areas of verbs, pronouns, and modifiers. If you are not sure when to use *lie* and when to use *lay*, when to use *who* and when to use *whom*, or when to use *good* and when to use *well*, this book can help you. If you are not sure whether the standard expression is *between you and I* or *between you and me*, or if you are not sure about the difference between a colon and a semicolon, you will find the answers here. That line of *if* statements could be applied to almost every page in this book. Perhaps you are not sure of the correct answer to most of these questions. The good news is that by the end of the course, you will be sure—and if your "sure" is still a bit shaky, then you will know where to find the rules, examples, and discussion in this book.

The text in Part II follows a pattern: principles, examples, exercises, and writing activity. Again, you learn by practicing sound principles.

Part III: Using the Writing Process

The third part, Using the Writing Process, presents writing as a process, not as something that is supposed to emerge complete on demand. Writing begins with a topic, either generated or provided, and moves through stages of exploration, organization, development, revision, and editing. If you have suffered, at least at times, from writer's block, this book is for you. If you have sometimes produced material that was organized poorly so that you did not receive full credit for what you knew, then this book is for you. If you have sometimes had ideas, but you did not fully develop them, so your work was judged as "sketchy" or "lacking in content," then this book is for you.

Part IV: Writing Paragraphs and Essays: Instruction, with Integrated Reading Selections

Individual chapters in Part IV feature forms of writing that are commonly used in college assignments: descriptive narration, exemplification, analysis by division, process analysis, cause and effect, comparison and contrast, and argument. The writing instruction includes integrated reading selections by professional and student authors, cartoons, photographs, exercises, and suggested topics. Reading-based writing offers you an opportunity to polish your critical-thinking skills as you compose responses to what you read, much as you do in classes across the curriculum.

Strategies for Self-Improvement

Here are some strategies you can follow to make the best use of this book and to jump-start the improvement in your writing skills.

1. *Be active and systematic in learning.* Take advantage of your instructor's expertise by being an active class member—one who takes notes, asks questions, and contributes to discussion. Become dedicated to systematic learning: Determine your needs, decide what to do, and do it. Make learning a part of your everyday thinking and behavior.

2. *Read carefully.* Underlining and annotating will help you focus for immediate understanding and prepare you for quizzes, discussion, and reading-based writing assignments.

3. *Read widely.* Samuel Johnson, a great English scholar, once said he did not want to read anything by people who had written more than they had read. William Faulkner, a Nobel Prize winner in literature, said, "Read, read, read. Read everything—trash, classics, good and bad, and see how writers do it." Read to learn technique, to acquire ideas, and to be stimulated to write. Especially read to satisfy your curiosity and to receive pleasure.

4. *Keep a journal.* Keep a journal, even though it may not be required in your particular class. It is a good practice to jot down your observations in a notebook. Here are some topics for daily, or almost daily, journal writing:

   • Summarize, evaluate, or react to reading assignments.
   • Summarize, evaluate, or react to what you see on television and in movies and what you read in newspapers and in magazines.

- Describe and narrate situations or events you experience.
- Write about career-related matters you encounter in other courses or on the job.

Your journal entries may read like an intellectual diary, a record of what you are thinking about at certain times. Keeping a journal will help you to understand reading material better, to develop more language skills, and to think more clearly—as well as to become more confident and to write more easily so that writing becomes a comfortable, everyday activity. Your entries may also provide subject material for longer, more carefully crafted pieces. The most important thing is to get into the habit of writing something each day.

5. *Evaluate your writing skills.* Use the Self-Evaluation Chart on the inside front cover of this book to assess your writing skills by listing problem areas you need to work on. You may be adding to these lists throughout the entire term. Drawing on your instructor's comments, make notes on matters such as organization, development, content, spelling, vocabulary, diction, grammar, sentence structure, punctuation, and capitalization. Use this chart for self-motivated study assignments and as a checklist in all stages of writing. As you master each problem area, you can erase it or cross it out.

Most of the elements you record in your Self-Evaluation Chart probably are covered in *Sentences, Paragraphs, and Beyond.* The table of contents, the index, and the Correction Chart on the inside cover of this book will direct you to the additional instruction you decide you need.

- *Organization/Development/Content*: List aspects of your writing, including the techniques of all stages of the writing process, such as freewriting, brainstorming, and clustering; the phrasing of a good topic sentence or thesis; and the design, growth, and refinement of your ideas.
- *Spelling/Vocabulary/Diction*: List common words marked as incorrectly spelled on your college assignments. Here, *common* means words that you use often. If you are misspelling these words now, you may have been doing so for years. Look at your list. Is there a pattern to your misspellings? Consult Chapter 12 for a set of useful rules. Whatever it takes, master the words on your list. Continue to add troublesome words as you accumulate assignments. If your vocabulary is imprecise or your diction is inappropriate (if you use slang, trite expressions, or words that are too informal), note those problems as well.
- *Grammar/Sentence Structure*: List recurring problems in your grammar or sentence structure. Use the symbols and page references listed on the Correction Chart (inside cover of this book) or look up the problem in the index.
- *Punctuation/Capitalization*: Treat these problems the same way you treat grammar problems. Note that the punctuation and capitalization section in Chapter 11 numbers some rules; therefore, you can often give exact locations of the remedies for your problems.

Here is an example of how you might use your chart.

Self-Evaluation Chart

Organization/ Development/ Content	Spelling/ Vocabulary/ Diction	Grammar/ Sentence Structure	Punctuation/ Capitalization
needs more specific support such as examples, 336	avoid slang, 287	fragments, 95	difference between semicolons and commas, 219
refine outline, 279	avoid clichés such as "be there for me," 287	subject-verb agreement, 135	comma after long introductory modifier, 211, #22
use clear topic sentence, 276	it's, its, 250	comma splice, 108	comma in compound sentence, 72, #1
	you're, your, 251	vary sentence patterns, 87	
	receive, rule on, 250		

6. *Use the Writing Process Worksheet.* Record details about each of your assignments, such as the due date, topic, length, and form. The worksheet will also remind you of the stages of the writing process: explore, organize, and write. A blank Writing Process Worksheet for you to photocopy for assignments appears on page 6. Discussed in Chapter 16, it illustrates student work in Chapters 18–24. Your instructor may ask you to complete the form and submit it with your assignments.

STUDENT COMPANION SITE *For additional practice, visit www.cengage .com/devenglish/ brandon/spb6e.*

7. *Take full advantage of the Student Companion Site and other technology.* Using a computer will enable you to write, revise, and edit more swiftly as you move, alter, check, and delete material with a few keystrokes. The Student Companion Site offers additional exercises and instruction. Many colleges have writing labs with good instruction and facilities for networking and researching complicated topics. The Internet, used wisely, can provide resource material for compositions.

8. *Be positive.* To improve your English skills, write with freedom, but revise and edit with rigor. Work with your instructor to set attainable goals, and proceed at a reasonable pace. Soon, seeing what you have mastered and checked off your list will give you a sense of accomplishment.

Finally, do not compare yourself with others. Compare yourself before your learning experiences with yourself after your learning experiences, and, as you improve, consider what you are—a student on the path toward more effective writing, a student on the path toward success.

Writing Process Worksheet

Name _____ **Title** _____ **Due Date** _____

Use the back of this page or separate paper if you need more space.

Assignment In the space below, write whatever you need to know about your assignment, including information about the topic, audience, pattern of writing, length, whether to include a rough draft or revised drafts, and whether your paper must be typed.

Stage One **Explore** Freewrite, brainstorm (list), cluster, or take notes as directed by your instructor.

Stage Two **Organize** Write a topic sentence or thesis; label the subject and focus parts.

Write an outline or an outline alternative. For reading-based writing, include quotations and references with page numbers as support in the outline.

Stage Three **Write** On separate paper, write and then revise your paragraph or essay as many times as necessary for **c**oherence, **l**anguage (usage, tone, and diction), **u**nity, **e**mphasis, **s**upport, and **s**entences (**CLUESS**). Read your work aloud to hear and correct any grammatical errors or awkward-sounding sentences.

Edit any problems in fundamentals, such as **c**apitalization, **o**missions, **p**unctuation, and **s**pelling (**COPS**).

Part I

CONNECTING READING WITH WRITING

....

Reading and writing are joined without seam. Reading activates your memory and provides you with substance for writing. Writing helps you examine your ideas and clarify what you have read. Reading and writing often blend as reading-based writing and together are the essence of critical thinking.

Chapter 1

From Reading to Writing

FLOW OF WRITING

Reading-Based Writing

THE WRITING COMPONENT

Reading-based writing was invented to help you easily fill those intimidating blank pages with thoughtful statements centered around what you have read, commonly called the *source*, or *text*. *Text* is a broad term that includes items as diverse as photos, advertisements, online postings, and movies as sources for what is called *text-based writing*, but in this book we are concerned with writing about reading, naturally called *reading-based writing*. For instruction in this book, reading-based writing comes in three forms: summary, reaction, and two-part response. In writing a summary, you use your own words to restate the main ideas in what you have read. In writing a reaction, you comment critically on what you have read, while giving credit for the ideas and words you borrow. Then, in composing a two-part response, you write both a summary and a reaction, but you separate them to show your instructors that you know the difference between the two forms.

THE READING COMPONENT

Reading-based writing can also make you a better reader. When you are reading, you concentrate more because you are thinking about how you will be using the reading content in writing. When you are writing, your mind reflects back on what you have read, running ideas critically by your windows of experiences and your banks of knowledge. Reading-based writing represents the complete *you* as a thinking, feeling person in relation to what you have read. In fact, reading-based writing is what we call the essence, or core, of critical thinking.

READING-BASED WRITING AND OTHER APPROACHES IN WRITING

Reading-based writing will serve you well in classrooms across your campus and also in your career. Of course, this book presents a range of writing approaches that may not make use of reading-based writing, including those called *personal experience*, *individual perspective*, *cross-curricular*, *career-related*, and *reading-related*. All of these approaches are presented in this book with instruction, examples, exercises, and suggested topics and prompts. Some approaches overlap, but each has a main thrust with variations imposed by particular writing objectives.

Reading Techniques and Reading-Based Writing Forms

Reading-based writing is presented in this introductory chapter because all writing instruction in this book involves reading in some way. The abundant student and professional readings (more than fifty) were selected to stimulate thought and discussion, to provide content for writing, and to inform writing by strong examples of techniques and forms. Even reading-based writing has its own different forms, and reading itself has its own techniques. Those techniques and forms are shown here in a concise outline of the instruction that covers the remainder of this chapter:

I. Reading techniques
   A. Underlining
   B. Annotating

      C. Outlining

      D. Taking notes

  II. Reading-based writing forms

      A. Summary

      B. Reaction

      C. Two-part response

Reading Techniques

UNDERLINING

One way to build concentration in reading is to develop a relationship with the reading material. Imagine you are reading a chapter of several pages, and you decide to underline and write in the margins. Immediately, the underlining takes you out of the passive, television-watching frame of mind. You are involved. You are participating. It is now necessary for you to discriminate, to distinguish more important from less important ideas. Perhaps you have thought of underlining as a method designed only to help you with reviewing. That is, when you study the material the next time, you will not have to reread all of the material; instead, you can review only the most important, underlined parts. However, even while you are underlining, you are benefiting from an imposed concentration, because this procedure forces you to think, to focus. Consider the following guidelines for underlining:

1. Underline the main ideas in paragraphs. The most important statement, the topic sentence, is likely to be at the beginning of the paragraph.

2. Underline the support for those main ideas.

3. Underline answers to questions that you bring to the reading assignment. These questions may have come from the end of the chapter, from subheadings that you turn into questions, or from your independent concern about the topic.

4. Underline only the key words. You would seldom underline all the words in a sentence and almost never a whole paragraph.

Does that fit your approach to underlining? Possibly not. Most students, in their enthusiasm to do a good job, overdo underlining.

Maybe you have had this experience: You start reading about something you have not encountered before. The idea seems important. You highlight it. The next idea is equally fresh and significant. You highlight it. A minute or two later, you have changed the color of the page from white to yellow, but you haven't accomplished anything.

The trick is how to figure out what to underline. You would seldom underline more than about 30 percent of a passage, although the amount would depend on your purpose and the nature of the material. Following the preceding four rules will be useful. Learning more about the principles of sentence, paragraph, and essay organization will also be helpful. These principles are presented in Chapters 2 through 17.

Consider this passage with effective underlining.

YOUTH AND THE COUNTERCULTURE

Main idea

1   Rock music helped tie this international subculture together. Rock grew out of the black music culture of rhythm and blues, which was flavored with country and western

Support   to make it more accessible to white teenagers. The mid-1950s signaled a break-

Support   through as Billy Hailey called on record buyers to "Rock Around the Clock" and Elvis

Support   Presley warned them to keep off his "Blue Suede Shoes." In the 1960s, the Beatles thrilled millions of young people, often to their parents' dismay. Like Elvis, the Beatles suggested personal and sexual freedom that many older people found disturbing.

Main idea

2   It was Bob Dylan, a young folksinger turned rock poet with an acoustic guitar, who best expressed the radical political as well as cultural aspirations of the

Support   "younger generation." In a song that became a rallying cry, Dylan sang that "the times they are a'changing." The song captured the spirit of growing alienation

Support   between the generation whose defining experiences had been the Great Depression and World War II and the generation ready to reject the complacency of the

Closing statement   1950s. Increasing discontent with middle-class conformity and the injustices of racism and imperialism fueled the young leaders of social protest and reflected a growing spirit of rebellion.

(John P. McKay et al., *A History of Western Society*)

EXERCISE 1   Underlining

Using the four rules of underlining on page 11, mark the following paragraphs.

THE LEADERSHIP OF MARTIN LUTHER KING JR.

1   On December 1, 1955, in Montgomery, Alabama, a black woman named Rosa Parks was arrested for refusing to give up her bus seat to a white man. In protest, Montgomery blacks organized a year-long bus boycott. The boycott forced white city leaders to recognize the blacks' determination and economic power.

2   One of the organizers of the bus boycott was a Baptist minister, the Reverend Martin Luther King Jr. King soon became a national leader in the growing civil rights movement. With stirring speeches and personal courage, he urged blacks to demand their rights. At the same time, he was completely committed to nonviolence. Like Gandhi, . . . he believed that justice could triumph through moral force.

3   In April 1963, King began a drive to end segregation in Birmingham, Alabama. He and his followers boycotted segregated businesses and held peaceful marches and demonstrations. Against them, the Birmingham police used electric cattle prods, attack dogs, clubs, and fire hoses to break up marches.

4   Television cameras brought those scenes into the living rooms of millions of Americans, who were shocked by what they saw. On May 10, Birmingham's city leaders gave in. A committee of blacks and whites oversaw the gradual desegregation of the city and tried to open more jobs for blacks. The victory was later marred by grief, however, when a bomb exploded at a Birmingham church, killing four black children.

(Steven L. Jantzen, *World History: Perspectives on the Past*)

ANNOTATING

Annotating, a practice related to underlining, is writing in the margins. You can do it independently, although it usually appears in conjunction with underlining to mark the understanding and to extend the involvement.

Writing in the margins represents intense involvement because it makes the reader a writer. If you read material and write something in the margin as a reaction to it, then in a way you have had a conversation with the author. The author has made a statement and you have responded. In fact, you may have added something to the text; therefore, for your purposes you have become a co-author or collaborator. The comments you make in the margin are of your own choosing according to your interests and the purpose you bring to the reading assignment. Your response in the margin may merely echo the author's ideas, it may question them critically, it may relate them to something else, or it may add to them.

In the following example, you can see how the reader has reinforced the underlining by commenting in the margin.

WOMEN AND WITCHCRAFT
Mary Beth Norton

Salem witchcraft— broad interest

1   The Salem witchcraft crisis of 1692 to 1693, in which a small number of adolescent girls and young women accused hundreds of older women (and a few men) of having bewitched them, has fascinated Americans ever since. It has provided material for innumerable books, plays, movies, and television productions. To twentieth-century Americans, the belief in witchcraft in the seventeenth-century colonies is difficult to explain or understand; perhaps that is why the Salem episode has attracted so much attention. For those interested in studying women's experiences, of course, witchcraft incidents are particularly intriguing. The vast majority of suspected witches were female, and so, too, were many of

Why mostly women?

their accusers. Although colonial women rarely played a role on the public stage, in witchcraft cases they were the primary actors. What accounts for their prominence under these peculiar circumstances?

Historical/cultural background

2   To answer that question, the Salem crisis must be placed into its proper historical and cultural context. People in the early modern world believed in witchcraft because it offered a rationale for events that otherwise seemed random and

Without modern science

unfathomable. In the absence of modern scientific knowledge about such natural phenomena as storms and diseases, and clear explanations for accidents of various sorts, the evil actions of a witch could provide a ready answer to a person or community inquiring about the causes of a disaster.

Witch hunts in Europe— the extent

3   Therefore, witchcraft accusations—and some large-scale "witch hunts"—were not uncommon in Europe between the early fourteenth and the late seventeenth centuries (1300 to 1700). In short, the immigrants to the colonies came from a culture in which belief in witchcraft was widespread and in which accusations could result in formal prosecutions and executions. Recent research has demonstrated that the Salem incident, although the largest and most important witch hunt in New England, was just one of a number of such episodes in the American colonies.

Question—repeated

4   But why were witches women? Admittedly, historians have not yet answered that question entirely satisfactorily. Certain observations can be made: women gave birth to new life and seemed to have the potential to take life away. In

Answers: 1

     2

     3

Women seen as "out of their place"

Western culture, <u>women were seen</u> as <u>less rational than men</u>, <u>more linked</u> to the "natural" world, in which <u>magic</u> held sway. <u>Men</u>, who <u>dominated European society</u>, <u>defined</u> the characteristics of a <u>"proper woman,"</u> who was <u>submissive</u> and <u>accepted a subordinate position</u>. The <u>stereotypical witch</u>, usually described as an <u>aggressive</u> and <u>threatening older woman</u>, represented the <u>antithesis</u> of that <u>image</u>. These broad categories need further refinement, and historians are currently looking closely at the women who were accused of practicing witchcraft to identify the crucial characteristics that set them apart from their contemporaries and made them a target for accusations.

(Mary Beth Norton, *Major Problems in American Women's History*)

EXERCISE 2   Underlining and Annotating

Mark the following paragraphs with underlining and annotation. Compare your marks with those of your classmates.

BUDDHA TAUGHT NONVIOLENCE

1   Buddha gave his first sermon to the five wisdom seekers who had been his companions. That sermon was a landmark in the history of world religions. Buddha taught the four main ideas that had come to him in his enlightenment, calling them the Four Noble Truths.

2   *First Noble Truth:* Everything in life is suffering and sorrow.

3   *Second Noble Truth:* The cause of all this pain is people's self-centered cravings and desires. People seek pleasure that cannot last and leads only to rebirth and more suffering.

4   *Third Noble Truth:* The way to end all pain is to end all desires.

5   *Fourth Noble Truth:* People can overcome their desires and attain enlightenment by following the Eightfold Path.

6   The Eightfold Path was like a staircase. According to Buddha, those who sought enlightenment had to master one step at a time. The steps of the Eightfold Path were right knowledge, right purpose, right speech, right action, right living, right effort, right mindfulness, and right meditation. By following the Eightfold Path, anyone could attain *nirvana* (nur-VAHN-uh), Buddha's word for release from pain and selfishness.

7   Buddha taught his followers to treat all living things (humans, animals, and even insects) with loving kindness. A devout Buddhist was not even supposed to swat a mosquito.

8   Buddhists and Hindus both sought to escape from the woes of this world, but their paths of escape were very different. Unlike traditional Hinduism, Buddhism did not require complex rituals. Moreover, Buddha taught in everyday language, not in the ancient Sanskrit language of the Vedas and the Upanishads, which most Indians in 500 BCE. could no longer understand. Buddha's religion was also unique in its concern for all human beings—women as well as men, lowborn as well as highborn.

OUTLINING

Outlining can pertain to both reading and writing. Among the writing that will be suggested as assignments in this book are outlines, summaries, and reactions. In some instances, you may use all three forms after reading a passage. The three forms are also associated with reading and critical thinking, in that they contribute to reading comprehension and use systematic and analytical thought. The reading below is followed by student Leon Batista's outline. Note the parallel structure in his outline.

THE ROMAN TOGA

1   Practicality has never been a requirement of fashion. The Roman toga was an uncomfortable garment. It was hot in summer, cold in winter, and clumsy for just about any activity but standing still. The toga was, however, practical in one way: It was easy to make, since it involved no sewing. Not even a buttonhole was needed. An adult's toga was basically a large wool blanket measuring about 18 by 7 feet. It was draped around the body in a variety of ways without the use of buttons or pins.

2   In the early days of the Roman republic, both women and men wore togas. Women eventually wore more dresslike garments, called *stolas*, with separate shawls. For men, however, the toga remained in fashion with very little change.

3   Soon after the republic was formed, the toga became a symbol of Roman citizenship. Different styles of togas indicated a male citizen's place in society. For example, a young boy would wear a white toga with a narrow purple band along the border. When his family decided he was ready for adult responsibilities, he would don a pure white toga. On that day, usually when he was about 16, his family would take him to the Forum, where he would register as a full citizen. For the rest of his life, he would wear a toga at the theater, in court, for religious ceremonies, and on any formal occasion. At his funeral his body would be wrapped in a toga to mark him, even in death, as a Roman citizen.

(Steven L. Jantzen, *World History: Perspectives on the Past*)

I. Practicality
   A. Not practical
      1. Hot in summer
      2. Cold in winter
      3. Clumsy
   B. Practical
      1. Easy to make
      2. Easy to put on and take off
II. Fashion in Roman republic
   A. Worn by men and women
      1. Changes little with men
      2. Alternates with stolas and shawls for women
   B. Symbol of citizenship
      1. One style for young male
      2. Another style for adult male
         a. Presented at point of adulthood
         b. Worn on all occasions

EXERCISE 3   Organizing an Outline

Use the outline form to organize these sentences about college English into an outline.

1. It can help you express yourself more effectively in speaking and writing.

2. It can help you with your reading.

3. It will present the difference between fact and opinion.

4. It can help you to recognize and avoid logical fallacies.

5. It will offer complex courses in the interpretation of literature.

6. It will teach that a fact is something that can be verified.

7. It will offer courses in reading skills.

8. It will teach that an opinion is a subjective view.

9. It will offer courses in composition.

10. It will offer instruction in inductive and deductive thinking.

11. It will offer courses that involve discussion.

12. It can help you think critically.

13. College English can benefit you in many ways.

14. It will help you understand causes and effects.

Main idea: _____

   I. _____

      A. _____

      B. _____

  II. _____

      A. _____

      B. _____

 III. _____

      A. _____

         1. _____

         2. _____

      B. _____

      C. _____

      D. _____

TAKING NOTES

Taking notes for reading-based writing in this book should be little more than marking and annotating passages in reading selections and jotting down the useful points for support in your outline as you organize your summary or reaction. While writing, you will use those notes for support as you refer directly to what you have read and use some quotations from the reading. You will also give credit to the source you are reading, and—if your instructor requires you to do so—you will use documentation, including page numbers and identification of your source(s) for those ideas and words you borrow.

If you were doing a longer writing assignment based on numerous sources outside this book, use cards that group and coordinate borrowed ideas in relation to a basic outline of the ground you expect to cover. Of course, as you carefully and critically read sources in this book, you will naturally underline significant passages (often only a few words) and annotate your reactions to what you read. Those annotations will vary according to your interests, background, and immediate needs for writing. The sooner you settle on a topic and its natural divisions, the better, because then you will be able to take notes more purposefully

If you already have at least a general topic before you read, you can easily formulate some basic questions to help you focus. Most reading-based writing prompts at the ends of Chapters 18–24 divide topics into parts that can serve as divisions for your outline. Reading some of the prompts and the entries called "Mindset: Lock It In" before you read the selections will also be useful in helping you concentrate.

Here is an example of a reading-based writing prompt for the essay "Low Wages, High Skills" by Katherine S. Newman, on pages 371–375.

"Low Wages, High Skills" [title of Newman's essay]

> Write a two-part response to the essay. Focus your critical thinking on Newman's idea that those who work at Burger Barn have transferable skills. Relate those specific skills to what you have experienced in a low-paying service job. Use direct references to and quotations from the essay. Agree or disagree with Newman.

Putting together a simple outline in advance and allowing some writing space between lines will provide you with places to pencil in references and quotes, with page numbers. Then when you write your outline or reaction, you can just incorporate your notes without having to refer back to the reading(s).

Here is an example of how you can place notes inside outlines. It is an excerpt from, student Alex Mylonas's reading-based reaction to the short story "The Use of Force" by William Carlos Williams. During his first reading, Alex underlined and annotated freely; then later he selected phrases as support in his outline, which he submitted with a long paragraph assignment.

II. The inner conflict
    A. Doctor versus himself
        1. Wants to be professional
        2. Loses self-control
           "attractive little thing," p. 333

"damned little brat," p. 333

 3. Loses sight of objective

 "got beyond reason," p. 334

 B. Emotional (brutal) side wins

 "It was a pleasure to attack her," p. 335

 "blind fury," p. 335

Reading-Based Writing Forms

WRITING A SUMMARY

A **summary** is a rewritten, shortened version of a piece of writing in which you use your own wording to express the main ideas. Learning to summarize effectively will help you in many ways. Summary writing reinforces comprehension skills in reading. It requires you to discriminate among the ideas in the target reading passage. Summaries are usually written in the form of a well-designed paragraph. Frequently, they are used in collecting material for research papers and in writing conclusions to essays.

The following rules will guide you in writing effective summaries.

1. Cite both the author and title of the text.

2. Reduce the length of the original by about two-thirds, although the exact reduction will vary, depending on the content of the original.

3. Concentrate on the main ideas and include details only infrequently.

4. Change the original wording without changing the idea.

5. Do not evaluate the content or give an opinion in any way (even if you see an error in logic or fact).

6. Do not add ideas (even if you have an abundance of related information).

7. Do not include any personal comments (that is, do not use *I*, referring to self).

8. Use quotations only infrequently. (If you do use quotations, enclose them in quotation marks.)

9. Use author tags ("says York," "according to York," or "the author explains") to remind the reader that you are summarizing the material of another writer.

10. Begin with the main idea (as you usually do in middle paragraphs) and cover the main points in an organized fashion while using complete sentences.

The following is a summary of "The Roman Toga," written by the student who prepared the sample outline. The writing process used by Batista was direct and systematic. When first reading the material, he had underlined key parts and written comments and echo phrases in the margin. Then he wrote his outline. Finally, referring to both the marked passage and the outline, he wrote this summary. Had he not been assigned to write the outline, he would have done so anyway, as preparation for writing his summary.

SUMMARY OF "THE ROMAN TOGA"
BY STEVEN L. JANTZEN

According to Steven Jantzen in *World History: Perspectives on the Past*, the toga was the main form of dress for citizens of the Roman republic, despite its being "hot in summer, cold in winter, and clumsy" to wear. Perhaps the Romans appreciated the simplicity of wearing a piece of woolen cloth about eighteen by seven feet "without the use of buttons or pins." Jantzen explains that the women also wore another garment similar to a dress called the *stola*, but Roman male citizens were likely to wear only the toga—white with a purple edge for the young and solid white for the adult. This apparel was worn from childhood to death.

EXERCISE 4   Evaluating a Summary

Compare this summary with the original passage and with the student summary you just read. Then mark the instances of poor summary writing by underlining and by using rule numbers from the preceding list.

SUMMARY ABOUT ONE OF MY FAVORITE GARMENTS

For citizens of the Roman republic, the toga was the main form of dress, despite its being hot in summer, cold in winter, and clumsy to wear. Frankly, I don't see why a bright bunch of people like the Romans couldn't have come up with a better design. Perhaps the Romans appreciated the simplicity of wearing a piece of woolen cloth about eighteen by seven feet without buttons or pins; but I've read elsewhere that the togas were sometimes stolen at the public baths. The women also wore another garment similar to a dress called the *stola*, but the Roman male citizen was likely to wear only the toga—white with a purple edge for the young and solid white for the adult. For the rest of his life, he would wear a toga at the theater, in court, for religious ceremonies, and on any formal occasion. At his funeral, his body would be wrapped in a toga to mark him, even in death, as a Roman citizen.

WRITING A REACTION

The following three paragraphs are further examples of reading-related writing: the reaction and the two-part response.

A reaction concentrates on the content in a reading selection or selections. It includes personal experience and other information only to explain, validate, or challenge the ideas in that content.

In the following reaction, student Shanelle Watson takes a basic idea from the original passage and finds historical parallels. She begins and ends her paragraph with references to the content of the reading selection.

STICKS AND STONES
Shanelle Watson

Reading "Women and Witchcraft" by Mary Beth Norton reminded me of a long line of indignities against women. If something goes wrong, and women can be blamed, they are. For centuries if a woman did not have babies, it was said *she* could not, although the man was just as likely as the woman to be the cause of her childlessness. If, heaven forbid, the woman kept having female babies, that woman, it was said, couldn't produce a male. Yet we know now that it is the male who determines the sex of the child. If the child was not bright, as recently as a hundred years ago some doctors said it was because the woman was reading during pregnancy and took away the brain power from the fetus. As a result, many women were not allowed to open a book during pregnancy. Of course, because it was believed that women were so weak, husbands were allowed to beat their wives, but, according to English law, the stick could be no thicker than the man's thumb, hence "the rule of thumb." Even voting was argued against by some who said that the typical woman, controlled by emotions, would allow her husband to tell her how to vote, and each married man would then have two votes. It is no wonder that three hundred years ago men looked around and, finding many misfortunes, decided that women were the culprits and should be punished. Sticks were not enough. It was time for stones.

WRITING A TWO-PART RESPONSE

As you have seen, the reaction includes an idea or ideas from a reading or is written with the assumption that readers have read the original piece. However, your instructor may prefer that you separate the forms and present a clear, concise summary followed by another type of reading-related writing. This format is especially useful for critical reactions or problem-solving assignments because it requires you to understand and repeat another's views or experiences before responding. The two-part response also helps you avoid the common problem of writing only a summary of the text when your instructor wants you to both summarize and evaluate or to otherwise react. When writing a summary and a critical reply to a reading assignment, be sure you know whether your instructor wants you to separate your summary from your reaction.

   The following reading-based writing first summarizes and then, in a separate paragraph of reaction, analyzes, evaluates, and interprets the original passage.

"WOMEN AND WITCHCRAFT" BY MARY BETH NORTON: A SUMMARY AND A REACTION
Jeanne Garcia

Part 1: Summary

   Americans have long been fascinated by the Salem witchcraft plight in 1692 to 1693. One perplexing factor is that most of the people accused and many who blamed them were women. In "Women and Witchcraft," Mary Beth Norton says the whole issue should be placed in a historical context. In those times, much was unknown about the causes of disasters and illnesses, and the people came to believe that these things could be attributed to evil supernatural forces. Consequently, from about 1300 to 1700 "witchhunts" occurred, and Salem was just one of the locations. Historians are not certain about why women were often victims and accusers. They may have been involved because they had the power to produce life and, therefore, maybe had "the potential to take life away." Women were thought to be more emotional than rational and even connected to nature, as in magic. Moreover, the stereotypical witch was characterized as a mature, assertive woman, unlike the "proper woman" of the time "who was submissive and accepted a subordinate position." Norton says that historians now seek to discover the precise causes that made assertive women the victims of persecution as witches.

Part 2: Reaction

The "witchcraft crisis of 1692 to 1693," which Mary Beth Norton discusses in "Women and Witchcraft," is not so surprising to some of us who look back after three hundred years at the way some men treat some women. One does not have to read between Norton's lines. She makes it clear that "usually" the people were "aggressive and threatening older wom[e]n." The charges came mainly from adolescent girls and young women, but the power structure was adult men. Out of ignorance, the men, often with female accomplices, were looking around to find reasons for the misfortunes—bad weather, diseases, and accidents—that their society faced. It is a fact that if people are foolish and desperate enough to look for witches, they are foolish and desperate enough to find them. And they did: They found mainly a few old women who did not know their place, individuals of a gender associated with the emotions. If these women had been meek and mild, if they had been properly submissive to the menfolk, and if they had still been young and sexy, they would not have been vulnerable. But they were what they were—mature and relatively independent women, who seemed to be different—and that made them witches to those who were said not to be emotionally based—the men.

Kinds of Support for Reading-Based Writing

In your reading-based writing assignments, you are likely to use three methods in developing your ideas: explanations, direct references to the reading selection, and quotations from the reading selection.

- Your explanations will often be expressed in patterns, such as causes and effects, comparison and contrast, definition, or exemplification. These forms are presented in depth and related to reading-based writing in Chapters 18 through 24. Your discussion of personal experience will be used only to explain, validate, or challenge ideas from the reading selection.
- Your references will point your reader(s) directly toward original ideas in sources. The more specific the references, the more helpful they will be to your readers.
- Your quotations will be words borrowed from sources and credited to those sources. You will use quotation marks around those words, which will appear as sentences or as partial sentences blended with your own words.

Basic Formal Documentation in Reading-Based Writing

Borrowing words or ideas without giving credit to the originator is called **plagiarism** and is not acceptable scholarship, regardless of whether it is intentional. To help you in learning to give credit accurately, your instructor may ask you to document your reading-based writing formally, even though the text is readily available and assigned. Formal documentation means you must indicate the location of all the original ideas you have borrowed, even if you have changed the words.

CITATIONS

STUDENT COMPANION SITE
For additional practice, visit www.cengage .com/devenglish/ brandon/spb6e.

Documenting sources for reading-based writing should be done with care. This book uses a system called MLA (Modern Language Association) Style with the 2009 Update. You can find detailed information by keying in "MLA Style 2009" on a search engine such as Google. Your Student Companion Site also has further instructions. Mainly, you need to remember that when using material from a source, you must give enough information so that the reader will recognize it or be able to find it in its original context. Here are the most common principles of documentation that can be used for textbook or other restricted sources, whether it is quoted, paraphrased (restated), or summarized.

If you use the author's name in introducing a quotation, then usually give only the page number.

> **Example:** Suzanne Britt says that "neat people are bums and clods at heart" (255).

If you use the author's name in introducing a borrowed idea, then usually give only the page number.

> **Example:** Suzanne Britt believes that neat people are weak in character (255).

If you do not use the author's name to introduce a quotation or an idea, then usually give both the author's name and the page number.

> **Example:** Music often helps Alzheimer's patients think more clearly (Weiss 112).

WORKS CITED

Work(s) Cited lists the sources used, meaning those that appear in citations, as shown in the previous section. Each kind of publication has its own order of parts and punctuation.

Here is an example of a Work Cited entry for this book, pertaining to the student writing on pages 325–326. It is "A Work in an Anthology" (covered in even more detail on the Internet, although this may be all you will need for this course). Note the punctuation between parts and the order of those parts: author's name (last, first), title of composition (quotation marks for a short work; italics for a long work); editor(s) of the anthology; name of the anthology; edition if there is one; place of publication; publisher; date of publication; pages on which the selection appears, and medium of publication.

Work Cited

Ortiz, Charles C. "Not Invulnerable." *Sentences, Paragraphs, and Beyond: With Integrated Readings*. 6th ed. Ed. Lee Brandon and Kelly Brandon. Boston: Cengage, 2011. 325–26. Print.

Example of Reading-Based Writing

STUDENT READING-BASED PARAGRAPH (EXTRACTED FROM AN ESSAY)

Student Lydia Hsiao was asked to read and then write a reading-based reaction to a reading selection taken from Maxine Hong Kingston's *The Woman Warrior*. This paragraph taken from Hsiao's short essay illustrates how to document sources.

STRUGGLING AGAINST SILENCE
Lydia Hsiao

Maxine Hong Kingston and I came from a strict Chinese background and were taught that "a ready tongue is an evil" (Kingston 252). We were also taught to keep to ourselves. We were never taught to communicate with those outside our culture. This background may have caused my self-consciousness and my paralyzing fear of being embarrassed. During my first year in the United States, I was constantly teased about my Chinese accent. If I mispronounced a word during class, I could not help but be disgusted by my own mistakes, causing me even greater embarrassment. Kingston says, "[They] scare the voice away" (254). The result was that, like Kingston, my potential was for years undiscovered. In the same way Kingston allowed silence to "[paint] layers of black over [her life]" (254), silence continued to create a thicker darkness in my life. It first embarrassed me; then it soon robbed me of my self-esteem. As Kingston says, "[Talking] takes up that day's courage" (252). It was almost as if silence was more than a curtain. It seemed to grow its own body and walk beside me. That silence became my sinister friend, taking advantage of my willingness to accept this cruel school life, tricking me into believing that home was the only place I could find my voice. The monster silence kept me quiet.

Work Cited

Kingston, Maxine Hong. "Silence." *Rereading America*. Ed. Gary Colombo, Robert Cullan, and Bonnie Lisle. New York: Bedford/St. Martin's, 1998. 252–55. Print.

Essays for Discussion and Writing

The following essays, the first by a professional writer and the second by a student, demonstrate many of the elements of good writing that we have been exploring. To help you evaluate and write in response to the selections, they are underlined and annotated. Both are accompanied by a set of discussion and critical-thinking questions and then by several reading-based writing suggestions. Taking a look at the questions and writing suggestions before you read each essay may help you focus your reading.

PROFESSIONAL ESSAY

. . . .

American Space, Chinese Place

YI-FU TUAN

What can you learn about people by studying the design of their homes? According to Yi-Fu Tuan, you can learn a great deal.

Americans: space

1   Americans have a sense of space, not of place. Go to an American home in exurbia, and almost the first thing you do is drift toward the picture window. How curious that the first compliment you pay your host inside his house is to say how lovely it is outside his house! He is pleased that you should admire his vistas.

Space symbol

The distant horizon is not merely a line separating earth from sky, it is a symbol of the future. The American is not rooted in his place, however lovely: His eyes are drawn by the expanding space to a point on the horizon, which is his future.

Symbols for place

2   By contrast, consider the traditional Chinese home. Blank walls enclose it. Step behind the spirit wall and you are in a courtyard with perhaps a miniature garden around the corner. Once inside the private compound you are wrapped in an ambiance of calm beauty, an ordered world of buildings, pavement, rock, and decorative vegetation. But you have no distant view: Nowhere does space open out before you. Raw nature in such a home is experienced only as weather, and

Chinese: place

the only open space is the sky above. The Chinese is rooted in his place. When he has to leave, it is not for the promised land on the terrestrial horizon, but for another world altogether along the vertical, religious axis of his imagination.

3   The Chinese tie to place is deeply felt. Wanderlust is an alien sentiment. The Taoist classic *Tao Te Ching* captures the idea of rootedness in place with these words: "Though there may be another country in the neighborhood so close that they are within sight of each other and the crowing of cocks and barking of dogs in one place can be heard in the other, yet there is no traffic between them; and throughout their lives the two peoples have nothing to do with each

Farmers—high rank

other." In theory if not in practice, farmers have ranked high in Chinese society. The reason is not only that they are engaged in the "root" industry of producing food but that, unlike pecuniary merchants, they are tied to the land and do not abandon their country when it is in danger.

4   Nostalgia is a recurrent theme in Chinese poetry. An American reader of translated Chinese poems may well be taken aback—even put off—by the frequency as well as the sentimentality of the lament for home. To understand the strength of this sentiment, we need to know that the Chinese desire for stabil-

Chinese: cause of rootedness

ity and rootedness in place is prompted by the constant threat of war, exile, and the natural disasters of flood and drought. Forcible removal makes the Chinese keenly aware of their loss. By contrast, Americans move, for the most part, voluntarily. Their nostalgia for home town is really longing for childhood to which they cannot return: In the meantime the future beckons and the future is "out there," in open space. When we criticize American rootlessness we tend

American: ideals, effects

to forget that it is a result of ideals we admire, namely, social mobility and optimism about the future. When we admire Chinese rootedness, we forget the word "place" means both location in space and position in society: To be tied to

Chinese: effects
Thesis

place is also to be bound to one's station in life, with little hope of betterment. Space symbolizes hope; place, achievement and stability.

EXERCISE 5   Discussion and Critical Thinking

1. According to the author, if you visit a traditional American home, what will your host invite you to enjoy? Why?

2. On the contrary, if you visit a Chinese home, what will your host invite you to enjoy? Why?

3. Why do the Chinese admire their farmers?

4. In the same vein, what station in life do Americans, in contrast with Chinese, admire?

5. What are the different views, good and bad, held by Chinese and Americans on moving?

6. Do these characterizations of Chinese apply also to Chinese-American immigrants? How do they apply to different generations of Chinese Americans?

EXERCISE 6   Writing a Response to a Reading

On separate paper, complete one of the assignments below. Use references and quotations in reactions.

- Write a summary.

- Write a reaction. Include enough summary to establish clear and logical connections between the text and your own ideas.

- Write a two-part response composed of a summary separated from a reaction. In your reaction, consider answers to discussion questions above.

STUDENT ESSAY
....

Everyone Pays the Price

HADLEY MCGRAW

Sitting in a college classroom, Hadley McGraw doesn't remind one of the stereotypical gang member. Apparently tattoo- and puncture-free, she is fair-skinned, well-groomed, and soft-spoken. She does her homework, contributes to class discussion, and writes well. So much for stereotypes!

1   It is ten o'clock and time for me to start my day. I put an X on my calendar to signify that another twenty-four hours has passed. I now have one hundred and nine days until Martin, my boyfriend, comes home. He has been in jail for the last year. I guess you could say I was not surprised by his sentence. This is not the first time, and I am afraid it will not be the last. Eighteen months of our three-and-a-half-year relationship, he has spent in correctional institutions. Martin is a gang member. He has been a gang member for nine years now. *Thesis* Gang membership of a loved one affects everyone around that person. Three-and-a-half years later I live each day in fear and grief.

Topic sentence

2   I guess what attracted me to Martin at first was his bad-boy image and his carefree way of life. He was good looking and well known. He was tough and exciting. I, however, was good and obedient. I had been told often that I was pretty. I made good grades and came from a good home. My parents, still married and drug-free, lived comfortably in a middle-class neighborhood. Martin, *Causes* on the contrary, came from a broken home. His parents hated each other. His father was a cold, heartless man, and his mother was a "flakey" drug addict. His uncles and cousins were all members of a very large gang that "controlled" an area where he lived. Soon he too was a gang member.

3   Martin quit school when he was a freshman and spent his days on a street corner drinking Olde English forty-ouncers. Soon I was joining him. I began ditching school to hang out. In no time, I was a gang member myself, and as I look back, I see what an awful person I became. We used drugs all day and all night. *Effects* I did not care about anything and neither did he. I left home and devastated my family and lost my friends. I didn't care because I had a new family and new friends. Martin spent his nights committing crimes and dealing drugs. I was by his side, carrying his gun. The drugs made him irritable and violent, and small disagreements turned into huge battles between us. Jail sentences made him angrier and closer to his gang. Each day Martin became farther from me. Life was a nonstop party with his homeboys, and I was his woman. It was exciting and risky. It was self-destructive.

Topic sentence

4   My breaking point was one year ago. Martin and I were at a party. Everyone was drinking and joking. Oldies were playing and a noisy, wild game of poker was taking place. Suddenly a car was approaching us rapidly. Martin told me to run and hide, so I did. The homeboys began reaching for their guns. I heard five gunshots before the car drove away. I ran to the front of the house where Martin's cousin lay bleeding. I tried to wake him, speak to him. He wasn't responding. I screamed for an ambulance. Finally Martin appeared from behind *Effects* a car and ran inside to call 911. When the ambulance arrived, I was hysterical and covered in blood. They took Martin's cousin to the hospital where he was pronounced dead. Because of the gunshot wounds, the funeral was a closed casket affair and very hard on everyone. It made Martin stronger, meaner, and colder, and it made me wiser. Martin was out committing crimes again, and two months later would be jailed again.

5   It is hard for me to imagine what I did to myself, knowing that any day I could have died senselessly. It is even harder for me to accept the fact that my boyfriend would die for a dirty, trashy street gang, but not for me.

Topic sentence	6

6 <u>This last year I have been moving back to the right track. I have gotten sober,</u> started college, and returned home. <u>I have nightmares</u> about things I have seen and things I have done. I struggle every day to stay sober, to do the right thing. I am doing a lot of thinking. <u>I live each day in fear for Martin's safety as well as my own.</u> I fear for our future in a society that does not understand us. I count down the days until Martin can see the sunlight. <u>I pray every day that this time will be the last time he goes to jail.</u> <u>I pray Martin will trade his gun for me, even get an education.</u> I cry every night and try to live every day.

Effects

EXERCISE 7   Discussion and Critical Thinking

1. Why did McGraw become associated with Martin and finally become a gang member?

2. Were there deeper reasons for her dropping out of mainstream, middle-class society and joining a gang? Explain.

3. What were the effects on McGraw's life and the lives of those who were close to her?

4. What happened before the killing to set the stage for her change?

5. To what extent has she changed?

6. Why doesn't she leave Martin? Discuss.

7. What is your reaction to the statement "I fear for our future in a society that does not understand us" (paragraph 6)?

EXERCISE 8   Suggestions for Reading-Based Writing

On separate paper, complete one of the following reading-based responses. Use references and quotations in reactions.

1. Write a summary of McGraw's essay.

2. Write a two-part response composed of labeled summary and reaction parts.

3. Write a reaction in which you examine each part of McGraw's experience and discuss the relationship of the parts. Concentrate on the stages of her changes for bad and good. As you emphasize stages, resist any temptation to write only a summary. Another approach would be to imagine that McGraw has written this essay to you, and now you are writing a paragraph or an essay of advice to her. Direct your advice to her through what she has written, using references and quotations.

EXERCISE 9   Incorporating Quotations

Work with these three ways of incorporating quotations: (1) Introduce the sentence as it is. (2) Select a key part of a sentence and blend it with your words in a new sentence. (3) Paraphrase (reword) the sentence.

Examples:

1. McGraw: "I fear for our future in a society that does not understand us" (paragraph 6). Quote an entire sentence:
   One of her last statements is confusing: "I fear for our future in a society that does not understand us."

2. McGraw: "It was self-destructive" (paragraph 3).
   Select a key part of a sentence and blend it with your words:
   McGraw admits that her life then "was self-destructive."

3. McGraw: "I did not care about anything and neither did he" (paragraph 3).
   Paraphrase (reword) the sentence:
   They were not concerned about anything.

Quotations for you to incorporate:

1. McGraw: "His parents hated each other" (paragraph 2).
   Quote an entire sentence:

2. McGraw: "I could have died senselessly" (paragraph 5).
   Select a key part of a sentence and blend it with your words:

3. McGraw: "This last year I have been moving back to the right track" (paragraph 6). Paraphrase (reword) the sentence:

Journal Writing

Your journal entries are likely to be concerned primarily with the relationship between the reading material and you—your life experiences, your views, your imagination. The reading material will give you something of substance to write about, but you will be writing especially for yourself, developing confidence and ease in writing so that writing becomes a comfortable part of your everyday activities, as speaking already is.

These journal entries will be part of your intellectual diary, recording what you are thinking about a certain issue. They will help you understand the reading material; help you develop your writing skills, in uncovering ideas that can be used on other assignments; and help you think more clearly and imaginatively. Because these entries are of a more spontaneous nature than the more structured writing assignments, organization and editing are likely to be of less concern.

Each journal entry should be clearly dated and, if reading related, should specify the title and author of the original piece.

Even if your instructor wants you to concentrate on what you read for your journal writing, he or she might not want you to be restricted to the material in this text. Fortunately, you are surrounded by reading material in newspapers, magazines, and, of course, textbooks from other courses. These topics can serve you well, especially if you want to begin your journal writing now.

Cross-Curricular and Career-Related Writing

STUDENT COMPANION SITE
For additional practice, visit www.cengage .com/devenglish/ brandon/spb6e.

This textbook includes cross-curricular and career-related writing topics at the end of Chapters 18 through 24. These suggestions offer a wide range of subject material to those of you who would like to write about subjects you have encountered across campus, at work, and in your search for a career. Some of that writing may include ideas coming directly from your reading. Those ideas can be documented with a listing of the source, which usually includes the name of the author, title of the work, place of publication, publisher, date, page numbers, and medium of publication. The citations for quotations or specific references can be made in the same fashion as the ones for textbook sources.

WRITER'S GUIDELINES: From Reading to Writing

1. Underlining helps you to read with discrimination, and focus.

   - Underline the main ideas in paragraphs.
   - Underline the support for those ideas.
   - Underline answers to questions that you bring to the reading assignment.
   - Underline only the key words.

2. Annotating enables you to actively engage the reading material.

   - Number parts if appropriate.
   - Make comments according to your interests and needs.

3. Outlining the passages you read sheds light on the relationship of ideas, including the major divisions of the passage and their relative importance.

4. Taking notes will provide you with support when you write your reading-based paragraph or essay.

5. Summarizing helps you concentrate on main ideas. A summary

   - cites the author and title of the text.
   - is usually shorter than the original by about two-thirds, although the exact reduction will vary depending on the content of the original.
   - concentrates on the main idea and important supporting points.
   - changes the original wording without changing the idea.
   - includes details only infrequently.
   - does not evaluate the content or give an opinion in any way (even if the original contains an error in logic or fact).
   - does not add ideas (even if the writer of the summary has an abundance of related information).

- does not include any personal comments by the writer of the summary (therefore, no use of *I*, referring to self).
- seldom contains quotations (although, if it does, only with quotation marks).
- includes some author tags ("says York," "according to York," or "the author explains") to remind the reader(s) that it is a summary of the material of another writer.

6. Two other types of reading-based writing are

- the reaction, which shows how the reading relates to you, your experiences, and your views; also, it is often a critique of the worth and logic of the piece.
- the two-part response, which includes a summary and a reaction that are separate.

7. Most ideas in reading-based papers are developed in one or more of these three ways:

- explanation
- direct references
- quotations

8. Documenting is giving credit to borrowed ideas and words.

- formal by giving credit in MLA style
- informal by just referring to what you have read

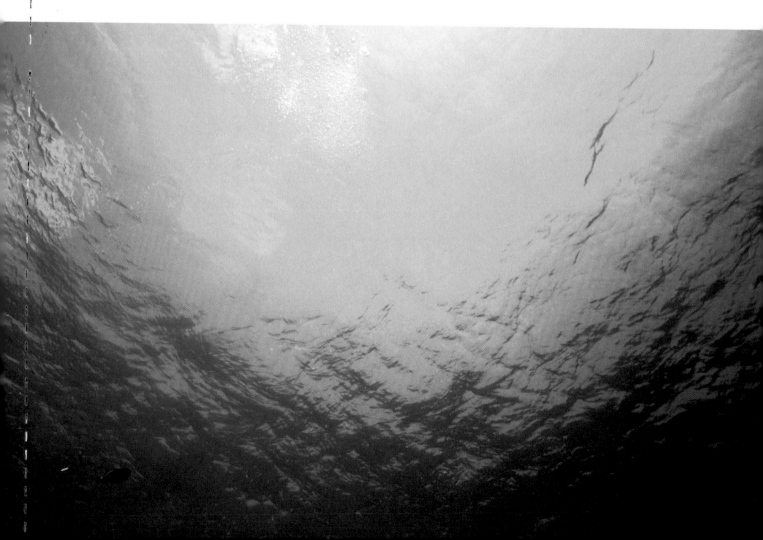

Part II WRITING SENTENCES

Almost all of your most important writing will be in sentences. Good sentences, those you write correctly and effectively, will convey what you intend to say and perhaps even enhance the message. Incorrect and awkward sentences will detract from your message. Even an original, insightful idea may be discredited if it is carried by weak phrasing, faulty mechanics, or poor word choice. Chapters 2 through 13 will help you get full credit for communicating your ideas.

Chapter 2

Parts of Speech

FLOW OF WRITING

MICROTHEME	Writing Activity in Miniature

EXERCISE A

Before you work on this chapter, write a Microtheme on the following topic. Write small enough to leave room for marking later. **After** you have studied this chapter, return to your Microtheme and complete Exercise B to practice what you have learned.

Suggested Microtheme Topic: Write a Microtheme of 80 to 100 words on what you would do if you won a million dollars in the lottery. Be specific in naming what you would buy, whom you would help, and how you would change your lifestyle.

EXERCISE B

Connecting Your Learning Objectives with Your Microtheme

Complete this exercise after you have studied this chapter.

1. Pick three sentences and identify the part of speech for each word.
2. Check to make certain you have not confused adjectives with pronouns.
3. Check to make certain you have not confused prepositions with conjunctions.

Principles for Identification

To classify a word as a part of speech, we observe two simple principles:

- The word must be in the context of communication, usually in a sentence.
- We must be able to identify the word with others that have similar characteristics—the eight parts of speech: nouns, pronouns, adjectives, verbs, adverbs, prepositions, conjunctions, or interjections.

The first principle is important because some words can be any of several parts of speech. The word *round*, for example, can function as five:

1. I watched the potter *round* the block of clay. [verb]

2. I saw her go *round* the corner. [preposition]

3. She has a *round* head. [adjective]

4. The astronauts watched the world go *round*. [adverb]

5. The champ knocked him out in one *round*. [noun]

NOUNS

- **Nouns** are naming words. Nouns may name persons, animals, plants, places, things, substances, qualities, or ideas—for example, *Bart, armadillo, Mayberry, tree, rock, cloud, love, ghost, music, virtue.*
- Nouns are often pointed out by noun indicators. These noun indicators—*the, a, an*—signal that a noun is ahead, although there may be words between the indicator and the noun itself.

the slime	*a* werewolf	*an* aardvark
the green slime	*a* hungry werewolf	*an* angry aardvark

PRONOUNS

A **pronoun** is a word that is used in place of a noun.

- Some pronouns may represent specific persons or things:

I	she	they	you
me	her	them	yourself
myself	herself	themselves	yourselves
it	he	we	who
itself	him	us	whom
that	himself	ourselves	

- Indefinite pronouns refer to nouns (persons, places, things) in a general way:

each	everyone	nobody	somebody

- Other pronouns point out particular things:

	Singular	**Plural**

Singular
this, that
This is my treasure.
That is your junk.

Plural
these, those
These are my jewels.
Those are your trinkets.

- Still other pronouns introduce questions.

    Which is the best CD player?

    What are the main ingredients of a Twinkie?

VERBS

Verbs show action or express being in relation to the subject of a sentence. They customarily occur in set positions in sentences.

- **Action verbs** are usually easy to identify.

    The aardvark *ate* the crisp, tasty ants. [action verb]

    The aardvark *washed* them down with a snoutful of water. [action verb]

- The **being** verbs are few in number and are also easy to identify. The most common *being* verbs are *is, was, were, are,* and *am.*

    Gilligan *is* on an island in the South Pacific. [*being* verb]

    I *am* his enthusiastic fan. [*being* verb]

- The form of a verb expresses its tense, that is, the time of the action or being. The time may be in the present or past.

    Roseanne *sings* "The Star-Spangled Banner." [present]

    Roseanne *sang* "The Star-Spangled Banner." [past]

- One or more **helping verbs** may be used with the main verb to form other tenses. The combination is called a *verb phrase.*

    She *had sung* the songs many times in the shower. [Helping verb and main verb indicate a time in the past.]

    She *will be singing* the song no more in San Diego. [Helping verbs and main verb indicate a time in the future.]

- Some helping verbs can be used alone as main verbs: *has, have, had, is, was, were, are, am.* Certain other helping verbs function only as helpers: *will, shall, should, could.*

    The most common position for the verb is directly after the subject or after the subject and its modifiers.

    At high noon only two men [subject] *were* on Main Street.

    The man with a faster draw [subject and modifiers] *walked* away alone.

ADJECTIVES

Adjectives modify nouns and pronouns. Most adjectives answer the questions *What kind? Which one?* and *How many?*

- Adjectives answering the *What kind?* question are descriptive. They tell the quality, kind, or condition of the nouns or pronouns they modify.

red convertible	*dirty* fork
noisy muffler	*wild* roses
The rain is *gentle*.	Bob was *tired*.

- Adjectives answering the *Which one?* question narrow or restrict the meaning of a noun. Some of these are pronouns that become adjectives by function.

my money	*our* ideas	the *other* house
this reason	*these* apples	

- Adjectives answering the *How many?* question are, of course, numbering words.

some people	*each* pet	*few* goals
three dollars	*one* glove	

- The words *a*, *an*, and *the* are adjectives called *articles*. As "noun indicators," they point out persons, places, and things.

ADVERBS

Adverbs modify verbs, adjectives, and other adverbs. Adverbs answer the questions *How? Where? When?* and *To what degree?*

Modifying Verbs: They <u>did</u> their work <u>quickly</u>.
                               v   adv

                               He <u>replied</u> <u>angrily</u>.
                                      v   adv

Modifying Adjectives: They were <u>somewhat</u> <u>happy</u>.
                                              adv   adj

- Adverbs that answer the *How?* question are concerned with manner or way.

  She ate the snails *hungrily*.

  He snored *noisily*.

- Adverbs that answer the *Where?* question show location.

  They drove *downtown*.

  He stayed *behind*.

  She climbed *upstairs*.

- Adverbs that answer the *When?* question indicate time.

  The ship sailed *yesterday*.

  I expect an answer *soon*.

- Adverbs that answer the *To what degree?* question express extent.

  She is *entirely* correct.

  He was *somewhat* annoyed.

Most words ending in *-ly* are adverbs.

> He completed the task *skillfully*. [adverb]

> She answered him *courteously*. [adverb]

However, there are a few exceptions.

> The house provided a *lovely* view of the valley. [adjective]

> Your goblin mask is *ugly*. [adjective]

PREPOSITIONS

A **preposition** is a word or group of words that function as a connective. The preposition connects its object(s) to some other word(s) in the sentence. A preposition and its object(s)—usually a noun or pronoun—with modifiers make up a **prepositional phrase**.

> Bart worked <u>against</u> great <u>odds</u>.
> prep   object
> prepositional phrase

> Everyone <u>in</u> his <u>household</u> cheered his effort.
> prep   object
> prepositional phrase

Some of the most common prepositions are the following:

about	around	between	for	of	toward
above	before	beyond	from	off	under
across	behind	but	in	on	until
after	below	by	into	over	upon
against	beneath	despite	like	past	with
among	beside	down	near	to	

Some prepositions are composed of more than one word and are made up from other parts of speech:

according to	as far as	because of	in spite of
ahead of	as well as	in back of	instead of
along with	aside from	in front of	together with

Caution: Do not confuse adverbs with prepositions.

> I went *across* slowly. [without an object—adverb]

> I went *across* the field. [with an object—preposition]

> We walked *behind* silently. [without an object—adverb]

> We walked *behind* the mall. [with an object—preposition]

CONJUNCTIONS

A **conjunction** connects and shows a relationship between words, phrases, or clauses. A phrase is two or more words acting as a part of speech. A clause is a group of words with a subject and a verb. An independent clause can stand by itself: *She plays bass guitar.* A dependent clause cannot stand by itself: *when she plays bass guitar.*

There are two kinds of conjunctions: coordinating and subordinating.

Coordinating conjunctions connect words, phrases, and clauses of equal rank: noun with noun, adjective with adjective, verb with verb, phrase with phrase, main clause with main clause, and subordinate clause with subordinate clause. The seven common coordinating conjunctions are *for*, *and*, *nor*, *but*, *or*, *yet*, and *so*. (An easy way to remember them is to think of the acronym FANBOYS, which is made up of the first letter of each conjunction.)

Two Nouns: Bring a <u>pencil</u> <u>and</u> some <u>paper</u>.
                  noun   conj   noun

Two Phrases: Did she go <u>to the store</u> <u>or</u> <u>to the game</u>?
                    prep phrase   conj   prep phrase

Paired conjunctions such as *either/or*, *neither/nor*, or *both/and* are usually classed as coordinating conjunctions.

<u>Neither</u> the coach <u>nor</u> the manager was at fault.
conj   conj

Subordinating conjunctions connect dependent clauses with main clauses. The most common subordinating conjunctions include the following:

after	because	provided	whenever
although	before	since	where
as	but that	so that	whereas
as if	if	till	wherever
as long as	in order that	until	
as soon as	notwithstanding	when	

Sometimes the dependent clause comes *before* the main clause, where it is set off by a comma.

<u>Although</u> <u>she</u> <u>was</u> in pain, she stayed in the game.
conj   sub   v
└──────┬──────┘
dependent clause

Sometimes the dependent clause comes *after* the main clause, where it usually is *not* set off by a comma.

She stayed in the game <u>because</u> <u>she</u> <u>was needed</u>.
conj   sub   v
└──────┬──────┘
dependent clause

Caution: Certain words can function as either conjunctions or prepositions. It is necessary to look ahead to see if the word introduces a clause with a subject and verb—conjunction function—or takes an object—preposition function. Some of the words with two functions are these: *after*, *for*, *since*, *until*.

After the concert was over, we went home. [clause follows—conjunction]

After the concert, we went home. [object follows—preposition]

INTERJECTIONS

An **interjection** conveys strong emotion or surprise. When an interjection appears alone, it is usually punctuated with an exclamation mark.

Wow!   Curses!   Cowabunga!   Yabba dabba doo!

When it appears as part of a sentence, an interjection is usually followed by a comma.

Oh, I did not consider that problem.

The interjection may sound exciting, but it is seldom appropriate for college writing.

EXERCISE 1   Identifying Parts of Speech

Identify the part of speech of each italicized word or group of words by placing the appropriate abbreviations in the blanks.

n	noun	pro	pronoun
v	verb	adj	adjective
adv	adverb	conj	conjunction
prep	preposition		

_____ _____ **1.** The *turtle* can be defined as a reptile *with* a shell.

_____ _____ **2.** It is a *toothless* creature that *can smell* and see well.

_____ _____ **3.** Some live *mostly* in the water, whereas others live mostly *in* places as dry as the desert.

_____ _____ **4.** Both sea *and land* turtles will burrow and hibernate.

_____ _____ **5.** Turtles are well known *for their* longevity.

_____ _____ **6.** *Some live* to be more than a hundred years old.

_____ _____ **7.** *Many* people purchase turtles for *pets*.

_____ _____ **8.** Young turtles *eat chopped* raw meat, greens, fish, and worms.

_____ _____ **9.** *They* need both sunlight *and* shade.

_____ _____ **10.** *Some* people paint their *pet* turtles, a practice that can damage the turtles' shells.

_____ _____ **11.** *Most* turtles are not *suitable* for pets.

_____ _____ **12.** The snapping turtle *is* one such *species*.

_____ _____ **13.** *It* can be *vicious* when cornered.

_____ _____ **14.** The *common* snapper weighs up to sixty pounds and can snap off a set of fingers *with* one bite.

_____ _____ **15.** Folklore holds that *when* a snapping turtle bites someone, it will not let go *until* it hears thunder.

_____ _____ **16.** Stories *circulate* about a farmer who cut off the head of a snapping turtle that was biting someone, *yet* even without its body, the snapper would not let go.

_____ _____ **17.** The box turtle is a *gentle creature* and makes a good pet.

_____ _____ **18.** It has a *hooked* beak, red eyes, and a splotchy *yellow* and brown shell.

_____ _____ **19.** It eats worms, snails, berries, *and* other *fruit*.

_____ _____ **20.** In the summer in the Midwest, one *can find* many box turtles crawling about, their solemn beaks red from a *meal* of blackberries.

EXERCISE 2   Identifying Parts of Speech

Identify the part of speech of each italicized word or group of words by placing the appropriate abbreviations in the blanks.

n	noun	pro	pronoun
v	verb	adj	adjective
adv	adverb	conj	conjunction
prep	preposition		

_____ _____ **1.** *Before* gunpowder was invented, soldiers *often* wore armor.

_____ _____ **2.** The armor *protected* the soldiers against *sharp* blows.

_____ _____ **3.** Early armor was designed *from* layers of animal *hide*.

_____ _____ **4.** The *first* designs were in the form *of* shields.

_____ _____ **5.** Other designs *covered* the *entire* body.

_____ _____ **6.** Whole battles were *sometimes* won or *lost* because of armor.

_____ _____ **7.** *Armor* craftsmen had *important* positions in society.

_____ _____ **8.** Chain mail *armor* was made *of* small connected rings.

_____ _____ **9.** *Japanese* armor of the 1500s was made *of* thousands of fishlike scales.

_____ _____ **10.** Most European armor was made of *large* metal plates shaped to the *body*.

_____ _____ **11.** *Some* of it was designed with precious metals and decorated with *artistic* patterns.

_____ _____ **12.** The metal was *heavy, and* soldiers needed special assistance in mounting their horses.

_____ _____ **13.** Because the metal was *so* strong, knights *often* tried to unseat their opponents instead of trying to pierce the armor.

_____ _____ **14.** One famous soldier fell off his horse *and* into a stream *fifteen* inches deep.

_____ _____ **15.** His armor *filled* with water *and* he drowned.

_____ _____ **16.** *During* the crusades, European soldiers wore their *metal* armor into the deserts.

_____ _____ **17.** The *armor* often became so hot the soldiers fell off their horses *in* exhaustion.

_____ _____ **18.** With the development of the longbow *and* gunpowder, traditional armor *lost* its popularity.

_____ _____ **19.** Lightweight *armor* has been used in *modern* warfare.

_____ _____ **20.** The helmet is one *carryover* from earlier *designs*.

CHAPTER REVIEW   Identifying Parts of Speech

To classify a word as a part of speech, we observe two simple principles:

- The word must be in the context of communication, usually in a sentence.
- We must be able to identify the word with others that have similar characteristics—the eight parts of speech: nouns, pronouns, adjectives, verbs, adverbs, prepositions, conjunctions, or interjections.

CHAPTER REVIEW   Exercise

REVIEW 1   **Identifying Parts of Speech**

Identify the part of speech of each italicized word or group of words by placing the appropriate abbreviations in the blanks.

n	noun	pro	pronoun
v	verb	adj	adjective
adv	adverb	conj	conjunction
prep	preposition		

_____ _____ **1.** *For* about forty years, the Three Stooges were a popular *comedy* team.

_____ _____ **2.** They were *often* accused of making films *in* bad taste, but no one accused them of being good actors.

_____ _____ **3.** For decades they *made seven* or more pictures a year.

_____ _____ **4.** Actually six *different* actors *played* the parts.

_____ _____ **5.** The *most* famous threesome *was* Moe, Curley, and Larry.

_____ _____ **6.** The Stooges specialized *in physical* comedy.

_____ _____   **7.** They *took* special *delight* in hitting each other in the head and poking each other's eyes.

_____ _____   **8.** Moe was the on-screen *leader* of this *zany* group.

_____ _____   **9.** He assumed leadership in each film *because he* was more intelligent than the others, which isn't saying much.

_____ _____   **10.** Curley was not bright, but he made up for his *dumbness* by having the *hardest* head in the world, at least in the world of Stooge movies.

_____ _____   **11.** Larry *often got caught* between the flailing arms and kicking feet of Moe and Curley.

_____ _____   **12.** The movies made *by* the Stooges *usually* came in two reels and were shown along with feature-length films.

_____ _____   **13.** The Stooge movies *were given* such *titles* as *Half-Wits*, *Three Hams on Rye*, *Slap Happy Sleuths*, and *Matri Phony*.

_____ _____   **14.** They made fun of *dignity* and physically abused each other with all kinds *of* lethal instruments, but they never got hurt.

_____ _____   **15.** They received *little respect* from the filmmaking community.

_____ _____   **16.** Only Moe saved *his* money *and* became wealthy.

_____ _____   **17.** Apparently Curley *at* times lived his *movie* role off stage.

_____ _____   **18.** After a *brief* marriage, Curley's wife *left* him, saying he punched, poked, pinched, and pushed her and left cigar butts in the sink.

STUDENT COMPANION SITE
For additional practice, visit www.cengage .com/devenglish/ brandon/spb6e.

_____ _____   **19.** Moe tried to gain *respectability* as a character actor, but the audiences could never accept *him* in serious roles.

_____ _____   **20.** A whole new television *audience has made* the Three Stooges the stars they never were in their lifetimes.

MICROTHEME

To practice your skills acquired in this chapter, return to the Microtheme on page 33 and complete Exercise B.

Chapter 3

Subjects and Verbs

FLOW OF WRITING

MICROTHEME	Writing Activity in Miniature

EXERCISE A

Before you work on this chapter, write a Microtheme on the following topic. Write small enough to leave room for marking later. **After** you have studied this chapter, return to your Microtheme and complete Exercise B to practice what you have learned.

Suggested Microtheme Topic: Write a Microtheme of 80 to 100 words about an event that took place in no more than five minutes. Perhaps it had a special meaning as a discovery, a reason for change, or a transformation. The event could be outstanding because of the pain, pleasure, or insight it gave you.

EXERCISE B

Connecting Your Learning Objectives with Your Microtheme

Complete this exercise after you have studied this chapter.

1. Underline the subjects and circle the verbs in your first two sentences.
2. Check to make certain you have not confused objects of prepositions with subjects.
3. Check to make certain you have not confused verbs with adverbs.

The two most important parts of any sentence are the subject and the verb. The **subject** is who or what causes the action or expresses a state of being. The **verb** indicates what the subject is doing or is being. Many times, the subject and verb taken together carry the meaning of the sentence. Consider this example:

> The <u>woman</u> <u>left</u> for work.
>   subject   verb

The subject *woman* and the verb *left* indicate the basic content of the sentence while providing structure.

Subjects

The **simple subject** of a sentence is usually a single noun or pronoun.

> The judge's <u>reputation</u> for order in the courtroom is well known.
>   simple subject

The **complete subject** is the simple subject with all its modifiers—that is, with all the words that describe or qualify it.

> <u>The judge's reputation for order in the courtroom</u> is well known.
>   complete subject

To more easily understand and identify simple subjects of sentences, you may want to review the following information about nouns and pronouns.

NOUNS

Nouns are naming words. Nouns may name persons, animals, plants, places, things, substances, qualities, or ideas—for example, Bart, armadillo, Mayberry, tree, rock, cloud, love, ghost, music, virtue.

PRONOUNS

A **pronoun** is a word that is used in place of a noun.

• Pronouns that can be used as subjects of sentences may represent specific persons or things and are called **personal pronouns**:

I	we
you	you
he, she, it	they

> **Example:** <u>They</u> recommended my sister for the coaching position.
>   subject

• **Indefinite pronouns** refer to nouns (persons, places, things) in a general way:

each	everyone	nobody	somebody

> **Example:** <u>Everyone</u> wants a copy of that photograph.
>   subject

• Other pronouns point out particular things:

Singular: *this*, *that*	**Plural:** *these*, *those*
This is my treasure.	*These* are my jewels.
That is your junk.	*Those* are your trinkets.

- Still other pronouns introduce questions:

    Which is the best iPod?

    What are the main ingredients in a Twinkie?

    Who understands this computer command?

Note: To be the subject of a sentence, a pronoun must stand alone.

    This is a treasure. [Subject is *this*; pronoun stands alone.]

    This *treasure* is mine. [Subject is *treasure*. *This* is an **adjective**—a word that describes a noun; *this* describes *treasure*.]

COMPOUND SUBJECTS

A subject may be **compound**. That is, it may consist of two or more subjects, usually joined by *and* or *or*, that function together.

    The *prosecutor* and the *attorney* for the defense made opening statements.

    He and his *friends* listened carefully.

    Steven, *Juan*, and *Alicia* attended the seminar. [Note the placement of commas for three or more subjects.]

IMPLIED SUBJECTS

A subject may be **implied**, or understood. An **imperative sentence**—a sentence that gives a command—has *you* as the implied subject.

    (You) Sit in that chair, please.

    (You) Now take the oath.

    (You) Please read the notes carefully.

TROUBLE SPOT: PREPOSITIONAL PHRASES

A **prepositional phrase** is made up of a preposition (a word such as *at, in, of, to, with*) and one or more nouns or pronouns with their modifiers: *at the time, by the jury, in the courtroom, to the judge and the media, with controlled anger*. Be careful not to confuse the subject of a sentence with the noun or pronoun (known as the object of the preposition) in a prepositional phrase. The object of a preposition cannot be the subject of a sentence.

    The <u>car</u> <u>with the dents</u> is mine.
        subject   prepositional
                   phrase

The subject of the sentence is *car*. The word *dents* is the object of the preposition *with* and cannot be the subject of the sentence.

    <u>Most</u> <u>of the pie</u> has been eaten.
     subject prepositional
              phrase

The <u>person</u> <u>in the middle</u> <u>of the crowd</u> has disappeared.
    subject   prepositional   prepositional
            phrase   phrase

TROUBLE SPOT: THE WORDS *HERE* AND *THERE*

The words *here* and *there* are adverbs (used as filler words) and cannot be subjects.

There is no <u>problem</u>.
          subject

Here is the <u>issue</u>.
       subject

EXERCISE 1   Finding Subjects

Circle the subjects in the following sentences. You will have to supply the subject of one sentence.

1. Mahatma Gandhi gave his life for India and for peace.

2. Through a practice of nonviolent resistance, he led his people to freedom from the British.

3. Ponder his preference for behavior rather than accomplishment.

4. There was only good in his behavior and in his accomplishments.

5. His fasts, writings, and speeches inspired the people of India.

6. He taught his people self-sufficiency in weaving cloth and making salt for themselves against British law.

7. Gandhi urged the tolerance of all religions.

8. Finally, the British granted freedom to India.

9. Some leaders in India and a few foreign agitators questioned the freedom of religion.

10. Gandhi, the Indian prince of peace, was killed by an intolerant religious leader.

EXERCISE 2   Finding Subjects

Circle the subjects in the following sentences. You will have to supply the subject of one sentence.

1. More than two hundred years ago, some tractors were powered by steam.

2. They could travel at about three miles per hour for about ten minutes.

3. Consider that information in relation to the following material.

4. There was a great future for these self-powered vehicles.

5. About a hundred years later, in 1897, Freelan O. Stanley and his associates produced the Stanley steamer, the best-known steam automobile.

6. Around the same time, William Morrison built an electric car.

7. Without polluting the atmosphere, it could go twenty miles an hour.

8. After traveling for about fifty miles, its batteries had to be recharged.

9. Meanwhile in Germany, Gottlieb Daimler, Karl Benz, and their engineers were developing the internal-combustion engine.

10. In the 1890s, the first successful gasoline-powered automobiles took to the roads.

Verbs

Verbs show action or express being in relation to the subject of a sentence.

TYPES OF VERBS

Action verbs indicate movement or accomplishment in idea or deed. Someone can "consider the statement" or "hit the ball." Here are other examples:

> She *sees* the arena.
>
> He *bought* the book.
>
> They *adopted* the child.
>
> He *understood* her main theories.

***Being* verbs** indicate existence. Few in number, they include *is, was, were, am,* and *are.*

> The movie *is* sad.
>
> The book *was* comprehensive.
>
> They *were* responsible.
>
> I *am* concerned.
>
> We *are* organized.

VERB PHRASES

Verbs may occur as single words or as phrases. A **verb phrase** is made up of a main verb and one or more helping verbs such as the following:

is	was	can	have	do	may	shall
are	were	could	had	does	might	should
am		will	has	did	must	
		would				

Here are some sentences that contain verb phrases:

> The judge *has presided* over many capital cases.
>
> His rulings seldom *are overturned* on appeal.

TROUBLE SPOT: WORDS SUCH AS *NEVER*, *NOT*, AND *HARDLY*

Never, *not*, *hardly*, *seldom*, and so on, are modifiers, not verbs.

The attorney could *not* win the case without key witnesses.
[*Not* is an adverb. The verb phrase is *could win*.]

The jury could *hardly* hear the witness. [*Hardly* is an adverb; *could hear* is the verb phrase.]

COMPOUND VERBS

Verbs that are joined by a word such as *and* or *or* are called **compound verbs**.

As a district attorney, Barbara *had presented* and *had won* famous cases.

She *prepared* carefully and *presented* her ideas with clarity.

We *will go* out for dinner or *skip* it entirely.

TROUBLE SPOT: VERBALS

Do not confuse verbs with verbals. **Verbals** are verblike words in certain respects, but they do not function as verbs. They function as other parts of speech. There are three kinds of verbals.

An **infinitive** is made up of the word *to* and a verb. An infinitive provides information, but, unlike the true verb, it is not tied to the subject of the sentence. It acts as a modifier or a noun.

His drive *to succeed* would serve him well.

He wanted *to get* a bachelor's degree.

His main objective was *to get* a bachelor's degree.

In the first example, *to succeed* is an infinitive acting as a modifier. In the second and third examples, *to get* is an infinitive acting as a noun.

A **gerund** is a verblike word ending in *-ing* that acts as a noun.

Retrieving her e-mail was her main objective.

She thought about *retrieving* her e-mail.

Retrieving in each sentence acts as a noun.

A **participle** is a verblike word that usually has an *-ing* or an *-ed* ending.

Walking to town in the dark, he lost his way.

Wanted by the FBI, she was on the run.

The *starved* dog barked for food.

In the first example, the word *walking* answers the question *when*. In the second example, the word *wanted* answers the question *which one*. In the third example, *starved* describes the dog. *Walking*, *wanted*, and *starved* are describing words; they are not the true verbs in the sentences.

EXERCISE 3   Finding Verbs

Underline the verb(s) in each sentence.

1. Chimpanzees live and travel in social groups.

2. The composition of these groups varies in age and gender.

3. The habitat of the chimpanzees is mainly forests.

4. They spend more time in the trees than on the ground.

5. Each night they make a nest of branches and leaves in trees.

6. Sometimes a proud male will beat on his chest.

7. Chimpanzees are violent at times but usually live peacefully.

8. After finding food, a chimp hoots and shakes branches.

9. Other chimps hear the commotion and go to the food source.

10. Chimp tools, such as leaf sponges and sticks, are primitive.

EXERCISE 4   Finding Verbs

Underline the verb(s) in each sentence.

1. Chimpanzees share many features with human beings.

2. More than 90 percent of basic genetic make-up is shared.

3. Both human beings and chimps can use reason.

4. Chimps have a remarkable talent for communication.

5. Chimps do not have the capacity for human speech.

6. However, chimps can use other symbols.

7. In one experiment, chimps learned American Sign Language.

8. Chimps can learn a complex system of language.

9. Chimp scholar Washoe has learned more than 160 signs and can ask questions.

10. Another chimp, Lana, uses a computer.

Location of Subjects and Verbs

Although the subject usually appears before the verb, it may follow the verb instead:

Into the court <u>stumbled</u> the <u>defendant</u>.
    verb   subject

> From tiny acorns <u>grow</u> mighty <u>oaks</u>.
>   verb   subject

> There <u>was</u> little <u>support</u> for him in the audience.
>   verb   subject

> Here <u>are</u> your <u>books</u> and your <u>papers</u>.
>   verb   subject   subject

Verb phrases are often broken up in a question. Do not overlook a part of the verb that is separated from another in a question such as "Where had the defendant gone on that fateful night?" If you have trouble finding the verb phrase, recast the question, making it into a statement: "The defendant *had gone* where on that fateful night?" The result will not necessarily be a smooth or complete statement, but you will be able to see the basic elements more easily.

> *Can* the defense lawyer *control* the direction of the trial?

Change the question to a statement to find the verb phrase:

> The defense lawyer *can control* the direction of the trial.

As you will see in Chapter 4, a sentence may have more than one set of subjects and verbs. In the following passage, the subjects are circled; the verbs are underlined.

> (We) <u>should be</u> careful to get out of an experience only the wisdom (that) <u>is</u> in it—and <u>stop</u> there; lest (we) <u>be</u> like the cat (that) <u>sits</u> down on a hot stove lid. (She) <u>will</u> never <u>sit</u> down on a hot stove lid again—and (that) <u>is</u> well; but also (she) <u>will</u> never <u>sit</u> down on a cold one any more.
>
> (Mark Twain, *Epitaph for His Daughter*)

EXERCISE 5   Finding Subjects and Verbs

Circle the subject(s) and underline the verb(s) in the following sentences. You will have to supply the subject for one sentence.

1. Read this exercise and learn about the Aztec empire in Mexico.

2. Aztec cities were as large as those in Europe at that time.

3. Government and religion were important concerns.

4. There was little difference between the two institutions.

5. They built huge temples to their gods and sacrificed human beings.

6. The religious ceremonies related mainly to their concerns about plentiful harvests.

7. Aztec society had nobles, commoners, serfs, and slaves.

8. The family included a husband, a wife, children, and some relatives of the husband.

9. At the age of ten, boys went to school, and girls either went to school or learned domestic skills at home.

10. The Aztecs wore loose-fitting garments, they lived in adobe houses, and they ate tortillas.

11. Scholars in this culture developed a calendar of 365 days.

12. Huge Aztec calendars of stone are now in museums.

13. The Aztec language was similar to that of the Comanche and Pima Indians.

14. The Aztec written language was pictographic and represented ideas and sounds.

15. Both religion and government required young men to pursue warfare.

16. By pursuing warfare, the soldiers could capture others for slaves and sacrifice, and enlarge the Aztec empire.

17. In 1519, Hernando Cortez landed in Mexico.

18. He was joined by Indians other than Aztecs.

19. After first welcoming Cortez and his army, the Aztecs then rebelled.

20. The Spaniards killed Emperor Montezuma II, and then they defeated the Aztecs.

EXERCISE 6   Finding Subjects and Verbs

Circle the subject(s) and underline the verb(s) in the following sentences.

1. Who are the Eskimos?

2. Where did they come from?

3. How do they live?

4. How has their way of life changed in the last century?

5. These questions are all important.

6. There may be different views on some of the answers.

7. They live in the Arctic from Russia east to Greenland.

8. Their ancestors came from Siberia in Northern Asia.

9. They have learned to live in a land of perpetual snow.

10. The word *Eskimo* means *eaters of raw meat* in a Native American language.

11. Their own name for themselves is *Inuit* or *Yuit*, meaning *people*.

12. For hundreds of years, their homes during hunting and fishing excursions were made of blocks of ice or packed snow and are called *igloos*.

13. They ate the raw flesh of caribou, seals, whales, and fish.

14. During the 1800s, the whalers enlisted the Eskimos as helpers.

15. Later the traders came and bought furs from the Eskimos.

16. The traders and whalers brought guns, tools, technology, and disease to the Eskimos.

17. The Eskimos used their new harpoons and guns, and killed more game.

18. Their simple, traditional way of life changed.

19. Now most Eskimos live in settlements.

20. Despite the many changes, Eskimos still treasure their ancient ways.

CHAPTER REVIEW Subjects and Verbs

The **subject** carries out the action or expresses the state of being in a sentence. The **verb** indicates what the subject is doing or is being.

SUBJECTS

You can recognize the **simple subject** by asking who or what causes the action or expresses the state of being found in the verb.

1. The **simple subject** can be single or compound.

My *friend* and *I* have much in common. [compound subject]

My *friend* brought a present. [single subject]

2. The command, or **imperative**, sentence has a "you" as the implied subject and no stated subject.

(*You*) Read the notes.

3. Although the subject usually appears before the verb, it may follow the verb.

There was *justice* in the verdict.

4. The object of a preposition cannot be a subject.

The *chairperson* [subject] of the department [object of the preposition] directs the discussion.

VERBS

Verbs show action or express being in relation to the subject.

1. **Action verbs** suggest movement or accomplishment in idea or deed.

He *dropped* the book. [movement]

He *read* the book. [accomplishment]

2. *Being* **verbs** indicate existence.

> They *were* concerned.

3. Verbs may occur as single words or phrases.

> He *led* the charge. [single word]

> She *is leading* the charge. [phrase]

4. A **verb phrase** may be separated in a question.

> Where *had* the defendant *gone* on that fateful night?

5. **Compound verbs** are joined by a word such as *and* or *or*.

> She *worked* for twenty-five years and *retired*.

6. Words such as *never*, *not*, and *hardly* are not verbs; they modify verbs.

7. Verbals are not verbs; **verbals** are verblike words that function as other parts of speech.

> *Singing* [gerund acting as a noun subject] is fun.

> I want *to sing*. [infinitive acting as a noun object]

> *Singing* [participle acting as a modifier], he walked in the rain.

CHAPTER REVIEW Exercises

REVIEW 1   ### Finding Subjects and Verbs

Circle the subject(s) and underline the verb(s) in the following sentences. You will have to supply the subject for one sentence.

1. Read this exercise carefully.

2. What causes earthquakes?

3. How much damage can they do?

4. Earthquakes shake the earth.

5. There is no simple answer to the question of cause.

6. The earth is covered by rock plates.

7. Instead of merely covering, they are in constant motion.

8. These plates bump into each other and then pass over each other.

9. The rocks are squeezed and stretched.

10. They pull apart or pile up and cause breaks in the earth's surface.

11. These breaks are called *faults*.

12. The formation of a fault is an earthquake.

13. During the breaking or shifting, a seismic wave travels across the earth's surface.

14. These quaking vibrations are especially destructive near the point of the breaking or shifting.

15. Their force is equal to as much as ten thousand times that of an atomic bomb.

16. For many years, scientists have tried to predict earthquakes.

17. There has been little success in their endeavors.

18. Earthquakes are identified only after the fact.

19. Some states, such as California, experience many earthquakes.

20. Somewhere in the earth, a quake of some magnitude is almost certainly occurring now.

REVIEW 2

Finding Subjects and Verbs

Circle the subject(s) and underline the verb(s) in the following sentences. You will have to supply the subject for one sentence.

1. Consider this information about Puerto Rico.

2. Just where is Puerto Rico?

3. What do the words *Puerto Rico* mean?

4. Are Puerto Ricans U.S. citizens?

5. How is Puerto Rico different from our states?

6. Will it ever become a state?

7. The Commonwealth of Puerto Rico is located southeast of Florida.

8. *Puerto Rico* means "rich port."

9. Puerto Rico became a U.S. territory in 1898 after the Spanish-American War.

10. It became a commonwealth with its own constitution in 1952.

11. Puerto Ricans are citizens of the United States.

12. They cannot vote in presidential elections and do not pay federal income taxes.

13. On several occasions, they have voted not to become a state.

14. However, there are many in favor of statehood.

15. The majority of the citizens speak Spanish.

16. Their economy is based on manufacturing, fishing, and agriculture.

17. The Caribbean National Forest is treasured by Puerto Ricans and visitors.

18. In this tropical rain forest parrots and orchids can be seen.

19. Tourists by the thousands visit the Phosphorescent Bay at La Parguera.

20. On moonless nights, the phosphorescent plankton light the water.

REVIEW 3

Writing Sentences with Subjects and Verbs

Using the topic of *work*, write five sentences. For variety, include one sentence with a compound subject, one with a compound verb, one with the verb before the subject, and one with the subject followed by a prepositional phrase. Circle the subjects and underline the verbs.

1. _____

_____

2. _____

_____

3. _____

_____

4. _____

_____

5. _____

_____

STUDENT COMPANION SITE

For additional practice, visit www.cengage .com/devenglish/ brandon/spb6e.

MICROTHEME

To practice your skills acquired in this chapter, return to the Microtheme on page 43 and complete Exercise B.

Kinds of Sentences

MICROTHEME	Writing Activity in Miniature

EXERCISE A

Before you work on this chapter, write a Microtheme on the following topic. Write small enough to leave room for marking later. **After** you have studied this chapter, return to your Microtheme and complete Exercise B to practice what you have learned.

Suggested Microtheme Topic: Write a Microtheme of 80 to 100 words about the best or the worst decision you made during the past three years.

EXERCISE B

Connecting Your Learning Objectives with Your Microtheme

Complete this exercise after you have studied this chapter.

1. Examine your Microtheme to make sure you have used a variety of sentence structures.
2. Mark one simple sentence (S), one compound sentence (CP), and one complex (CX) sentence. Revise sentences for variety if necessary.

The four kinds of basic sentences in English are simple, compound, complex, and compound-complex. The terms may be new to you, but if you can recognize subjects and verbs, with a little instruction and practice you should be able to identify and write any of the four kinds of sentences. The only new idea to master is the concept of the *clause*.

Clauses

A **clause** is a group of words with a subject and a verb that functions as a part or all of a complete sentence. The two kinds of clauses are independent (main) and dependent (subordinate).

Independent Clause: I have the money.

Dependent Clause: When I have the money

INDEPENDENT CLAUSES

An **independent (main) clause** is a group of words with a subject and a verb that can stand alone and make sense. An independent clause expresses a complete thought by itself and can be written as a separate sentence.

Sabrina plays the bass guitar.

The manager is not at fault.

DEPENDENT CLAUSES

A **dependent clause** is a group of words with a subject and a verb that depends on the main clause to give it meaning.

since Carlotta came home [no meaning alone]

Since Carlotta came home, her mother has been happy. [has meaning]
dependent clause   independent clause

because she was needed [no meaning alone]

Kachina stayed in the game because she was needed. [has meaning]
independent clause   dependent clause

RELATIVE CLAUSES

One type of dependent clause is called a **relative clause**. A relative clause begins with a relative pronoun, a pronoun such as *that*, *which*, or *who*. Relative pronouns *relate* the clause to another word in the sentence.

that fell last night [no meaning alone]

The snow that fell last night is nearly gone. [has meaning]
dependent clause
independent clause

In the sentence above, the relative pronoun *that* relates the dependent clause to the subject of the sentence, *snow*.

who stayed in the game [no meaning alone]

Kachina was the only one who stayed in the game.
       independent clause   dependent clause

In the sentence above, the relative pronoun *who* relates the dependent clause to the word *one*.

TROUBLE SPOT: PHRASES

A **phrase** is a group of words that go together. It differs from a clause in that a phrase does not have a subject and a verb. In Chapter 3, we discussed prepositional phrases (*in the house, beyond the horizon*) and saw some verbal phrases (infinitive phrase: *to go home*; participial phrase: *disconnected from the printer*; and gerund phrase: *running the computer*).

EXERCISE 1   Identifying Clauses and Phrases

Identify the following groups of words as an independent, or main, clause (has a subject and verb and can stand alone); a dependent clause (has a subject and verb but cannot stand alone); or a phrase (a group of words that go together but do not have a subject and verb). Use these abbreviations: IC (independent clause), DC (dependent clause), or P (phrase).

_____   **1.** Under the table

_____   **2.** After I scanned the document

_____   **3.** I scanned the document.

_____   **4.** To find a fossil

_____   **5.** Mr. Darwin found a fossil.

_____   **6.** Over the bridge and through the woods

_____   **7.** We chased the wind over the bridge and through the woods.

_____   **8.** Which is on the floor

_____   **9.** Find your new socks.

_____   **10.** Because of the new guidelines

_____   **11.** Standing on the corner

_____   **12.** Why are we standing on the corner?

Writing Sentences

This section covers sentence types according to this principle: On the basis of the number and kinds of clauses it contains, a sentence may be classified as simple, compound, complex, or compound-complex. In the examples in the following list, the dependent clauses are italicized, and the independent clauses are underlined.

Type	Definition	Example
Simple	One independent clause	<u>She did the work well.</u>
Compound	Two or more independent clauses	<u>She did the work well</u>, and <u>she was paid well.</u>
Complex	One independent clause and one or more dependent clauses	*Because she did the work well*, <u>she was paid well.</u>
Compound-complex	Two or more independent clauses and one or more dependent clauses	*Because she did the work well*, <u>she was paid well</u>, and <u>she was satisfied.</u>

SIMPLE SENTENCES

A **simple sentence** consists of one independent clause and no dependent clauses. It may contain phrases and have more than one subject or verb.

The *lake looks* beautiful in the moonlight. [one subject and one verb]

The *Army, Navy,* and *Marines sent* troops to the disaster area. [three subjects and one verb]

We sang the old songs and *danced* happily at their wedding. [one subject and two verbs]

My *father, mother,* and *sister came* to the school play, *applauded* the performers, and *attended* the party afterward. [three subjects and three verbs]

EXERCISE 2   Writing Simple Sentences

Write six simple sentences. The first five have been started for you.

1. This school _____

_____

2. My desk _____

_____

3. My friend _____

_____

4. In the evening, I _____

_____

5. Last night the _____

_____

6. _____

_____

COMPOUND SENTENCES

A **compound sentence** consists of two or more independent clauses with no dependent clauses. Take, for example, the following two independent clauses:

He opened the drawer. He found his missing disk.

Here are two ways to join the independent clauses to form a compound sentence.

1. The two independent clauses can be connected by a connecting word called a *coordinating conjunction*. The coordinating conjunctions are *for, and, nor, but, or, yet, so.* (Remember the acronym FANBOYS.) Use a comma before the coordinating conjunction (FANBOYS) between two independent clauses (unless the clauses are extremely short).

He opened the drawer, *and* he found his missing disk.

He opened the drawer, *so* he found his missing disk.

2. Another way to join independent clauses to form a compound sentence is to put a semicolon between the clauses.

He opened the drawer; he found his missing disk.

EXERCISE 3   Writing Compound Sentences

Write five compound sentences using coordinating conjunctions. The sentences have been started for you. Then write the same five compound sentences without the coordinating conjunctions. Use a semicolon to join the independent clauses.

1. He played well in the first quarter, but he _____

_____

_____

2. She was happy for a while, and then _____

_____

_____

3. The dog is our best friend, for _____

_____

_____

4. She is not the best player, nor is _____

_____

_____

5. I will try to help, but _____

_____

_____

6. _____

_____

_____

7. _____

_____

_____

8. _____

_____

_____

9. _____

_____

_____

10. _____

_____

_____

COMPLEX SENTENCES

A **complex sentence** consists of one independent clause and one or more dependent clauses. In the following sentences, the dependent clauses are italicized.

When lilacs are in bloom, we love to visit friends in the country. [one dependent clause and one independent clause]

Although it rained last night, we decided to take the path *that led through the woods*. [one independent clause and two dependent clauses]

Punctuation tip: Use a comma after a dependent clause that appears before the main clause.

When the bus arrived, we quickly boarded.

A relative clause (see page 57) can be the dependent clause in a complex sentence.

I knew the actress *who played that part in the 1980s*.

EXERCISE 4   Writing Complex Sentences

Write six complex sentences. The first five have been started for you.

1. Although he did the work quickly, _____

_____

2. _____

_____ because we got caught in a storm.

3. After you go to the party, _____

_____

4. Because you are smart, _____

_____

5. _____

_____ when he turned to leave.

6. _____

_____

COMPOUND-COMPLEX SENTENCES

A **compound-complex sentence** consists of two or more independent clauses and one or more dependent clauses.

Compound-Complex Sentence:	Albert enlisted in the Army, and Robert, who was his older brother, joined him a day later.
Independent Clauses:	Albert enlisted in the Army Robert joined him a day later
Dependent Clause:	who was his older brother
Compound-Complex Sentence:	Because Mr. Yamamoto was a talented teacher, he was voted teacher of the year, and his students prospered.
Independent Clauses:	he was voted teacher of the year his students prospered
Dependent Clause:	Because Mr. Yamamoto was a talented teacher

EXERCISE 5   Writing Compound-Complex Sentences

Write six compound-complex sentences. The first five have been started for you.

1. Because he was my friend, I had to defend him, and I _____

   _____

2. Although he started late, he finished rapidly, and he _____

   _____

3. She had not eaten since the clock struck twelve, and she _____

   _____

4. The man who was sick tried to rise, but _____

   _____

5. If you want to leave, _____

   _____

6. _____

   _____

Procedure for Sentence Analysis

Here is a systematic approach to sentence analysis some students find helpful.

1. Underline all the verbs and circle all the subjects in the sentence.

2. Draw a box around each clause.

3. Label each box as either IC (independent clause) or DC (dependent clause).

4. Add up the number of each kind of clause and apply the following formula. (See the chart on page 59 for a more detailed explanation and examples.)

   One IC = Simple

   Two or more ICs = Compound

   One IC and one or more DCs = Complex

   Two or more ICs and one or more DCs = Compound-Complex

   Example:

   DC

   | Although (he) underline{played} well all season, |

   IC

   | his (team) lost ten games and finished in last place. |

   1 DC + 1 IC = Complex

EXERCISE 6   Identifying Types of Sentences

Indicate the kind of sentence by writing the appropriate letter(s) in the blank.

S	**simple**
CP	**compound**
CX	**complex**
CC	**compound-complex**

Underline the verbs and circle the subjects. Consider using labeled boxes as shown in the previous example.

_____ **1.** The most popular sport in the world is soccer.

_____ **2.** People in ancient China and Japan had a form of soccer, and even Rome had a game that resembled soccer.

_____ **3.** The game as it is played today got its start in England.

_____ **4.** In the Middle Ages, whole towns played soccer on Shrove Tuesday.

_____ **5.** Goals were built at opposite ends of town, and hundreds of people who lived in those towns would play on each side.

_____ **6.** Such games resembled full-scale brawls.

7. The first side to score a goal won and was declared village champion.

_____ **8.** Then both sides tended to the wounded, and they didn't play again for a whole year.

_____ **9.** The rules of the game were written in the late 1800s at British boarding schools.

_____ **10.** Now nearly every European country has a national soccer team, and the teams participate in international tournaments.

EXERCISE 7   Identifying Types of Sentences

Indicate the kind of sentence by writing the appropriate letter(s) in the blank.

S	**simple**
CP	**compound**
CX	**complex**
CC	**compound-complex**

Underline the verbs and circle the subjects. Consider using labeled boxes as shown on page 63.

_____ 1. Leonardo da Vinci was one of the greatest painters of the Italian Renaissance.

_____ 2. His portrait *Mona Lisa* and his religious scene *The Last Supper* rank among the most famous pictures ever painted.

_____ 3. Da Vinci was trained to be a painter, but he was also one of the most versatile geniuses in all of history.

_____ 4. His interests and achievements spread into an astonishing variety of fields that are usually considered scientific specialties.

_____ 5. Da Vinci studied anatomy, astronomy, botany, and geology, and he designed machines and drew plans for hundreds of inventions.

_____ 6. He recorded his scientific observations and his ideas for inventions in notebooks.

_____ 7. About 4,200 pages still exist; they are filled with brilliant drawings that reveal da Vinci's powers of observation and skill as a draftsman.

_____ 8. His recorded ideas were ahead of their time; for example, he drew plans for a flying machine, and he came up with the parachute, too.

_____ 9. These drawings rank among da Vinci's greatest masterpieces.

_____ 10. Although scientists of his day believed in an Earth-centered universe, da Vinci's notebooks reveal his understanding of the Earth's movement around the Sun.

EXERCISE 8   Identifying Types of Sentences

Indicate the kind of sentence by writing the appropriate letter(s) in the blank.

S   simple
CP   compound
CX   complex
CC   compound-complex

Underline the verbs and circle the subjects. Consider using labeled boxes as shown on page 63.

_____ 1. The American Society of Civil Engineers (ASCE) compiled a list of the seven wonders of the modern world.

_____ 2. These engineering experts based their decisions on several factors; for example, they evaluated the pioneering quality of structures' design or construction, the structures' contributions to humanity, and the engineering challenges that were overcome to build the structures.

_____ 3. One structure on the list is the 31-mile Channel Tunnel, or Chunnel, which connects England and France through a system of tunnels under the English Channel.

_____ 4. Another marvel is the Panama Canal; it took 42,000 workers ten years to dig a canal across Panama to connect the Atlantic and Pacific oceans.

_____ 5. Although it was completed back in 1937, San Francisco's Golden Gate Bridge remains the world's tallest suspension bridge.

_____ 6. The bridge's construction involved many difficulties, for workers faced strong tides, frequent storms and fog, and the problem of blasting rock under deep water for earthquake-resistant foundations.

_____ 7. Two of the structures on the ASCE's list of wonders are buildings.

_____ 8. One of them is New York's Empire State Building, and the other is the CN Tower in Toronto, Canada.

_____ 9. Even though it is no longer the tallest building in the world, the well-engineered Empire State Building held that record for forty years, and its construction revolutionized the skyscraper construction industry.

_____ 10. The Itaipu Dam at the Brazil/Paraguay border and the dams, floodgates, and storm surge barriers of the Netherlands' North Sea Protection Works illustrate humanity's ability to master the forces of nature, so they are the sixth and seventh items on the list.

EXERCISE 9   Identifying Types of Sentences

Indicate the kind of sentence by writing the appropriate letter(s) in the blank.

S	**simple**
CP	**compound**
CX	**complex**
CC	**compound-complex**

Underline the verbs and circle the subjects. Consider using labeled boxes as shown on page 63.

_____ **1.** Around 500 BCE, the Mayans began to create their civilization in the southern Gulf Coast region and present-day Guatemala.

_____ **2.** The result was remarkable for its brilliant achievements.

_____ **3.** Although they had no wheeled vehicles and no beasts of burden such as horses or oxen, they moved great pieces of stone to build their temples.

_____ **4.** They had no iron tools; however, because they shaped their stone blocks so skillfully, their pyramids still stand.

_____ **5.** The pyramids were the center of Mayan religious ceremonies.

_____ **6.** The Mayans built many city-states, and the ruins of at least eighty have been found.

_____ **7.** The tallest pyramid was as high as a twenty-story building.

_____ **8.** A small temple was constructed at the top, where priests conducted ceremonies.

_____ **9.** These pyramids were surrounded by plazas and avenues.

_____ **10.** The Mayans were able to build complex structures and to invent an accurate calendar because they knew mathematics well.

CHAPTER REVIEW   Kinds of Sentences

On the basis of number and kinds of clauses, sentences may be classified as simple, compound, complex, and compound-complex.

CLAUSES

1. A **clause** is a group of words with a subject and a verb that functions as a part or all of a complete sentence. There are two kinds of clauses: independent (main) and dependent (subordinate).

2. An **independent (main) clause** is a group of words with a subject and a verb that can stand alone and make sense. An independent clause expresses a complete thought by itself and can be written as a separate sentence.

  I have the money.

3. A **dependent clause** is a group of words with a subject and a verb that depends on a main clause to give it meaning.

  When you are ready

TYPES OF SENTENCES

Type	Definition	Example
Simple	One independent clause	Susan was having trouble with her spelling.
Compound	Two or more independent clauses	Susan was having trouble with her spelling, and she purchased a computer with a spell checker.
Complex	One independent clause and one or more dependent clauses	Because Susan was having trouble with her spelling, she purchased a computer with a spell checker.
Compound-complex	Two or more independent clauses and one or more dependent clauses	Because Susan was having trouble with her spelling, she purchased a computer with a spell checker, and the results made her expenditure worthwhile.

PUNCTUATION

1. Use a comma before a coordinating conjunction (FANBOYS) between two independent clauses.

The movie was good, *but* the tickets were expensive.

2. Use a comma after a dependent clause that appears before the main clause.

When the bus arrived, we quickly boarded.

3. Use a semicolon between two independent clauses in one sentence if there is no coordinating conjunction.

The bus arrived; we quickly boarded.

CHAPTER REVIEW Exercises

REVIEW 1   ## Identifying Types of Sentences

Indicate the kind of sentence by writing the appropriate letter(s) in the blank.

S	**simple**
CP	**compound**
CX	**complex**
CC	**compound-complex**

Underline the verbs and circle the subjects. Consider using labeled boxes as shown on page 63.

_____ **1.** For more than forty years, dolphins have served in the U.S. Navy.

_____ **2.** Dolphins use *echolocation,* which involves transmitting sound waves at objects and then reading the "echoes" from those objects.

_____ **3.** They can distinguish a BB pellet from a kernel of corn from fifty feet away.

_____ **4.** They can also tell the difference between natural and human-made objects, so the navy has trained dolphins to detect explosive anti-ship mines.

_____ **5.** After unmanned undersea vehicles use sonar to identify suspicious objects, a dolphin and his team of humans go into watery combat zones to evaluate those objects.

_____ **6.** When a dolphin positively identifies a mine, the location is marked, and divers arrive later to remove the mine.

_____ **7.** During the 2003 war with Iraq, dolphins helped to disarm 100 mines and underwater booby traps planted in the water near the port city of Umm Qasr.

_____ **8.** The dolphins are not in jeopardy because they are trained to stay a safe distance from the mines.

_____ **9.** Dolphins also protected warships during the Vietnam War; in 1970, for example, the presence of five navy dolphins prevented enemy divers from destroying an army pier.

_____ **10.** Many people do not realize that dolphins have used their extraordinary abilities to protect American lives during wartime, so the navy considers them to be very valuable assets.

REVIEW 2

Identifying Types of Sentences

Indicate the kind of sentence by writing the appropriate letter(s) in the blank.

S   **simple**
CP   **compound**
CX   **complex**
CC   **compound-complex**

Underline the verbs and circle the subjects. Consider using labeled boxes as shown on page 63.

_____ **1.** Most hummingbirds weigh less than a nickel.

_____ **2.** Because they're so tiny, people think of them as cute, sweet little birds.

_____   3. However, hummingbirds are very mean, and they have been dubbed the "junkyard dogs" of the bird world.

_____   4. A male hummingbird will fiercely guard a nectar feeder or a patch of flowers, and if any other hummingbirds come near, he will attack them.

_____   5. The bird will threaten intruders, chase them, ram them in mid-air, and try to stab them with its beak.

_____   6. Hummingbirds can even intimidate birds like hawks, which are a hundred times their size.

_____   7. These territorial birds can be vicious, but they do have a good reason.

_____   8. They expend a lot of energy; as a matter of fact, their hearts beat 1,200 times a minute, and their wings beat at over 2,000 revolutions per minute.

_____   9. To survive, a hummingbird must consume 7 to 12 calories per day; in human terms, that would be 204,300 calories per day, which is the amount in 171 pounds of hamburger.

_____   10. If you had to round up that much grub every day, you, too, might get very protective of your food source.

REVIEW 3   ## Writing Types of Sentences

Write a paragraph or two (a total of about ten sentences) on the topic of food (eating or preparing). Then examine your sentences and mark at least one example of each kind: simple (S), compound (CP), complex (CX), and compound-complex (CC). If any kinds are not represented, do some simple sentence revision.

STUDENT COMPANION SITE
For additional practice, visit www.cengage .com/devenglish/ brandon/spb6e.

MICROTHEME

To practice your skills acquired in this chapter, return to the Microtheme on page 56 and complete Exercise B.

Combining Sentences

FLOW OF WRITING

MICROTHEME   Writing Activity in Miniature

EXERCISE A

Before you work on this chapter, write a Microtheme on the following topic. Write small enough to leave room for marking later. **After** you have studied this chapter, return to your microtheme and complete Exercise B to practice what you have learned.

Suggested Microtheme Topic: Write a Microtheme of 80 to 100 words about the breakup of a relationship. It could be a friendship, romance, or school or work situation. Concentrate on causes or effects.

EXERCISE B

Connecting Your Learning Objectives with Your Microtheme

Complete this exercise after you have studied this chapter.

1. Check to make sure you have combined the sentences that could and should be combined. Revise as necessary.
2. Check to make sure you have properly used commas and semicolons in compound, complex, and compound-complex sentences.

The simple sentence, the most basic sentence in the English language, can be exceptionally useful and powerful. Some of the greatest statements in literature have been presented in the simple sentence. Its strength is in its singleness of purpose. However, a piece of writing made up of a long series of short, simple sentences is likely to be monotonous. Moreover, the form may suggest a separateness of ideas that does not serve your purpose well. If your ideas are closely associated and some are equal in importance and some not, you may be able to combine sentences to show a clearer relationship among those ideas.

Coordination: The Compound Sentence

If you intend to communicate two equally important and closely related ideas, you certainly will want to place them close together, probably in a **compound sentence**.

Suppose we take two simple sentences that we want to combine:

I am very tired. I worked very hard today.

We have already looked at coordinating conjunctions as a way of joining independent clauses to create compound sentences. Depending on which coordinating conjunction you use, you can show different kinds of relationships. (The following list is arranged according to the FANBOYS acronym discussed in Chapter 4. Only the first conjunction joins the original two sentences.)

For shows a reason:

I am very tired, *for* I worked very hard today.

And shows equal ideas:

I am very tired, *and* I want to rest for a few minutes.

Nor indicates a negative choice or alternative:

I am not tired, *nor* am I hungry right now.

But shows contrast:

I am very tired, *but* I have no time to rest now.

Or indicates a choice or an alternative:

I will take a nap, *or* I will go out jogging.

Yet indicates contrast:

I am tired, *yet* I am unable to relax.

So points to a result:

I am tired, *so* I will take a nap.

PUNCTUATION WITH COORDINATING CONJUNCTIONS

When you combine two sentences by using a coordinating conjunction, drop the first period, change the capital letter that begins the second sentence to a small letter, and insert a comma before the coordinating conjunction.

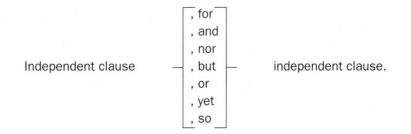

EXERCISE 1   Combining Sentences: Compound

Combine the following pairs of sentences by deleting the first period, changing the capital letter that begins the second sentence to a small letter, and inserting a comma and an appropriate coordinating conjunction from the FANBOYS list. Feel free to reword the sentences as necessary.

1. James Francis "Jim" Thorpe, a Sac and Fox Indian, was born in 1888 near Prague, Oklahoma. At the age of sixteen, he left home to enroll in the Carlisle Indian School in Pennsylvania.

2. He had had little experience playing football. He led his small college to victories against championship teams.

3. He had scarcely heard of other sports. He golfed in the 70s, bowled above 200, and played varsity basketball and lacrosse.

4. In the 1912 Olympic Games for amateur athletes at Stockholm, Jim Thorpe entered the two most rigorous events, the decathlon and the pentathlon. He won both.

5. King Gustav V of Sweden told him, "You, Sir, are the greatest athlete in the world." Jim Thorpe said, "Thanks, King."

6. Later it was said he had once been paid fifteen dollars a week to play baseball, making him a professional athlete. The Olympic medals were taken from him.

7. Soon a Major League baseball scout did offer Thorpe a respectable contract, He played in the National League for six seasons.

8. Not content to play only one sport, he also earned a good salary for his time in professional football. After competing for fifteen years, he said he had never played for the money.

9. Many regard Jim Thorpe as the greatest athlete of the twentieth century. He excelled in many sports at the highest levels of athletic competition.

10. Off the playing fields, he was known by his friends as a modest, quiet man. On the fields, he was a person of joyful combat.

EXERCISE 2   Combining Sentences: Compound

Combine the following pairs of sentences by deleting the first period, changing the capital letter that begins the second sentence to a small letter, and inserting a comma and an appropriate coordinating conjunction from the FANBOYS list. Feel free to reword the sentences as necessary.

1. Sailing on its maiden voyage, the *Titanic* was considered unsinkable. On April 14, 1912, it struck an iceberg.

2. The ship sank 1,600 miles northeast of New York City. About 1,500 lives were lost.

3. The *Titanic* had been designed with great care. Its structure included sixteen watertight compartments.

4. Four of the compartments could be flooded without the ship's sinking. On that night five of the compartments flooded.

5. There were not enough lifeboats for the passengers. Lifeboats were considered unnecessary.

6. The management of the *Titanic* was supremely confident about the safety of the passengers. No lifeboat drills were required.

7. The killer iceberg was spotted just before the crash. It was too late.

8. At the time of the collision, another ship, the *Californian*, was only twenty miles away. The radio operator aboard the *Californian* was not on duty.

9. Some people behaved heroically. Others thought only of saving themselves.

10. Most of the survivors were women and children. The victims included the rich and famous.

SEMICOLONS AND CONJUNCTIVE ADVERBS

In Chapter 4, we saw that a semicolon can join independent clauses to make a compound sentence. Here are two more simple sentences to combine:

> We were late. We missed the first act.

We can make one compound sentence of them by joining the two clauses with a semicolon:

> We were late; we missed the first act.

We can also use words called **conjunctive adverbs** after semicolons to make the relationship between the two clauses clearer. Look at how the conjunctive adverb *therefore* adds the idea of "as a result."

> We were late; *therefore*, we missed the first act.

Conjunctive adverbs include the following words and phrases: *also, consequently, furthermore, hence, however, in fact, moreover, nevertheless, now, on the other hand, otherwise, soon, therefore, similarly, then, thus.*

Consider the meaning you want when you use a conjunctive adverb to coordinate ideas.

As a result of: *therefore, consequently, hence, thus, then*

To the contrary or with reservation: *however, nevertheless, otherwise, on the other hand*

In addition to: *moreover, also*

To emphasize or specify: *in fact, for example*

To compare: *similarly*

PUNCTUATION WITH SEMICOLONS AND CONJUNCTIVE ADVERBS

When you combine two sentences by using a semicolon, replace the first period with a semicolon and change the capital letter that begins the second sentence to a small letter. If you wish to use a conjunctive adverb, insert it after the semicolon and put a comma after it. (However, no comma follows *then, now, thus,* and *soon.*) The first letters of ten common conjunctive adverbs make up the acronym HOTSHOT CAT.

Independent clause
; however,
; otherwise,
; therefore,
; similarly,
; hence,
; on the other hand,
; then
; consequently,
; also,
; thus
independent clause.

EXERCISE 3   Combining Sentences: Compound

Combine the following pairs of sentences by replacing the first period with a semicolon, changing the capital letter that begins the second sentence to a small letter, and inserting a conjunctive adverb if appropriate, followed by a comma. Consider the list of conjunctive adverbs (HOTSHOT CAT and others). Do not use a conjunctive adverb in every sentence.

1. The legendary island of Atlantis has fascinated people for centuries, It probably never existed.

2. According to the Greek writer Plato, the people of Atlantis were very ambitious and warlike, They planned to conquer all of the Mediterranean.

3. Initially, they were successful in subduing areas to the west, They became wealthy.

4. Then the people of Atlantis became proud, They became corrupt and wicked.

5. They were confident and attacked Athens. Athens and its allies defeated the invaders.

6. The story of Atlantis is probably just a tale. Many people have believed it.

7. Some writers have tried to link the legend with such real places as America and the Canary Islands. No link has been found.

8. The Minoan civilization on Crete was destroyed by tidal waves. A similar fate may have befallen Atlantis.

9. Some people speculate about a volcanic explosion on Atlantis. A volcanic eruption did destroy part of the island Thera in the Eastern Mediterranean in 1500 BCE.

10. Some writers have conjectured that American Indians migrated to the New World by way of Atlantis. Archaeologists dispute that idea.

EXERCISE 4   Combining Sentences: Compound

Combine the following pairs of sentences by replacing the first period with a semicolon, changing the capital letter that begins the second sentence to a small letter, and inserting a conjunctive adverb if appropriate, sometimes followed by a comma. Consider the list of conjunctive adverbs (HOTSHOT CAT and others). Do not use a conjunctive adverb in every sentence.

1. Camels can cover much distance in heat with little or no water. They are well adapted to the desert.

2. They can walk easily on soft sand and carry heavy loads. They are useful pack animals for human beings traveling in the desert.

3. The typical desert offers little vegetation. That circumstance does not affect the camel.

4. A camel stores food in one or two humps of fat on its back. When food is scarce, the camel uses that fat for energy.

5. The Arabian camel has one hump. The Bactrian has two.

6. Camels are known for their bad temper. Most people are not surprised when camels bite, kick, and spit.

7. Camels grunt and groan when a passenger climbs aboard. Once under way, they carry their loads patiently.

8. Camels have mouth linings as tough as leather. They can eat a thorny cactus without injuring themselves.

9. In the 1850s the U.S. Army imported camels for desert transportation. The development of the railroads made camels unnecessary.

10. Working camels in Africa live for as long as fifty years. In circuses and zoos they die by the age of thirty.

Subordination: The Complex Sentence

Whereas a compound sentence contains independent clauses that are equally important and closely related, a **complex sentence** combines ideas of unequal value. The following two sentences can be combined as either a compound sentence or a complex sentence, depending on whether the writer thinks the ideas are of equal value.

My neighbors are considerate. They never play loud music.

Combined as a compound sentence, suggesting that the ideas are of equal value, the new sentence looks like this:

My neighbors are considerate, and they never play loud music.
    independent clause   independent clause
      (main idea)   (main idea)

Here are the same two ideas combined as a complex sentence, suggesting that the ideas are of unequal value:

Because my neighbors are considerate, they never play loud music.
    dependent clause   independent clause
   (less important idea)   (main idea)

Although both the compound and complex forms are correct, the complex form conveys the ideas more precisely because one idea does seem to be more important—one idea depends on the other.

Thus if you have two sentences with closely related ideas and one is clearly more important than the other, consider combining them in a complex sentence. Compare these two paragraphs:

1. This version contains six simple sentences, implying that the ideas are of equal value:

   (1) I was very upset. (2) The Fourth of July fireworks were especially loud. (3) My dog ran away. (4) The animal control officer made his morning rounds. (5) He found my dog in another part of town. (6) I was relieved.

2. This version consists of two simple sentences and two complex sentences, showing that some ideas are more important than others:

(1) I was very upset. (2) Because the Fourth of July fireworks were especially loud, my dog ran away. (3) When the animal control officer made his morning rounds, he found my dog in another part of town. (4) I was relieved.

You will probably consider Version 2 superior to Version 1. In Version 1, sentences 2 and 3 are closely related, but 3 is more important. Sentences 4 and 5 are closely related, but 5 is more important. In Version 2, the revision made each pair into a complex sentence.

Although you could combine sentences 1 and 2, the result would be illogical because the wrong idea would be conveyed:

> **Illogical Combination:**   I was very upset because the Fourth of July fireworks were especially loud.

The person was very upset because the dog ran away, not because the fireworks were especially loud.

SUBORDINATING CONJUNCTIONS

As you learned in Chapter 4, a complex sentence is composed of one independent clause and one or more dependent clauses. In combining two independent clauses to write a complex sentence, your first step is to decide on a word that will best show the relationship between the clauses. Words that show the relationship of a dependent clause to an independent one are called **subordinating conjunctions**. The italicized words in the following sentences are subordinating conjunctions. Consider the meaning as well as the placement of each one. Note that the first letters of the words spell out BAT WASHTUB. Remembering that acronym will help you write complex and compound-complex sentences.

Because the storm hit, the game was canceled.

After the storm passed, the dogs began to bark.

That he won is a certainty.

While Colette told her joke, the class was moved to fits of hysterics.

Vernon did not volunteer to work on the holiday, *although* the pay was good.

No one has visited Patty *since* she moved into town.

How he won is a secret.

They decided to wait *till* the cows came home.

They refused to work *unless* they were allowed to wear chef's hats.

Before the session ended, all the "hep cats" blew some sweet sounds.

Other subordinating conjunctions include the following:

as	if	so that	where
as if	in order that	than	whereas
even if	provided that	when	wherever
even though	rather than	whenever	whether

PUNCTUATION WITH SUBORDINATING CONJUNCTIONS

If the dependent clause comes *before* the independent clause, set it off with a comma.

Before Mike wrote his final draft, he looked over his outline.

If the dependent clause comes *after* or *within* the independent clause, set it off only if the clause is not necessary to the meaning of the independent clause or if the dependent clause begins with the word(s) *although*, *though*, or *even though*.

We went home *after* the concert had ended.

Vincent continued painting, *although* he had repainted the cabinet twice.

PUNCTUATION WITH RELATIVE PRONOUNS

As you learned in Chapter 4, a relative clause begins with a relative pronoun, a pronoun such as *that*, *which*, or *who*.

The decision <u>that I made</u> is final.
       relative clause

A student <u>who uses a computer</u> can save time in revising.
       relative clause

Set off the dependent (relative) clause with commas when it is not necessary to the sentence. Do not set off the clause if it is necessary for the meaning of the sentence.

Everyone *who tries* will pass this class. [The dependent clause is necessary because one would not say, "Everyone will pass this class."]

Juan, *who tries*, will pass this class. [The dependent clause is not necessary because one can say, "Juan will pass this class."]

The relative pronoun *which* usually refers to things. The word *which* almost always indicates that a clause is not necessary for the meaning of the sentence. Therefore, a clause beginning with *which* is almost always set off by commas.

My car, *which* is ten years old, has a flat tire.

The relative pronoun *that* also usually refers to things. However, the word *that* almost always indicates that the clause *is* necessary for the meaning of the sentence. Therefore, a clause beginning with *that* usually is *not* set off by commas.

The car *that* has a flat tire is ten years old.

The relative pronouns *who* and *whom*, as well as *whoever* and *whomever*, usually refer to people. Clauses that begin with those relative pronouns are not set off by commas if they are necessary for the meaning of the sentence; if they are not necessary, they are set off.

A person *who* has a way with words is often quoted. [necessary for the meaning of the sentence]

Uncle Colby, *whom* I quote often, has a way with words. [not necessary for the meaning of the sentence]

EXERCISE 5   Combining Sentences: Complex

Combine the following pairs of sentences into one complex sentence. Insert an appropriate subordinating conjunction or relative pronoun, add or fix punctuation, and make other minor changes as needed. Sentences that should be combined by using a relative pronoun are indicated.

1. (relative pronoun) The freeway congestion was under study. The problem occured every Friday at noon.

2. The vacationers had a good time, The bears destroyed a few tents and ate people's food.

3. The teenagers loved their senior prom. The band played badly.

4. Farmers gathered for miles around. Jeff had grown a fifty-pound cucumber.

5. Back-seat drivers make unwanted suggestions in the nag-proof model. They can be ejected from the vehicle.

6. (relative pronoun) The marriage counselor gave bad advice. He charged only half price.

7. (relative pronoun) The robots would not do their work. They needed fresh batteries.

8. The hurricane was expected to hit during the night. The residents checked their flashlights.

9. The ice sculptor displayed his work in the dining hall. The customers applauded.

10. Someone stole the artwork of ice. No evidence was found.

EXERCISE 6   Combining Sentences: Complex

Combine the following pairs of sentences into one complex sentence. Insert an appropriate subordinating conjunction or relative pronoun, add or fix punctuation, and make other minor changes as needed. Sentences that should be combined by using a relative pronoun are indicated.

1. (relative pronoun) Mary Hayes was one of the first female soldiers in American warfare. She is better known as Molly Pitcher.

2. (relative pronoun) At the outbreak of the War of Independence, Mary was the wife of John Hayes. He soon joined the army.

3. Following established practice, Mary Hayes also went to war. She was the wife of a soldier.

4. He performed military duties. She washed and mended clothes and cooked meals.

5. John Hayes's regiment fought at the Battle of Monmouth. The day was hot.

6. Mary Hayes brought the soldiers water in pitchers. Some men started calling her Molly Pitcher, "Molly" for "Mary" and "Pitcher" for what she carried.

7. She was immediately proud of the name. Others started using it.

8. John Hayes suffered a heat stroke. Mary Hayes took over his job, firing his cannon.

9. A cannonball sailed between her knees and tore her dress. She refused to stop fighting.

10. Following the war, Mary Hayes received a pension for soldiers, She was truly a patriotic veteran.

Coordination and Subordination: The Compound-Complex Sentence

At times you may want to show the relationship of three or more ideas within one sentence. If that relationship involves two or more main ideas and one or more supporting ideas, the combination can be stated in a **compound-complex sentence** (two or more independent clauses and one or more dependent clauses).

<u>Before Kafka learned how to operate a word processor,</u>
dependent clause

<u>he had trouble with his typewritten assignments,</u>
independent clause

but now <u>he produces clean, attractive pages</u>.
independent clause

In our previous discussion of the complex sentence, we presented this group of six sentences:

I was very upset. The Fourth of July fireworks were especially loud. My dog ran away. The animal control officer made his morning rounds. He found my dog in another part of town. I was relieved.

We then converted the group of six sentences to four.

I was very upset. Because the Fourth of July fireworks were especially loud, my dog ran away. When the animal control officer made his morning rounds, he found my dog in another part of town. I was relieved.

But what if we wanted to show an even closer relationship of ideas? One solution would be to combine the two complex sentences in this way (the italicized sentence is compound-complex):

I was very upset. *Because the Fourth of July fireworks were especially loud, my dog ran away; but when the animal control officer made his morning rounds, he found my dog in another part of town.* I was relieved.

PUNCTUATION OF COMPLICATED COMPOUND OR COMPOUND-COMPLEX SENTENCES

If a compound or compound-complex sentence has one or more commas in the first clause, you may want to use a semicolon before the coordinating conjunction between the two clauses. Its purpose is to show the reader very clearly the division between the two independent clauses. The preceding example illustrates this use of the semicolon.

EXERCISE 7   Combining Sentences: Compound-Complex

Combine each group of sentences into one compound-complex sentence. Use the rules of sentence combining and punctuation discussed in this chapter.

1. A grumpy bear had stalked the grounds. Summer camp had been a great experience for the campers. They vowed to return.

2. The stuffed cabbage ran out. The party ended. The guests went home.

3. It was a costume party. All the guests dressed as movie legends. Ten were Elvis impersonators.

4. A new Elvis theme park opened in our town, I attended, I think I saw the King.

5. My father encouraged me to take up a hobby. I began collecting stamps. Now my hobby has become a business.

6. They were in a wilderness camp. They were not allowed to bring pets. They were allowed to bring toys.

7. He had no leather shoes to wear. Young Stu could not go to the prom. He hoped there would be a prom next year.

8. People were hungry. They ate massive quantities of hot dogs at the game. They knew the dogs were made of mystery meat.

9. The ambulance drivers were taking a break. A man had a choking fit. The drivers came to his rescue.

10. The film was filled with scenes of violence. It included a charming love story. The public liked it.

EXERCISE 8   Combining Sentences: Compound-Complex

Combine each group of sentences into one compound-complex sentence. Use the rules of sentence combining and punctuation discussed in this chapter.

1. Helen Keller suffered a serious childhood illness. She became blind and deaf. At first her parents did not know what to do.

2. Her parents would not give up despite discouraging advice. They advertised for a teacher. A tutor named Anne Sullivan agreed to help.

3. Young Helen began to discover the world through her sense of touch. She learned the alphabet. She started connecting words with objects.

4. Her physical condition was irreversible. Her progress was rapid. In three years she could read Braille.

5. She could not talk. She used sign language for speech. She used a special typewriter to write.

6. She reached the age of ten. She took speech lessons from a teacher of the deaf. In six years she could speak well enough to be understood.

7. She attended college. She still needed help. Anne Sullivan continued as her tutor and interpreter.

8. She graduated from college with honors. She became involved in programs to help the deaf and blind communicate. She wrote books and articles about problems of the disabled.

9. The effects of World War II presented special problems. Helen Keller helped disabled people in other countries. She helped soldiers blinded in the war.

10. Helen Keller died in 1968. She had an international reputation as a humanitarian. Her books had been translated into more than fifty languages.

Other Ways to Combine Ideas

In this chapter, you have learned how to combine simple sentences into compound, complex, and compound-complex sentences that show the coordination and subordination of ideas. You can use other methods of combining ideas, as well. Here are four you may want to use in your own writing.

1. Use an **appositive**, which is a noun or noun phrase that immediately follows a noun or pronoun and renames it.

   Kyoko is the leading scorer on the team. Kyoko is a quick and strong player.

   Kyoko, *a quick and strong player*, is the leading scorer on the team.

2. Use a **prepositional phrase**, a preposition followed by a noun or pronoun object.

   Dolly Parton wrote a song about a coat. The coat had many colors.

   Dolly Parton wrote a song about a coat *of many colors*.

3. Drop the subject in the sentence that follows and combine the sentences.

   Some items are too damaged for recycling. They must be discarded.

   Some items are too damaged for recycling *and* must be discarded.

4. Use a **participial phrase**, a group of words that includes a participle, which is a verbal that usually ends in *-ing* or *-ed*.

   Jamal rowed smoothly. He reached the shore.

   Rowing smoothly, Jamal reached the shore.

EXERCISE 9   Combining Sentences

Combine each group of sentences into a single sentence in the ways indicated.

Use an appositive.

1. Ernest Hemingway won the Nobel Prize for literature in 1954. He was mainly

   an American writer of fiction.

2. Ernest spent his childhood summers in Michigan. He was the second of six

   children of Clarence and Grace Hemingway.

Use a prepositional phrase.

3. After high school he became a reporter. He worked for the Kansas City *Star*.

4. During World War I he volunteered to serve as a Red Cross ambulance driver. The Red Cross unit was stationed in Italy.

Drop the subject of the second sentence.

5. In 1920 he returned to journalism with the Toronto *Star.* He met his future first wife, Hadley Richardson.

6. Hemingway and his wife moved to France. They lived in a walk-up flat in the Latin Quarter of Paris.

Use a participial phrase.

7. Hemingway Worked conscientiously on his writing. He soon became a leader of the so-called Lost Generation.

8. He always sought adventure. He hunted, fished, loved, drank, fought, and wrote his way through the next three decades.

Use any of the above ways.

9. During World War II Hemingway armed his fishing boat and hunted for German submarines. He patrolled the waters of the Caribbean.

10. He died as a life-weary, broken man in 1961 at his home in Ketchum, Idaho. He was suffering from both physical and psychological problems.

Omissions: When Parts Are Missing

Do not omit words that are needed to make your sentences clear and logical. Of the many types of undesirable construction in which necessary words are omitted, the following are the most common.

1. **Subjects.** Do not omit a necessary subject in a sentence with two verbs.

   Illogical: The cost of the car was $12,000 but would easily last me through college. (subject of *last*)

   Logical: The cost of the car was $12,000, but the car would easily last me through college.

2. **Verbs**. Do not omit verbs that are needed because of a change in the number of the subject or a change of tense.

   Illogical: The bushes were trimmed and the grass mowed.

   Logical: The bushes were trimmed and the grass was mowed.

Illogical: True honesty always has and always will be admired by most people. (tense)

Logical: True honesty always has been and always will be admired by most people.

3. *That* **as a conjunction**. The conjunction *that* should not be omitted from a dependent clause if there is danger of misreading the sentence.

Misleading: We believed Eric, if not stopped, would hurt himself.

Clear: We believed that Eric, if not stopped, would hurt himself.

4. **Prepositions**. Do not omit prepositions in idiomatic phrases, in expressions of time, and in parallel phrases.

Illogical: Weekends the campus is deserted. (time)

Logical: During weekends the campus is deserted.

Illogical: I have neither love nor patience with untrained dogs. (parallel phrases)

Logical: I have neither love for nor patience with untrained dogs.

Illogical: Glenda's illness was something we heard only after her recovery.

Logical: Glenda's illness was something we heard about only after her recovery.

EXERCISE 10   Omissions

Identify the kinds of omissions by writing one of the following words in the blanks to the right: preposition, verb, subject, that. Insert the necessary words in the sentences.

1. Charles had neither love nor patience with small pets.   _____

2. Because he was careless, a branch caught on the trigger of his gun, and went off.   _____

3. In the newspaper, the radio, and TV, the story was the same.   _____

4. We saw the car, if not stopped, would hit the tree.   _____

5. Because Jim had not worked that summer, money was scarce in the fall and expenses burdensome.   _____

6. Harry's ignorance was one of the things that we learned the trip.   _____

7. We believed the lie, if not revealed, would harm people. _____

8. The truck was creeping up the hill, and had no
thought at all of the traffic behind. _____

9. I do not believe and never have that a person's life
is not his or her own responsibility. _____

10. When Joe got his second wind, his breathing slowed, and
was able to go on running without fatigue. _____

Variety in Sentences: Types, Order, Length, Beginnings

Sentences can be written in a variety of ways to achieve freshness and clarity. Much of this polishing takes place during revision. Here are a few techniques for the main variations.

Types

You have learned that all four types of sentences are sound. Your task as a writer is to decide which one to use for a particular thought. That decision may not be made until you revise your composition. Then you can choose on the basis of the relationship of ideas:

Simple: a single idea
Compound: two closely related ideas
Complex: one idea more important than the other
Compound-complex: a combination of compound and complex

These types were all discussed in Chapter 4. This chapter provides further practice, as you combine sentences.

Order

You will choose the order of parts and information according to what you want to emphasize. Typically the most emphatic location is at the end of any unit.

Length

Uncluttered and direct, short sentences commonly draw attention. But that focus occurs only when they stand out from longer sentences. Therefore, you would usually avoid a series of short sentences.

Beginnings

A long series of sentences with each beginning containing a subject followed by a verb may become monotonous. Consider beginning sentences in different ways:

With a prepositional phrase: *In the distance* a dog barked.

With a transitional connective (conjunctive adverb) such as *then*, *however*, or *therefore*: *Then* the game was over.

With a coordinating conjunction such as *and* or *but*: *But* no one moved for three minutes. (Caution: Use this beginning sparingly.)

With a dependent clause: *Although he wanted a new Corvette,* he settled for a used Ford Taurus.

With an adverb: *Carefully* he removed the thorn from the lion's paw.

EXERCISE 11   Providing Sentence Variety

Revise the following passage to achieve better sentence variety through changes in types of sentences, order of information, length of sentences, and beginnings of sentences. Also, combine sentences for improved expression. Compare your revisions with those of others in your class. There is no single correct way of making these changes.

POWER RANGERS TO THE RESCUE
Leewan Yeomans

I do promotions on the weekends for TV's "Power Rangers." I'm Trini. She's supposed to be Chinese. I'm Chinese-American, the kids think I'm the real Ranger when I take off my mask. I've never felt very much like a Ranger except for one occasion. It was a weekend promotion, held at a park. We were doing our routine. I looked around and saw a little boy collapse. I guess he had been in distress for a while. Wearing the mask, I could hardly see anything. Anyway, this little boy was lying there, thrashing around and trying to throw up, No one was doing anything. The Pink Ranger started running around trying to find the child's parents. No one answered. I ran over when no one touched the boy, took off my mask, and put my finger in his mouth to clear his throat. There I found the problem. He had been chewing on, or maybe blowing up, a long balloon. He had swallowed it. I pulled it out of his throat. It was almost a foot long. The whole spectacle must have looked like a magic trick. The child still wasn't breathing well. The paramedics were called. They quickly helped him back to good health. His parents, who lived across the street, came to carry him home. We Rangers put our masks back on. The audience cheered us as if we had planned the whole scene. We resumed our routine. It was just another day of work for the Power Rangers.

CHAPTER REVIEW   Combining Sentences

COORDINATION

If you want to communicate two equally important and closely related ideas, place them close together, probably in a **compound sentence** (two or more independent clauses).

1. When you combine two sentences by using a coordinating conjunction (FAN-BOYS), drop the first period, change the capital letter of the second sentence to a small letter, and insert a comma before the coordinating conjunction.

I like your home. I can visit for only three months.

I like your home, *but* I can visit for only three months.

2. When you combine two sentences by using a semicolon, replace the first period with a semicolon and change the capital letter that begins the second sentence to a small letter. If you wish to use a conjunctive adverb, insert it after the semicolon and usually follow it with a comma.

I like your home. I can visit for only three months.

I like your home; I can visit for only three months.

I like your home; *however,* I can visit for only three months.

SUBORDINATION

If you have two ideas that are closely related, but one is secondary or dependent on the other, you may want to use a **complex sentence**.

My neighbors are considerate. They never play loud music.

Because my neighbors are considerate, they never play loud music.

1. If the dependent clause comes first, set it off with a comma.

Because my dog has no hands or words, he licks me to show affection.

2. If the dependent clause comes after the main clause, set it off with a comma only if you use some form of the word *though* or if the words are not necessary to convey the basic meaning in the sentence.

Edmund Hillary was knighted by Queen Elizabeth II because he was one of the first two men to climb Mt. Everest.

Other mountain climbers soon duplicated his feat, *though* they received less recognition.

3. One type of dependent clause is called a **relative clause**. A relative clause begins with a relative pronoun, a pronoun such as *that*, *which*, or *who*. Relative pronouns *relate* the clause to another word in the sentence.

Orlando purchased a used computer. It had hardly been touched.

Orlando purchased a used computer *that* had hardly been touched.

4. A relative clause should be set off with commas when it is not necessary to the sentence. Do not set the clause off if it is necessary for the meaning of the sentence.

> **Necessary:**   No one who fails the eye test will get a driver's license.
>
> **Unnecessary:**   Mr. McGoo, who failed his eye test, did not get a driver's license.

COORDINATION AND SUBORDINATION

At times you may want to show the relationship of three or more ideas within one sentence. If that relationship involves two or more main ideas and one or more supporting ideas, the combination can be stated in a **compound-complex sentence** (two or more independent clauses and one or more dependent clauses).

> Kafka produced illegible handwritten papers. At that time he had not learned how to operate a computer. Now he hands in clean, attractive pages.
>
> Before Kafka learned how to operate a computer, he produced illegible handwritten papers, but now he hands in clean, attractive pages.

Use punctuation consistent with that of the compound and complex sentences.

OTHER WAYS TO COMBINE IDEAS

1. Use an **appositive phrase**, a group of words that immediately follows a noun or pronoun and renames it.

> Garth Brooks claims Yukon, Oklahoma, as his hometown. He is a famous singer.
>
> Garth Brooks, a famous singer, claims Yukon, Oklahoma, as his hometown.

2. Use a **prepositional phrase**, a preposition followed by a noun or pronoun object.

> John Elway led the Denver Broncos to two Super Bowl victories. Both triumphs occurred in the 1990s.
>
> John Elway led the Denver Broncos to two Super Bowl victories *in the 1990s.*

3. Drop the subject in the sentence that follows and combine the sentences.

> Emily Dickinson's poetry went mostly unpublished during her lifetime. It was finally discovered and celebrated more than a half century later.
>
> Emily Dickinson's poetry went mostly unpublished during her lifetime *but was finally discovered and celebrated more than a half century later.*

4. Use a **participial phrase**, a group of words that includes a participle, which is a verbal that usually ends in *-ing* or *-ed*.

> The turtle plodded without rest stops. It won the race against the rabbit.
>
> *Plodding without rest stops*, the turtle won the race against the rabbit.

CHAPTER REVIEW Exercises

REVIEW 1   ## Combining Sentences

Combine two or more sentences from each group by using any pattern.

1. The Mercury Comet was judged the winner. It had imitation zebra-skin seat covers. It had an eight-ball shift knob.

2. Koko had a great plan to make some money. She had financial problems. She could not develop her plan.

3. The mixture could not be discussed openly. Competitors were curious. Corporate spies were everywhere.

4. Babette's bowling ball is special. It is red and green. It is decorated with her phone number in metal-flake.

5. The young bagpiper liked Scottish food. He enjoyed doing Scottish dances. Wearing a kilt in winter left him cold.

6. Ruby missed the alligator farm. She fondly remembered the hissing and snapping of the beasts as they scrambled for raw meat. Her neighbors were indifferent to the loss.

7. Many people are pleased to purchase items with food preservatives. Others are fearful. They think these chemicals may also preserve consumers.

8. Lauren loves her new in-line roller skates. They look and perform much like ice skates. They are not as safe as her conventional roller skates.

9. Fish sold at Discount Fish Market were not of the highest quality. Some of them had been dead for days without refrigeration. They were suitable only for bait.

10. Earl wanted to impress his date. He splashed on some cologne. He put on his motorcycle leathers and a flying scarf.

REVIEW 2

Combining Sentences

Use appropriate methods to combine sentences as needed. Add and delete words sparingly.

Muhammad Ali, was arguably the greatest heavyweight boxing champion. He won the title on four occasions. He loved to perform for the press. He made up sayings and poems about himself and his opponents. He said he would "float like a butterfly and sting like a bee." Ali announced that he would win each fight. He even named the round. He became a Black Muslim. He refused induction into the armed services. He was convicted of a crime for having done so. As a result he lost his championship. Later the decision was reversed by the U.S. Supreme Court. He won back the championship by defeating George Foreman in 1974. In 1978 he lost it to Leon Spinks. He won it back one more time the next year. He retired in 1980. Then fought once more for the title. He quit for good.

REVIEW 3

Combining Sentences

Use appropriate methods to combine sentences as needed. Add and delete words sparingly.

REBA MCENTIRE: NO SECRETS TO HER SUCCESS

Good singers can be found anywhere, even in a local lounge or pizza parlor. Great singers are rare. They have the "something special" qualities. The qualities just seem to work together. Country singer Reba McEntire is definitely one of the greats. The reasons are obvious: voice, songs, and style. Her voice is like no other. Her Oklahoma "twangy" accent is known by everyone in country music. She is able to jump from note to note. She can cover two octaves with ease. Her voice is rich and sensitive, yet powerful. Reba sings. She takes up all the oxygen in the room. The songs she sings are another reason for her greatness. Her lyrics deal with the issues. Those issues really touch the heart. They inspire the mind. They make even the men cry. Her song "Is There Life Out There?" encourages women and men everywhere to follow their dreams, no matter what those dreams may be. That song came out. Reba got thousands of letters from people. The people thanked her for writing such a positive song during difficult times. The final reason

for her greatness is her style. It is all its own, from her spunky attitude right down to her steel-toed boots. This fiery redhead really knows how to get the crowd going. She has been performing for about thirty years. She has produced more than twenty albums. With all those qualities, Reba McEntire will be around for a long, long time.

MICROTHEME

To practice your skills acquired in this chapter, return to the Microtheme on page 71 and complete Exercise B.

Chapter 6

Correcting Fragments, Comma Splices, and Run-Ons

FLOW OF WRITING

MICROTHEME	Writing Activity in Miniature

EXERCISE A

Before you work on this chapter, write a Microtheme on the following topic. Write small enough to leave room for marking later. **After** you have studied this chapter, return to your Microtheme and complete Exercise B to practice what you have learned.

Suggested Microtheme Topic: Write a Microtheme of 80 to 100 words about a problem on campus, such as registration, class schedules, counseling, student activities, or parking. Use at least one example of the problem and suggest a solution.

EXERCISE B

Connecting Your Learning Objectives with Your Microtheme

Complete this exercise after you have studied this chapter.

1. Check to make sure you have used no fragments. If you have, correct them. If in doubt, underline subjects and verbs.

2. Check to make sure you have used no comma splices. If you have, correct them. If in doubt, try placing a period in the questionable spot and see if you have two sentences.

In Chapter 3, you learned about subjects and verbs. In Chapters 4 and 5, you identified and wrote different kinds of sentences. With the information you now have, you will be able to spot and correct three problems in sentence structure that sometimes creep into and insidiously destroy what is otherwise good writing. Those problems are sentence fragments, comma splices, and run-on sentences.

Fragments

A correct sentence signals completeness. The structure and punctuation provide those signals. For example, if I say to you, "She left in a hurry," you do not necessarily expect me to say anything else, but if I say, "In a hurry," you do. If I say, "Tomorrow I will give you a quiz on the reading assignment," and I leave the room, you will merely take note of my words. But if I say, "Tomorrow when I give you a quiz on the reading assignment," and I leave the room, you will probably be annoyed, and you may even chase after me and ask me to finish my sentence. Those examples illustrate the difference between completeness and incompleteness.

A **fragment** is a word or group of words without a subject ("Is going to town.") or without a verb ("He going to town.") or without both ("Going to town."). A fragment can also be a group of words with a subject and verb that cannot stand alone ("When he goes to town."). Although the punctuation signals a sentence (a capital letter at the beginning and a period at the end), the structure of a fragment signals incompleteness. If you said it or wrote it to someone, that person would expect you to go on and finish the idea.

Other specific examples of common unacceptable fragments are these:

- *Dependent clause only*: When she came.
- *Phrase(s) only*: Waiting there for some help.
- *No subject in main clause*: Went to the library.
- *No verb in main clause*: She being the only person there.

ACCEPTABLE FRAGMENTS

Sometimes fragments are used intentionally. When we speak, we often use the following fragments:

- *Interjections*: Great! Hooray! Whoa!
- *Exclamations*: What a day! How terrible! What a bother!
- *Greetings*: Hello. Good morning. Good night. Good evening.
- *Questions*: What for? Why not? Where to?
- *Informal conversation*: (What time is it?) Eight o'clock. Really.

In novels, plays, and short stories, fragments are often used in conversation among characters. However, unless you are writing fiction, you need to be able to identify fragments in your college assignments and turn those fragments into complete sentences.

DEPENDENT CLAUSES AS FRAGMENTS:
CLAUSES WITH SUBORDINATING CONJUNCTIONS

In Chapter 5, you learned that words such as *because*, *although*, *that*, *while*, *after*, *since*, *how*, *till*, *unless*, *before* (**BAT WASHTUB**) are or can be subordinating conjunctions, words that show the relationship of a dependent clause to an independent one. A dependent clause punctuated like a sentence (capital letter at the beginning; period at the end) is a sentence fragment.

> *While the ship was sinking.*

You can choose one of many ways to fix that kind of fragment.

Incorrect:	They continued to dance. *While the ship was sinking.*
Correct:	They continued to dance *while the ship was sinking.*
Correct:	*While the ship was sinking*, they continued to dance.
Correct:	The ship was sinking. They continued to dance.
Correct:	The ship was sinking; they continued to dance.

In the first two correct sentences above, the dependent clause *while the ship was sinking* has been attached to an independent clause. Note that a comma is used when the dependent clause appears at the beginning of the sentence. In the next two sentences, the subordinating conjunction *while* has been omitted. The two independent clauses can then stand alone as sentences or as parts of a sentence, joined by a semicolon.

DEPENDENT CLAUSES AS FRAGMENTS: CLAUSES WITH RELATIVE PRONOUNS

You learned in Chapter 4 that words such as *that*, *which*, and *who* can function as relative pronouns, words that relate a clause back to a noun or pronoun in the sentence. Relative clauses are dependent. If they are punctuated as sentences (begin with a capital letter; end with a period), they are incorrect. They are really sentence fragments.

> *Which is lying on the floor.*

The best way to fix such a fragment is to attach it as closely as possible to the noun to which it refers.

Incorrect:	That new red sweater is mine. *Which is lying on the floor.*
Correct:	The new red sweater, *which is lying on the floor*, is mine.

Reminder: Some relative clauses are restrictive (necessary to the meaning of the sentence) and should not be set off with commas. Some are nonrestrictive (not necessary to the meaning of the sentence), as in the example above, and are set off by commas.

EXERCISE 1   Correcting Fragments

Underline and correct each fragment. Some items may be correct as is.

1. When Leroy Robert Paige was seven years old. He was carrying luggage at a railroad station in Mobile, Alabama.

2. He was a clever young fellow. Who invented a contraption for carrying four satchels (small suitcases) at one time.

3. After he did that. He was always known as Satchel Paige.

4. His fame rests on his being arguably the best baseball pitcher. Who ever played the game.

5. Because of the so-called Jim Crow laws. He, as an African-American, was not allowed to play in the Major Leagues. Until 1948 after the Major League color barrier was broken.

6. By that time he was already forty-two. Although he was in excellent condition.

7. He had pitched. Wherever he could, mainly touring around the country.

8. When he faced Major Leaguers in exhibition games. He almost always won.

9. Because people liked to see him pitch. He pitched almost every day. While he was on tour.

10. One year he won 104 games. During his career he pitched 55 no-hitters and won more than 2,000 games.

11. He pitched his last game in the majors at the age of fifty-nine.

12. In 1971 he was the first African-American player. Who was voted into the Baseball Hall of Fame in a special category for those. Who played in the old Negro Leagues.

EXERCISE 2   Correcting Fragments

Underline and correct each fragment. Some items may be correct as is.

1. When the Beatles began releasing hit records in the early 1960s. No one realized how profound an influence they would have on rock music and world culture.

2. Years after Paul McCartney, John Lennon, George Harrison, and Ringo Starr formed a band. Rock music finally became an accepted art form.

3. As they experimented with new techniques, instruments, and musical effects. They made highly innovative music.

4. When the band incorporated the sitar into songs like "Norwegian Wood." They created the swirling, swishing sound now known as "flanging."

5. Because their songs are so interesting. Radio stations have played them for new generations of fans.

6. The Beatles have also inspired and influenced other musical artists. That impact has continued for over four decades.

7. In addition, the band's films anticipated the music video. Which is the essential promotional tool of today's musicians.

8. Their influence extended beyond their music. That influence included hair and fashion.

9. After "Beatlemania" hit the United States in 1964. Long hair soon became standard for rock-and-roll stars.

10. When the Beatles used Eastern instruments like the sitar. They also introduced elements of Eastern philosophy into popular music culture.

PHRASES AS FRAGMENTS

Although a phrase may carry an idea, a phrase is a fragment because it is incomplete in structure. It lacks both a subject and a verb. See Chapter 3 for verbal phrases and prepositional phrases, and see Chapter 5 for appositive phrases.

Verbal Phrase

Incorrect: *Having studied hard all evening.* John decided to retire.

Correct: *Having studied hard all evening,* John decided to retire.

The italicized part of the incorrect example is a **verbal phrase**. As you learned in Chapter 3, a verbal is verblike without being a verb in sentence structure. Verbals include verb parts of speech ending in *-ed* and *-ing*. To correct a verbal phrase fragment, attach it to a complete sentence (independent clause). When the phrase begins the sentence, it is usually set off by a comma.

Prepositional Phrase

Incorrect:	*For the past ten hours*. I have been designing my home page.
Correct:	*For the past ten hours*, I have been designing my home page.

In this example, the fragment is a **prepositional phrase**—a group of words beginning with a preposition, such as *in*, *on*, *of*, *at*, and *with*, that connects a noun or pronoun object to the rest of the sentence. To correct a prepositional phrase fragment, attach it to a complete sentence (independent clause). If the prepositional phrase is long and begins the sentence, it is usually set off by a comma.

Appositive Phrase

Incorrect:	He lived in the small town of Whitman. *A busy industrial center near Boston.*
Correct:	He lived in the small town of Whitman, *a busy industrial center near Boston.*
Incorrect:	Many readers admire the work of the nineteenth-century American poet. *Emily Dickinson.*
Correct:	Many readers admire the work of the nineteenth-century American poet *Emily Dickinson.*

In these examples, the fragment is an **appositive phrase**—a group of words following a noun or pronoun and renaming it. To correct an appositive phrase fragment, connect it to a complete sentence (an independent clause). An appositive phrase fragment is set off by a comma or by commas only if it is not essential to the meaning of the sentence.

EXERCISE 3   Correcting Fragments

Underline and correct each fragment.

1. As a subject of historical record. Dancing seems to be a natural human act.

2. Even prehistoric cave paintings depict dancing figures. Scrawled outlines of people in motion.

3. Dancing takes many forms, but mainly it is a matter of moving rhythmically. In time to music.

4. Most children jump up and down when they are excited. They sway back and forth when they are contented.

5. Having studied the behavior of many ethnic groups. Anthropologists confirm that dancing reveals much. About a group's culture.

6. People dance for various reasons. Such as to entertain others, to relax, to inspire others, and to celebrate life.

7. One stylized form of dancing is the ballet. A story told with graceful, rhythmic movement and music.

8. Folk dances relate stories. Of the dancers' culture.

9. Young people can get to know each other at social dances. While enjoying themselves.

10. Each generation of social dancers seems to have its own style. Sometimes a modified revival, such as swing.

EXERCISE 4   Correcting Fragments

Underline and correct each fragment.

1. Reflecting religious concerns. Ceremonial dances are still conducted in some cultures to promote good crops or successful warfare.

2. In the 1800s, an American Christian group called the Shakers performed a whirling, shaking dance. A ceremony to shake out the devil.

3. In the 1900s. Whirling Dervishes and Ghost Dancers believed that their dancing protected them in battle.

4. In Australia and North America. Aborigines had dances that imitated the movement of animals to be hunted.

5. Some of those dances are still performed. With few significant changes of style.

6. In Africa and the South Pacific. Groups have dances that signify the achievement of maturity.

7. In the United States and in many other countries. Young people gain popular- ity. By learning and demonstrating popular dance steps and movements.

8. It is hard to imagine human beings without dance. An activity transcending all time and cultures.

9. With the birth of rock 'n' roll music. Dancing styles became freer.

10. During the past hundred years. Dozens of dances, such as the lindy, twist, hustle, Charleston, big apple, frug, and mashed potato, have had their times of popularity.

EXERCISE 5   Correcting Fragments

Correct the following phrase fragments by adding subjects and verbs and, perhaps, by changing or adding words. The story line is simple. Driving his Honda Civic, Joe took Theresa to the opening-day baseball game at Dodger Stadium. They arrived with high hopes, settled into their seats, had expectations, saw the game begin, and spotted some rain clouds. The questions in the boxes will help you follow the plot.

Example: A special date with Theresa.

Who had a special date with Theresa?

Joe had a special date with Theresa.

1. A Honda Civic with custom wheels and low profile tires.

What did he polish?

_____

_____

2. To pick up Theresa for their date.

What did he do then?

_____

_____

3. To go to the opening-day baseball game at Dodger Stadium.

Where did Theresa want to go on the date?

_____

_____

4. A never-to-be-forgotten experience.

What satisfaction did she hope for?

_____

_____

5. Being seen on big-screen Diamond Vision in the stadium.

What special experience did Theresa dream of?

_____

_____

6. With the first sound of the bat on ball.

When did they arrive?

_____

_____

7. Buying peanuts and Crackerjacks.

Who bought peanuts and Crackerjacks and for whom?

_____

_____

8. A baseball glove to catch a well-hit ball.

What did Theresa bring so that she might catch a well-hit ball?

_____

_____

9. To hear and see heroes up close.

What portable electronic device did Theresa bring so that she could follow the action on the field?

_____

_____

10. Seeing the rain clouds.

Noticing the change in weather, what did they fear?

_____

_____

EXERCISE 6   Correcting Fragments

Correct the following phrase fragments by adding subjects and verbs and, perhaps, by changing or adding words. Continuing from Exercise 5 is the story of Joe and Theresa at a baseball game where they got caught in a rainstorm. They ran for cover, contemplated leaving, waited, saw the game continue, watched the players slide in the mud, celebrated the Dodgers' victory, headed for the parking lot, and finally found Joe's car. The questions in the boxes will help you follow the plot.

Example: In the last of the fourth inning.

> What began to fall from the clouds?

In the last of the fourth inning, *rain began to fall.*

1. Running for shelter.

> What happened to them as they ran through the rain?

_____

_____

2. Shivering and waiting for sunshine.

> Where did they wish they were?

_____

_____

3. To delay the game.

> What did the umpires decide to do?

_____

_____

4. To leave or not to leave.

> What question did Joe and Theresa consider?

_____

_____

5. In less than an hour.

> What happened to the rain?

_____

_____

6. With the players back on the field.

> Following the change of weather, what happened to the game?

_____

_____

7. Sliding into bases on the wet field.

> What became easy for the players?

_____

_____

8. Winning the game at the end of the eleventh inning.

   How did the Dodgers delight their fans?

   _____

   _____

9. Finding Joe's Honda in the parking lot.

   What problem did Joe and Theresa have in finding the car?

   _____

   _____

10. By the light of the moon.

    How did they find the car?

    _____

    _____

FRAGMENTS AS WORD GROUPS WITHOUT SUBJECTS OR WITHOUT VERBS

Incorrect: Ayana studied many long hours. And received the highest grade in the class. [without subject]

Correct: Ayana studied many long hours and received the highest grade in the class.

Incorrect: Few children living in that section of the country. [without verb]

Correct: Few children live in that section of the country.

Each sentence must have an independent clause, a group of words that contains a subject and a verb and that can stand alone. As you may recall from the discussion of subjects in Chapter 3, a command or direction sentence, such as "Think," has an understood subject of *you*.

EXERCISE 7   Correcting Fragments

The fragments in the following passage need either a subject or a verb. Underline the fragments and correct them.

(1) Two ice hotels the ultimate place for "chilling out." (2) One of these hotels in Quebec, Canada. (3) The other being in Sweden. (4) These structures built of 4,500 tons of snow and 250 tons of ice, like giant igloos. (5) The hotels' rooms even including furniture made of ice. (6) Room temperatures do not rise above 27 degrees Fahrenheit. (7) But outside temperatures well below freezing. (8) The hotels' ice walls actually trapping and holding some of the heat inside. (9) Guests

sleep in thick sleeping bags piled with animal skins for warmth. (10) In the hotels' bars, even the glasses are made of ice. (11) Drinks served "in the rocks" instead of "on the rocks." (12) Construction in December of every year. (13) In January, the hotels open for business. (14) Stay open until late March. (15) Then begin to melt. (16) These are two hotels having to be totally rebuilt every year.

EXERCISE 8   Correcting Fragments

The fragments in the following passage need either a subject or a verb. Underline the fragments and correct them.

(1) Susan B. Anthony among the leaders in the early days of the women's rights movement. (2) Her parents being Quakers, who believed in the equality of the sexes. (3) As a young woman, wanted to argue against alcohol abuse. (4) Was not allowed to speak at rallies because she was a woman. (5) Susan B. Anthony not to be silenced. (6) She joined other women in fighting for women's rights in education, voting, and property ownership. (7) Also fought for the abolition of slavery. (8) When black men were given the right to vote in 1869, she was pleased. (9) However, was disappointed that women did not receive the same consideration. (10) For about sixty years, she was active in the National Woman Suffrage Movement. (11) Died fourteen years before the 19th Amendment gave women the right to vote. (12) In 1979, she was recognized for her civic contributions. (13) Placed her picture on a one-dollar coin.

EXERCISE 9   Correcting Fragments

The following fragments need either a subject or a verb. Correct them.

1. One of the two main industries in Florida which is tourism.
2. People going to Florida to visit Disney World.
3. Others who go to watch sporting events such as the Orange Bowl.
4. Tourists regarding the Everglades National Park as a natural wonder.
5. St. Augustine having the oldest house in the United States.
6. Many Major League baseball teams to Florida for spring training.
7. Can see a living coral reef formation at a state park.
8. Tours, demonstrations, and displays at the John F. Kennedy Space Center.
9. Some people who visit Florida for the pleasant weather and good beaches.
10. Circus World which offers opportunities for amateurs.

EXERCISE 10   Correcting Fragments

The following fragments need either a subject or a verb. Correct them.

1. Australia as the "down under" country because it is south of the equator.

2. It being colonized by the English.

3. The first English residents being convicts.

4. The aborigines moving away from their traditional lands.

5. Had lived there for many thousands of years.

6. The population of Australia now well beyond twenty million.

7. More than two hundred thousand aborigines.

8. Many people living in the southeastern part of the country.

9. The inner region as the outback.

10. Australia being known for its unusual animals.

EXERCISE 11   Correcting Fragments

Identify each of the following as a fragment (FRAG) or a complete sentence (OK). Correct the fragments. (They may be any of the kinds you have studied in this chapter: dependent clause, phrase, or word group without a subject or without a verb.) You can correct some fragments by adding them to a complete sentence.

_____ 1.   Asia which developed much earlier than the West.

_____

_____ 2.   More than five thousand years ago, Asia had an advanced

civilization.

_____

_____ 3.   People there who invented writing and created literature.

_____

_____ 4.   Involved in the development of science, agriculture, and religion.

_____

_____ 5.   The birthplace of the major religions of the world.

_____

_____ 6.   The most common religion in Asia being Hinduism.

_____

_____ 7.   The second most common religion is Islam.

_____

_____ 8.   Asia is the most populous continent.

_____

_____ **9.** With almost four billion people.

_____

_____ **10.** Hong Kong and Bangladesh which are among the most densely

populated places in the world.

_____

_____ **11.** Asia having many ethnic groups.

_____

_____ **12.** Including the Chinese, the Indians, the Arabs, the Turks, and

the Jews.

_____

_____ **13.** The Chinese have different groups.

_____

_____ **14.** Speaking many dialects.

_____

_____ **15.** Although they have different dialects.

_____

_____ **16.** There is a national language.

_____

_____ **17.** A language called Mandarin.

_____

_____ **18.** Cultural differences exist in Taiwan.

_____

_____ **19.** The main difference being between the Chinese from the

mainland and the Taiwanese.

_____

_____ **20.** Despite the difference, all Chinese have much culture in common.

_____

Comma Splices and Run-Ons

The comma splice and the run-on are two other kinds of faulty "sentences" that give false signals to the reader. In each instance, the punctuation suggests that there is only one sentence, but, in fact, there is material for two.

The **comma splice** consists of two independent clauses with only a comma between them:

The weather was disappointing, we canceled the picnic. [A comma by itself cannot join two independent clauses.]

The **run-on** differs from the comma splice in only one respect: It has no comma between the independent clauses. Therefore, the run-on is two independent clauses with *nothing* between them:

The weather was disappointing we canceled the picnic. [Independent clauses must be properly connected.]

Because an independent clause can stand by itself as a sentence and because two independent clauses must be properly linked, you can use a simple technique to identify the comma splice and the run-on. If you see a sentence that you think may contain one of these two errors, ask yourself this question: "Can I insert a period at some place in the word group and still have a sentence on either side?" If the answer is yes and there is no word such as *and* or *but* following the inserted period, then you have a comma splice or a run-on to correct. In our previous examples of the comma splice and the run-on, we could insert a period after the word *disappointing* in each case, and we would still have an independent clause—therefore, a sentence—on either side.

FOUR WAYS TO CORRECT COMMA SPLICES AND RUN-ONS

Once you identify a comma splice or a run-on in your writing, you need to correct it. There are four different ways to fix these common sentence problems: Use a comma and a coordinating conjunction, use a subordinating conjunction, use a semicolon, or make each clause a separate sentence.

1. Use a comma and a coordinating conjunction.

Incorrect: We canceled the picnic the weather was disappointing. [run-on]

Correct: We canceled the picnic, *for* the weather was disappointing. [Here we inserted a comma and the coordinating conjunction *for.*]

Knowing the seven coordinating conjunctions will help you in writing sentences and correcting sentence problems. Remember the acronym FANBOYS: *for, and, nor, but, or, yet, so.*

EXERCISE 12   Correcting Comma Splices and Run-Ons

Identify each word group as a comma splice (CS), a run-on (RO), or a complete sentence (OK), and make needed corrections using commas and coordinating conjunctions.

Example: ___CS___ He did the assignment, ^and^ his boss gave him a bonus.

_____ **1.** In 1846 a group of eighty-two settlers headed for California with

much optimism, a hard road lay ahead.

_____ **2.** They had expected to cross the mountains before winter they

were in good spirits.

_____ 3. They would not arrive in California before winter nor would some

of them get there at all.

_____ 4. When they encountered a heavy snowstorm, they stopped to

spend the winter they still thought they would be safe.

_____ 5. They made crude shelters of logs and branches, some also

used moss and earth.

_____ 6. They had trouble managing they had not encountered such prob-

lems before.

_____ 7. They ran out of regular food, they ate roots, mice, shoe leather,

and their horses.

_____ 8. Thirty-five members of the Donner Party died that winter, the

survivors were so hungry that they ate the dead bodies.

_____ 9. They were weak, sick, and depressed they did not give up.

_____ 10. Fifteen people set out to get help seven survived and returned

to rescue friends and relatives.

EXERCISE 13   Correcting Comma Splices and Run-Ons

**Identify each word group as a comma splice (CS), a run-on (RO), or a complete
sentence (OK), and make needed corrections using commas and coordinating
conjunctions.**

_____ 1. Comedian Woody Allen once observed that no one gets out of

this world alive, we all know that no human is immortal.

_____ 2. But several famous dead people have managed to continue to

look alive they (or their admirers) had their bodies preserved

and put on display.

_____ 3. Philosopher Jeremy Bentham wanted his body preserved, his

wishes were carried out when he died in 1832.

_____ 4. Bentham left a lot of money to London's University College,

the college couldn't have the money unless it agreed to let

Bentham's body attend its annual board of directors meetings.

_____ **5.** Bentham's dressed-up body was posed sitting in an armchair in his hand was his favorite walking stick.

_____ **6.** Every year for ninety-two years, the college complied with Bentham's instructions the board's minutes for those years record Bentham as "present but not voting."

_____ **7.** Bentham's body is still at University College, it's on display now in a permanent exhibit.

_____ **8.** Soviet Union leader V. I. Lenin has been dead and on display since 1924 Russians and tourists can still visit his lifelike body enclosed in a glass coffin in Moscow.

_____ **9.** The corpse of People's Republic of China founder Mao Tse-Tung was preserved for posterity, too, in his mausoleum, an elevator raises his glass coffin from underground to a public viewing area every morning.

_____ **10.** Other famous people turned into modern mummies were national leaders Joseph Stalin, Eva Perón, and Ho Chi Minh, and opera singer Enrico Caruso.

---

2. Use a subordinating conjunction.

Incorrect: The weather was disappointing, we canceled the picnic.

Correct: *Because* the weather was disappointing, we canceled the picnic.

By inserting the subordinating conjunction *because*, you can transform the first independent clause into a dependent clause and correct the comma splice. Knowing the most common subordinating conjunctions will help you in writing sentences and correcting sentence problems. Here is a list of the subordinating conjunctions you saw in Chapter 5.

after	if	until
although	in order that	when
as	provided that	whenever
as if	rather than	where
because	since	whereas
before	so that	wherever
even if	than	whether
even though	unless	while

EXERCISE 14   Correcting Comma Splices and Run-Ons

Identify each word group as a comma splice (CS), a run-on (RO), or a complete sentence (OK), and correct the errors by making a dependent clause.

_____ 1. Roberto Clemente grew up poor in Puerto Rico, he would become rich and famous.

_____ 2. As a child he was determined to play baseball he used a tree limb to slug an old tennis ball wrapped with yarn.

_____ 3. Clemente excelled in youth and sandlot teams, he signed a contract to play professional baseball.

_____ 4. He played for the Pittsburgh Pirates between 1955 and 1972, he was once selected the Most Valuable Player and twice had the highest hitting average in the National League.

_____ 5. Often regarded as the best right fielder of all time, he won twelve Gold Gloves for his defensive play, and it was said he could throw out runners from his knees.

_____ 6. Clemente said that he was taught good values by his family and that he respected the poor because they had learned about life from their suffering.

_____ 7. Clemente became wealthy, he always found time to help the less fortunate.

_____ 8. He liked to take an active part in his humanitarian work, in 1972 he decided to fly on an airplane he had chartered to take supplies to earthquake victims in Nicaragua.

_____ 9. The airplane crashed all aboard were killed.

_____ 10. He was a great baseball player and a great human being many schools and parks have been named after him.

EXERCISE 15   Correcting Comma Splices and Run-Ons

Identify each word group as a comma splice (CS), a run-on (RO), or a complete sentence (OK), and correct the errors by making a dependent clause.

_____ 1. Jesse Owens won four gold medals in the 1936 Olympics he became a famous person.

_____ 2. The 1936 Olympics were held in Nazi Germany Owens was placed at a disadvantage.

_____ 3. Hitler believed in the superiority of the Aryans, he thought Owens would lose.

_____ 4. Jesse Owens won Hitler showed his disappointment openly.

_____ 5. Owens broke a record for the 200-meter race that had stood for thirty-six years.

_____ 6. Owens then jumped a foot farther than others in the long jump Hitler left the stadium.

_____ 7. Before the day was at last over, Owens had also won gold medals in the 100-meter dash and the 400-meter relay.

_____ 8. Hitler's early departure was a snub at Owens, but he did not care.

_____ 9. Owens returned to the United States, he engaged in numerous exhibitions, including racing against a horse.

_____ 10. In his later years Owens became an official for the U.S. Olympic Committee, he never received the recognition that many contemporary athletes do.

3. Use a semicolon.

Incorrect: The weather was disappointing, we canceled the picnic.

Correct: The weather was disappointing; we canceled the picnic.

Correct: The weather was disappointing; *therefore*, we canceled the picnic.

This comma splice was corrected by a semicolon. The first correct example shows the semicolon alone. The second correct example shows a semicolon followed by the conjunctive adverb *therefore*. The conjunctive adverb is optional, but, as we have already seen, conjunctive adverbs can make the relationship between independent clauses stronger. Here is the list of conjunctive adverbs you saw in Chapter 5.

however	hence	also
otherwise	on the other hand	thus
therefore	then	
similarly	consequently	

Consider using the acronym HOTSHOT CAT, made up of the first letter of each of these common conjunctive adverbs. The acronym will help you remember them. Other conjunctive adverbs include *in fact*, *for example*, *moreover*, *nevertheless*, *furthermore*, *now*, and *soon*.

EXERCISE 16   Correcting Comma Splices and Run-Ons

Identify each word group as a comma splice (CS), a run-on (RO), or a complete sentence (OK). Make corrections with a semicolon, and add a conjunctive adverb if appropriate.

_____ **1.** Harry Houdini is often referred to as a magician, he was more famous as an escapologist.

_____ **2.** He initially performed card tricks and other common routines of illusion, he developed some special nonescape acts.

_____ **3.** One of his spectacular nonescape acts was making an elephant and its trainer disappear they were actually lowered into an empty swimming pool under the stage.

_____ **4.** Soon Houdini grew bored with conventional magic, and he perfected some escape tricks.

_____ **5.** Houdini learned to swallow and then regurgitate keys and tools, he could break free from restraints under water.

_____ **6.** Houdini could also dislocate both shoulders at will he could escape easily from a straitjacket.

_____ **7.** Houdini's most famous trick involved the Chinese Water Torture Cell, a steel and glass water-filled box in which he was chained and suspended upside down.

_____ **8.** As an active member of a group of skeptics, he exposed spiritualists who claimed to contact the dead.

_____ **9.** He decided to put his beliefs to a test, shortly before his death, he gave his wife a secret code and told her he would try to contact her from the grave.

_____ **10.** Each Halloween night for a decade after he died, his wife and friends met and waited for a signal from Houdini, she gave up, saying, "Ten years is long enough to wait for any man."

EXERCISE 17   Correcting Comma Splices and Run-Ons

Identify each word group as a comma splice (CS), a run-on (RO), or a complete sentence (OK). Make corrections with a semicolon, and add a conjunctive adverb if appropriate.

_____ **1.** Ants are highly social insects they live in colonies.

_____ **2.** They work for the benefit of the group, cooperation is important.

_____ **3.** Ants have different roles they will, in some species, have different sizes and shapes.

_____ **4.** An ant will be a queen, a worker, or a male, there is not an identity problem among ants.

_____ **5.** A worker may be a soldier whose job is to defend the nest that ant has large mandibles, or teeth.

_____ **6.** The worker that is a janitor will have the job of cleaning the nest her head is big for pushing waste material through the tunnel.

_____ **7.** The queen is very large because she must lay many eggs.

_____ **8.** The workers are all female, their job is to do all of the work.

_____ 9. The males have only one function, and that function is to mate with the queen.

_____ 10. In some species, the workers may change roles in their work, the males only mate and die young.

---

4. **Make each clause a separate sentence.**

Incorrect: The weather was disappointing, we canceled the picnic.

Correct: The weather was disappointing. We canceled the picnic.

This method is at once the simplest and most common method of correcting comma splices and run-ons. To correct the comma splice, replace the comma with a period, and begin the second sentence (the second independent clause) with a capital letter. For a run-on, insert a period between the two independent clauses and begin the second sentence with a capital letter.

EXERCISE 18   Correcting Comma Splices and Run-Ons

Identify each word group as a comma splice (CS), a run-on (RO), or a complete sentence (OK), and make corrections with a period and a capital letter.

_____ 1. About a hundred and fifty years ago, British soldiers wore a bright red coat, they also wore a black hat and white trousers.

_____ 2. The soldiers looked good in parades the queen was very proud.

_____ 3. On the battlefield, the situation was different, and the uniform was regarded differently.

_____ 4. The coat could be seen at a great distance enemies aimed at the red coats.

_____ 5. This had long been a problem, even in the days of the American Revolution.

_____ 6. No one in high position was willing to change the colors of the uniform the soldiers decided to take action.

_____ 7. A solution was at hand, the soldiers would wear the red coats but change the colors.

_____ **8.** At the time of their experiment, they were serving in India, they

would use natural elements to solve their problem.

_____ **9.** In the dry season, they would rub yellow-brown dust on their

uniforms, and in the wet season they would use mud.

_____ **10.** They liked the camouflage color so much that they finally

changed the color of their uniforms to the drab color they called

it _khaki_, the Indian word for _dust_.

EXERCISE 19   Correcting Comma Splices and Run-Ons

Identify each word group as a comma splice (CS), a run-on (RO), or a complete sentence (OK), and make corrections with a period and a capital letter.

_____ **1.** The world's fastest steel-track roller coaster is the Top Thrill

Dragster, it's at the Cedar Point Amusement Park in Ohio.

_____ **2.** Riders rocket out of a starting gate they reach a speed of 120

miles per hour in four seconds.

_____ **3.** The second-fastest roller coaster is in Japan, it goes a mere

106.8 miles per hour.

_____ **4.** Wooden roller coasters are downright pokey in comparison the

fastest reaches speeds of only 78.3 miles per hour.

_____ **5.** If you're looking for the biggest drop, the Top Thrill Dragster has

that distinction, too.

_____ **6.** The largest drop on the Top Thrill Dragster is 400 feet, compare

that to the largest drop on a wooden coaster, which is only

214 feet.

_____ **7.** The longest roller coaster ride of them all is the Steel Dragon

2000 in Japan, that coaster is 8,133 feet long.

_____ **8.** You want the steepest angle of descent, you can choose

from several steel-track coasters that allow you to plummet

downward at a 90-degree angle.

_____ **9.** The steepest wooden coasters average about 55 degrees as

a matter of fact, the steepest of all is only 61 degrees.

_____ **10.** Most of the world's record-setting roller coasters were opened

between 2000 and 2003 thrill-seekers hope they'll continue to

get faster and steeper.

Techniques for Spotting Problem Sentences

1. For the fragment, ask yourself: "If someone were to say or write this to me, would I expect the person to add to the statement or rephrase it?"

2. In checking for the comma splice or run-on, ask yourself, "Is there a point in this word group at which I can insert a period and create a sentence on either side?" The question is not necessary if there is a coordinating conjunction (FANBOYS) at that point.

3. If you have trouble with comma splices and run-ons, check these constructions as you revise:

  a. A comma preceded by a noun or pronoun followed by a noun or pronoun
  b. A sentence beginning with a subordinating conjunction

4. If you have trouble with fragments, look for these clues:

  a. A word group with a single verb ending in *-ing*
  b. A word group without both a subject and a verb

5. Use the grammar checker on your computer to alert you to possible problem sentences. Then use instruction from this book to make the necessary corrections.

CHAPTER REVIEW   Correcting Fragments, Comma Splices, and Run-Ons

FRAGMENTS

1. A correct sentence signals completeness; a **fragment** signals incompleteness—it doesn't make sense. You expect the speaker or writer of a fragment to say or write more or to rephrase it.

2. A **dependent clause** cannot stand by itself because it begins with a subordinating word.

> *Because* he left.

> *When* she worked.

> *Although* they slept.

3. A **verbal phrase**, a **prepositional phrase**, and an **appositive phrase** may carry ideas, but each is incomplete because it lacks a subject and a verb.

Verbal Phrase:	*having completed his initial research*
Sentence:	*Having completed his initial research*, he refined his outline.
Prepositional Phrase:	*in the store*
Sentence:	She worked *in the store*.
Appositive Phrase:	*a successful business*
Sentence:	Marks Brothers, *a successful business*, sells clothing.

4. Each complete sentence must have an **independent clause**, a group of words that contains a subject and a verb, and can stand alone.

> He enrolled for the fall semester.

COMMA SPLICES AND RUN-ONS

1. The **comma splice** consists of two independent clauses with only a comma between them.

> Maria exceeded her sales quota, she received a bonus. [A comma by itself cannot join two independent clauses.]

2. The **run-on** differs from the comma splice in only one respect: It has no comma between the independent clauses.

> Maria exceeded her sales quota she received a bonus. [Independent clauses must be properly connected.]

CORRECTING COMMA SPLICES AND RUN-ONS

1. Use a comma and a **coordinating conjunction** (*for, and, nor, but, or, yet, so*) to correct the comma splice or run-on.

> Maria exceeded her sales quota, *and* she received a bonus.

2. Use a **subordinating conjunction** (such as *because, after, that, when, although, since, how, till, unless, before*) to make one clause dependent and correct the comma splice or run-on.

> *Because* Maria exceeded her sales quota, she received a bonus.

3. Use a **semicolon** (with or without a conjunctive adverb such as *however, otherwise, therefore, similarly, hence, on the other hand, then, consequently, also, thus*) to correct the comma splice or run-on.

> Maria exceeded her sales quota; *therefore*, she received a bonus.

> Maria exceeded her sales quota; she received a bonus.

4. Use a period to replace a comma and add a capital letter (to correct a comma splice), or use a period between two independent clauses and add a capital letter (to correct a run-on).

> Maria exceeded her sales quota. She received a bonus.

CHAPTER REVIEW Exercises

REVIEW 1   Correcting Fragments, Comma Splices, and Run-Ons

Correct each fragment, comma splice, and run-on by using one of the methods you learned. Select the method you think is most effective for smoothness of expression and emphasis. You may find it helpful to read the material aloud as you work.

Dinosaurs were giant lizardlike animals, they lived more than a hundred million years ago. Some had legs like lizards and turtles, some had legs more like birds. The ones with legs like birds. Could walk easily with raised bodies. They varied in size, many were huge. The largest, the diplodocus, about ninety feet long, equal to the distance between the bases in baseball. Weighing more than ten elephants. The smallest weighed no more than two pounds and was no bigger than a chicken. Some dinosaurs ate meat, almost certainly some dinosaurs ate other dinosaurs. Used their strong claws and fierce teeth to tear at their victims. Dinosaurs were different. In design as well as size. They had horns, spikes, bills, armorlike plates, clublike tails, bony crests, and teeth in many sizes and shapes their heads were proportionately tiny or absurdly large. Their mouths varied. Depending on their eating habits.

Correcting Fragments, Comma Splices, and Run-Ons

Correct each fragment, comma splice, and run-on by using one of the methods you learned. Select the method you think is most effective for smoothness of expression and emphasis.

Deserts are often referred to as wastelands. It is true that not as many plants grow there as in a temperate zone, it is also true that animals do not live there in great numbers. However, many plants and animals live and do quite well in the desert. Because of their adaptations.

Not all deserts have the same appearance, many people think of the desert as a hot, sandy area. Actually, sand covers only about 20 percent of the desert. Some deserts have mountains some others have snow.

Because deserts are dry for most of the year. Plants must conserve and store water. Several kinds of cacti can shrink during a dry season and swell during a rainy season. Some shrubs simply drop their leaves and use their green bark to manufacture chlorophyll. Seeds sometimes lying in the desert for several years before sprouting to take advantage of a rainfall.

Animals have quite effectively adjusted to the desert, some animals obtain moisture from the food they eat and require no water. One animal of the desert, the camel, produces fat. Which it stores in its hump. The fat allows the camel to reserve more body heat it needs little water. Still other animals feed only at night or are inactive for weeks or even months.

STUDENT COMPANION SITE
For additional practice, visit www.cengage .com/devenglish/ brandon/spb6e.

About 15 percent of the land of the earth is covered by deserts. That area increasing every year. Because of overgrazing by livestock. Also because of the destruction of forests. Areas that were once green and fertile will now support little life and only a small population of human beings.

MICROTHEME

To practice your skills acquired in this chapter, return to the Microtheme on page 94 and complete Exercise B.

Verbs

MICROTHEME	Writing Activity in Miniature

EXERCISE A

Before you work on this chapter, write a Microtheme on the following topic. Write small enough to leave room for marking later. **After** you have studied this chapter, return to your Microtheme and complete Exercise B to practice what you have learned.

Suggested Microtheme Topic: Write a Microtheme of 80 to 100 words about people's driving habits that bother you. Give at least one real-life example.

EXERCISE B

Connecting Your Learning Objectives with Your Microtheme

Complete this exercise after you have studied this chapter.

1. Check to make sure your verbs are correct in form and consistent in tense.
2. Check to make sure your subjects and verbs agree.
3. Check to make sure you have used strong verbs in the appropriate voice and mood.

This chapter covers the use of standard verbs. To some, the word *standard* implies "correct." A more precise meaning is "that which is conventional among educated people." Therefore, a standard verb is the right choice in most school assignments, most published writing, and most important public-speaking situations. We all change our language when we move from these formal occasions to informal ones: We don't talk to our families in the same way we would speak at a large gathering in public; we don't write letters to friends the same way we write a history report. Even with informal language, we would seldom change from standard to nonstandard usage.

Regular and Irregular Verbs

Verbs can be divided into two categories, called *regular* and *irregular*. Regular verbs are predictable, but irregular verbs—as the term suggests—follow no definite pattern.

The forms for both regular and irregular verbs vary to show time.

- **Present-tense verbs** show an action or a state of being that is occurring at the present time: I *like* your hat. He *is* at a hockey game right now. Present-tense verbs can also imply a continuation from the past into the future: She *drives* to work every day.
- **Past-tense verbs** show an action or a state of being that occurred in the past: We *walked* to town yesterday. Tim *was* president of the club last year.
- **Past-participle verbs** are used with helping verbs such as *has, have,* and *had:* Georgina *had studied* hard before she took the test.

REGULAR VERBS

Present Tense

For *he, she,* and *it,* regular verbs in the present tense add an *-s* or an *-es* to the base word. The following chart shows the present tense of the base word *ask,* which is a regular verb.

	Singular	Plural
First Person:	I ask	we ask
Second Person:	you ask	you ask
Third Person:	he, she, it asks	they ask

If the verb ends in *-y,* you might have to drop the *-y* and add *-ies* for *he, she,* and *it.*

	Singular	Plural
First Person:	I try	we try
Second Person:	you try	you try
Third Person:	he, she, it tries	they try

Past Tense

For regular verbs in the past tense, add *-ed* to the base form.

Base Form (Present)	Past
walk	walked
answer	answered

If the base form already ends in *-e*, add just *-d*.

Base Form (Present)	Past
smile	smiled
decide	decided

If the base form ends in a consonant followed by *-y*, drop the *-y* and add *-ied*.

Base Form (Present)	Past
fry	fried
amplify	amplified

Regardless of how you form the past tense, regular verbs in the past tense do not change forms. The following chart shows the past tense of the base word *like*, which is a regular verb.

	Singular	Plural
First Person:	I liked	we liked
Second Person:	you liked	you liked
Third Person:	he, she, it liked	they liked

Past Participles

The past participle uses the helping verbs *has*, *have*, or *had* along with the past tense of the verb. For regular verbs, the past-participle form of the verb is the same as the past tense.

Base Form	Past	Past Participle
happen	happened	happened
hope	hoped	hoped
cry	cried	cried

Here is a list of some common regular verbs, showing the base form, the past tense, and the past participle. The base form can also be used with such helping verbs as *can*, *could*, *do*, *does*, *did*, *may*, *might*, *must*, *shall*, *should*, *will*, and *would*.

Base Form (Present)	Past	Past Participle
answer	answered	answered
ask	asked	asked
cry	cried	cried
decide	decided	decided
dive	dived (dove)	dived
finish	finished	finished
happen	happened	happened
learn	learned	learned
like	liked	liked
love	loved	loved
need	needed	needed
open	opened	opened
start	started	started
suppose	supposed	supposed
walk	walked	walked
want	wanted	wanted

IRREGULAR VERBS

Irregular verbs do not follow any definite pattern.

Base Form (Present)	Past	Past Participle
shake	shook	shaken
make	made	made
begin	began	begun

Some irregular verbs that sound similar in the present tense don't follow the same pattern.

Base Form (Present)	Past	Past Participle
ring	rang	rung
swing	swung	swung
bring	brought	brought

Present Tense

For *he*, *she*, and *it*, irregular verbs in the present tense add an *-s* or an *-es* to the base word. The following chart shows the present tense of the base word *break*, which is an irregular verb.

	Singular	Plural
First Person:	I break	we break
Second Person:	you break	you break
Third Person:	he, she, it breaks	they break

If the irregular verb ends in *-y*, you might have to drop the *-y* and add *-ies* for *he*, *she*, and *it*.

	Singular	Plural
First Person:	I fly	we fly
Second Person:	you fly	you fly
Third Person:	he, she, it flies	they fly

Past Tense

Like past-tense regular verbs, past-tense irregular verbs do not change their forms. The following chart shows the past tense of the irregular verb *do*.

	Singular	Plural
First Person:	I did	we did
Second Person:	you did	you did
Third Person:	he, she, it did	they did

For irregular verbs in the past tense, use the following list of irregular verbs.

Past Participles

Use the past-tense form with the helping verbs *has*, *have*, and *had*.

Here is a list of some common irregular verbs, showing the base form (present), the past tense, and the past participle. Like regular verbs, the base forms can be used with such helping verbs as *can*, *could*, *do*, *does*, *did*, *may*, *might*, *must*, *shall*, *should*, *will*, and *would*.

Irregular Verbs

Base Form (Present)	Past	Past Participle
arise	arose	arisen
awake	awoke (awaked)	awoken (awaked)
be (is)	was, were	been
become	became	become
begin	began	begun
bend	bent	bent
blow	blew	blown
burst	burst	burst
buy	bought	bought
catch	caught	caught
choose	chose	chosen
cling	clung	clung
come	came	come
cost	cost	cost
creep	crept	crept
deal	dealt	dealt
do	did	done
drink	drank	drunk
drive	drove	driven
eat	ate	eaten
feel	felt	felt
fight	fought	fought
fling	flung	flung
fly	flew	flown
forget	forgot	forgotten
freeze	froze	frozen
get	got	got (gotten)
go	went	gone
grow	grew	grown
hang	hung	hung
have	had	had
hit	hit	hit
know	knew	known
lead	led	led
leave	left	left
lose	lost	lost
make	made	made
mean	meant	meant
put	put	put
read	read	read
ride	rode	ridden
ring	rang	rung
see	saw	seen
sew	sewed	sewn (sewed)
shine	shone	shone
shoot	shot	shot

Base Form (Present)	Past	Past Participle
sing	sang	sung
sink	sank	sunk
sleep	slept	slept
slink	slunk	slunk
speak	spoke	spoken
spend	spent	spent
spread	spread	spread
steal	stole	stolen
stink	stank (stunk)	stunk
sweep	swept	swept
swim	swam	swum
swing	swung	swung
take	took	taken
teach	taught	taught
tear	tore	torn
think	thought	thought
throw	threw	thrown
thrust	thrust	thrust
wake	woke (waked)	woken (waked)
weep	wept	wept
write	wrote	written

EXERCISE 1 Selecting Verbs

Underline the correct verb form.

1. In the twentieth century, two jilted men on opposite sides of the country (create, created) amazing structures to soothe their broken hearts.

2. In 1908, Baldasare Forestiere (built, builded) a four-room underground apartment in Fresno, California.

3. Then, he (goes, went) to his native Italy and (ask, asked) his childhood sweetheart to join him in America.

4. When she refused, a sorrowful Baldasare (returns, returned) to the United States and (threw, throwed) himself into his digging.

5. By the time Baldasare died in 1946, he had (digged, dug) for thirty-eight years and had (construct, constructed) ninety underground rooms over ten acres.

6. Just after World War II, Edward Leedskalnin (began, begins) building a castle from enormous coral rocks in Florida City, Florida.

7. He had been (jilted, jilten) in 1920 by his 16-year-old fiancée, Agnes.

8. Edward (hopes, hoped) that Agnes would come back to him when he

   (became, become) famous for his project, which he moved to Homestead,

   Florida.

9. Edward (works, worked) on his castle for sixteen years in the dark of night,

   and no one (knows, knowed) how the five-foot-tall man moved twenty-five-ton

   blocks.

10. Unfortunately, Agnes never (seen, saw) Coral Castle, and she did not

    (change, changed) her mind about marrying Edward.

EXERCISE 2   Selecting Verbs

Underline the correct verb form.

1. If you want to save money, professional tightwads urge you to reconsider the

   things you've always (throwed, thrown) away.

2. For instance, ties that are worn out can (become, became) tails for kites or

   leashes for dogs.

3. You may not have (realize, realized) that you can (use, used) toothbrushes to

   clean shoes.

4. Your golfing pals will wonder why they've never (thinked, thought) of using

   their own old socks as golf club covers.

5. A clear, plastic yogurt lid can (become, became) a frame for a school photo

   if you add a magnet.

6. Bridesmaid dresses can be cut up and (sew, sewn) together to create

   decorative throw pillows that would dazzle Martha Stewart.

7. Two old license plates can be (reborn, reborned) as a roof for a birdhouse.

8. And don't you dare toss this textbook; it can be (used, use) to wrap fish.

9. Strapped to the chest, it can (stop, stopped) small-caliber bullets.

10. When (dropped, dropt) from sufficient height, a single copy has been (known,

    knowed) to kill small rodents.

"Problem" Verbs

The following pairs of verbs are especially troublesome and confusing: *lie* and *lay*, *sit* and *set*, *rise* and *raise*. One way to tell them apart is to remember which word in each pair takes a direct object. A direct object answers the question *whom* or *what* in connection with a verb. The words *lay*, *raise*, and *set* take a direct object.

> He *raised* the window. [He *raised* what?]

Lie, *rise*, and *sit*, however, cannot take a direct object. We cannot say, for example, "He rose the window." In the following examples, the italicized words are objects.

Present Tense	Meaning	Past Tense	Past Participle	Example
lie	to rest	lay	lain	I lay down to rest.
lay	to place something	laid	laid	We laid the *books* on the table.
rise	to go up	rose	risen	The smoke rose quickly.
raise	to lift, to bring forth	raised	raised	She raised the *question*.
sit	to rest	sat	sat	He sat in the chair.
set	to place something	set	set	They set the *basket* on the floor.

EXERCISE 3   Selecting Verbs

Underline the correct verb form.

1. This story is about Bill "Chick" Walker, who (lossed, lost) all he owned at the Wagon Wheel Saloon in Las Vegas.

2. Chick had (laid, layed) one thousand dollars on the red 21 at the roulette table.

3. For that spin, he (done, did) an amazing thing—he (won, wins).

4. But after a while, Chick (became, become) stupid, and his luck (ran, run) out.

5. Before he had (ate, eaten) breakfast, he accepted free drinks from the charming Trixie, who (served, serve) cocktails.

6. His judgment was soon (ruined, ruint) by the drinks, and he (put, putted) all his money on one spin.

7. That wager (cost, costed) Chick everything, and he couldn't (raise, rise) any more money.

8. Moreover, Trixie would not (sit, set) with him because she (like, liked) only winners.

9. Chick drained his glass, (rose, raised) from his red-tufted vinyl barstool, and (head, headed) for the parking lot.

10. There he (known, knew) Bonnie Lou would be waiting for him because she (lust, lusted) for losers.

EXERCISE 4   Selecting Verbs

Underline the correct verb form.

1. According to legend, a vampire (lays, lies) in his coffin during the daylight hours.

2. Like a teenager, he (sets, sits) his own schedule: He sleeps all day and stays out all night.

3. He cannot (rise, raise) until after the sun sets.

4. Then the bloodsucker can (rise, raise) the coffin's lid and (set, sit) up.

5. He (rises, raises) from his bed hungry.

6. But don't bother (setting, sitting) a place for him at the dinner table.

7. He goes out hunting for victims who have unwisely (lain, laid) down their cruci-fixes, wooden stakes, and garlic necklaces.

8. He pounces quickly so that the victim has no time to (rise, raise) an alarm.

9. If he (lies, lays) his hands upon you, you're a goner.

10. But when the sun begins to (rise, raise) in the sky, this monster must hurry back to bed to (lie, lay) his head down.

EXERCISE 5   Using Verbs in Sentences

Use each of these words in a sentence of ten words or more.

1. *lie, lay* (rest), *lain, laid* _____

_____

_____

_____

_____

_____

2. *sit, sat, set* _____

_____

_____

_____

_____

_____

3. *is, was, were* _____

_____

_____

_____

_____

_____

4. *do, does* (or *don't, doesn't*) _____

_____

_____

_____

_____

_____

The Twelve Verb Tenses

Some languages, such as Chinese and Navajo, have no verb tenses to indicate time. English has a fairly complicated system of tenses, but most verbs pattern in what are known as the simple tenses: past, present, and future. Altogether there are twelve tenses in English. The four sections that follow illustrate those tenses in sentences. The charts place each verb on a timeline. The charts also explain what the different tenses mean and how to form them.

SIMPLE TENSES

Present: I, we, you, they *drive*.
He, she, it *drives*.

Past: I, we, you, he, she, it, they *drove*.

Future: I, we, you, he, she, it, they *will drive*.

PERFECT TENSES

Present Perfect: I, we, you, they *have driven*.
He, she, it *has driven*.

Past Perfect: I, we, you, he, she, it, they *had driven*.

Future Perfect: I, we, you, he, she, it, they *will have driven*.

PROGRESSIVE TENSES

Present Progressive: I *am driving*.
He, she, it *is driving*.
We, you, they *are driving*.

Past Progressive: I, he, she, it *was driving*.
We, you, they *were driving*.

Future Progressive: I, we, you, he, she, it, they *will be driving*.

PERFECT PROGRESSIVE TENSES

Present Perfect Progressive: I, we, you, they *have been driving*.
He, she, it *has been driving*.

Past Perfect Progressive: I, we, you, he, she, it, they *had been driving*.

Future Perfect Progressive: I, we, you, he, she, it, they *will have been driving*.

Simple Tenses

Tense	Time Line	Time	Verb Form
Present I *drive* to work. She *drives* to work.	past —— xxx —— future Now	Present, may imply a continuation from past to future	Present: *drive* *drives*
Past I *drove* to work.	x Now	Past	Past: *drove*
Future I *will drive* to work.	x Now	Future	Present preceded by *will*: *will drive*

Perfect Tenses

Tense	Time Line	Time	Verb Form
Present Perfect I *have driven* to work.	past —— xxx —— future Now	Completed recently in the past, may continue to the present	Past participle preceded by *have* or *has*: *have driven*
Past Perfect I *had driven* to work before I moved to the city. [event]	Event x o Now	Prior to a specific time in the past	Past participle preceded by *had*: *had driven*
Future Perfect I *will have driven* to work thousands of times by December 31. [event]	Event x o Now	At a time prior to a specific time in the future	Past participle preceded by *will have*: *will have driven*

Progressive Tenses

Tense	Time Line	Time	Verb Form
Present Progressive I *am driving* to work.	 past —xxx— future Now	In progress now	Progressive (*-ing* ending) preceded by *is*, *am*, or *are*: *am driving*
Past Progressive I *was driving* to work.	 xxx Now	In progress in the past	Progressive (*-ing* ending) preceded by *was* or *were*: *was driving*
Future Progressive I *will be driving* to work.	 xxx Now	In progress in the future	Progressive (*-ing* ending) preceded by *will be*: *will be driving*

Perfect Progressive Tenses

Tense	Time Line	Time	Verb Form
Present Perfect Progressive I *have been driving* to work.	past —xxx— future Now	In progress up to now	Progressive (*-ing* ending) preceded by *have been* or *has been*: *have been driving*
Past Perfect Progressive I *had been driving* when I began ride-sharing. [event]	Event xxx o Now	In progress before another event in the past	Progressive (*-ing* ending) preceded by *had been*: *had been driving*
Future Perfect Progressive By May 1 [event], I *will have been driving* to work for six years.	Event xxx o Now	In progress before another event in the future	Progressive (*-ing* ending) preceded by *will have been*: *will have been driving*

EXERCISE 6   Choosing Verb Tense

Underline the correct verb form.

1. In the eighteenth century, Benjamin Franklin (is saying, said) that compound interest was the "eighth wonder of the world."

2. Today, taking advantage of compound interest (is, was) still one way to grow a fortune.

3. I wish I (had, had been) started investing years ago.

4. If I (will have, could have) saved $2,000 per year from age 21 on, I (would have, would have had) over a million dollars now.

5. I (have, had) never realized this until I did the math.

6. So I (have decided, could have been deciding) to begin investing money every month from now on.

7. Yesterday, I (determined, have determined) an amount I should save each week.

8. I hope that you (will have considered, are considering) doing the same thing.

9. By the time we're ready to retire, we (were, may be) millionaires.

10. Someday we (will worry, worried) about how to pay the bills.

EXERCISE 7   Choosing Verb Tense

Underline the correct verb form.

1. We (study, are studying) William Shakespeare's play *Romeo and Juliet*.

2. The teenagers Romeo and Juliet (met, had met) at a party.

3. By the time the party was over, they (fell, had fallen) in love.

4. Unfortunately, though, their families (feud, were feuding), so Romeo and Juliet (hid, had hidden) their affection for one another.

5. They secretly (married, had married) and (planned, had planned) to run away together.

6. But long before Juliet met Romeo, Juliet's father (decided, had decided) that she would marry a man named Paris.

7. The night before her wedding, Juliet (took, had taken) a potion that made her appear dead.

8. This tale (has, has had) a tragic ending because before Romeo found Juliet in her tomb, he (was not informed, had not been informed) that she wasn't really dead.

9. So he (committed, had committed) suicide, and Juliet (stabbed, had stabbed) herself when she awoke to find his body.

10. If I review this exercise, I (have, will have) a hanky ready to dry my tears.

Subject-Verb Agreement

This section is concerned with number agreement between subjects and verbs. The basic principle of **subject-verb agreement** is that if the subject is singular, the verb should be singular, and if the subject is plural, the verb should be plural. In the examples under the following ten major guidelines, the simple subjects and verbs are italicized.

1. Do not let words that come between the subject and verb affect agreement.

   - Modifying phrases and clauses frequently come between the subject and verb:

     The various *types* of drama *were* not *discussed*.

     Angela, who is hitting third, *is* the best player.

     The *price* of those shoes *is* too high.

   - Certain prepositions can cause trouble. The following words are prepositions, not conjunctions: *along with*, *as well as*, *besides*, *in addition to*, *including*, *together with*. The words that function as objects of prepositions cannot also be subjects of the sentence.

     The *coach*, along with the players, *protests* the decision.

   - When a negative phrase follows a positive subject, the verb agrees with the positive subject.

     Phillip, not the other boys, *was* the culprit.

2. Do not let inversions (verb before subject, not the normal order) affect the agreement of subject and verb.

   - Verbs and other words may come before the subject. Do not let them affect the agreement. To understand subject-verb relationships, recast the sentence in normal word order.

     Are Jabir and his *sister* at home? [question form]

     Jabir and his *sister are* at home. [normal order]

   - A sentence filler is a word that is grammatically independent of other words in the sentence. The most common fillers are *there* and *here*. Even though a sentence filler precedes the verb, it should not be treated as the subject.

     There *are* many *reasons* for his poor work. [The verb *are* agrees with the subject *reasons*.]

3. A singular verb agrees with a singular indefinite pronoun. (See page 163.)

   - Most indefinite pronouns are singular.

     Each of the women *is* ready at this time.

     Neither of the women *is* ready at this time.

     One of the children *is* not paying attention.

- Certain indefinite pronouns do not clearly express either a singular or plural number. Agreement, therefore, depends on the meaning of the sentence. These pronouns are *all*, *any*, *none*, and *some*.

  All of the melon *was* good.

  All of the melons *were* good.

  None of the pie *is* acceptable.

  None of the pies *are* acceptable.

4. Two or more subjects joined by *and* usually take a plural verb.

   The *captain* and the *sailors were* happy to be ashore.

   The *trees* and *shrubs need* more care.

- If the parts of a compound subject mean one and the same person or thing, the verb is singular; if the parts mean more than one, the verb is plural.

  The *secretary* and *treasurer is* not present. [one]

  The *secretary* and the *treasurer are* not present. [more than one]

- When *each* or *every* modifies singular subjects joined by *and*, the verb is singular.

  Each *boy* and each *girl brings* a donation.

  Each *woman* and *man has asked* the same questions.

5. Alternative subjects—that is, subjects joined by *or*, *nor*, *either/or*, *neither/ nor*, *not only/but also*—should be handled in the following manner:

- If the subjects are both singular, the verb is singular.

  Rosa or *Alicia* is responsible.

- If the subjects are plural, the verb is plural.

  Neither the *students* nor the *teachers were* impressed by his comments.

- If one of the subjects is singular and the other subject is plural, the verb agrees with the nearer subject.

  Either the Garcia *boys* or their *father goes* to the hospital each day.

  Either their *father* or the Garcia *boys go* to the hospital each day.

6. Collective nouns—*team*, *family*, *group*, *crew*, *gang*, *class*, *faculty*, and the like—take a singular verb if the noun is considered a unit, but they take a plural verb if the group is considered as a number of individuals.

   The *team is playing* well tonight.

   The *team are getting* dressed. [In this sentence, the individuals are acting not as a unit but separately. If you don't like the way the sentence sounds, substitute "The members of the team are getting dressed."]

7. Titles of books, essays, short stories, and plays; a word spoken of as a word; and the names of businesses take a singular verb.

> *The Canterbury Tales was written* by Geoffrey Chaucer.

> *Ives is* my favorite name for a pet.

> *Markle Brothers has* a sale this week.

8. Sums of money, distances, and measurements are followed by a singular verb when a unit is meant. They are followed by a plural verb when the individual elements are considered separately.

> *Three dollars was* the price. [unit]

> *Three dollars were* lying there. [individual]

> *Five years is* a long time. [unit]

> The *first five years were* difficult ones. [individual]

9. Be careful of agreement with nouns ending in *-s*. Several nouns ending in *-s* take a singular verb—for example, *aeronautics, civics, economics, ethics, measles, mumps.*

> *Mumps is* an unpleasant disease.

> *Economics is* my major field of study.

10. Some nouns have only a plural form and so take only a plural verb—for example, *clothes, fireworks, scissors, trousers.*

> His *trousers are* badly wrinkled.

> Marv's *clothes were* stylish and expensive.

EXERCISE 8   Making Subjects and Verbs Agree

Underline the verb that agrees in number with the subject.

1. "Two Kinds" (is, are) a short story by Amy Tan.

2. My trousers (is, are) wrinkled.

3. Twenty pounds (is, are) a lot to lose in one month.

4. Physics (is, are) a difficult subject to master.

5. *60 Minutes* (is, are) a respected television program.

6. Sears (is, are) having a giant sale.

7. The scissors (is, are) very sharp.

8. Five miles (is, are) too far to walk.

9. The class (is, are) stretching their muscles.

10. My dog and my cat (is, are) sleeping on the couch.

EXERCISE 9   Making Subjects and Verbs Agree

Underline the verb that agrees in number with the subject.

1. Even after the devastation caused by Hurricane Katrina, New Orleans (is, are) the site of one of the most celebrated parties in the United States.

2. Though the event was temporarily scaled back, Mardi Gras (is, are) an event that refuses to die.

3. Mardi Gras, which means "Fat Tuesday," (is, are) always forty-six days before Easter.

4. But twelve days before that, the crowd (begins, begin) to grow.

5. All of the bands in the state of Louisiana (converges, converge) on New Orleans.

6. A visitor, along with just about all of the city's residents, (enjoys, enjoy) nonstop jazz and blues music.

7. Cajun and Creole food (satisfies, satisfy) the revelers' hungry appetites.

8. There (is, are) numerous parades, but the best ones (occurs, occur) during the last five days of the celebration.

9. Each of the spectacular parade floats (is, are) decorated and (carries, carry) riders wearing costumes.

10. Four miles (is, are) the length of a typical parade route.

11. Beads, coins, cups, and an occasional medallion (is, are) tossed from the floats into the crowd.

12. People who line the parade route (tries, try) to catch as many trinkets as they can.

13. One float, the best of all of that parade's floats, (wins, win) an award.

14. Some of the most popular festivities, besides a good parade, (is, are) the masked balls.

15. Every one of the costumes (is, are) outrageous and unique.

16. *Cajun Mardi Gras Masks* (is, are) a book that will give you some ideas.

17. The celebration (is, are) a happening of fun and frenzy.

18. After dark, there (is, are) fireworks in the night sky.

19. Neither the participants nor the curious onlooker (wants, want) the party to end.

20. (Is, Are) these days of merrymaking something you'd enjoy?

Consistency in Tense

Consider this paragraph:

> We (1) went downtown, and then we (2) watch a movie. Later we (3) met some friends from school, and we all (4) go to the mall. For most of the evening, we (5) play video games in arcades. It (6) was a typical but rather uneventful summer day.

Does the shifting verb tense bother you (to say nothing about the lack of development of ideas)? It should! The writer makes several unnecessary changes. Verbs 1, 3, and 6 are in the past tense, and verbs 2, 4, and 5 are in the present tense. Changing all verbs to past tense makes the paragraph much smoother.

> We went downtown, and then we watched a movie. Later we met some friends from school, and we all went to the mall. For most of the evening, we played video games in arcades. It was a typical but rather uneventful summer day.

In other instances you might want to maintain a consistent present tense. There are no inflexible rules about selecting a tense for certain kinds of writing, but you should be consistent, changing tense only for a good reason.

The present tense is most often used in writing about literature, even if the literature was written long in the past:

> *Moby Dick* is a novel about Captain Ahab's obsession with a great white whale. Ahab *sets* sail with a full crew of sailors who *think* they *are going* on merely another whaling voyage. Most of the crew *are* experienced seamen.

The past tense is likely to serve you best in writing about your personal experiences and about historical events (although the present tense can often be used effectively to establish the feeling of intimacy and immediacy):

> In the summer of 1991, Hurricane Bob *hit* the Atlantic coast region. It *came* ashore near Cape Hatteras and *moved* north. The winds *reached* a speed of more than ninety miles per hour on Cape Cod but then *slackened* by the time Bob *reached* Maine.

EXERCISE 10   Making Verbs Consistent in Tense

Correct verbs as needed in the following paragraph to achieve consistency in tense. Most verbs will be past tense.

Lizzie Borden was famous for being arrested and tried for the gruesome ax murder of her father and stepmother. On August 4, 1892, when Andrew Borden was taking a nap in his home, someone hits him in the head eleven times with a hatchet. His wife, Abby Borden, had already been killed in an upstairs bedroom with the same weapon. The police investigate and conclude that Andrew's thirty-two-year-old daughter Lizzie is the murderess. Lizzie is arrested but pleaded not guilty to the crimes. Her sensational trial was followed by people all over the country. The prosecution presents an overwhelming amount of circumstantial evidence. Many people thought that she is guilty. Nonetheless, Lizzie's jury acquitted her. The case remains unsolved to this day.

EXERCISE 11   Making Verbs Consistent in Tense

Correct verbs as needed in the following paragraph to achieve consistency in tense. Most verbs will be past tense.

Guam is located in the Mariana chain of islands. It is first inhabited by the Chamorro people approximately 4,000 years ago. This island is an American territory since 1898, when the Spanish give up control after losing the Spanish American War. The Japanese occupy the island during World War II until it is recaptured by the United States in July 1944. Today the island was a popular tourist spot for Asians as well as being a site for several U.S. military bases. A beautiful tropical island, Guam looked much like the Hawaiian Islands. The original inhabitants come from Indonesia around 4,000 years ago. From those times came the belief in Taotao Mona, spirits of the ancient Chamorros; today most residents of Guam were Christian. People born in Guam are American citizens. In fact, the motto of Guam was "Where America's Day Begins."

Active and Passive Voice

Which of these sentences sounds better to you?

Ken Griffey Jr. slammed a home run.

A home run was slammed by Ken Griffey Jr.

Both sentences carry the same message, but the first expresses it more effectively. The subject (*Ken Griffey Jr.*) is the actor. The verb (*slammed*) is the action. The direct object (*home run*) is the receiver of the action. The second sentence lacks the vitality of the first because the receiver of the action is the subject; the one who performs the action is embedded in the prepositional phrase at the end of the sentence.

The first sentence demonstrates the active voice. It has an active verb (one that leads to the direct object), and the action moves from the beginning to the end of the sentence. The second sentence exhibits the passive voice (with the action reflecting back on the subject). When given a choice, you should usually select the active voice. It promotes energy and directness.

The passive voice, although not usually the preferred form, does have its uses.

- When the doer of the action is unknown or unimportant:

    My car was stolen. [The doer, a thief, is unknown.]

- When the receiver of the action is more important than the doer:

    My neighbor was permanently disabled by an irresponsible drunk driver. [The neighbor's suffering, not the drunk driver, is the focus.]

As you can see, the passive construction places the doer at the end of a prepositional phrase (as in the second example) or does not include the doer in the statement at all (as in the first example). In the first example, the receiver of the action (the car) is in the subject position. The verb is preceded by *was*, a *to be* helper. Here is another example:

    The book was read by her. [passive]

    She read the book. [active]

Weak sentences often involve the unnecessary and ineffective use of the passive form; Exercises 12 and 13 give you practice in identifying the passive voice and changing it to active.

EXERCISE 12   Using Active and Passive Voice

Identify each sentence as either active voice (A) or passive voice (P). If a sentence with the passive form would be more effective in the active voice, rewrite it.

_____ 1. For centuries, pirates have harassed ships on all of the world's oceans.

_____ 2. Piracy has been defined as armed robbery on the high seas.

_____ 3. Cargo was seized and coastal towns were plundered by pirates.

_____ 4. Also, people were kidnapped and held for ransom by pirates.

_____ 5. Captains of pirate ships often flew a flag with a white skull and crossbones on a black background.

_____ 6. The swashbuckling pirate of our imagination was created by writers such as Rafael Sabatini and Lord Byron.

_____ 7. The romantic portrait of a sword-wielding, treasure-hunting ruffian in gold earrings was given to readers by books like _Captain Blood_ and poems like "The Corsair."

_____ 8. As a result, pirates have often been perceived by people as ruthless but adventurous heroes.

_____ 9. Actually, though, a drunken, violent, and short life was lived by these desperate criminals.

_____ 10. The decline of piracy was caused by the development of national navies in the nineteenth century.

EXERCISE 13   Using Active and Passive Voice

Identify each sentence as either active voice (A) or passive voice (P). If a sentence with the passive form would be more effective in the active voice, rewrite it.

_____ 1. A story was reported by the _Las Vegas SUN_ newspaper.

_____ 2. An accident was experienced by the Flying Elvises during a skydive in Boston.

_____ 3. Elvis Presley, King of Rock 'n' Roll, was impersonated by these high-flying stuntmen.

_____ 4. Fringed white jumpsuits, slicked-back hair, and sunglasses were worn by the four-member skydiving team.

_____ 5. The toughest part of the act involved keeping their hair in place as they fell.

_____ 6. But this time, the four Elvi were blown off course.

_____ 7. A miscalculation was made by the jumpers on that windy day.

_____ **8.** Two of the Elvi hit the water in Boston Harbor.

_____ **9.** A street and a yacht club were struck by the two other Elvi.

_____ **10.** The accident was observed by about 1,600 confused but amused people.

Strong Verbs

Because the verb is an extremely important part of any sentence, it should be chosen with care. Some of the most widely used verbs are the *being* verbs: *is, was, were, are, am*. We couldn't get along in English without them, but writers often use them when more forceful and effective verbs are available.

Consider these examples:

Weak Verb: He *is* the leader of the people.

Strong Verb: He *leads* the people.

Weak Verb: She *was* the first to finish.

Strong Verb: She *finished* first.

EXERCISE 14   Using Strong Verbs

Replace the weak verbs with stronger ones in the following sentences. Delete unnecessary words to make each sentence even more concise if you can.

1. Like most people, Bob is afraid of public speaking.

2. Public speaking is the one thing most people fear more than death!

3. Bob is full of worry about looking foolish.

4. Bob is in need of more learning about public speaking.

5. So Bob is now in attendance at Santa Ana College.

6. He is a student who has enrolled in a speech class.

7. Preparation of a speech is something that Bob learns how to do.

8. Bob is now a person who can control his anxiety.

9. To relax, Bob is taking deep breaths.

10. Bob is a confident giver of speeches.

EXERCISE 15   Using Strong Verbs

Replace the weak verbs with stronger ones in the following sentences. Delete unnecessary words to make each sentence even more concise if you can.

1. Mickey Mantle was the hitter of many home runs.

2. The chef was a man with a fondness for food.

3. To graduate in two years is my plan.

4. John Hancock was the first signer of the Declaration of Independence.

5. Juanita is the organizer of the event.

6. Cooking is something she likes to do.

7. Carl was the owner of the restaurant.

8. Tiger Woods will be the winner of the tournament.

9. They were in love with each other.

10. His passion for her was in a state of demise.

Subjunctive Mood

Mood refers to the intention of the verb. Three moods are relevant to our study: indicative, imperative, and subjunctive.

The **indicative mood** expresses a statement of fact.

I considered the issue.

I was tired.

The **imperative mood** expresses a command (and has a *you* understood subject).

Go to the store.

The **subjunctive mood** expresses a statement as contrary to fact, conditional, desirable, possible, necessary, or doubtful. In current English the subjunctive form is distinguishable only in two forms: The verb *to be* uses *be* throughout the present tense and *were* throughout the past tense.

He requires that we *be* [instead of *are*] on time.

If she *were* [instead of *was*] the candidate, she would win.

In other verbs, the final *s* is dropped in the third-person singular (*he*, *she*, *it*) of the present tense to make all forms the same in any one tense.

I request that he *report* [instead of *reports*] today.

Here are examples of the common forms:

If I *were* [instead of *was*] you, I wouldn't do that. [contrary to fact]

She behaves as if she *were* [instead of *was*] not certain. [doubt]

I wish I *were* [instead of *was*] in Texas. [wish]

EXERCISE 16   Selecting Subjunctive Verbs

Underline the subjunctive verbs.

1. If she (was, were) a few years older, he would ask her out.

2. I wish I (was, were) a wealthy woman.

3. If I (was, were) rich, I'd buy you a pony.

4. They act as if they (are, were) immortal.

5. She requested that her check (is, be) mailed to her.

6. If you wish you (are, were) thinner, try this new diet.

7. You talk as if you (are, were) not coming back.

8. My attorney requested that I (am, be) released on bail.

9. Let's pretend that your theory (was, were) true.

10. If I (was, were) younger, I'd wear bikinis.

CHAPTER REVIEW   Verbs

1. **Standard usage** is appropriate for the kind of writing and speaking you are likely to do in your college work and future career.

2. Whereas **regular verbs** are predictable—having an *-ed* ending for past and past-participle forms—**irregular verbs**, as the term suggests, follow no definite pattern.

   raise, raised, raised [regular]; *see, saw, seen* [irregular]

3. Certain verbs (present-tense here) can be troublesome and should be studied with care (page 128).

   lie, lay   sit, set   rise, raise

4. If the subject of a sentence is singular, the verb should be singular; if the subject is plural, the verb should be plural.

   The *price* of the shoes *is* high.

   The *advantages* of that shoe *are* obvious.

5. There are no inflexible rules about selecting a tense for certain kinds of writing, but you should be consistent, changing tense only for a good reason.

6. Usually you should select the present tense to write about literature.

    Herman Melville's character Bartleby the Scrivener *fails* to communicate.

    Select the past tense to write about yourself or something historical.

    I *was* eighteen when I *decided* I *was* ready for independence.

7. English has twelve verb tenses. (See pages 131–133 for names, examples, functions, and forms.)

8. The **active-voice** expression (subject, active verb, and sometimes object) is usually preferred over the **passive-voice** expression (subject as the receiver of action, with doer unstated or at the end of a prepositional phrase).

    She *read* the book. [active]

    The book *was read* by her. [passive]

9. In your revision, replace weak verbs with strong ones.

    He *was* the first to leave. [weak verb]

    He *left* first. [strong verb]

10. The **subjunctive mood** expresses a statement that is contrary to fact, conditional, desirable, possible, necessary, or doubtful. *Be* is used throughout the present tense and *were* throughout the past.

    He requires that we *be* [not *are*] on time.

    I wish I *were* [not *was*] home.

    In other verbs, the final *s* is dropped in the third-person singular (*he*, *she*, *it*) of the present tense.

    I request that he *report* [instead of *reports*] today.

CHAPTER REVIEW   Exercises

| REVIEW 1 | **Changing Verb Tense** |

Change the verbs from present to past tense.

1. Frederick Douglass is the leading spokesman of African-Americans in the 1800s.

2. Born a slave, he is befriended by his master's wife and begins to educate himself.

3. As a young man, he runs away to New Bedford, Massachusetts.

4. He works as a common laborer for some time.

5. At the Massachusetts Antislavery Society in 1841, he gives a speech on the importance of freedom.

6. His speech is so well received that he was hired to lecture on his experience as a slave.

7. While traveling on the lecture circuit, he often protests various forms of segregation.

8. He insists on sitting in "Whites Only" areas on the railroad.

9. He successfully protests against segregated schools in Rochester, New York.

10. In 1845 he publishes *Narrative of the Life of Frederick Douglass*, his autobiography.

REVIEW 2

Making Subjects and Verbs Agree

Underline the verb that agrees in number with the subject.

1. The result of the defendant's corrupt business dealings (was, were) soon felt.

2. The mayor and most citizens (was, were) deeply affected.

3. There (was, were) no justification for the defendant's behavior.

4. Neither of the defendant's parents (was, were) willing to defend him.

5. Neither the judge nor the jury members (was, were) very sympathetic with the defense's case.

6. Ethics (was, were) apparently an unknown field of study to the defendant.

7. Each and every day (was, were) consumed with intense debate.

8. In the penalty phase, the judge said that ten years (was, were) the correct sentence.

9. Then the judge added, "Fifty thousand dollars (is, are) the right sum for restitution."

10. The defendant, along with his attorney, (was, were) not pleased.

REVIEW 3   ## Correcting Verb Problems

Correct problems with verb form, tense, agreement, strength, and voice. As a summary of a novel, this piece should be mostly in the present tense.

SUMMARY OF *THE OLD MAN AND THE SEA*

Santiago, one of many local fishermen, have not caught a fish in eighty-four days. Young Manolin, despite the objections of his parents, has a belief in the old man. His parents says Santiago is unlucky, and they will not let their son go fishing with him.

The next day Santiago sit sail. Soon he catch a small tuna, which he used for bait. Then a huge marlin hit the bait with a strike. The old man cannot rise the fish to the surface, and it pulled the boat throughout the rest of the day and during the night.

During the second day, Santiago's hand is injured by the line and he become extremely tired, but he holds on. When the fish moves to the surface, Santiago notes that it was two feet longer than his skiff. It is the biggest fish he has ever saw. He thinks in wonder if he will be up to the task of catching it. With the line braced across his shoulders, he sleeped for a while. As he dreams gloriously of lions and porpoises and of being young, he is awaken by the fish breaking water again, and Santiago is sure the fish is tiring. He lays in the boat and waits.

On the third day, the fish came to the surface. Santiago pull steadily on the line, and finally it is harpooned and killed by Santiago. The fish is tied to the skiff by him. But sharks attacked and mutilate the huge marlin. Using an oar, he beats on the sharks courageously with all his strength, but they strips the fish to a skeleton.

With the bones still tied to the skiff, the exhausted old man returned to shore. Other fishermen and tourists marvel at the eighteen-foot skeleton of the fish as the old man lays asleep. The young boy knew he has much to learn from the old man and is determined to go fishing with him.

REVIEW 4

Using Strong Verbs

Replace the weak verbs with stronger ones in the following sentences. Delete unnecessary words to make each sentence even more concise if you can.

1. Whitney is in the process of rebuilding her desktop.

2. Anika is a person who is capable of leading our group.

3. Matthew was the scorer of the last touchdown.

4. Maria is a worker at the department store.

5. Jonathan is one who attracts favorable attention.

6. Lauren has a smile that is sweet.

7. Shane is waiting for the next train.

8. Jarrett is a swift runner.

9. Jannell was the second to finish the race.

10. This review is something that makes me think.

REVIEW 5

Writing Sentences with Correct Verbs

Each of the following verbs appears in its base form. Change the verb form to the tense specified in parentheses and include it in a sentence of ten or more words. (See pages 122–126 for verb forms.)

1. eat (to past) _____

    _____

    _____

2. begin (to future) _____

    _____

    _____

3. see (to past perfect) _____

    _____

    _____

4. walk (to future perfect) _____

    _____

    _____

5. speak (to present perfect) _____

_____

_____

6. go (to future progressive) _____

_____

_____

7. drink (to present progressive) _____

_____

_____

8. dance (to past progressive) _____

_____

_____

9. fly (to present perfect progressive) _____

_____

_____

10. grow (to past perfect progressive) _____

_____

_____

11. choose (to future perfect progressive) _____

_____

_____

STUDENT COMPANION SITE
For additional practice, visit www.cengage .com/devenglish/ brandon/spb6e.

MICROTHEME

To practice your skills acquired in this chapter, return to the Microtheme on page 121 and complete Exercise B.

Pronouns

FLOW OF WRITING

MICROTHEME	Writing Activity in Miniature

EXERCISE A

Before you work on this chapter, write a Microtheme on the following topic. Write small enough to leave room for marking later. **After** you have studied this chapter, return to your Microtheme and complete Exercise B to practice what you have learned.

Suggested Microtheme Topic: Write a Microtheme of 80 to 100 words about needed changes in procedures, management, products, or services in your workplace; if you do not have a job, write about needed changes at home or in a class.

EXERCISE B

Connecting Your Learning Objectives with Your Microtheme

Complete this exercise after you have studied this chapter.

1. Underline all pronouns and consider their position in sentence structure.
2. Make sure that pronouns are in the correct cases, objective or subjective.
3. Check to make sure that pronouns agree in person, number, and gender.
4. Draw a line from each pronoun to its antecedent to make sure that it has clear reference.

hould you say, "Between you and *I*" or "Between you and *me*"? What about "Let's you and *I* do this" or "Let's you and *me* do this"? Are you confused about when to use *who* and *whom*? Is it "Everyone should wear *their* coat, or *his* coat, or *his or her* coat"? Is there anything wrong with saying, "When *you* walk down the streets of Laredo"?

The examples in the first paragraph represent the most common problems people have with pronouns. This chapter will help you identify the standard forms and understand why they are correct. The result should be additional expertise and confidence in your writing.

Pronoun Case

Case is the form a pronoun takes as it fills a position in a sentence. Words such as *you* and *it* do not change, but others do, and they change in predictable ways. For example, *I* is a subject word and *me* is an object word. As you refer to yourself, you will select a pronoun that fits a certain part of sentence structure. You say, "*I* will write the paper," not "*Me* will write the paper," because *I* is in the subject position. But you say, "She will give the apple to *me*," not "She will give the apple to *I*" because *me* is in the object position. These are the pronouns that change:

Subject	Object
I	me
he	him
she	her
we	us
they	them
who, whoever	whom, whomever

SUBJECTIVE CASE

	Singular	Plural
First Person:	I	we
Second Person:	you	you
Third Person:	he, she, it	they
	who	

Subjective-case pronouns can fill two positions in a sentence.

1. Pronouns in the subjective case may fill subject positions.

   a. Some will be easy to identify because they are at the beginning of the sentence.

      I dance in the park.

      He dances in the park.

> *She* dances in the park.
>
> *We* dance in the park.
>
> *They* dance in the park.
>
> *Who* is dancing in the park?

b. Others will be more difficult to identify because they are not at the beginning of a sentence and may not appear to be part of a clause. The words *than* and *as* are signals for these special arrangements, which can be called incompletely stated clauses.

> He is taller than *I* (am).
>
> She is younger than *we* (are).
>
> We work as hard as *they* (do).

The words *am*, *are*, and *do*, which complete the clauses, have been omitted. We are actually saying, "He is taller than *I am*," "She is younger than *we are*," and "We work as hard as *they do*." The italicized pronouns are subjects of "understood" verbs.

2. Pronouns in the subjective case may refer back to the subject.

a. They may follow a form of the verb *to be*, such as *was*, *were*, *am*, *is*, and *are*.

> I believe it is *he*.
>
> It was *she* who spoke.
>
> The victims were *they*.

b. Some nouns and pronouns refer back to an earlier noun without referring back through the verb.

> The leading candidates—Pedro, Darnelle, Steve, Kimilieu, and *I*—made speeches.

OBJECTIVE CASE

	Singular	Plural
First Person:	me	us
Second Person:	you	you
Third Person:	him, her, it	them
	whom	

Objective-case pronouns can also fill two positions in sentences.

1. Pronouns in the objective case may fill object positions.

   a. They may be objects after the verb. A direct object answers the question *what* or *whom* in connection with the verb.

      We brought *it* to your house. [*What* did we bring? *it*]

      We saw *her* in the library. [*Whom* did we see? *her*]

   An indirect object answers the question *to whom* in connection with the verb.

      I gave *him* the message. [*To whom* did I give the message? *to him*]

      The doctor told *us* the test results. [*To whom* did the doctor tell the results? *to us*]

   b. They may be objects after prepositions.

      The problem was clear to *us*.

      I went with Steve and *him*.

2. Objective-case pronouns may also refer back to object words.

   They had the results for us—Judy and *me*.

   The judge addressed the defendants—John and *her*.

TECHNIQUES FOR DETERMINING CASE

Here are three techniques that will help you decide which pronoun to use when the choice seems difficult.

1. If you have a compound element (such as a subject or an object of a preposition), consider only the pronoun part. The sound alone will probably tell you the answer.

   She gave the answer to Yoshi and (I, *me*).

   Yoshi and the pronoun make up a compound object of the preposition *to*. Disregard the noun, *Yoshi*, and ask yourself, "Would I say, 'She gave the answer *to me* or *to I*'?" The way the words sound would tell you the answer is *to me*. Of course, if you immediately notice that the pronoun is in an object position, you need not bother with sound.

2. If you are choosing between *who* (subject word) and *whom* (object word), look to the right to see if the next verb has a subject. If it does not, the pronoun probably *is* the subject, but if it does, the pronoun probably is an object.

   The person (*who*, whom) works hardest will win. [*Who* is the correct answer because it is the subject of the verb *works*.]

   The person (who, *whom*) we admire most is José. [*Whom* is the correct answer because the next verb, *admire*, already has a subject, *we*. *Whom* is an object.]

A related technique works the same way. If the next important word after *who* or *whom* in a statement is a noun or pronoun, the correct word will almost always be *whom*. However, if the next important word is not a noun or pronoun, the correct word will be *who*.

To apply this technique, you must disregard qualifier clauses such as "I think," "it seems," and "we hope."

> Tyrone is a natural leader (*who*, whom) has charisma. [*Who* is the correct answer; it is followed by something other than a noun or pronoun.]

> Tyrone is a natural leader (*who*, whom), we think, has charisma. [*Who* is the correct answer; it is followed by the qualifier clause *we think*, which is then followed by something other than a noun or pronoun.]

> Tyrone is a natural leader (who, *whom*) we supported. [*Whom* is the correct answer; it is followed by a pronoun.]

3. *Let's* is made up of the words *let* and *us* and means "you *let us*"; therefore, when you select a pronoun to follow it, consider the two original words and select another object word—*me*.

> Let's you and (I, *me*) take a trip to Westwood. [Think of "You let us, you and me, take a trip to Westwood." *Us* and *me* are object words.]

EXERCISE 1   Selecting Pronouns

Underline the correct pronouns.

1. We admired his beer can collection, so he left it to (I, me) and (she, her) in his will.

2. (He, Him) and (I, me) found true love via the Lovers-R-Us.com online dating service.

3. He deserves to win more than (her, she).

4. The final showdown will be between (they, them) and (we, us).

5. No one can beat (we, us), so let's you and (I, me) apply to be contestants on the *Wheel of Fortune* game show.

6. (Us, We) attorneys resent being compared to sharks.

7. The show delighted and amazed (us, we) puppet enthusiasts.

8. The individual (who, whom) gave his mother a vacuum cleaner for Mother's Day deserves a tongue-lashing.

9. You can hire (whoever, whomever) you choose.

10. Between you and (I, me), I didn't care for the twenty-minute drum solo.

EXERCISE 2   Selecting Pronouns

Underline the correct pronouns.

1. (She, Her) and (I, me) went to the Ripley's Believe It or Not Museum.

2. (We, Us) young people are fascinated by the weird, the gross, and the creepy.

3. I would rather go to the museum with you than with (she, her).

4. There are those (who, whom) would urge you not to waste your money to see oddities like shrunken heads and a portrait of John Wayne made of dryer lint.

5. Robert L. Ripley, an eccentric newspaper cartoonist (who, whom) loved to travel, collected strange things.

6. He is the man (who, whom) we can thank for acquiring many of the artifacts now housed in forty-four "Odditoriums" in ten different countries.

7. (Who, Whom) wouldn't be entertained by a stuffed six-legged cow or pictures of two-headed lambs and other freaks of nature?

8. And don't forget the bizarre videos, like the one of a man (who, whom) swallows and then regurgitates a live mouse.

9. I feel sorry for (whoever, whomever) misses the replica of the *Mona Lisa* made out of croutons.

10. Just between you and (I, me), though, the wax figures of bizarre accident victims, like the man impaled on a crowbar, were a little unnerving.

EXERCISE 3   Selecting Pronouns

Underline the correct pronouns.

1. (Who, Whom) did the judges crown Zucchini Queen?

2. To (who, whom) did the wealthy widow leave her vast fortune?

3. She was a woman (who, whom) loved cats, so her pets inherited her estate.

4. For (who, whom) are you buying this handsome set of Ginsu knives?

5. I know someone (who, whom) actually likes school cafeteria food.

6. (Who, Whom) is going to get the blue ribbon for the best pickles?

7. Seventeenth-century poet John Donne warned, "Ask not for (who, whom) the bell tolls; it tolls for thee."

8. How do I know (who, whom) to trust?

9. She addressed her love letter "To (Who, Whom) It May Concern."

10. The winner of the Spelling Bee was the child (who, whom) spelled the word *sesquipedalian* correctly.

EXERCISE 4   Selecting Pronouns

Underline the correct pronouns.

1. (Who, Whom) is next in line for the throne?

2. (Who, Whom) should I call if I need help assembling my antigravity machine?

3. We all know (who, whom) put the superglue on the boss's chair.

4. With (who, whom) are you dancing next?

5. The sailor (who, whom) swabbed the deck did an excellent job.

6. When her husband suggested that it would be fun to host a party for one hundred of their closest friends, she replied, "Fun for (who, whom)?"

7. (Who, Whom) did you marry in Las Vegas' drive-thru wedding chapel?

8. The contestant (who, whom) tripped on her evening gown and fell still managed to win first runner-up.

9. He will call the plumber, (who, whom) will know what to do.

10. "*What* you know is not as important as (who, whom) you know," he confided.

EXERCISE 5   Selecting Pronouns

Underline the correct pronouns.

1. Let's you and (I, me) consider some stories called urban legends.

2. These are stories heard by people like you and (I, me), which are passed on as if they were true.

3. We hear them from people (who, whom) have heard them from others.

4. You have probably heard more of them than (I, me), but I'll tell some anyway.

5. One is about a guard dog named Gork (who, whom) was found choking in his owner's bedroom.

6. The owner, (who, whom) loved Gork dearly, took him to the veterinarian, left him, and headed home.

7. While driving home, the owner answered his cell phone, asking "To (who, whom) am I speaking?"

8. "This is your vet calling. Just between you and (I, me), you have a big problem here."

9. "Gork has someone's detached finger stuck in his throat, and I've called the police, (who, whom) are on their way to your house."

10. Eventually the police arrested an angry armed man (who, whom) they suspected had broken into the owner's house, where Gork had bitten off and choked on the intruder's finger while the intruder, (who, whom) had crawled into a closet, passed out from loss of blood.

EXERCISE 6   Selecting Pronouns

Underline the correct pronouns.

1. Another famous urban legend, involving two motorists, was told to my sister and (me, I) years ago.

2. Between you and (I, me), the story is sexist, but this is the way (we, us) heard it.

3. A motorist, (who, whom) was named Al, needed someone to push his car, so he called on Sue, his neighbor, (who, whom) lived next door.

4. "I need a push to get my car started," he said to her. "Let's you and (I, me) work together, and I'll be grateful forever."

5. "You're a special person (who, whom) I've always wanted to befriend," she said happily. "Tell me what to do."

6. "My car has an automatic transmission, which means the car won't start at less than thirty-five miles per hour," said Al, (who, whom) talked fast.

7. Al sat in his car as happy as (her, she) when he looked in his rear-view mirror and saw (she, her) heading toward his back bumper at a high speed.

8. After the collision, Al stumbled out of his car and confronted Sue, (who, whom), despite her injuries, was smiling.

9. "Look what you've done to you and (I, me)!" Al yelled.

10. "Let's you and (I, me) review what you said," she answered coolly. "You said, 'thirty-five miles per hour,' and that's exactly what I was doing."

EXERCISE 7   Selecting Pronouns

Underline the correct pronouns.

1. My brother can tell this urban legend better than (I, me), but here is my version.

2. A man (who, whom) always wanted a 1958 Corvette saw one advertised in the newspaper for twenty dollars.

3. Within an hour he had purchased the car from a person named Lola, but before he drove away, he said, "(Who, Whom) is the person (who, whom) authorized you to make the sale?"

4. "It's my husband, Jake, (whom, who) I now despise because he ran away with his secretary."

5. "Last week," Lola went on, "he sent this fax: 'I've spent all my money here in Las Vegas, and Flo and (me, I) need your help.'"

6. "'Please sell my Corvette and send me the money. Just between you and (I, me), I miss you lots.'"

7. The man (who, whom) bought the Corvette said, "And now you're going to send Flo and (he, him) the money?"

8. "That's right, but he didn't tell me the price. So now I'm sending twenty dollars to this jerk (whom, who) I thought I loved."

9. That urban legend was told to my family and (I, me) when I was a wide-eyed child.

10. Some people insist that the buyer was a friend of someone (whom, who) they know.

Pronoun-Antecedent Agreement

Every pronoun refers to an earlier noun, which is called the **antecedent** of the pronoun. The antecedent is the noun that the pronoun replaces. The pronoun brings the reader back to the earlier thought. Here are some examples:

I tried to buy *tickets* for the concert, but *they* were all sold.

Roger painted a *picture* of a pickup truck. *It* was so good that *he* entered *it* in an art show.

A **pronoun** agrees with its antecedent in person, number, and gender. **Person**—first, second, or third—indicates perspective, or point of view. **Number** indicates singular or plural. **Gender** indicates masculine, feminine, or neuter.

Subject Words

	Singular	Plural
First Person:	I	we
Second Person:	you	you
Third Person:	he, she, it	they
	who	

Object Words

	Singular	Plural
First Person:	me	us
Second Person:	you	you
Third Person:	him, her, it	them
	whom	

AGREEMENT IN PERSON

Avoid needless shifting of person, which means shifting of point of view, such as from *I* to *you*. First person, second person, and third person indicate perspectives from which you can write. Select one point of view and maintain it, promoting continuity and consistency. Needless shifting of person, meaning changing perspectives without reasons important for your content and purpose, is distracting and awkward. Each point of view has its appropriate purposes.

First Person

Using the word *I* and its companion forms *we*, *me*, and *us*, the first-person point of view emphasizes the writer, who is an important part of the subject of the composition. Choose first person for friendly letters, accounts of personal experience, and, occasionally, business correspondence, such as a letter of application for a job, which requires self-analysis.

Observe the presence of the writer and the use of *I* in this example.

> *I* could tell that the wedding would not go well when the caterers started serving drinks before the ceremony and the bride began arguing with her future mother-in-law. After the sound system crashed, the band canceled, and *I* wished *I* had not come.

Second Person

Using or implying the word *you*, the second-person point of view is fine for informal conversation, advice, and directions. Although it is occasionally found in academic writing, most instructors prefer that you use it only in process analysis, instructions in how to do something.

In this example, note that the word *you* is sometimes understood and not stated.

> To juggle three balls, first *you* place two balls (A and B) in one hand and one ball (C) in the other. Then toss one of the two balls (A), and before *you* catch it with your other hand, toss the single ball (C) from that hand. Before that ball (C) lands in the other hand, toss the remaining inactive ball (B). Then pick up the balls and repeat the process until the balls no longer fall to the ground.

Third Person

Referring to subject material, individuals, things, or ideas, the third-person point of view works best for most formal writing, be it academic or professional. Third-person pronouns include *he*, *she*, *it*, *they*, *him*, *her*, and *them*. Most of your college writing—essay exams, reports, compositions that explain and argue, critiques, and research papers—will be from this detached perspective with no references to yourself.

In this example, written in the third person, the name *Bartleby* is replaced by forms of *he*.

> *Bartleby*, one of Herman Melville's most memorable characters, has befuddled critics for more than a century. At a point in *his* life chosen for

no obvious reason, *he* decides not to work, not to cooperate with others, and not to leave the premises of *his* employer because *he* "prefer[s] not to." Most readers do not know what to make of *him*.

Correcting Problems of Agreement in Person

Most problems with pronoun agreement in person occur with the use of *you* in a passage that should have been written in the first or third person. If your composition is not one of advice or directions, the word *you* is probably not appropriate and should be replaced with a first- or third-person pronoun.

If you are giving advice or directions, use *you* throughout the passage, but if you are not, replace each *you* with a first- or third-person pronoun that is consistent with the perspective, purpose, and content of the passage.

Inconsistent:	*I* love to travel, especially when *you* go to foreign countries.
Consistent:	*I* love to travel, especially when *I* go to foreign countries.
Inconsistent:	When *you* are about to merge with moving traffic on the freeway, *one* should not stop *his or her* car.
Consistent:	When *you* are about to merge with moving traffic on the freeway, *you* should not stop *your* car.
Consistent:	When *one* is about to merge with moving traffic on the freeway, *one* should not stop *his or her* car. [using third-person pronouns, including the indefinite pronoun *one*]
Consistent:	When *drivers* are about to merge with moving traffic on the freeway, *they* should not stop *their* cars. [using third-person plural pronouns to match plural noun]

EXERCISE 8   Selecting Correct Pronouns: Person

Each of the following sentences has one or more needless changes in pronoun person. Correct each problem by crossing out the inconsistent pronoun and substituting a consistent one. Change verb forms, also, if necessary.

1. People fishing on the Amazon River know that when you hook a blood-thirsty piranha, you have to be careful of its razor-sharp teeth.

2. Some people think you can make it rain by washing your car.

3. Some of my friends have no idea where Peru is located, but you know the words to all of the Beatles' songs.

4. I got her to admit that astrology is hooey, but you couldn't convince her to stop reading her daily horoscope.

5. Every male knows that you will seldom hear a woman laugh at the antics of the Three Stooges.

6. She knew that the seating-chart mistake was her fault because you should not place a baron above a count.

7. The magicians forgot that you can't fool everyone all of the time.

8. Wise people remind us that if you don't know history, you are doomed to repeat it.

9. They should have known that you can't keep a good woman down.

10. Pyromaniac chefs love to flambé, especially when you light the Baked Alaska on fire.

EXERCISE 9   Selecting Correct Pronouns: Person

Complete the following sentences while maintaining agreement in person. Use at least one personal pronoun in each completion.

First Person

1. I know that it's important to drink enough water, so _____

   _____

2. However, I sometimes drink too many sodas and cups of coffee, and _____

   _____

3. Hydrating my body properly causes _____

   _____

Second Person

1. If you want to make sure your body is properly hydrated, _____

   _____

2. Your body functions better when _____

   _____

3. Health experts recommend drinking eight glasses of water per day; therefore,

   _____

Third Person

1. Health-conscious people always make sure that _____

   _____

2. Healthy people know that when they drink eight glasses of water per day, _____

   _____

3. When people feel thirsty, _____

   _____

AGREEMENT IN NUMBER

Most problems with pronoun-antecedent agreement involve **number**. The main principle is simple: If the antecedent (the word the pronoun refers back to) is singular, use a singular pronoun. If the antecedent is plural, use a plural pronoun.

1. A singular antecedent requires a singular pronoun.

   Hoang forgot *his* notebook.

2. A plural antecedent requires a plural pronoun.

   Many *students* cast *their* votes today.

3. A singular indefinite pronoun as an antecedent takes a singular pronoun. Most indefinite pronouns are singular. The following are common indefinite singular pronouns: *anybody, anyone, each, either, everybody, everyone, no one, nobody, one, somebody, someone.*

   Each of the girls brought *her* book.

   When *one* makes a promise, *one* [or *he or she*] should keep it.

4. A plural indefinite pronoun as an antecedent takes a plural pronoun.

   Few knew *their* assignments.

5. Certain indefinite pronouns do not clearly express either a singular or plural number. Agreement, therefore, depends on the meaning of the sentence. These pronouns are *all, any, none,* and *some.*

   All of the grapefruit *was* good.

   All of the grapefruits *were* gone.

   None of the cake *is* acceptable.

   None of the cakes *are* acceptable.

6. Two or more antecedents, singular or plural, take a plural pronoun. Such antecedents are usually joined by *and* or by commas and *and*.

   Howard and his *parents* bought *their* presents early.

   Students, instructors, and the *administration* pooled *their* ideas at the forum.

7. Alternative antecedents—that is, antecedents joined by *or*, *nor*, *whether/or*, *either/or*, *neither/nor*, *not only/but also*—require a pronoun that agrees with the nearer antecedent.

> Neither Sam nor his *friends* lost *their* way.
>
> Neither his friends nor *Sam* lost *his* way.

8. In a sentence with an expression such as *one of those _____ who*, the antecedent is usually the plural noun that follows.

> He is one of those *people who* want *their* money now.

9. In a sentence with the expression *the only one of those _____ who*, the antecedent is usually the singular word *one*.

> She is the *only one of* the members *who* wants *her* money now.

10. When collective nouns such as *team*, *jury*, *committee*, and *band* are used as antecedents, they take a singular pronoun if they are considered as units.

> The *jury* is doing *its* best to follow the judge's directions.

When individual behavior is suggested, antecedents take a plural form.

> The *jury* are putting on *their* coats.

11. The words *each*, *every*, and *many a(n)* before a noun make the noun singular.

> *Each child* and *adult* was *his or her* own authority.
>
> *Each* and *every person* doubted *himself or herself*.
>
> *Many a* person is capable of knowing *himself or herself*.

EXERCISE 10   Selecting Correct Pronouns: Number

Underline the correct pronouns.

1. The band always ends (its, their) concert with a lively tuba solo.

2. Each and every American should save money, or (they, he or she) may not have enough for retirement.

3. Each camper must bring (their, his or her) own shaving cream.

4. If the class doesn't go on the field trip, (it, they) will miss the mummy exhibit.

5. Each of those farmers knows that (he, they) must rotate (his, their) crops.

6. Pauline and Reggie left (their, his or her) hearts in San Francisco.

7. Everyone should leave (their, his or her) world a better place.

8. Neither the bride nor the bridesmaids could control (her, their) giggles during the ceremony.

9. He is one of those men who likes to drive (his, their) car fast.

10. Every rose has (its, their) thorn, every dog has (its, his or her) day, and every cloud has (its, his or her) silver lining.

EXERCISE 11   Selecting Correct Pronouns: Number

Underline the correct pronouns.

1. An army of ants made (its, their) way toward the unsuspecting picnickers.

2. The company alienated many of (its, their) faithful customers by raising prices.

3. The crowd of onlookers booed (its, their) disapproval when the knight was thrown from his horse.

4. Judy is the only one of the girls who has dared to dye (her, their) hair purple.

5. Neither the pilot nor the flight attendants realized (his or her, their) mistake.

6. A parent knows when (his or her, their) child is not being honest.

7. The U.S. Marines wants (their, its) equipment in top condition.

8. The camel offers good desert transportation because of (its, their) relatively low need for water.

9. Each of the women wanted (her, their) groceries bagged in paper instead of plastic.

10. Several members of the chess team are setting up (its, their) boards.

AGREEMENT IN GENDER

A pronoun should agree with its antecedent in gender, if the gender of the antecedent is specific. Masculine and feminine pronouns are gender-specific: *he, him, she, her*. Others are neuter: *I, we, me, us, it, they, them, who, whom, that, which*. The words *who* and *whom* refer to people. *That* can refer to ideas, things, and people but usually does not refer to individuals. *Which* refers to ideas and things but never to people.

My *girlfriend* gave me *her* best advice. [feminine]

Mighty *Casey* tried *his* best. [masculine]

The *people* with *whom* I work are loud. [neuter]

Indefinite singular pronouns used as antecedents require, of course, singular pronouns. Handling the gender of these singular pronouns is not as obvious; opinion is divided.

1. Traditionally, writers have used the masculine form of pronouns to refer to the indefinite singular pronouns when the gender is unknown.

Everyone should work until *he* drops.

2. To avoid a perceived sex bias, use *he or she* or *his or her* instead of just *he* or *his.*

   Everyone should work until *he or she* drops.

3. Although option 1 is more direct, it is illogical to many listeners and readers, and option 2 used several times in a short passage can be awkward. To avoid those possible problems, writers often use plural forms.

   All people should work until *they* drop.

In any case, avoid using a plural pronoun with a singular indefinite pronoun; such usage violates the basic principle of number agreement.

   Incorrect: *Everyone* should do *their* best.

   Correct: *Everyone* should do *his or her* best.

   Correct: *People* should do *their* best.

EXERCISE 12   Selecting Correct Pronouns: Gender and Number

Underline the correct pronoun for gender and number.

1. All of the people in the aerobics class were swearing through clenched teeth as (he or she, they) completed (his or her, their) five hundredth leg lift.

2. Every lifeguard at the swimming pool likes being paid as (he or she, they) works on (his or her, their) tan.

3. The Boy Scout troop was proud of (its, their) handiwork: a full-size cabin made entirely of popsicle sticks.

4. All employees have been instructed to always wash (his or her, their) hands before returning to work.

5. That woman and her husband are mulching (his or her, their) flower beds with cut-up credit cards.

6. A disgruntled glassblower might very well refuse to let (their, his or her) spouse have a Tupperware party.

7. Each mermaid will be carefully measured so that (her, their) scales fit properly.

8. The winners of the carnival game got to select (his or her, their) prizes from a smorgasbord of stuffed animals.

9. George, the human cannonball, had to admit that (his, their) career might be a short one.

10. Does everyone who lives in Florida paint (his or her, their) house pink?

EXERCISE 13   Selecting Correct Pronouns: Gender and Number

Correct the faulty pronouns for problems in gender and number.

1. A person which enjoys taking risks might become a firefighter.

2. Everyone will now pause to offer their thanks to the man who invented the air conditioner.

3. A smart motorcyclist keeps their mouth closed to avoid incoming bugs.

4. The individual which said she was abducted by aliens appeared on a news program.

5. My grandmother was one of the pioneers that lived in a sod house.

6. Practically every person is bothered by their particular pet peeve.

7. Around these parts, the wooly worm is thought to predict the severity of the upcoming winter by the thickness of their coat.

8. In the summer, a cricket can reveal the temperature if you count the number of their chirps over 15 seconds.

9. Someone which adds thirty-seven to the number of the cricket's chirps will know exactly how hot it is in degrees Fahrenheit.

10. So far, the only thing the cockroach has been able to reveal is the lack of success of the restaurant they call home.

Pronoun Reference

A pronoun must refer clearly to its antecedent. Because a pronoun is a substitute word, it can express meaning clearly and definitely only if its antecedent is easily identified.

In some sentence constructions, gender and number make the reference clear.

> Dimitri and Poloma discussed *his* absences and *her* good attendance. [gender]

> If the three older boys in the *club* carry out those plans, *it* will break up. [number]

Avoid ambiguous reference. The following sentences illustrate the kind of confusion that results from structuring sentences with more than one possible antecedent for the pronoun.

Unclear: Kim gave David *his* money and clothes.

Clear: Kim gave his own money and clothes to David.

Unclear: Sarah told her sister that *her* car had a flat tire.

Clear: Sarah said to her sister, "Your car has a flat tire."

When using a pronoun to refer to a general idea, make sure that the reference is clear. The pronouns used frequently in this way are *this, that, which,* and *it.* The best solution may be to recast the sentence to omit the pronoun in question.

Unclear: Gabriella whistled the same tune over and over, *which* irritated me.

Clear: Gabriella whistled the same tune over and over, a *habit* that irritated me.

Recast: Her whistling the same tune over and over irritated me.

EXERCISE 14   Showing Clear Pronoun References

Label each sentence as V if the pronoun reference is vague or OK if it is clear.

_____ **1.** (a) The middle-aged golfers insisted on wearing knickers during the tournament, which looked ridiculous.

_____   (b) During the tournament, the middle-aged golfers insisted on wearing knickers, a fashion that looked ridiculous.

_____ **2.** (a) I went back to the grocery store and told the manager that my melon was moldy.

_____   (b) I went back to the grocery store and told them that my melon was moldy.

_____ **3.** (a) The judge sentenced him to watch reruns of the old *Brady Bunch* sitcom, which was unnecessarily cruel.

_____   (b) The judge sentenced him to watch reruns of the old *Brady Bunch* sitcom, a penalty that was unnecessarily cruel.

_____ **4.** (a) Carmen told her grandmother that she was in need of dance lessons.

_____   (b) Carmen said to her grandmother, "I'm in need of dance lessons."

_____ **5.** (a) Her grandmother agreed with Carmen that it was indeed time for her to learn to salsa.

_____   (b) Her grandmother replied that it was indeed time for Carmen to learn to salsa.

_____ **6.** (a) Rex's last tattoo covered his last few inches of available skin, which has left him without a goal and slightly depressed.

_____ (b) Rex's last tattoo covered his last few inches of available skin, a situation that has left him without a goal and slightly depressed.

_____ 7. (a) The zookeeper told her assistant to go clean out the lion's cage.

_____ (b) The zookeeper said to the assistant, "I have to go clean out the lion's cage."

_____ 8. (a) Jason made an appointment at the dentist's office so that they could polish his gold tooth until it gleamed.

_____ (b) Jason made an appointment at the dentist's office so that the hygienist could polish his gold tooth until it gleamed.

_____ 9. (a) The twelve-year-old girl told Mrs. McDonald that she didn't know the first thing about raising children.

_____ (b) The twelve-year-old girl told Mrs. McDonald, "I don't know the first thing about raising children."

_____ 10. (a) The girls called the boys names and pelted them with mud, which inexplicably failed to stir the boys' ardor.

_____ (b) The girls called the boys names and pelted them with mud, all of which inexplicably failed to stir the boys' ardor.

EXERCISE 15   Choosing Correct Pronouns: Reference and Agreement

Identify and correct the problems with pronoun reference and agreement.

1. I eat fast food only three times a week, which is un-American to some.

2. The supervisors told the staff members that they would be getting a big raise.

3. If a woman is looking for quality men, you should enroll in our English class.

4. She called to find out the store's hours, but they didn't answer.

5. When he smashed into the pyramid of cat food with his shopping cart, it was destroyed.

6. It says in the newspaper that an elephant is on the loose.

7. I tend to submit my assignments late, which hurts my grade.

8. The Great Oz told the Tin Man that he already possessed the thing he craved most.

9. They say that the horse named Cheese Whiz may win the Triple Crown.

10. Spiderman told Superman that he may have given up on love too soon.

CHAPTER REVIEW   Pronouns

1. Case is the form a pronoun takes as it fills a position in a sentence.

2. Subjective-case pronouns are *I*, *he*, and *she* (singular) and *we* and *they* (plural). *Who* can be either singular or plural.

Subjective-case pronouns can fill subject positions.

We dance in the park.

It was *she* who spoke. [referring back to and meaning the same as the subject]

3. Objective-case pronouns are *me*, *him*, and *her* (singular) and *us* and *them* (plural). *Whom* can be either singular or plural.

Objective-case pronouns fill object positions.

We saw *her* in the library. [object of verb]

They gave the results to *us*. [object of a preposition]

4. Three techniques are useful for deciding which pronoun case to use.

a. If you have a compound element (such as a subject or an object of a preposition), consider only the pronoun part.

They will visit you and (I, *me*). [Consider: They will visit *me*.]

b. If the next important word after *who* or *whom* in a statement is a noun or pronoun, the word choice will be *whom*; otherwise, it will be *who*. Disregard qualifier clauses such as *It seems* and *I feel*.

The person *whom* judges like will win.

The person *who* works hardest will win.

The person *who*, we think, worked hardest won. [ignoring the qualifier clause]

c. *Let's* is made up of the words *let* and *us* and means "*You let us*"; therefore, when you select a pronoun to follow it, consider the two original words and select another object word—*me*.

Let's you and *me* go to town.

5. A pronoun agrees with its antecedent in person, number, and gender.

   a. Avoid needless shifting in **person**, which means shifting in point of view, such as from *I* to *you*.

   "*I* was having trouble. *You* could see disaster ahead." Change to "*I* was having trouble. *I* could see disaster ahead."

   b. Most problems with pronoun-antecedent agreement involve **number**. The principles are simple: If the antecedent (the word the pronoun refers back to) is singular, use a singular pronoun. If the antecedent is plural, use a plural pronoun.

   Royce forgot *his* notebook.

   Many students cast *their* votes.

   Someone lost *his or her* [not *their*] book.

   c. The pronoun should agree with its antecedent in **gender**, if the gender of the antecedent is specific. Masculine and feminine pronouns are gender-specific: *he, him, she, her.* Others are neuter: *I, we, me, us, it, they, them, who, whom, that, which.* The words *who* and *whom* refer to people. *That* can refer to ideas, things, and people but usually does not refer to individuals. *Which* refers to ideas and things but not to people. To avoid a perceived sex bias, you can use *he or she* or *his or her* instead of just *he* or *his*; however, many writers simply make antecedents and pronouns plural.

   Everyone should revise *his or her* composition carefully.

   Students should revise *their* compositions carefully.

6. A pronoun must refer clearly to its antecedent. Because a pronoun is a substitute word, it can express meaning clearly and definitely only if its antecedent is easily identified.

CHAPTER REVIEW Exercises

REVIEW 1   Selecting Correct Pronouns: Case

Underline the correct pronouns.

1. Between you and (me, I), pronouns are not that difficult.
2. Those (who, whom) have much trouble may not have studied the rules.
3. Let's you and (I, me) consider those pesky rules.
4. The opportunity offered to you and (I, me) should not be wasted.
5. (We, Us) students can learn about these pronoun problems together.
6. To (whom, who) should I give credit for my success?
7. Some of the credit should go to you and (me, I).
8. I know you didn't study harder than (I, me).
9. Now I know that the person (who, whom) studies will prosper.
10. You and (I, me) should now celebrate.

| REVIEW 2 | **Selecting Correct Pronouns: Person** |

Each of the following sentences has one or more needless changes in pronoun person. Correct each problem by crossing out the inconsistent pronoun and substituting a consistent one. Change verb form, also, if necessary.

1. Everybody knows that you should remove high heels before attempting to catch a tossed bridal bouquet.

2. All people have faults, no matter who you are.

3. He tried to give her an engagement ring with a huge stone, but one could tell that the "diamond" was imitation.

4. When the metal detector's crackling indicates the possibility of loose change in the sand, you feel alive.

5. A job applicant should realize that smacking your gum noisily while answering the interviewer's questions is a no-no.

6. There was a time when almost every woman longed for a prince charming to whisk you away.

7. A man can never have too many trucker caps in your collection.

8. A cowboy knows that you can always depend on your trusted steed.

9. I didn't think you could donate your brain to science.

10. An ad campaign in Paris is trying to convince the French that you should exercise less and eat more fast food.

| REVIEW 3 | **Selecting Correct Pronouns: Number** |

Some of the following sentences have a problem with pronoun-antecedent number agreement. If a sentence is correct, label it C. If not, correct it.

_____ 1. The famous singing group The Village People encouraged its audience to sing along to its hit "YMCA."

_____ 2. Trudy and the other trick-or-treaters all chose the hula dancer as her Halloween costume.

_____ 3. Someone with very large feet left their footprints at the scene of the flour factory explosion.

_____ 4. The sinister Olaf and his devilish sidekick will stop at nothing to carry out his evil plans.

_____ 5. The girls who run the drink stand refuse to reveal the secret ingredient in her lemonade.

_____ 6. There will be a stampede of determined shoppers as soon as the stores in the mall open its doors.

_____ 7. The phones began ringing in the Complaint Department when the company began using cheaper vinegar in their pickles.

_____ 8. The members of the Polar Bear Club eagerly anticipate its next plunge into icy Canadian waters.

_____ 9. Few of the men would admit his fondness for fondue.

_____ 10. None of the monkeys in the tree could be coaxed down from its perch.

REVIEW 4

Selecting Correct Pronouns: Gender

Correct the faulty pronoun-antecedent gender agreement in the following sentences. One sentence is correct. Rewrite the sentences as necessary.

1. An individual who does not want to get their hair wet should not sit right next to the killer whale's tank.

2. A gambler should cash in their chips while they are ahead.

3. People shouldn't do the crime if he or she doesn't want to do the time.

4. André the Giant, one of the most popular wrestlers of all time, entertained their fans for many years.

5. The physicists liked to unwind by going up on the roof of his or her office building and seeing what gravity can do to a watermelon.

6. Many a bounty hunter has had to work both weekends and holidays to get their job done.

7. None of the hot dog connoisseurs could resist the once-in-a-lifetime opportunity to take his or her family to Frankfurt, the birthplace of the frankfurter.

8. The members of the band wanted to add some polka classics to their speed metal repertoire.

9. Each of Martha Stewart's viewers eagerly awaits the secret to keeping their compost pile smelling lemony fresh.

10. Each and every Elvis fan hopes to make a pilgrimage to Graceland before they die.

REVIEW 5

Selecting Correct Pronouns: References

Identify and correct the problems with pronoun reference.

1. He joined the Marine Corps, and that straightened him out.

2. Martin told Juan, that he needed to learn to ride a unicycle.

3. They say that you can fool some of the people some of the time, but you can't fool all of the people all of the time.

4. They say that senior citizens should get a flu shot every year.

5. Betty Sue told Rhonda Ann that her sauerkraut was the best in town.

6. When their son began drum lessons, they soundproofed the walls, but it still got through.

7. In the school cafeteria, you can choose among slop, gruel, or mystery meat.

8. Fay told her daughter that she was grouchy.

9. They say that time heals all wounds.

10. He told her he was planning to become a juggler, which made her laugh.

REVIEW 6

Writing Sentences with Correct Pronouns

Write a sentence using each of the following words. Do not use the word as the first one in the sentence. One sentence should contain the word *between* before a pronoun such as "between you and _____."

1. she _____

   _____

   _____

2. her _____

_____

_____

3. him _____

_____

_____

4. us _____

_____

_____

5. who _____

_____

_____

6. whom _____

_____

_____

7. me _____

_____

_____

8. I _____

_____

_____

9. they _____

_____

_____

10. them _____

_____

_____

STUDENT COMPANION SITE

For additional practice, visit www.cengage .com/devenglish/ brandon/spb6e.

MICROTHEME

To practice your skills acquired in this chapter, return to the Microtheme on page 151 and complete Exercise B.

Chapter 9

Adjectives and Adverbs

FLOW OF WRITING

MICROTHEME	Writing Activity in Miniature

EXERCISE A

Before you work on this chapter, write a Microtheme on the following topic. Write small enough to leave room for marking later. **After** you have studied this chapter, return to your Microtheme and complete Exercise B to practice what you have learned.

Suggested Microtheme Topic: Write a Microtheme of 80 to 100 words about three items you would place in a time capsule to be opened in fifty years. Explain why the items are significant.

EXERCISE B

Connecting Your Learning Objectives with Your Microtheme

Complete this exercise after you have studied this chapter.

1. Underline adjectives and adverbs, and make sure they are necessary and well-selected.
2. Be sure you have not dangled or misplaced modifiers. If in question, you should underline the modifier and draw a line to the word being modified.

Adjectives modify (describe) nouns and pronouns and answer the questions *Which one? What kind?* and *How many?*

Which one? The <u>new</u> <u>car</u> is mine.
                adj   n

What kind? <u>Mexican</u> <u>food</u> is my favorite.
            adj   n

How many? A <u>few</u> <u>friends</u> are all one needs.
              adj   n

Adverbs modify verbs, adjectives, and other adverbs and answer the questions *How? Where? When? Why?* and *To what degree?* Most words ending in *-ly* are adverbs.

Where? The cuckoo <u>flew</u> <u>south</u>.
               v   adv

When? The cuckoo <u>flew</u> <u>yesterday</u>.
             v   adv

Why? The cuckoo <u>flew</u> <u>because of the cold weather</u>.
           v   adv phrase

How? The cuckoo <u>flew</u> <u>swiftly</u>.
           v   adv

<u>Without adjectives and adverbs</u>, <u>even</u> John Steinbeck, the <u>famous</u>
     adv phrase   adv   adj

<u>Nobel Prize–winning</u> author, <u>surely</u> could <u>not</u> have described the
     adj   adv   adv

<u>crafty</u> octopus <u>very</u> <u>well</u>.
 adj   adv adv

We have two concerns regarding the use of adjectives and adverbs (modifiers) in writing. One is a matter of **diction**, or word choice—in this case, how to select adjectives and adverbs that will strengthen the writing. The other is how to identify and correct problems with modifiers.

Selecting Adjectives and Adverbs

If you want to finish the sentence "She was a(n) _____ speaker," you have many adjectives to select from, including these:

distinguished	irritating	profound	persuasive
influential	colorful	polished	long-winded
adequate	boring	abrasive	humorous

If you want to finish the sentence "She danced _____," you have another large selection, this time adverbs such as the following:

comically	catatonically	slowly	zestfully
gracefully	awkwardly	carnally	smoothly
mechanically	limply	serenely	frantically

Adjectives and adverbs can be used to enhance communication. If you have a thought, you know what it is, but when you deliver that thought to someone else, you may not say or write what you mean. Your thought may be eloquent and your word choice weak. Keep in mind that no two words mean exactly the same thing. Further, some words are vague and general. If you settle for a common word such as *good* or a slang word such as *neat* to characterize something you like, you will be limiting your communication. Of course, those who know you best may understand fairly well; after all, people who are really close may be able to convey ideas using only grunts and gestures.

But what if you want to write to someone you hardly know to explain how you feel about an important issue? Then the more precise the word, the better the communication. By using modifiers, you may be able to add significant information. Keep in mind, however, that anything can be overdone; therefore, use adjectives and adverbs wisely and economically.

Your first resource in searching for more effective adjectives should be your own vocabulary storehouse. Another resource is a good thesaurus (book of synonyms). Finally, you may want to collaborate with others to discuss and share ideas.

Supply the appropriate modifiers in the following exercises, using a dictionary, a thesaurus, or the resources designated by your instructor.

EXERCISE 1   Supplying Adjectives

Provide adjectives to modify these nouns. Use only single words, not adjective phrases.

1. A(n) _____ dog

2. A(n) _____ comedian

3. A(n) _____ voice

4. A(n) _____ neighbor

5. A(n) _____ ballplayer

6. A(n) _____ party

7. A(n) _____ singer

8. A(n) _____ date

9. A(n) _____ car

10. A(n) _____ job

EXERCISE 2   Supplying Adverbs

Provide adverbs to modify these verbs. Use only single words, not adverb phrases.

1. sleep _____

2. run   _____

3. talk _____

4. walk _____

5. kiss _____

6. smile _____

7. drive _____

8. leave _____

9. laugh _____

10. eat _____

Comparative and Superlative Forms

For making comparisons, most adjectives and adverbs have three different forms: the positive (one), the comparative (comparing two), and the superlative (comparing three or more).

ADJECTIVES

1. Some adjectives follow a regular pattern.

Positive (one)	Comparative (comparing two)	Superlative (comparing three or more)
nice	nicer	nicest
rich	richer	richest
big	bigger	biggest
tall	taller	tallest
lonely	lonelier	loneliest
terrible	more terrible	most terrible
beautiful	more beautiful	most beautiful

These are usually the rules:

a. Add *-er* (or *-r*) to short adjectives (one or two syllables) to rank units of two.

> Julian is *nicer* than Sam.

b. Add *-est* (or *-st*) to short adjectives (one or two syllables) to rank units of three or more.

> Of the fifty people I know, Julian is the *kindest*.

c. Add the word *more* to long adjectives (three or more syllables) to rank units of two.

> My hometown is *more beautiful* than yours.

d. Add the word *most* to long adjectives (three or more syllables) to rank units of three or more.

> My hometown is the *most beautiful* in all America.

2. Some adjectives are irregular in the way they change to show comparison.

Positive (one)	Comparative (comparing two)	Superlative (comparing three or more)
good	better	best
bad	worse	worst

ADVERBS

1. Some adverbs follow a regular pattern.

Positive (one)	Comparative (comparing two)	Superlative (comparing three or more)
clearly	more clearly	most clearly
quickly	more quickly	most quickly
carefully	more carefully	most carefully
thoughtfully	more thoughtfully	most thoughtfully

a. Add -er to some one-syllable adverbs for the comparative form and add -est for the superlative form.

> My piglet runs *fast*. [positive]
>
> My piglet runs *faster* than your piglet. [comparative]
>
> My piglet runs *fastest* of all known piglets. [superlative]

b. Add the word *more* to form comparisons of longer adverbs and the word *most* to form the superlative forms.

> Shanelle reacted *happily* to the marriage proposal. [positive]
>
> Shanelle reacted *more happily* to the marriage proposal than Serena. [comparative]
>
> Of all the women Clem proposed to, Shanelle reacted *most happily*. [superlative]

c. In some cases, the word *less* may be substituted for *more*, and the word *least* for *most*.

> Mort's views were presented *less effectively* than Al's. [comparative]
>
> Of all the opinions that were shared, Mort's views were presented *least effectively*. [superlative]

2. Some adverbs are irregular in the way they change to show comparisons.

Positive (one)	Comparative (comparing two)	Superlative (comparing three or more)
well	better	best
far	farther (distance)	farthest (distance)
	further	furthest
badly	worse	worst

Using Adjectives and Adverbs Correctly

1. Avoid double negatives. Words such as *no, not, none, nothing, never, hardly, barely,* and *scarcely* should not be combined.

   Double Negative: I do *not* have *no* time for recreation. [incorrect]

   Single Negative: I have *no* time for recreation. [correct]

   Double Negative: I've *hardly never* lied. [incorrect]

   Single Negative: I've *hardly* ever lied. [correct]

2. Do not confuse adjectives with adverbs. Among the most commonly confused adjectives and adverbs are *good/well, bad/badly,* and *real/really.* The words *good, bad,* and *real* are always adjectives. *Well* is sometimes an adjective. The words *badly* and *really* are always adverbs. *Well* is usually an adverb.

   To distinguish these words, consider what is being modified. Remember that adjectives modify nouns and pronouns and that adverbs modify verbs, adjectives, and other adverbs.

   Incorrect: I feel *badly* today. [We're concerned with the condition of *I.*]

   Correct: I feel *bad* today. [The adjective *bad* modifies the pronoun *I.*]

   Incorrect: She feels *well* about that choice. [We're concerned with the condition of *she.*]

   Correct: She feels *good* about that choice. [The adjective *good* modifies the pronoun *she.*]

   Incorrect: Ted plays the piano *good.* [The adjective *good* modifies the verb *plays,* but adjectives should not modify verbs.]

   Correct: Ted plays the piano *well.* [The adverb *well* modifies the verb *plays.*]

   Incorrect: He did *real* well. [Here the adjective *real* modifies the adverb *well,* but adjectives should not modify adverbs.]

   Correct: He did *really* well. [The adverb *really* modifies the adverb *well.*]

3. Do not use an adverb such as *very, more,* or *most* before adjectives such as *perfect, round, unique, square,* and *straight.*

   Incorrect: It is *more* round.

   Correct: It is round.

   Correct: It is *more nearly* round.

4. Do not double forms, such as *more lonelier* or *most loneliest.*

   Incorrect: Julie was *more nicer* than Jake.

   Correct: Julie was *nicer* than Jake.

5. Do not confuse standard and nonstandard forms of adjectives and adverbs.

   • **Accidently.** This is a substandard form of *accidentally.*

- **All ready, already.** *All ready* means "completely prepared." *Already* means "previously."

    We are *all ready* to give the signal to move out. [prepared]

    When he arrived at the station, we had *already* left. [previously]

- **All right, alright.** *All right* (two words) means "correct," "yes," "fine," "certainly." *Alright* is a substandard spelling of "all right."

    Yes, I am *all right* now.

- **All together, altogether.** *All together* means "in a group." *Altogether* means "completely," "wholly," "entirely."

    The boys were *all together* at the end of the field.

    The manuscript is *altogether* too confusing.

Be careful to place such words as *also, almost, even, just, hardly, merely, only,* and *today* in the right position to convey the intended meaning. As these words change position in the sentence, they may also change the meaning of the sentence.

I *only* advised him to act cautiously.
I advised *only* him to act cautiously.
Only I advised him to act cautiously.
I advised him *only* to act cautiously.

EXERCISE 3   Selecting Adjectives and Adverbs

Underline the correct adjective or adverb.

1. Betty Skelton was one of the (most, more) successful female stunt pilots of the 1940s and 1950s.

2. In the 1930s and 1940s, the public was (real, really) interested in watching acrobatic air shows.

3. Skelton was (not hardly, hardly) going to sit there and watch the men have all the fun.

4. She wanted (bad, badly) to learn to fly, and she was (real, really) adventurous, so she learned to perform daredevil feats.

5. Her small, agile airplane, which was named Little Stinker, performed tricks (well, good).

6. One of her (better, best) stunts was the inverted ribbon cut.

7. It was a (real, really) thrill to watch her fly upside down twelve feet off the ground and use her propeller to slice a foil strip strung between two poles.

8. The crowd could (not hardly, hardly) contain its excitement.

9. She earned only $25 for each air show, so the pay was (bad, badly).

10. But according to Betty, her six-year acrobatic flying career was the (more, most) enjoyable time in her life.

EXERCISE 4   Selecting Adjectives and Adverbs

Correct any problems with adjectives and adverbs in the following sentences.

1. The Pinewood Derby is a real big model car racing event for Cub Scouts.

2. The cars are hand carved from pine wood and should never weigh no more than five ounces.

3. The boys race their cars to see whose is faster.

4. Some Cub Scout packs give awards for the fastest and more beautiful cars.

5. Dads can even compete to see who is the better car builder by racing in the dads' division.

6. Those scouts who do good in their opening heats can go on to compete for trophies.

7. The cars glide down wood tracks powered only by gravity, so weight distribution and friction are real important issues.

8. Racing Pinewood Derby cars has become one of the more popular events on the scouting calendar.

9. Websites and books are devoted to details of car design, such as how to create more perfect axles.

10. The Pinewood Derby was designed for kids, but that does not never mean that the adults are not enthusiastic racers themselves.

EXERCISE 5   Selecting Adjectives and Adverbs

Underline the correct word or words.

1. In the early 1900s, if you were (real, really) (good, well) at tug-of-war, you could have competed in the Olympics.

2. Tug-of-war used to be an Olympic sport, but it's not (no, any) more.

3. I can (not, not hardly) believe that sports like golf and croquet used to be part of the Olympic Games, too.

4. Today, one of the (odder, oddest) of all of the Olympic sports is curling.

5. No, it's not a competition to see which hairdresser can create the (more, most) beautiful style.

6. And curling enthusiasts get (real, really) angry if you compare their sport to shuffleboard on ice.

7. But when people see curlers sweeping the ice with brooms to help a 42-pound rock glide better, they often conclude that the sport is one of the (stranger, strangest) they've ever seen.

8. Another odd Olympic sport is for those who can ski and shoot rifles (good, well).

9. In the biathlon, the athlete who takes home the gold is the one who hits targets (best, better) and skis (faster, fastest).

10. The triathlon combines swimming, cycling, and running, but a blend of cross-country skiing and marksmanship seems (more, most) odd.

EXERCISE 6   Selecting Adjectives and Adverbs

Correct any problems with adjectives and adverbs in the following sentences.

1. After her eighth cup of coffee, she is one of the most liveliest women in the office.

2. He wanted the fry cook job real bad, but his interview didn't go good.

3. As he strolled through Bronco Bob's Bar and Boot Shop, he knew that he had never seen a more perfect setting for a square dance.

4. He was real sorry for eating her artistic masterpiece, so he offered his sincere apologies.

5. Of the two weightlifters, Carlos is best at clean-and-jerk lifts.

6. She looks well in Spandex and sequins.

7. After her divorce, she finally felt happily.

8. The skater fell during every one of her jumps, so she performed pretty bad.

9. My baby cries louder than that baby.

10. In a blind taste test, most consumers said that Squirt was the better of the three leading brands of imitation cheese food.

Dangling and Misplaced Modifiers

Modifiers should clearly relate to the word or words they modify.

1. A modifier that fails to modify a word or group of words already in the sentence is called a **dangling modifier**.

Dangling:	*Walking down the street*, a snake startled him. [Who was walking down the street? The person isn't mentioned in the sentence.]
Correct:	*Walking down the street*, Don was startled by a snake.
Correct:	As *Don* walked down the street, *he* was startled by a snake.
Dangling:	*At the age of six*, my uncle died. [Who was six years old? The person isn't mentioned in the sentence.]
Correct:	*When I was six*, my uncle died.

2. A modifier that is placed so that it modifies the wrong word or words is called a **misplaced modifier**. The term also applies to words that are positioned so as to unnecessarily divide closely related parts of sentences such as infinitives (*to* plus verb) or subjects and verbs.

Misplaced:	The sick man went to a doctor *with a high fever*.
Correct:	The sick man *with a high fever* went to a doctor.
Misplaced:	I saw a great movie *sitting in my pickup*.
Correct:	*Sitting in my pickup*, I saw a great movie.
Misplaced:	Kim found many new graves *walking through the cemetery*.
Correct:	*Walking through the cemetery*, Kim found many new graves.
Misplaced:	I forgot all about my sick dog *kissing my girlfriend*.
Correct:	*Kissing my girlfriend*, I forgot all about my sick dog.
Misplaced:	They tried to *earnestly and sincerely* complete the task. [splitting of the infinitive *to complete*]
Correct:	They tried *earnestly and sincerely* to complete the task.
Misplaced:	My neighbor, *while walking to the store*, was mugged. [unnecessarily dividing the subject and verb]
Correct:	*While walking to the store*, my neighbor was mugged.

Try this procedure in working through Exercises 7, 8, and 9.

1. Circle the modifier.

2. Draw an arrow from the modifier to the word or words it modifies.

3. If the modifier does not relate directly to anything in the sentence, it is dangling; recast the sentence.

4. If the modifier does not modify the nearest word or words, or if it interrupts related sentence parts, it is misplaced; reposition it.

EXERCISE 7   Correcting Dangling and Misplaced Modifiers

Each of the following sentences has a dangling (D) or a misplaced (M) modifier. Identify the problems and correct them by rewriting the sentences.

_____ 1. Driving through the Brazilian rain forest, leafcutter ants were spotted going about their work.

_____ 2. This tribe of ants is one of the few creatures on this planet that grows food.

_____ 3. Leafcutter ants learned to cleverly farm over 50 million years ago.

_____ 4. Climbing trees, the leaves are cut down and bitten into the shape of half-moons.

_____ 5. Then each ant hoists a leaf and carries it back down the tree toward the nest, weighing ten times more than it does.

_____ 6. Marching home with their leaves, a parade of fluttering green flags is what the ants resemble.

_____ 7. Carried into the subterranean tunnels of the nest, the leafcutters deposit their cargo.

_____ 8. Taking over, the leaves are cleaned, clipped, and spread with secretions from tiny gardener ants' bodies.

_____ 9. Lined up in neat rows, the ants place fungus on the hunks of leaves.

_____ 10. Cultivated for food, the ants use the leaves as fertilizer for their fungus garden.

EXERCISE 8   Correcting Dangling and Misplaced Modifiers

Each of the following sentences has a dangling (D) or a misplaced (M) modifier. Identify the problems and correct them by rewriting the sentences.

_____   1. Changing the oil regularly, a car runs better and lasts longer.

_____   2. The crusty old sailor went to the fortune-teller with bad luck.

_____   3. The bartender decided to make an appointment to see a psy-chologist with a drinking problem.

_____   4. Reaching speeds of 180 miles per hour, the fans were thrilled by the race cars.

_____   5. I decided to sell my parrot with reluctance.

_____   6. Breathing deeply the intoxicating scent of new shoes, she felt her adrenaline begin to uncontrollably flow.

_____   7. Carlos was determined to quickly amass his fortune at the blackjack table and retire early.

_____   8. Swimming in a butter and garlic sauce, the diners relished every bite of the shrimp.

_____   9. He wanted to badly propose to her and make her his bride.

_____   10. I decided to foolishly purchase the solar-powered electric blanket.

EXERCISE 9   Correcting Dangling and Misplaced Modifiers

Each of the following sentences has a dangling (D) or a misplaced (M) modifier. Identify the problems and correct them by rewriting the sentences.

_____   1. I observed the parade of floats and marching bands on the rooftop.

_____   **2.** Flat busted, my piano had to be pawned for cash.

_____   **3.** The alleged burglar addressed the judge on his knees.

_____   **4.** Freshly snared from the ocean floor, he enjoyed the delicious lobster.

_____   **5.** Wearing a strapless velvet evening gown, Bob thought his wife looked ravishing.

_____   **6.** The student asked to see the school nurse with a sore throat.

_____   **7.** The lost child held on tight to the detective crying for his mommy.

_____   **8.** Cursing like a longshoreman, the baby finally arrived after her thirty-sixth hour of labor.

_____   **9.** By jumping on a trampoline, your heart gets a good cardiovascular workout.

_____   **10.** The outlaw phoned his granny in a pickle.

CHAPTER REVIEW   Adjectives and Adverbs

1. **Adjectives** modify (describe) nouns and pronouns and answer the questions *Which one? What kind?* and *How many?*

2. **Adverbs** modify verbs, adjectives, and other adverbs and answer the questions *Where? When? Why? How?* and *To what degree?* Most words ending in *-ly* are adverbs.

3. Anything can be overdone; therefore, use adjectives and adverbs like gravy, sparingly.

4. Some adjectives follow a regular pattern.

> *nice, nicer, nicest*
>
> *carefully, more careful, most careful*

These are usually the rules:

a. Add *-er* to short adjectives (one or two syllables) to rank units of two.

> Jethro is *shorter* than Cy.

b. Add *-est* to short adjectives (one or two syllables) to rank units of more than two.

Senator Goodyear is the *brightest* person in Congress.

c. Add the word *more* to long adjectives (three or more syllables) to rank units of two.

Your state is *more* prosperous than mine.

d. Add the word *most* to long adjectives (three or more syllables) to rank units of three or more.

Your state is the *most* prosperous state in the West.

e. Some adjectives are irregular in the way they change to show comparison.

good, better, best

bad, worse, worst

5. Some adverbs follow a regular pattern.

sadly, more sadly, most sadly

carefully, more carefully, most carefully

a. Add *-er* to some one-syllable adverbs for the comparative form and add *-est* for the superlative form.

Pierre works *hard*. [positive]

Pierre works *harder* than Simon. [comparative]

Pierre works *hardest* of all the students in the class. [superlative]

b. Add the word *more* to adverbs of two or more syllables for the comparative form and the word *most* to adverbs of two or more syllables for the superlative form.

Sultana proofread *carefully*. [positive]

Sultana proofread *more carefully* than Venny. [comparative]

Sultana proofread *most carefully* of all in the class. [superlative]

c. In some cases the word *less* may be substituted for *more* and the word *least* for *most*.

Martelle examined the contract *less carefully* during her second reading. [comparative]

Martelle examined the contract *least carefully* during her third reading. [superlative]

d. Some adverbs are irregular in the way they change to show comparisons.

well, better, best

badly, worse, worst

6. Use adjectives and adverbs correctly.

   a. Avoid double negatives. Words such as *no, not, none, nothing, never, hardly, barely,* and *scarcely* should not be combined.

   b. Do not confuse adjectives with adverbs. Among the most commonly confused adjectives and adverbs are *good/well, bad/badly,* and *real/really.* The words *good, bad,* and *real* are always adjectives. *Well* is sometimes an adjective. The words *badly* and *really* are always adverbs. *Well* is usually an adverb.

Incorrect:	Clint did *good.* [*Good* is not an adverb.]
Correct:	Joline felt *good.* [*Good* does not address the matter of feeling; it indicates the condition of the subject, *Joline.*]
Correct:	Clint did *well.* [Used here as an adverb, *well* modifies the verb *did.*]
Correct:	Sigmund said, "Carl, you are not a *well* person." [Used here as an adjective, *well* modifies the noun *person.*]
Incorrect:	Elvis was *real* happy with his new disguise. [*Happy* is an adjective modifying the noun *Elvis,* and *real* modifies that adjective. Because only adverbs modify adjectives, we need the word *really.*]
Correct:	Elvis was *really* happy with his new disguise.
Incorrect:	I feel *badly.* [*Badly* is an adverb but here indicates the condition of the subject; therefore, it modifies the pronoun *I.*]
Correct:	I feel *bad.* [*Bad* is an adjective modifying the pronoun *I.*]
Correct:	I explained that *badly.* [*Badly,* an adverb, modifies the verb *explained.*]

   c. Do not use an adverb such as *very, more,* or *most* before adjectives such as *perfect, round, unique, square,* and *straight.*

Incorrect:	It is *more square.*
Correct:	It is square.
Correct:	It is *more nearly square.*

   d. Do not double forms such as *more lonelier* or *most loneliest.*

Incorrect:	She is *more smarter* than I.
Correct:	She is *smarter* than I.

7. A **dangling modifier** gives information but fails to make clear which word or group of words it refers to.

Incorrect:	*Ignoring the traffic signals,* the car crashed into a truck. [The car is not ignoring; the driver is.]

Correct: *Ignoring the traffic signals*, the driver crashed his car into a truck.

8. A **misplaced modifier** is placed so that it modifies the wrong word or words.

Incorrect: The monkeys attracted the attention of the elegant women *who picked fleas off one another.*

Correct: The monkeys *who picked fleas off one another* attracted the attention of the elegant women.

CHAPTER REVIEW Exercises

REVIEW 1   Using Correct Modifiers

Correct problems with modifiers.

In 1951, Sir Hugh Beaver, who was the managing director of the Guinness Brewery, became embroiled in an argument about which bird was the faster game bird in Europe. He wondered if a book that supplied the answers to such burning questions would sell good. So, he worked with a fact-finding agency to compile what became *The Guinness Book of World Records*, first published in 1955. The book proved to be populerer than all other books climbing to the top of the British bestseller lists. Over the years, more than 94 million copies of the book's editions have been sold in 100 different countries and 37 different languages, making it the top-selling copyrighted book of all time. Today, of course, Guinness World Records is still a household name. The organization continues to be the better known collector and verifier of records set around the globe.

Some of the Guinness records—such as the oldest living person, largest animal, and worst flood—are set automatic without any special effort on the part of the record holder. Other people, though, intentional set records seeking a moment in the spotlight. These individuals think up some very creatively and often crazy stunts to perform, usual in front of large crowds. Rattling at full-throttle, one man won his place in history by juggling three chainsaws the longest (44 throws). Wearing only swimming trunks, a tub filled with ice was where another man set the record for the "Longest Full-body Ice

Contact Endurance" (66 minutes 4 seconds). And there's actual a record for

longest underwater pogo-stick jumping (3 hours 40 minutes), which was achieved

in the Amazon River. Apparently, as long as people want to know about these odd

accomplishments, Guinness World Records will be there to list them for us.

REVIEW 2

Writing Short Paragraphs Containing Adjectives and Adverbs

For each numbered item, write a short paragraph using the words in parentheses.

1. (good, better, best) _____

_____

_____

_____

_____

_____

2. (good, well) _____

_____

_____

_____

_____

_____

3. (more, most) _____

_____

_____

_____

_____

_____

_____

4. (bad, badly) _____

_____

_____

_____

_____

_____

_____

5. (real, really) _____

_____

_____

_____

_____

_____

_____

MICROTHEME

To practice your skills acquired in this chapter, return to the Microtheme on page 176 and complete Exercise B.

Chapter 10

Balancing Sentence Parts

FLOW OF WRITING

MICROTHEME	Writing Activity in Miniature

EXERCISE A

Before you work on this chapter, write a Microtheme on the following topic. Write small enough to leave room for marking later. **After** you have studied this chapter, return to your Microtheme and complete Exercise B to practice what you have learned.

Suggested Microtheme Topic: Write a microtheme of 80 to 100 words about a treasured possession, such as a car, an item of clothing, a piece of jewelry, or a family heirloom. Emphasize why the object is treasured by explaining how you acquired it.

EXERCISE B

Connecting Your Learning Objectives with Your Microtheme

Complete this exercise after you have studied this chapter.

1. Circle signal words and combination signal words.
2. Underline words that are parallel and linked by signal words and combination signal words.
3. Be sure that the parallel words are balanced in form and thought.

We are surrounded by balance. Watch a colorful cross-frame, or diamond, kite as it soars in the sky. If you draw an imaginary line from the top to the bottom of the kite, you will see corresponding parts on either side. If you were to replace one of the sides with a loose-flapping fabric, the kite would never fly. A similar lack of balance can also cause a sentence to crash.

Consider these statements:

"To be or not to be—that is the question." [dash added]

This line from *Hamlet*, by William Shakespeare, is one of the most famous lines in literature. Compare it to the well-balanced kite in a strong wind. Its parts are parallel and it "flies" well.

"To be or not being—that is the question."

It still vaguely resembles the sleek kite, but now the second phrase causes it to dip like an unbalanced kite. Lurching, the line begins to lose altitude.

"To be or death is the other alternative—that is the question."

The line slams to the floor. Words scatter across the carpet. We go back to the revision board.

The first sentence is forceful and easy to read. The second is more difficult to follow. The third is almost impossible to understand. We understand it only because we know what it should look like from having read the original. The point is that perceptive readers are as critical of sentences as kite-watchers are of kites.

Basic Principles of Parallelism

Parallelism as it relates to sentence structure is usually achieved by joining words with similar words: nouns with nouns, adjectives (words that describe nouns and pronouns) with adjectives, adverbs (words that describe verbs, adjectives, and other adverbs) with adverbs, and so forth.

Men, *women*, and *children* enjoy the show. [nouns]

The players are *excited*, *eager*, and *enthusiastic*. [adjectives]

The author wrote *skillfully* and *quickly*. [adverbs]

You can create parallel structure by joining groups of words with similar groups of words: prepositional phrase with prepositional phrase, clause with clause, sentence with sentence.

She fell *in love* and *out of love* in a few minutes. [prepositional phrases]

Who he was and *where he came from* did not matter. [clauses]

He came in a hurry. He left in a hurry. [sentences]

Parallelism means balancing one structure with another of the same kind. Faulty parallel structure is awkward and draws unfavorable attention to what is being said.

Nonparallel:	Vince Carter's reputation is based on his ability in *passing, shooting*, and *he is good at rebounds*.
Parallel:	Vince Carter's reputation is based on his ability in *passing, shooting*, and *rebounding*.

In the nonparallel sentence, the words *passing* and *shooting* are of the same kind (verblike words used as nouns), but the rest of the sentence is different. You do not have to know terms to realize that there is a problem of balance in sentence structure. Just read the material aloud. Then compare it with the statement in which *he is good at rebounds* has been changed to *rebounding* to make a sentence that is easy on the eye, ear, and brain.

Signal Words

Some words signal parallel structure. If you use *and*, the items joined by *and* should almost always be parallel. If they are not, then *and* is probably inappropriate.

The weather is hot *and* humid. [*and* joins adjectives]

The car *and* the trailer are parked in front of the house. [*and* joins nouns]

The same principle is true for *but*, although it implies a direct contrast. Where contrasts are being drawn, parallel structure is essential to clarify those contrasts.

He *purchased a Dodger Dog, but* I *chose the Stadium Peanuts*. [*but* joins contrasting clauses]

She *earned* an A in math *but failed* her art class. [*but* joins contrasting verbs]

You should regard all the coordinating conjunctions (FANBOYS: *for, and, nor, but, or, yet, so*) as signals for parallel structure.

EXERCISE 1   Identifying Signal Words and Parallel Elements

Underline the parallel elements—words, phrases, or clauses—and circle the signal words in the following sentences. The sentences in Exercises 1 through 9 are based on video review excerpts from *Movie Guide* by the Wherehouse; the film titles are shown in parentheses.

Example:	One by one they are <u>stalked</u>, <u>terrorized</u>, (and) <u>murdered</u>. (*The Howling*)

1. The residents become the target of vicious, relentless, and inexplicable attacks by hordes of birds. (*The Birds*)

2. A family moves into a supposedly haunted New York home, and it finds that the house is inoperative. (*The Amityville Horror*)

3. While the family members try to make a comfortable life for themselves and to ignore a few irritations, all hell breaks loose.

4. Muffy invited her college friends to her parents' secluded island home but neglected to tell them it might be the last day of their lives. (*April Fool's Day*)

5. A woman discovers that her young daughter has inherited an evil streak and has caused the death of several people. (*The Bad Seed*)

6. A physician surgically separates Siamese twins, and they hate him. (*Basket Case*)

7. One twin is normal, and the other is horribly deformed.

8. The deformed twin becomes an embittered and vindictive person.

9. In a final unreasoning, angry, and brutal assault, she rips the face off the doctor.

10. A slimy alien crashes to earth and devours everyone in its path. (*The Blob*)

EXERCISE 2   Identifying Signal Words and Parallel Elements

Underline the parallel elements—words, phrases, or clauses—and circle the signal words in the following sentences.

1. An old granny tells tales of wolves and of children of the night. (*The Company of Wolves*)

2. Several convicts from another planet escape and fly to the planet Earth. (*Critters*)

3. Krite eggs hatch bloodthirsty babies and the babies continue the family tradition. (*Critters 2*)

4. Four people become trapped in a shopping mall with walking flesh-eaters and a gang of motorcyclists. (*Dawn of the Dead*)

5. A mad scientist dreams of creating life and using his ingenious talents. (*Frankenstein*)

6. He succeeds in producing a monster with the brain of a friend, the emotions of a child, and the body of a giant.

7. Combining fact, fiction, and horror, this film is an imaginative tale of fear. (*Gothic*)

8. A man flees a disturbed past while being pursued by a lawman, a psychopathic killer, and the woman who still loves him. (*Night Breed*)

9. A man wants money he didn't earn, a sightless woman wants to see, and a man's past catches up with him. (*Night Gallery*)

10. Norman Bates attempts to put his life together and to put his old habits behind him. (*Psycho III*)

EXERCISE 3   Correcting Faulty Parallelism

Identify the sentences with parallel elements (P) and those with faulty parallelism (X). Correct the weak element. You need not rewrite the entire sentence.

_____ 1. Employees of a medical supply company release several zombies who like to roam the countryside and eating brains. (*Return of the Living Dead*)

_____ 2. A genetic experiment gone completely haywire spawns a new, hideous life form that breaks free and escaping into the sewer. (*Scared to Death*)

_____ 3. A young traveler finds madness, mystery, and he finds mayhem in the Louisiana bayou in this chilling Gothic tale. (*Sister, Sister*)

_____ 4. The Prince of Darkness has resurfaced in Los Angeles with a new look, a new life, a new love, and having an old enemy. (*To Die For*)

_____ 5. The Puttermans wanted clearer, more effective television reception. (*Terrorvision*)

_____ 6. They purchased a satellite dish, a good television set, and they sat down to watch.

_____ 7. Unfortunately for them, their new equipment brought monsters into their living room and upsetting their lives.

_____   8. Scientists have bred the combat weapons—beasts with the cunning of human beings, the strength of giants, and who had the bloodlust of predators. (*Watchers*)

_____   9. An explosion sets the mistakes free, and no one is safe.

_____   10. A group of teenagers go for a free late-night showing at a wax museum horror display but tragically becoming part of the show. (*Waxwork*)

EXERCISE 4   Correcting Faulty Parallelism

Identify the sentences with parallel elements (P) and those with faulty parallelism (X). Correct the weak element. You need not rewrite the entire sentence.

_____   1. This film gives a warm and nostalgic look back at the year 1963 and focuses on one summer night of cruising in a small town. (*American Graffiti*)

_____   2. It features greasers, geeks, good girls, and has cleancut characters.

_____   3. This film casts a cynical shadow on bad acting, bad special effects, and uses bad dialogue. (*Attack of the Killer Tomatoes*)

_____   4. Savage tomatoes roll around to terrorize the citizens and destroying their society.

_____   5. Alex Foley is a brash, street-smart Detroit detective and who follows the trail of a friend's murder. (*Beverly Hills Cop*)

_____   6. This zany comedy features a series of sketches that satirize movies, television, and ridicule other aspects of contemporary society. (*Kentucky Fried Movie*)

_____   7. Prince Alceem quickly finds a new job, new friends, new enemies, and has lots of trouble. (*Coming to America*)

_____   8. High school students struggle with independence, success, money, and to be mature in this off-beat comedy. (*Fast Times at Ridgemont High*)

_____ **9.** A bespectacled spectacle of a bookkeeper adores his pet fish and dreams of becoming one of these scaled wonders. (*The Incredible Mr. Limpet*)

_____ **10.** When his wish suddenly comes true, he fisheyes a lady fish and becoming an invaluable hero to the U.S. Navy.

EXERCISE 5   Completing Parallel Structures

Fill in the blanks in the following sentences with parallel elements.

1. The animated Disney classic concerns a little girl who follows a white rabbit to a land of wonder, _____, and _____. (*Alice in Wonderland*)

2. In this exciting and _____ family adventure, Benji is adopted by a loving family. (*Benji*)

3. When the two children are kidnapped, Benji is the only one who knows where they are and _____.

4. A daring family decides to move to Alaska and _____ completely apart from society. (*The Alaska Wilderness Adventure*)

5. This film takes us into the forest to share the excitement, _____, and _____ of a little deer. (*Bambi*)

6. The caped crusader and his faithful boy wonder fight for _____, _____, and _____. (*Batman*)

7. Acme Co.'s best customer uses his entire arsenal, but Road Runner _____ and _____. (*Road Runner*)

8. Coldheart has captured children and made them his slaves, and the Care Bears must outwit him with _____ and _____. (*The Care Bears in a Land Without Feeling*)

9. Van Dyke is delightful as a man whose old automobile suddenly develops the ability to _____ and _____. (*Chitty-Chitty Bang-Bang*)

10. The mistreated stepdaughter is transformed by her fairy godmother, who _____ her and _____ her to the royal ball. (*Cinderella*)

EXERCISE 6   Completing Parallel Structures

Fill in the blanks in the following sentences with parallel elements.

1. Schwarzenegger plays a _____, _____ killing machine. (*The Terminator*)

2. Nothing can stop him from his mission to find and _____ an innocent woman.

3. A man's dreams lead him to Mars in search of certain danger, his old _____, and a mysterious _____. (*Total Recall*)

4. A spaceship crash-lands on an unknown planet, and the three astronauts _____. (*Planet of the Apes*)

5. There, the apes are the rulers, and the _____.

6. Ultimately the alien grows to be an enormous size and _____ killing everyone on board. (*Alien*)

7. When unsuspecting guests check in at a hotel, they are surprised to find vicious ants who appear and _____ them with a vengeance. (*Ants*)

8. A futuristic ex-cop is drawn out of retirement to seek and _____ a group of renegade robots. (*Bladerunner*)

9. This is a touching and sometimes comical adventure of an _____ but _____ alien. (*E.T.*)

10. Max's somewhat cloudy origin is brought to light as the "creation" of an _____ and _____ computer-generated talk-show host. (*Max Headroom—The Original Story*)

Combination Signal Words

The words *and* and *but* are the most common individual signal words used with parallel constructions. Sometimes, however, **combination words** signal the need for parallelism or balance. The most common ones are *either/or*, *neither/nor*, *not only/but also*, *both/and*, and *whether/or*. Now consider this faulty sentence and a possible correction.

Nonparallel: *Either we will* win this game, *or let's* go out fighting.

Parallel: *Either we will* win this game, *or we will* go out fighting.

The correction is made by changing *let's* to *we will* to parallel the *we will* in the first part of the sentence. The same construction should follow the *either* and the *or*.

Nonparallel: Flour is used *not only* to bake cakes *but also in* paste.

Parallel: Flour is used *not only to bake* cakes *but also to make* paste.

The correction is made by changing *in* (a preposition) to *to make* (an infinitive). Now an infinitive follows both *not only* and *but also*.

EXERCISE 7   Identifying Combination Signal Words and Parallel Elements

Underline the parallel elements—words, phrases, or clauses—and circle the combination signal words in the following sentences.

1. Robin Hood not only robbed from the rich but also gave to the poor. (*Adventures of Robin Hood*)

2. Both Humphrey Bogart and Katharine Hepburn star in this movie about two unlikely people traveling together through the jungle rivers of Africa during World War II. (*The African Queen*)

3. Dr. Jekyll discovers a potion, and now he can be either himself or Mr. Hyde. (*Dr. Jekyll and Mr. Hyde*)

4. An Oklahoma family moves to California and finds neither good jobs nor compassion in the "promised land." (*The Grapes of Wrath*)

5. In this Christmas classic, Jimmy Stewart stars as a man who can either die by suicide or go back to see what life would have been like without him. (*It's a Wonderful Life*)

6. During the Korean War, army surgeons discover that they must either develop a lunatic lifestyle or go crazy. (*M*A*S*H*)

7. An advertising executive not only gets tied up with an obnoxious but boring salesman but also goes with him on a wacky chase across the country. (*Planes, Trains, and Automobiles*)

8. In this flawless integration of animation and live action, Roger and Eddie try to discover both who framed Roger and who is playing patty-cake with his wife. (*Who Framed Roger Rabbit?*)

9. A long-suffering black woman named Celie experiences not only heartaches
but also some joy as she rises from tragedy to personal triumph. (*The Color
Purple*)

10. An independent man learns that he is expected to give up either his dignity or
his life. (*Cool Hand Luke*)

EXERCISE 8   Correcting Faulty Parallelism

**Underline the parallel elements—words, phrases, or clauses—and circle the
combination signal words in the following sentences. If the elements are not
parallel, change them to achieve balance. You need not rewrite the entire
sentence.**

Example: (Either) the street punks would terrorize the school (or) a former
gang member would stop them. (*The Moment of Truth*)

1. A fanatical submarine captain makes a misguided effort to sink the ships of
both the allies and the enemy. (*20,000 Leagues Under the Sea*)

2. After a young woman is brutally attacked by a scurvy street gang, not only she
studies martial arts but also plans for absolute bloody revenge. (*Alley Cat*)

3. The main issue is whether a street-wise girl will find the killer or he will
escape. (*Avenging Angel*)

4. Either the Barbarian brothers will triumph or the evil world will win. (*The
Barbarians*)

5. Neither the Joker nor anyone else can get the last laugh on Batman. (*Batman*)

6. Two youngsters are shipwrecked in the South Pacific and not only they mature
but also slowly make a surprising discovery. (*Blue Lagoon*)

7. A neighborhood gang will either reign, or Danny McGavin will. (*Colors*)

8. After Conan's parents were murdered, he swore that he would either get
revenge or die trying. (*Conan the Barbarian*)

9. The question is whether Harry will kill the psychopath or the psychopath will
kill him. (*Dirty Harry*)

10. Neither Mumbles nor Breathless Mahoney communicated well with Dick Tracy.

(*Dick Tracy*)

EXERCISE 9   Correcting Faulty Parallelism

Underline the parallel elements—words, phrases, or clauses—and circle the combination signal words in the following sentences. If the elements are not parallel, change them to achieve balance. You need not rewrite the entire sentence.

1. James Bond protects the U.S. gold reserve both with some wonderfully ingenious gadgets and a few unusually lovely ladies. (*Goldfinger*)

2. Two convicts decide that either they must escape from Devil's Island or die. (*Papillon*)

3. These prehistoric people are not only competing in a quest for fire but also in a struggle for dominance. (*Quest for Fire*)

4. Whether one side won or the other, human beings would benefit.

5. Neither his poor physical condition nor his reputation would discourage Rocky Balboa. (*Rocky*)

6. Both Al Capone and Bugs Moran neglected to pass out Valentine's Day cards in 1934. (*The St. Valentine's Day Massacre*)

7. It was neither a bird nor was it a plane; it was Superman. (*Superman— The Movie*)

8. The pilot loved both the experience of flying and to be around a certain beautiful astrophysicist. (*Top Gun*)

9. A computer whiz kid manages not only to get himself hooked into a top-secret military computer but also finds the fate of the world in his hands. (*Wargames*)

10. Only one person would walk away from this friendship; it would be either the drug smuggler or it would be the cop. (*Tequila Sunrise*)

CHAPTER REVIEW   Balancing Sentence Parts

1. **Parallelism** is a balance of one structure with another of the same kind—nouns with nouns, verbs with verbs, adjectives with adjectives, phrases with phrases, and clauses with clauses.

> *Goats*, *chickens*, and *cows* [nouns] *roamed* the yard and *caused* [verbs] considerable confusion.

> Tanya walked *into the room* and *out of the room* with grace [prepositional phrases].

> *Tanya walked into the room*, and *she walked out of the room* with grace [independent clauses].

2. Faulty parallel structure is awkward and draws unfavorable attention to what is being said.

> *Hitting* home runs and *to catch* balls in the outfield were his main concerns. [should be *Hitting . . . and catching* or *To hit . . . and to catch*]

3. Some words signal parallel structure. All coordinating conjunctions (FANBOYS: *for, and, nor, but, or, yet, so*) can give such signals.

> My car is inexpensive *and* plain.

> My dog is ugly, *but* it is a good companion.

4. Combination words also signal the need for parallelism or balance. The most common ones are *either/or*, *neither/nor*, *not only/but also*, *both/and*, and *whether/or*.

> Patsy decided that propagating plants could be *either* a hobby *or* a business but not both. [A noun follows each of the combination words.]

CHAPTER REVIEW   Exercises

REVIEW 1   Correcting Faulty Parallelism

Eliminate awkwardness in the following passage by using parallel structure.

Ken Kesey wrote *One Flew Over the Cuckoo's Nest* as a novel. It was later made into a stage play and a film. The title was taken from a children's folk rhyme: "One flew east, one flew west, / One flew over the cuckoo's nest."

The narrator in the novel is Chief Bromden, the central character is Randle McMurphy, and Nurse Ratched is the villain. Bromden sees and can hear but does not speak. He is a camera with a conscience. McMurphy is both an outcast and serves as a leader, and he speaks out for freedom and as an individual. Nurse Ratched is the voice of repression. She is the main representative of what

Bromden calls the "Combine." She organizes, directs, controls, and, if necessary to her purposes, will destroy.

The setting is a mental institution where McMurphy has gone to avoid doing more rigorous time in the nearby prison. Discovering what the inmates are going through, he seeks to liberate them from their affliction and freeing them from Nurse Ratched's domination.

A battle of wills ensues, and the reader wonders who will win. The nurse has the whole system behind her, one that prevents the inmates from regaining self-esteem. McMurphy is a colorful, irreverent, expressive person and who appeals to the men's deepest need for self-respect and to be sane. She offers her therapy; his is also offered. She gives drugs. She also gives group therapy, which is tightly controlled by her to produce humiliation. McMurphy provides recreation in the form of first a fishing trip and then sex (for some).

McMurphy is eventually defeated by the system. Neither his energy was enough nor his intelligence when the Combine moves in. McMurphy is given a lobotomy and reduced to a mere body without a mind. Out of profound respect and deeply loving, Bromden destroys McMurphy's body and then escapes.

REVIEW 2

Completing Parallel Structures

Complete each of the following sentences by adding a construction that is parallel to the underlined construction.

1. We went to the zoo not only for <u>fun</u> but also for _____

_____

2. He attended Utah State University for <u>a good education</u> and _____

_____

3. For a college major, she was considering <u>English</u>, <u>history</u>, and _____

4. Mr. Ramos was <u>a good neighbor</u> and _____

5. My breakfast each day that week consisted of <u>a slice of bread</u>, <u>a glass of low-fat milk</u>, and_____

6. She decided that she must choose between <u>a social life</u> and _____

_____

7. Either <u>she would make the choice</u>, or _____

_____

8. Because we are mutually supportive, either <u>we will all have a good time</u>, or

_____

9. Like the Three Musketeers, our motto is "<u>All for one</u> and _____

_____

10. My intention was to <u>work for a year</u>, <u>save my money</u>, and _____

_____

REVIEW 3

Writing Sentences with Parallel Structure

Use each of these signal words or combined signal words in a sentence of ten or more words.

1. and _____

_____

_____

2. but _____

_____

_____

3. so _____

_____

_____

4. either/or _____

_____

_____

5. both/and _____

_____

_____

STUDENT COMPANION SITE

For additional practice, visit www.cengage .com/devenglish/ brandon/spb6e.

MICROTHEME

To practice your skills acquired in this chapter, return to the Microtheme on page 194 and complete Exercise B.

Chapter 11

Punctuation and Capitalization

FLOW OF WRITING

MICROTHEME — Writing Activity in Miniature

EXERCISE A

Before you work on this chapter, write a Microtheme on the following topic. Write small enough to leave room for marking later. **After** you have studied this chapter, return to your Microtheme and complete Exercise B to practice what you have learned.

Suggested Microtheme Topic: Write a Microtheme of 80 to 100 words as a plot summary of a film that you admire because of its dramatic and comedic content.

EXERCISE B

Connecting Your Learning Objectives with Your Microtheme

Complete this exercise after you have studied this chapter.

1. Use the chapter table of contents to look up any questionable marks of punctuation or capitalization.
2. Consider punctuation in relation to what you have learned about sentence structure in other chapters.

Understanding punctuation will help you to write better. If you are not sure how to punctuate a compound or a compound-complex sentence, then you probably will not write one. If you do not know how to show that some of your words come from other sources, you may mislead your reader. If you misuse punctuation, you will force your readers to struggle to get your message. So take the time to review and master the mechanics. Your efforts will be rewarded.

End Punctuation

PERIODS

1. Place a period after a statement.

The weather is beautiful today.

2. Place a period after common abbreviations.

Dr.   Mr.   Mrs.   Dec.   a.m.

Exceptions: FBI   UN   NAACP   FHA

3. Use an ellipsis—three periods within a sentence and four periods at the end of a sentence—to indicate that words have been omitted from quoted material.

He stopped walking and the buildings...rose up out of the misty courtroom....

(James Thurber, "The Secret Life of Walter Mitty")

QUESTION MARKS

1. Place a question mark at the end of a direct question.

Will you go to the country tomorrow?

2. Do *not* use a question mark after an indirect (reported) question.

She asked me what caused the slide.

EXCLAMATION POINTS

1. Place an exclamation point after a word or a group of words that expresses strong feeling.

Oh!   What a night!   Help!   Gadzooks!

2. Do not overwork the exclamation point. Do not use double exclamation points. Use the period or comma for mild exclamatory words, phrases, or sentences.

Oh, we can leave now.

EXERCISE 1   Using End Punctuation

Add end punctuation.

1. Have you ever heard of the Mummy's Curse

2. In 1923, twenty-four people entered the newly discovered tomb of Egypt's King Tutankhamen

3. Only weeks after they unearthed Tut's final resting place, the man who financed the dig died

4. By 1929, eleven people connected with the discovery of the tomb had also died early of unnatural causes

5. Holy sarcophagus, the tomb was cursed

6. I heard that an untimely death was in store for all of the tomb raiders

7. As each person on the expedition passed away, the newspapers shrieked, "The mummy's curse strikes again"

8. Did you know that within a decade, the press had linked thirty deaths to King Tut

9. Studies now show, though, that on average, the twenty-four people who entered the burial chamber lived to be seventy years old

10. I suppose that the legendary curse was a fiction created by the press

EXERCISE 2   Using End Punctuation

Add end punctuation.

1. Did you know that the U.S. Department of Commerce once kept a list of genuine haunted houses

2. There are thirty houses on the last version of this agency's list

3. Eeek, I just saw a government-certified ghost

4. San Diego's Whaley House is one of the places on the official list

5. Could this historic home be the most haunted house in America

6. At least four different spirits are active in this place

7. Oh, the sound of ghostly footsteps is driving me mad

8. Thomas and Anna Whaley have been dead for over a hundred years, but visitors still smell his cigars and her perfume

9. They also hear the Whaleys' disembodied voices and the tunes Anna played on her piano

10. Help, the ghost of Anna Whaley just materialized right in front of me

---

Commas

COMMAS TO SEPARATE

1. Use a comma to separate main clauses joined by one of the coordinating conjunctions—*for, and, nor, but, or, yet, so*. The comma may be omitted if the clauses are brief and parallel.

> We traveled many miles to see the game, *but* it was canceled.
>
> Mary left *and* I remained. [brief and parallel clauses]

2. Use a comma after introductory dependent clauses and long introductory phrases (generally, four or more words is considered long).

> *Before the arrival of the shipment*, the boss had written a letter protesting the delay. [two prepositional phrases]
>
> *If you do not hear from me*, assume that I am lost. [introductory dependent clause, an adverbial modifier]
>
> *In winter* we skate on the river. [short prepositional phrase, no comma]

3. Use a comma to separate words, phrases, and clauses in a series.

> *Red, white,* and *blue* were her favorite colors. [words]
>
> He ran *down the street, across the park,* and *into the arms of his father.* [prepositional phrases]
>
> *When John was asleep, when Mary was at work,* and *when Bob was studying,* Mother had time to relax. [dependent clauses]

4. However, when coordinating conjunctions connect all the elements in a series, the commas are omitted.

> He bought *apples* and *pears* and *grapes.*

5. Use a comma to separate coordinate adjectives not joined by *and* that modify the same noun.

> I need a *sturdy, reliable* truck.

6. Do not use a comma to separate adjectives that are not coordinate. Try the following technique to determine whether the adjectives are coordinate: Put *and* between the adjectives. If it fits naturally, the adjectives are coordinate; if it does not, they are not, and you do not need a comma.

She is a kind, beautiful person.

kind *and* beautiful [natural, hence the comma]

I built a red brick wall.

red *and* brick wall [not natural, no comma]

7. Use a comma to separate sentence elements that might be misread.

Inside the dog scratched his fleas.

Inside, the dog scratched his fleas.

Without benefit of the comma, the reader might initially misunderstand the relationship among the first three words.

COMMAS TO SET OFF

1. Use commas to set off (enclose) adjectives in pairs that follow a noun.

The scouts, *tired and hungry*, marched back to camp.

2. Use commas to set off nonessential (unnecessary for meaning of the sentence) words, phrases, and clauses.

My brother, *a student at Ohio State University,* is visiting me. [If you drop the phrase, the basic meaning of the sentence remains intact.]

Marla, *who studied hard*, will pass. [The clause is not essential to the basic meaning of the sentence.]

All students *who studied hard* will pass. [Here the clause *is* essential. If you remove it, you would have *All students will pass*, which is not necessarily true.]

I shall not stop searching *until I find the treasure*. [A dependent clause at the end of a sentence is usually not set off with a comma. However, a clause beginning with the word *though* or *although* will be set off regardless of where it is located.]

I felt unsatisfied, though we had won the game.

3. Use commas to set off parenthetical elements such as mild interjections (*oh, well, yes, no,* and others), most conjunctive adverbs (*however, otherwise, therefore, similarly, hence, on the other hand,* and *consequently,* but not *then, thus, soon, now,* and *also*), quotation indicators, and special abbreviations (*etc., i.e., e.g.,* and others).

Oh, what a silly question! [mild interjection]

It is necessary, *of course*, to leave now. [sentence modifier]

We left early; *however*, we missed the train anyway. [conjunctive adverb]

"When I was in school," *he said*, "I read widely." [quotation indicator]

Books, papers, pens, *etc.*, were scattered on the floor. [The abbreviation *etc.* should be used sparingly, however.]

4. Use commas to set off nouns used as direct address.

Play it again, *Sam*.

Please tell us the answer, *Jane*, so we can discuss it.

5. Use commas to separate the numbers in a date.

June 4, *1965*, is a day I will remember.

6. Do not use commas if the day of the month is not specified, or if the day is given before the month.

June 1965 was my favorite time.

One day I will never forget is 4 June 1965.

7. Use commas to separate the city from the state. No comma is used between the state and the zip code.

Walnut, CA 91789

8. Use a comma after both the city and the state when they are used together in a sentence.

Our family visited Anchorage, *Alaska*, last summer.

9. Use a comma following the salutation of a friendly letter and the complimentary closing in any letter.

Dear Saul,

Sincerely,

10. Use a comma in numbers to set off groups of three digits. However, omit the comma in dates, serial numbers, page numbers, years, and street numbers.

The total assets were *$2,000,000*.

I look forward to the year 2050.

EXERCISE 3   Using Commas

Insert commas where needed.

1. Edward Teach who was better known as Blackbeard terrorized the oceans on

the *Queen Anne's Revenge* from 1716 to 1718.

2. Blackbeard and his band of pirates ambushed ships took the passengers and

crew hostage and ransacked cabins in search of valuables.

3. They were looking for coins gold silver and jewelry.

4. Blackbeard ferocious and menacing quickly earned a reputation for being the

most frightening of all pirates.

5. To make himself look especially fierce he braided his long hair and bushy beard and tied the braids with black ribbons.

6. Before he fought in battles he wove slow-burning fuses into his hair and lit them to look demonic.

7. He was a large man who wore a red coat and adorned himself with numerous swords pistols and knives.

8. He spent the warmer months terrorizing the coasts of North and South Carolina and then he menaced the seas of the Caribbean in the winter.

9. Instead of the usual skull-and-crossbones Blackbeard's black flag had an image of a horned skeleton holding a spear and an hourglass.

10. When the crew of other ships saw this flag they usually surrendered without a fight.

11. Blackbeard captured a ship sailing from Charleston South Carolina and threatened to kill its passengers if the townspeople didn't give him a chest filled with medical remedies.

12. The townspeople paid the ransom so Blackbeard freed his prisoners.

13. The pirate captured over forty ships and caused the deaths of hundreds of people during his short lawless career.

14. By the spring of 1718 Blackbeard commanded four ships and three hundred pirates.

15. Blackbeard's favorite hideout was off Ocracoke Island one of a string of islands off the coast of North Carolina.

16. The British colonists there liked to buy the pirates' cheap stolen goods so they turned a blind eye to Blackbeard's activities.

17. Blackbeard's reign of terror ended however on November 22 1718.

18. The governor of Virginia fed up with Blackbeard's crimes sent Royal Navy ships to trap the pirates in Ocracoke Inlet.

19. During the brief but bloody battle Blackbeard was shot five times but he fought on until a Navy seaman slashed his throat from behind.

20. As a warning to other pirates the Navy captain cut off Blackbeard's head and hung it from the bow of his ship.

EXERCISE 4 Using Commas

Insert commas where needed.

1. In *Frankenstein* the original classic horror thriller written by Mary Shelley and published on October 3 1818 Victor Frankenstein was a gifted dedicated student.

2. While he studied science at the university he came upon the secret of how to create life.

3. Being more interested in simple practical matters than in theory he set out to construct a living breathing creature.

4. Victor who was very much concerned about process first needed to gather the materials necessary for his experiment.

5. He went all around town picking up body parts and he stored them in his laboratory.

6. The dissecting room at a local hospital provided him with the most basic articles and he was very grateful.

7. Local butcher shops had plenty of items perhaps including some spare ribs.

8. Finally he was ready to begin construction of a strange humanlike creature.

9. He made a creature that was eight feet tall four feet wide and very strong.

10. The face of the creature which could be described only as hideous was not easy to look upon.

11. One night while Victor was sleeping lightly the monster lonely and troubled came to his bedroom.

12. Victor screamed loudly and the monster ran away in disappointment.

13. Victor developed brain fever which was a result of the encounter.

14. When Victor recovered from his illness he discovered that one of his brothers had been murdered by an unknown person.

15. In despair and befuddlement Victor went to a remote wilderness to sort out his problems.

16. One day when he was out walking Victor saw a strange lumbering creature running into the mountains.

17. Victor chased the creature but he was unable to catch it.

18. Soon after he sat down to rest and the creature appeared before him.

19. It was Victor Frankenstein's monster who had come to talk to him.

20. With a great deal of self-pity the monster explained that he was very sad because people were unkind to him.

EXERCISE 5   Using Commas

Insert commas where needed.

1. Frankenstein's monster distraught and desperate told a story of acute loneliness.

2. After leaving Victor Frankenstein's house he had gone to live in the country.

3. He had tried diligently to help the simple gentle people by bringing them firewood.

4. They took the firewood; however they were at first frightened and then angry.

5. The monster very upset and dejected had gone back to the city.

6. There he killed Victor's innocent unsuspecting brother and he then cleverly tried to place the blame on someone else.

7. Listening to the monster in horror Victor Frankenstein realized what he had done in this act of creation.

8. The monster started making demands and it was clear that he would force Victor to carry them out.

9. He said that if Victor did not make a suitable female companion for him he would begin killing human beings at random.

10. Victor went away gathered up some more parts and started building a bride for the monster.

11. The monster waited in eager anticipation but he was to be sorely disappointed.

12. Victor became disgusted with his project and he destroyed all the tissue just before it came to life.

13. Needless to say the monster was deeply distressed by this unexpected shocking development.

14. Before the monster ran away he swore to get revenge on Victor's wedding night.

15. When Victor got married he armed himself fully for he expected a visit from the enraged vengeful monster.

16. On the night of the wedding the monster slipped into the bridal chamber and strangled the horrified unlucky bride.

17. Victor himself vowed to avenge the murder by killing the monster but the monster was nowhere to be found.

18. Victor finally died in a cabin in the desolate frozen lands of the North and much later his body was found by a friend.

19. The monster dropped by for one last visit for he wanted to complain about his unhappy life.

20. He said that Victor had created a man without a friend love or even a soul; and therefore Victor was more wicked than anyone.

EXERCISE 6   Using Commas

Insert commas where needed.

1. In August 1862 Confederate private Henry Clark was fighting in the Battle of Richmond Kentucky when he was hit in the thigh with an enemy shell.

2. Clark was taken prisoner and the Union medic who treated the soldier's wound discovered that the patient had a secret.

3. Henry Clark was actually a woman and her name was really Mary Ann Clark.

4. Federal troops gave her a dress to wear made her promise to return to the life of a lady and then released her.

5. Mary Ann replaced the dress with a uniform returned to the rebel army and was immediately promoted.

6. Clark seems to have openly served as a female officer but about four hundred other women disguised themselves as men to fight in the Civil War.

7. To get to the front lines women had to pass themselves off as men.

8. If a woman was detected of course she was sent home.

9. But both armies were desperate for troops and physical exams of new recruits were not thorough.

10. Being discovered was unlikely for soldiers slept in their uniforms and took baths infrequently.

11. Many of the women blended in by learning to cuss taking up gambling and even dating local girls.

12. Some of the females gave themselves away with their ladylike behaviors but most were detected only when they needed medical treatment.

13. Research shows that most of these female soldiers were not eccentric crazy or deranged.

14. According to a letter from Clark's mother Mary Ann joined the military to escape a bad marriage.

15. Martha Parks Lindley however joined because she could not part from her husband.

16. Their fellow soldiers thought that Lindley and his constant companion a "young man" named Jim Smith were just very close friends.

17. Charlotte Hope signed up to avenge the death of her fiancé who was killed in an 1861 raid.

18. Charlotte angry and grief-stricken vowed to kill one Union soldier for each of the twenty-one years her fiancé had lived.

19. Others wanted to be soldiers for the financial benefits for patriotic reasons or just for the thrill of it.

20. Apparently most of the women enlisted for the same reasons men joined.

Semicolons

The **semicolon** indicates a stronger division than the comma. It is used principally to separate independent clauses within a sentence.

1. Use a semicolon to separate independent clauses not joined by a coordinating conjunction.

   You must buy that car today; tomorrow will be too late.

2. Use a semicolon between two independent clauses joined by a conjunctive adverb such as one of the HOTSHOT CAT words (*however, otherwise, therefore, similarly, hence, on the other hand, then, consequently, accordingly, thus*).

   It was very late; *therefore,* I remained at the hotel.

3. Use a semicolon to separate main clauses joined by a coordinating conjunction if one or both of the clauses contain distracting commas.

   Byron, the famous English poet, was buried in Greece; *and* Shelley, who was his friend and fellow poet, was buried in Italy.

4. Use a semicolon in a series between items that themselves contain commas.

   He has lived in Covina, California; Reno, Nevada; Tribbey, Oklahoma; and Bangor, Maine.

EXERCISE 7   Using Semicolons and Commas

Insert semicolons and commas where needed.

1. In September 1991, two hikers saw the head and shoulders of a dead man protruding through the ice of the Italian Alps and they assumed that the man was just another Alpine accident victim.

2. Rescue workers were summoned they used jackhammers to extricate the man's body and his possessions from the ice.

3. But then an archaeologist saw the copper ax found beside the corpse he realized that the body was actually a spectacular archaeological discovery.

4. The snow and ice had naturally mummified the corpse and it had been frozen there on the mountain for about 5,300 years.

5. The Iceman was a well-preserved specimen of a Neolithic human his remains were the oldest human flesh ever found.

6. During the Neolithic period, metal tools had begun to replace stone tools consequently the Iceman carried both a flint dagger and a copper ax.

7. X-rays of the Iceman's body showed that he had been about forty years old when he died he had been killed by an arrow shot into his back.

8. He had also suffered other wounds for example his hand had been deeply cut and several of his ribs had been broken.

9. Archaeologists surmised that he may have been in a battle he fled the scene after being wounded.

10. In spite of his injuries he had begun ascending the mountain.

11. His broken ribs would have made climbing difficult so he must have thought he'd find safety at higher elevations.

12. The clothing, tools, and weapons found with the Iceman were also interesting for very few Neolithic artifacts have survived.

13. Feathers on his arrows revealed Neolithic people's understanding of ballistic principles obviously, they knew that feathers would make an arrow fly more accurately.

14. The embers he carried taught us how Neolithic people transported fire they wrapped the glowing coals in leaves and placed them in birch bark containers.

15. The Iceman also taught us about Neolithic clothing his leather shoes, for instance, were insulated with grass.

16. His people apparently did not weave cloth all of the Iceman's clothing was made from animal skins.

17. After archaeologists determined the age of the Iceman's ax they were forced to admit being wrong about the date copper smelting began.

18. Today, the Iceman is kept in a refrigerated vault in Italy his body remains encased in a glaze of ice to preserve it.

19. The Iceman has revealed a great deal about the Neolithic age but he has also raised new questions.

20. Archaeologists hope to continue to study and learn more from him so the Iceman will remain frozen in time.

EXERCISE 8   Using Semicolons and Commas

Insert semicolons and commas where needed.

1. Once upon a time, there was a young woman named Cyberella she lived in Oklahoma with an evil stepmother and an obnoxious stepsister.

2. One night at eleven her wretched stepfamily was snoring raucously and Cyberella was busily dusting the family computer, which someone had left running.

3. It was then that Cyberella inadvertently hit the Instant Internet button therefore the screen lit up.

4. She had never been permitted to use the Internet but she had enviously watched her evil stepfamily at the keyboard.

5. Cyberella created the screen name Cool4aday and logged on for fun and education naturally she started with the index of chat rooms.

6. She was delighted with her unexpected opportunity however she realized that the computer was programmed to go out of commission at midnight.

7. Now she was a free-spirited cyberspace explorer surfing the World Wide Web at midnight she would turn back into a servant ripping out cobwebs and capturing dust bunnies.

8. Cyberella spotted a chat room called "Talk to the Prince" feeling like a princess she joined in the conversation.

9. To her amazement she discovered that she was chatting with a real prince Prince Igor of Transylvania in fact he seemed to like her.

10. Prince Igor boldly invited Cyberella to accompany him to a private chat room breathlessly she said yes and followed him with demure keystrokes.

11. They chatted shyly and then passionately for almost an hour and soon the prince became royally enamored by the way she processed thought noticing that she wrote skillfully, using her spell checker and grammar checker in a most delicate way.

12. Cyberella wanted to tell Prince Igor explicitly what was in her heart therefore she often used the computer thesaurus feature, impressing him further with her highly eloquent diction.

13. Prince Igor was about to ask the royal marriage question then Cyberella heard the clock strike her computer went dark and she believed she would never again chat with her sweet prince.

14. Prince Igor was devastated and vowed to find this lovely correspondent he therefore directed his army to undertake a royal search that would properly but legally identify Cool4aday and expose all impostors.

15. The soldiers would test the computer-assisted writing skills of everyone in the world if necessary moreover they would even provide laptops for any computerless woman who looked as if she could possibly be the mystery writer.

16. Cyberella had informed Prince Igor that she was from the American Southwest a fact that enabled him to focus his search.

17. Following electronic clues, the soldiers visited Amarillo Texas Tucumcari New Mexico Tulsa Oklahoma and Window Rock Arizona.

18. At last a soldier came to Cyberella's house and was greeted by the obnoxious stepsister, who claimed that she was Cool4aday and began to chat online with Prince Igor however the stepsister forgot to use her spell checker and the prince flamed a rejection.

19. Then the soldier handed Cyberella a laptop computer and instructions of course both the wicked stepmother and the obnoxious stepsister scoffed.

20. Nevertheless, Cyberella was verified as Cool4aday and the prince was wildly elated therefore he declared an international holiday slapped his leg with glee and offered to grant her fondest wish.

21. "Does that mean I get this laptop for myself?" Cyberella asked and Prince Igor, a bit humbled by her response said "No, that means you get me for yourself."

22. "Oh, that's very, very nice but may I also have this laptop?" Cyberella asked striking a hard bargain as she fondly hugged the computer.

23. "Yes" Prince Igor said. "I'll even toss in a laser printer and I'll add a

few pounds of copy paper and a stack of Dungeon-and-Dragon software

customized in one of my own castles."

24. They got married and lived happily ever after for a while then the wicked

stepfamily tried to move into the palace but they were arrested and were no

longer allowed to use the Internet in Transylvania or Oklahoma until they had

passed a writing test which they never did.

Quotation Marks

Quotation marks are used principally to set off direct quotations. A direct quotation consists of material taken from the written work or the direct speech of others; it is set off by double quotation marks. Single quotation marks are used to set off a quotation within a quotation.

> **Double Quotation Marks:**   He said, "I don't remember."

> **Single Quotation Marks:**   He said, "I don't remember if she said, 'Wait for me.'"

1. Use double quotation marks to set off direct quotations.

> Lavonne said, "Give me the book."

> As Edward McNeil writes of the Greek achievement: "To an extent never before realized, mind was supreme over faith."

2. Use double quotation marks to set off titles of shorter pieces of writing such as magazine articles, essays, short stories, short poems, one-act plays, chapters in books, songs, and separate pieces of writing published as part of a larger work.

> The book *Literature: Structure, Sound, and Sense* contains a deeply moving poem titled "On Wenlock Edge."

> Have you read "The Use of Force," a short story by William Carlos Williams?

> My favorite Elvis song is "Don't Be Cruel."

3. Use double quotation marks to set off slang, technical terms, and special words.

> There are many aristocrats, but Elvis is the only true "King." [special word]

> The "platoon system" changed the game of football. [technical term]

4. Use double quotation marks in writing dialogue (conversation). Write each speech unit as a separate paragraph and set it off with double quotation marks.

> "Will you go with me?" he asked.

> "Yes," she replied. "Are you ready now?"

5. Use single quotation marks to set off a quotation within a quotation.

Professor Baxter said, "You should remember Shakespeare's words, 'Nothing will come of nothing.'"

6. Do *not* use quotation marks for indirect quotations.

Incorrect: He said that "he would bring the supplies."

Correct: He said that he would bring the supplies.

7. Do *not* use quotation marks for the title on your own written work. If you refer to that title in another piece of writing, however, you need the quotation marks.

Punctuation with Quotation Marks

1. A period or a comma is always placed *inside* the quotation marks.

Our assignment for Monday was to read Poe's poem "The Raven."

"I will read you the story," he said. "It's a good one."

2. A semicolon or a colon is always placed *outside* the quotation marks.

He read Robert Frost's poem "Design"; then he gave the examination.

He quoted Frost's "Stopping by Woods on a Snowy Evening": "But I have promises to keep."

3. A question mark, an exclamation point, or a dash (see page 227) is placed *outside* the quotation marks when it applies to the entire sentence and *inside* the quotation marks when it applies to the material in quotation marks.

He asked, "Am I responsible for everything?" [quoted question within a statement]

Did you hear him say, "I have the answer"? [statement within a question]

Did she say, "Are you ready?" [question within a question]

She shouted, "Impossible!" [quoted exclamation]

Roy screamed, "I'll flunk if I don't read Poe's short story 'The Black Cat'!" [exclamation that does not belong to the material inside the single quotation marks]

"I hope—that is, I—" he began. [dash within a quotation]

"Accept responsibility"—those were his words. [dash that does not belong to the material inside the quotation marks]

4. A single question mark is used in sentence constructions that contain a double question—that is, a quoted question following a question.

Mr. Rodriguez said, "Did he say, 'Are you going?'"

Italics

Italics (slanting type) is used to call special attention to certain words or groups of words. In handwriting, such words are <u>underlined</u>; computers provide italics.

1. Italicize (underline when handwriting) foreign words and phrases that are still listed in the dictionary as foreign.

   c'est la vie   Weltschmerz

2. Italicize (underline when handwriting) titles of books (except the Bible), long poems, plays, magazines, motion pictures, musical compositions, newspapers, and works of art.

   I think Hemingway's best novel is *A Farewell to Arms*.

   His source material was taken from *Time*, *Newsweek*, and the Los Angeles *Times*. [Sometimes the name of the city in titles of newspapers is italicized—for example, the *New York Times*.]

   The *Mona Lisa* is my favorite painting.

3. Italicize (underline when handwriting) the names of ships, airplanes, spacecraft, and trains.

   Ships: *Queen Mary   Lurline   Stockholm*

   Spacecraft: *Challenger   Voyager 2*

4. Italicize (underline when handwriting) to distinguish letters, figures, and words when they refer to themselves rather than to the ideas or things they usually represent.

   Do not leave the second *o* out of *sophomore*.

   Your *3*'s look like *5*'s.

EXERCISE 9   Using Quotation Marks and Italics

Insert quotation marks and italics (underlining) as needed.

1. Professor Jones said, Now we will read from The Complete Works of Edgar Allan Poe.

2. The enthusiastic students shouted, We like Poe! We like Poe!

3. The professor lectured for fifty-seven minutes before he finally said, In conclusion, I say that Poe was an unappreciated writer during his lifetime.

4. The next speaker said, I believe that Poe said, A short story should be short enough so that a person can read it in one sitting.

5. Then, while students squirmed, he read The Fall of the House of Usher in sixty-eight minutes.

6. Now we will do some reading in unison, said Professor Jones.

7. Each student opened a copy of The Complete Works of Edgar Allan Poe.

8. Turn to page 72, said Professor Jones.

9. What parts do we read? asked a student.

10. You read the words, or maybe I should say word, of the raven, said the

   professor.

EXERCISE 10   Using Quotation Marks and Italics

Insert quotation marks and italics (underlining) as needed.

1. The students were not pleased with their small part in the group reading of

   The Raven.

2. They made several derogatory comments about Professor Jones, even though

   he had written a learned textbook titled A Short, Brief, and Concise Study of

   English Rhetoric and the Art of Using English Effectively, Correctly, and Well.

3. As Professor Jones lit candles around a sculpted artwork, one student yelled,

   The poem says bust of Pallas, and that is not Pallas.

4. Professor Jones retorted archly, We didn't have a bust of Pallas in the depart-

   ment, so I brought a bust of Elvis from the chairperson's office.

5. Another student nodded approval and whispered to his enthralled companion,

   That prof is cool, real cool.

6. His companion, an English minor with a keen knowledge of grammar,

   whispered good-naturedly, Really cool is what you mean.

7. Yes, he said, that's what I mean. Sometimes I leave out my ly's and use the

   wrong words, and people think I'm a gashead.

8. The professor reached into his bag of props, took out a dark, feathered

   object, and said, I have brought a stuffed raven.

9. That's not a raven. That's a crow, said a student who was majoring in ornithology.

10. The professor waggled his finger playfully at his audience and said, I believe

   Coleridge once observed, Art sometimes requires the willing suspension of

   disbelief.

Dashes

The **dash** is used when a stronger break than the comma is needed. The dash is typed as two hyphens with no space before or after them (--).

1. Use a dash to indicate a sudden change in sentence construction or an abrupt break in thought.

> Here is the true reason—but maybe you don't care.

2. Use a dash after an introductory list. The words *these*, *those*, *all*, and occasionally *such* introduce the summarizing statement.

> English, French, history—these are the subjects I like.
>
> Dodgers, Giants, Yankees—such names bring back memories of exciting World Series games.

3. Use a dash to set off material that interrupts the flow of an idea, sets off material for emphasis, or restates an idea as an appositive.

> You are—I am certain—not serious. [interrupting]
>
> Our next question is—how much money did we raise? [emphasis]
>
> Dione plays the kazoo—an instrument with a buzz. [restatement]

4. Use a dash to indicate an unfinished statement or word or an interruption. Such interruptions usually occur in dialogue.

> Susan said, "Shall we—" [no question mark]
>
> "I only wanted—" Jason remarked. [no comma]

5. Do *not* use a dash in places in which other marks of punctuation would be more appropriate.

> **Incorrect:**   Lupe found the store—and she shopped.
>
> **Correct:**   Lupe found the store, and she shopped.
>
> **Incorrect:**   I think it is too early to go—
>
> **Correct:**   I think it is too early to go.

Colons

The **colon** is a formal mark of punctuation used chiefly to introduce something that is to follow, such as a list, a quotation, or an explanation.

1. Use a colon after a main clause to introduce a formal list, an emphatic or long restatement (appositive), an explanation, an emphatic statement, or a summary.

> These cars are my favorites: Cadillac, Chevrolet, Toyota, Oldsmobile, and Pontiac. [list]
>
> He worked toward one objective: a degree. [restatement or appositive]
>
> Let me emphasize one point: I do not accept late papers. [emphatic statement]

2. Use a colon to introduce a formal quotation or a formal question.

> Shakespeare's Polonius said: "Neither a borrower nor a lender be." [formal quotation]

> The question is this: Shall we surrender? [formal question]

3. Use a colon in the following conventional ways: to separate a title and subtitle, a chapter and verse in the Bible, and hours and minutes; and after the salutation in a formal business letter.

> Title and subtitle: *Korea: A Country Divided*
> Chapter and verse: Genesis 4:12
> Hour and minutes: 8:25 p.m.
> Salutation: Dear Ms. Chen:

Parentheses

1. Use parentheses to set off material that is not part of the main sentence but is too relevant to omit altogether. This category includes numbers that designate items in a series, amplifying references, explanations, directions, and qualifications.

> He offered two reasons for his losing: (1) he was tired, and (2) he was out of condition. [numbers]

> Review the chapters on the Civil War (6, 7, and 8) for the next class meeting. [references]

> Her husband (she had been married about a year) died last week. [explanation]

2. Use a comma, semicolon, or colon after the parentheses when the sentence punctuation requires their use.

> Although I have not lived here long (I arrived in 2006), this place feels like my only true home.

3. Use a period, a question mark, or an exclamation point in appropriate positions, depending on whether they go with the material within the parentheses or with the entire sentence.

> The greatest English poet of the seventeenth century was John Milton (1608–1674).

> The greatest English poet of the seventeenth century was John Milton. (Some might not agree; I myself favor Andrew Marvell.)

Brackets

Brackets are used within a quotation to set off editorial additions or corrections made by the person who is quoting.

> Churchill said: "It [the Yalta agreement] contained many mistakes."

EXERCISE 11   Using Dashes, Colons, Parentheses, Brackets, and Quotation Marks

Insert dashes, colons, parentheses, brackets, and quotation marks as needed.

1. Many of literature's great works poems, stories, and novels began as dreams.

2. Robert Louis Stevenson 1850–1894, the author of *Treasure Island*, often dreamed complete stories that he would later write.

3. He had the following to say of his tale about Jekyll and Hyde I dreamed the scene . . . in which Hyde, pursued for some crime, took the powder and underwent the change in the presence of his pursuers.

4. Mary Shelley 1797–1851 she was married to Romantic poet Percy Bysshe Shelley said that a nightmare gave her the idea for her novel *Frankenstein*.

5. English Romantic poet Samuel Taylor Coleridge, who is famous for the poem The Rime of the Ancient Mariner, is another literary artist inspired by a dream.

6. One of his best-known poems is titled Kubla Khan: Or, a Vision in a Dream.

7. This poem begins with these famous lines In Xanadu did Kubla Khan / A stately pleasure-dome decree.

8. Coleridge said that he fell asleep after reading in a history book Here the Khan Kubla another spelling of the name is *Kublai Khan* commanded a palace to be built and a stately garden thereunto. And thus ten miles of fertile ground were enclosed within a wall.

9. Poet, philosopher, and literary critic Coleridge had a fertile imagination and a huge intellect.

10. Unfortunately, though, he was interrupted as he composed his verse about Xanadu, and his vision completely evaporated, forcing him to subtitle the poem A Fragment.

EXERCISE 12   Using Dashes, Colons, Parentheses, Brackets, and Quotation Marks

Insert dashes, colons, parentheses, brackets, and quotation marks as needed.

1. Benjamin Franklin 1706–1790 was a remarkable man.

2. In his lifetime, Franklin served in many different roles statesman, scientist, philosopher, and publisher.

3. He rose from humble beginnings his father was a candle-maker to become America's first international celebrity.

4. His fame was due in part to his many inventions bifocals, swim fins, the odometer, the lightning rod, and the urinary catheter, among others.

5. Franklin was also an author his most famous publications were his autobiography and *Poor Richard's Almanack* who had a way with words.

6. In his *Almanack*, he included these clever sayings One today is worth two tomorrows; Early to bed and early to rise makes a man healthy, wealthy, and wise; and A penny saved is a penny earned.

7. In addition to *Poor Richard's* 1733–1758, Franklin published the *Pennsylvania Gazette* 1729–1766.

8. He is the one who left us with this astute aphorism Time is money.

9. Observant, witty, humorous Franklin also wrote, Three may keep a secret, if two of them are dead.

10. He wrote the following clever epitaph for himself The body of Benjamin Franklin, printer (like the cover of an old book, its contents worn out, and stript he used the old spelling of this word of its lettering and gilding), lies here, food for worms! Yet the work itself shall not be lost, for it will, as he believed, appear once more in a new and more beautiful edition, corrected and amended by its Author!

Apostrophes

The **apostrophe** is used with nouns and indefinite pronouns to show possession; to show the omission of letters and figures in contractions; and to form the plurals of letters, numerals, and words referred to as words.

1. A possessive shows that something is owned by someone. Use an apostrophe and *s* to form the possessive of a noun, singular or plural, that does not end in -*s*.

    man*'s* coat   women*'s* suits

2. Use an apostrophe alone to form the possessive of a plural noun ending in -*s*.

    girls' clothes   the Browns' house

3. Use an apostrophe and *s* or the apostrophe alone to form the possessive of singular nouns ending in -*s*. Use the apostrophe and *s* only when you would pronounce the *s*.

    James' hat *or* (if you would pronounce the *s*) James*'s* hat

4. Use an apostrophe and *s* to form the possessive of certain indefinite pronouns.

    everybody*'s* idea   one*'s* meat   another*'s* poison

5. Use an apostrophe to indicate that letters or numerals have been omitted.

    o'clock (short for *of the clock*) in the '90s (short for *1990s*)

6. Use an apostrophe with pronouns only when you are making a contraction. A contraction is a combination of two words. The apostrophe in a contraction indicates where a letter has been omitted.

    it is = it's

    she has = she's

    you are = you're

    If no letters have been left out, do not use an apostrophe.

    Incorrect: The dog bit it's tail. [not a contraction]

    Correct: The dog bit its tail.

    Incorrect: Whose the leader now?

    Correct: Who's the leader now? [a contraction of *who is*]

    Incorrect: Its a big problem.

    Correct: It's a big problem. [a contraction of *it is*]

7. Use an apostrophe to indicate the plural of letters, numerals, and words used as words.

    Dot your *i*'s. five *8*'s *and*'s

    Note that the letters, numerals, and words are italicized, but the apostrophe and *s* are not.

Hyphens

The **hyphen** brings two or more words together into a single compound word. Correct hyphenation, therefore, is essentially a spelling problem rather than one of punctuation. Because the hyphen is not used with any degree of consistency, consult your dictionary for current usage. Study the following as a beginning guide.

1. Use a hyphen to separate the parts of many compound nouns.

   brother-in-law   go-between

2. Use a hyphen between prefixes and proper names.

   all-American   mid-Atlantic

3. Use a hyphen to join two or more words used as a single adjective modifier before a noun.

   bluish-gray eyes   first-class service

4. Use a hyphen with spelled-out compound numbers up to ninety-nine and with fractions.

   twenty-six   two-thirds

Note: Dates, street addresses, numbers requiring more than two words, chapter and page numbers, time followed directly by a.m. or p.m., and figures after a dollar sign or before measurement abbreviations are usually written as figures, not words.

Capitalization

Following are some of the many conventions concerning the use of capital letters in English.

1. Capitalize the first word of a sentence.

2. Capitalize proper nouns and adjectives derived from proper nouns.

   Names of persons

   Edward Jones

   Adjectives derived from proper nouns

   a Shakespearean sonnet   a Miltonic sonnet

   Countries, nationalities, races, languages

   Germany   Spanish

   English   Chinese

   States, regions, localities, other geographical divisions

   California   the South   the Far East

   Oceans, lakes, mountains, deserts, streets, parks

   Lake Superior   Sahara Desert   Fifth Avenue

Educational institutions, schools, courses

>   Santa Ana College   Joe Hill School
>
>   Spanish 3   Rowland High School

Organizations and their members

>   Boston Red Sox   Boy Scouts   Audubon Society

Corporations, governmental agencies or departments, trade names

>   U.S. Steel Corporation   Treasury Department
>
>   Coca-Cola   White Memorial Library

Calendar references such as holidays, days of the week, months

>   Easter   Tuesday   January

Historic eras, periods, documents, laws

>   Romantic Age   First Crusade
>
>   Declaration of Independence   Geneva Convention

3. Capitalize words denoting family relationships when they are used before a name or substituted for a name.

>   He walked with his nephew and Aunt Grace.
>
>   *but*
>
>   He walked with his nephew and his aunt.
>
>   Grandmother and Mother are away on vacation.
>
>   *but*
>
>   My grandmother and my mother are away on vacation.

4. Capitalize abbreviations after names.

>   Henry White Jr.   Juan Gomez, M.D.

5. Capitalize titles of essays, books, plays, movies, poems, magazines, newspapers, musical compositions, songs, and works of art. Do not capitalize articles, short conjunctions, or prepositions unless they come at the beginning or the end of the title.

>   *Desire Under the Elms*   *Terminator*
>
>   *The Last of the Mohicans*   *Of Mice and Men*
>
>   "Blueberry Hill"

6. Capitalize any title preceding a name or used as a substitute for a name. Do not capitalize a title following a name.

>   Judge Wong   Alfred Wong, a judge
>
>   General Clark   Raymond Clark, a general
>
>   Professor Fuentes   Harry Fuentes, the biology professor

EXERCISE 13   Using Capital Letters, Hyphens, Apostrophes, and Quotation Marks

Correct capitalization and insert hyphens, apostrophes, and quotation marks as needed.

1. Ive heard that you intend to move to el paso, texas, my brother in law said.

2. My date of departure on united airlines is july 11, I answered.

3. Then youve only thirty three days remaining in california, he said.

4. My mother gave me some samsonite luggage, and dad gave me a ronson razor.

5. Jennifer does not know i am leaving for the university of texas.

6. Jennifer, my mothers dog, is one quarter poodle and three quarters cocker spaniel.

7. That dogs immediate concern is almost always food rather than sentimentality.

8. I wouldnt have received my scholarship without the straight *A*s from my elective classes.

9. I am quite indebted to professor jackson, a first rate teacher of english and several courses in speech.

10. I wasnt surprised when grandma gave me a box of stationery and a note asking me to write mother each friday.

EXERCISE 14   Using Capital Letters, Hyphens, Apostrophes, and Quotation Marks

Correct capitalization and insert hyphens, apostrophes, and quotation marks as needed.

1. Many young readers of *Harry Potter and the sorcerer's stone* and its sequels wish that Hogwarts school of witchcraft and wizardry were a real place.

2. They wish they could take classes like professor snapes course in making potions or professor mcGonagalls course in transfiguration.

3. In interviews, however, author j.k. rowling says, the setting is a fictional place.

4. Maybe she hasnt heard of flamel college, which was named after nicholas flamel, a first rate alchemist who lived in europe from 1330 to 1418.

8. Parentheses are used to set off material that is of relatively litt. to the main thought of the sentence. Such material—numbers, pa. cal material, figures, supplementary material, and sometimes explar. details—merely amplifies the main thought.

The years of the era (1961–1973) were full of action.

Several factors dictated his choice: (1) style, (2) purchase price, (3) safety features, and (4) operating expense.

9. Brackets are used within a quotation to set off editorial additions or corrections made by the person who is quoting.

"It [the Yalta Agreement] contained many mistakes."

10. The **apostrophe** is used with nouns and indefinite pronouns to show possession, to show the omission of letters and figures in contractions, and to form the plurals of letters, figures, and words referred to as words.

man's coat   girls' clothes   can't   five *and*'s   it's [contraction]

11. The **hyphen** is used to link two or more words together into a single compound word. Hyphenation, therefore, is essentially a spelling problem rather than a punctuation problem. Because the hyphen is not used with any degree of consistency, it is best to consult your dictionary to learn current usage.

a. Use a hyphen to separate the parts of many compound words.

about-face   go-between

b. Use a hyphen between prefixes and proper names.

all-American   mid-July

c. Use a hyphen with spelled-out compound numbers up to ninety-nine and with fractions.

twenty-six   one hundred   two-thirds

d. Use a hyphen to join two or more words used as a single adjective modifier before a noun.

first-class service   hard-fought game   sad-looking mother

12. English has many conventions concerning the use of capital letters. Although style and use of capital letters may vary, certain rules for capitalization are well established.

a. Capitalize the first word of a sentence.

b. Capitalize proper nouns and adjectives derived from proper nouns such as the names of persons, countries, nationalities and races, days of the week, months, and titles of books.

c. Capitalize words denoting family relationships when they are used before a name or substituted for a name.

The minister greeted Aunt May, my grandfather, and Mother.

5. Legend has it that flamel actually achieved every alchemists life long goal when he figured out how to turn other metals into gold.

6. Through the sacramento, california, institution named for him, would be witches and wizards can now earn credentials with names like diploma in magic and degree in esoteric arts.

7. Classes include crystal magic, developing psychic abilities, and pagan paths.

8. The person who described the college on its website wrote, we offer an unconventional curriculum.

9. The faculty of flamel college includes well known astrologers, witches, alchemists, and experts on ghosts and hauntings.

10. If you get straight *A*s in your courses, maybe you can command a few spirits to write your dissertation for you.

EXERCISE 15   Using Capital Letters and All Punctuation Marks

Correct capitalization and insert punctuation marks as needed.

will rogers 1879–1935 was a famous movie star newspaper writer and lecturer. Part cherokee indian he was born in what was then indian territory before oklahoma became a state. He is especially known for his humor and his social and political criticism. He said my ancestors may not have come over on the *mayflower*, but they met em at the boat. He said that when many oklahomans moved to california in the early 1930s the average IQ increased in both states. In his early years, he was a first class performer in rodeos circuses and variety shows. When he performed in variety shows he often twirled a rope. He usually began his presentations by saying, all I know is what I read in the papers. Continuing to be close to his oklahoma roots he appeared in fifty one silent movies and twenty one talking movies. At the age of fifty six he was killed in an airplane crash near Point Barrow Alaska. He was so popular and influential that his statue now stands in washington d.c. On another statue of him in Claremore Oklahoma is inscribed one of his most famous sayings I never met a man I didn't like.

CHAPTER REVIEW   Punctuation and Capitalization

1. There are three marks of **end punctuation**.

  a. Periods

    Place a period after a statement.

    Place a period after common abbreviations.

  b. Question marks

    Place a question mark at the end of a direct question.

    Do not use a question mark after an indirect question.

        She asked me what caused the slide.

  c. Exclamation points

    Place an exclamation point after a word or group of words that expresses strong feeling.

    Do not overwork the exclamation point. Do not use double exclamation points.

2. The **comma** is used to separate and to set off sentence elements.

  a. Use a comma to separate main clauses joined by one of the coordinating conjunctions—*for*, *and*, *nor*, *but*, *or*, *yet*, *so*.

        We went to the game, but it was canceled.

  b. Use a comma after long introductory modifiers. The modifiers may be phrases or dependent clauses.

        Before she and I arrived, the meeting was called to order.

  c. Use a comma to separate words, phrases, and clauses in a series.

        He ran down the street, across the park, and into the forest.

  d. Use a comma to separate coordinate adjectives not joined by *and* that modify the same noun.

        I need a sturdy, reliable truck.

  e. Use a comma to separate sentence elements that might be misread.

        Outside, the thunder rolled.

  f. Use commas to set off nonessential (unnecessary for the meaning of the sentence) words, phrases, and clauses.

        Maria, who studied hard, will pass.

  g. Use commas to set off nouns used as direct address.

        What do you intend to do, Hamlet?

  h. Use commas to separate the numbers in a date.

        November 11, 1918, is a day worth remembering.

  i. Use commas to separate the city from the state. No comma is used between the state and the zip code.

        Boston, MA 02110

3. The **semicolon** indicates a longer pause and stronger emphasis than the comma. It is used principally to separate main clauses within a sentence.

  a. Use a semicolon to separate main clauses not joined by a coordinating conjunction.

        You must buy that car today; tomorrow will be too late.

  b. Use a semicolon between two main clauses joined by a conjunctive adverb (such as *however*, *otherwise*, *therefore*, *similarly*, *hence*, *on the other hand*, *then*, *consequently*, *accordingly*, *thus*).

        It was very late; therefore, I remained at the hotel.

4. **Quotation marks** bring special attention to words.

  a. Quotation marks are used principally to set off direct quotations. A direct quotation consists of material taken from the written work or the direct speech of others; it is set off by double quotation marks. Single quotation marks are used to set off a quotation within a quotation.

        He said, "I don't remember if she said, 'Wait for me.'"

  b. Use double quotation marks to set off slang, technical terms, and special words.

        The "platoon system" changed the game of football. [technical term]

5. **Italics** (slanting type) are also used to call special attention to certain words or groups of words. In handwriting or typing, such words are underlined.

  a. Italicize (underline) foreign words and phrases that are still listed in the dictionary as foreign.

        la dolce vita　　*perestroika*

  b. Italicize (underline when handwriting) titles of books; long poems; plays; magazines; motion pictures; musical compositions; newspapers; works of art; names of aircraft and ships; and letters, numbers, and words referred to by their own name.

        War and Peace　　*Apollo 12*　　leaving the second *o* out of *sophomore*

6. The **dash** is used when a stronger pause than the comma is needed. It can also be used to indicate a break in the flow of thought and to emphasize words (less formal than the colon in this situation).

        I can't remember the town—now I do—it's Tupelo.

7. The **colon** is a formal mark of punctuation used chiefly to introduce something that is to follow, such as a list, a quotation, or an explanation.

        These cars are my favorites: Cadillac, Chevrolet, Toyota, Oldsmobile, and Pontiac.

5. Legend has it that flamel actually achieved every alchemists life long goal when he figured out how to turn other metals into gold.

6. Through the sacramento, california, institution named for him, would be witches and wizards can now earn credentials with names like diploma in magic and degree in esoteric arts.

7. Classes include crystal magic, developing psychic abilities, and pagan paths.

8. The person who described the college on its website wrote, we offer an unconventional curriculum.

9. The faculty of flamel college includes well known astrologers, witches, alchemists, and experts on ghosts and hauntings.

10. If you get straight *As* in your courses, maybe you can command a few spirits to write your dissertation for you.

EXERCISE 15   Using Capital Letters and All Punctuation Marks

Correct capitalization and insert punctuation marks as needed.

will rogers 1879–1935 was a famous movie star newspaper writer and lecturer. Part cherokee indian he was born in what was then indian territory before oklahoma became a state. He is especially known for his humor and his social and political criticism. He said my ancestors may not have come over on the *mayflower*, but they met em at the boat. He said that when many oklahomans moved to california in the early 1930s the average IQ increased in both states. In his early years, he was a first class performer in rodeos circuses and variety shows. When he performed in variety shows he often twirled a rope. He usually began his presentations by saying, all I know is what I read in the papers. Continuing to be close to his oklahoma roots he appeared in fifty one silent movies and twenty one talking movies. At the age of fifty six he was killed in an airplane crash near Point Barrow Alaska. He was so popular and influential that his statue now stands in washington d.c. On another statue of him in Claremore Oklahoma is inscribed one of his most famous sayings I never met a man I didn't like.

CHAPTER REVIEW Punctuation and Capitalization

1. There are three marks of **end punctuation**.

    a. Periods
      Place a period after a statement.
      Place a period after common abbreviations.

    b. Question marks
      Place a question mark at the end of a direct question.
      Do not use a question mark after an indirect question.

          She asked me what caused the slide.

    c. Exclamation points
      Place an exclamation point after a word or group of words that expresses strong feeling.
      Do not overwork the exclamation point. Do not use double exclamation points.

2. The **comma** is used to separate and to set off sentence elements.

    a. Use a comma to separate main clauses joined by one of the coordinating conjunctions—*for, and, nor, but, or, yet, so.*

          We went to the game, but it was canceled.

    b. Use a comma after long introductory modifiers. The modifiers may be phrases or dependent clauses.

          Before she and I arrived, the meeting was called to order.

    c. Use a comma to separate words, phrases, and clauses in a series.

          He ran down the street, across the park, and into the forest.

    d. Use a comma to separate coordinate adjectives not joined by *and* that modify the same noun.

          I need a sturdy, reliable truck.

    e. Use a comma to separate sentence elements that might be misread.

          Outside, the thunder rolled.

    f. Use commas to set off nonessential (unnecessary for the meaning of the sentence) words, phrases, and clauses.

          Maria, who studied hard, will pass.

    g. Use commas to set off nouns used as direct address.

          What do you intend to do, Hamlet?

    h. Use commas to separate the numbers in a date.

          November 11, 1918, is a day worth remembering.

    i. Use commas to separate the city from the state. No comma is used between the state and the zip code.

          Boston, MA 02110

3. The **semicolon** indicates a longer pause and stronger emphasis than the comma. It is used principally to separate main clauses within a sentence.

   a. Use a semicolon to separate main clauses not joined by a coordinating conjunction.

      You must buy that car today; tomorrow will be too late.

   b. Use a semicolon between two main clauses joined by a conjunctive adverb (such as *however, otherwise, therefore, similarly, hence, on the other hand, then, consequently, accordingly, thus*).

      It was very late; therefore, I remained at the hotel.

4. **Quotation marks** bring special attention to words.

   a. Quotation marks are used principally to set off direct quotations. A direct quotation consists of material taken from the written work or the direct speech of others; it is set off by double quotation marks. Single quotation marks are used to set off a quotation within a quotation.

      He said, "I don't remember if she said, 'Wait for me.'"

   b. Use double quotation marks to set off slang, technical terms, and special words.

      The "platoon system" changed the game of football. [technical term]

5. **Italics** (slanting type) are also used to call special attention to certain words or groups of words. In handwriting or typing, such words are underlined.

   a. Italicize (underline) foreign words and phrases that are still listed in the dictionary as foreign.

      la dolce vita   *perestroika*

   b. Italicize (underline when handwriting) titles of books; long poems; plays; magazines; motion pictures; musical compositions; newspapers; works of art; names of aircraft and ships; and letters, numbers, and words referred to by their own name.

      War and Peace   *Apollo 12*   leaving the second *o* out of *sophomore*

6. The **dash** is used when a stronger pause than the comma is needed. It can also be used to indicate a break in the flow of thought and to emphasize words (less formal than the colon in this situation).

      I can't remember the town—now I do—it's Tupelo.

7. The **colon** is a formal mark of punctuation used chiefly to introduce something that is to follow, such as a list, a quotation, or an explanation.

      These cars are my favorites: Cadillac, Chevrolet, Toyota, Oldsmobile, and Pontiac.

8. **Parentheses** are used to set off material that is of relatively little importance to the main thought of the sentence. Such material—numbers, parenthetical material, figures, supplementary material, and sometimes explanatory details—merely amplifies the main thought.

> The years of the era (1961–1973) were full of action.

> Several factors dictated his choice: (1) style, (2) purchase price, (3) safety features, and (4) operating expense.

9. **Brackets** are used within a quotation to set off editorial additions or corrections made by the person who is quoting.

> "It [the Yalta Agreement] contained many mistakes."

10. The **apostrophe** is used with nouns and indefinite pronouns to show possession, to show the omission of letters and figures in contractions, and to form the plurals of letters, figures, and words referred to as words.

> man's coat   girls' clothes   can't   five *and*'s   it's [contraction]

11. The **hyphen** is used to link two or more words together into a single compound word. Hyphenation, therefore, is essentially a spelling problem rather than a punctuation problem. Because the hyphen is not used with any degree of consistency, it is best to consult your dictionary to learn current usage.

   a. Use a hyphen to separate the parts of many compound words.

   > about-face   go-between

   b. Use a hyphen between prefixes and proper names.

   > all-American   mid-July

   c. Use a hyphen with spelled-out compound numbers up to ninety-nine and with fractions.

   > twenty-six   one hundred   two-thirds

   d. Use a hyphen to join two or more words used as a single adjective modifier before a noun.

   > first-class service   hard-fought game   sad-looking mother

12. English has many conventions concerning the use of capital letters. Although style and use of capital letters may vary, certain rules for capitalization are well established.

   a. Capitalize the first word of a sentence.

   b. Capitalize proper nouns and adjectives derived from proper nouns such as the names of persons, countries, nationalities and races, days of the week, months, and titles of books.

   c. Capitalize words denoting family relationships when they are used before a name or substituted for a name.

   > The minister greeted Aunt May, my grandfather, and Mother.

CHAPTER REVIEW   Exercises

REVIEW 1

Using Capital Letters and All Punctuation Marks

Correct capitalization and insert punctuation marks as needed.

1. everyone defines the term success differently how do you define it

2. according to american author and editor christopher morley the only success is
   being able to spend your life the way you want to spend it

3. margaret thatcher former leader of great britain said that success is being
   good at what youre doing but also having a sense of purpose

4. author vernon howard had this to say on the subject "you have succeeded in
   life when all you really want is only what you really need

5. albert einstein however believed that if *A* equals success in life then
   $A = x + y + z$

6. x is work *y* is play and *z* is keeping your mouth shut

7. one of the most well known quotes about success comes from philosopher
   ralph waldo emerson who wrote that to have succeeded is "to leave the world
   a bit better" and "to know that even one life has breathed easier because you
   have lived

REVIEW 2

Using Capital Letters and All Punctuation Marks

Correct capitalization and insert punctuation marks as needed.

Jack (Jackie) Roosevelt Robinson 1919–1972 was born in Pasadena California.
After excelling in sports in high school and community college he transferred to
UCLA, where he lettered in four sports baseball, basketball, football, and track.
In world war II he was commissioned second lieutenant in the army. After he was
discharged he joined the negro league as a player with the Kansas City Monarchs
for $100 a week. In 1947 he was offered a tryout with the Brooklyn dodgers.
Before no African-Americans had been allowed to participate in the minor or major
leagues. After signing a contract, Jackie Robinson was sent to the minor leagues
and there he played for one year with Montreal a team in the International

League. Following a year in which he was the best hitter in the league he was brought up to the major leagues. During the first year 1947 he showed his greatness and was named the rookie of the year. Two years later he was the most valuable player in the national league and won the batting title with a .342 average. Despite the initial bigoted opposition by some baseball fans and players he performed with dignity courage and skill. Nevertheless he was an independent proud person. In the book Players of Cooperstown Mike Tully wrote he Robinson refused to be someone he was not, refused to conform to an image of a man who 'knew his place.' Because sports is such a high profile activity Jackie Robinson is credited with playing a significant role in breaking down the racial barriers in society. In his ten years in the major leagues he helped his team reach the world series six times. He was inducted into the Baseball hall of fame in 1962.

REVIEW 3

Demonstrating Ability to Use Correct Punctuation

Demonstrate your ability to use correct punctuation by writing sentences that contain the following marks. Use the topics in parentheses.

Comma (travel)

1. To separate independent clauses in a compound sentence using coordinating conjunctions (FANBOYS)

   _____

   _____

   _____

2. For long introductory modifiers

   _____

   _____

   _____

3. To separate words in a series

   _____

   _____

   _____

Semicolon (a family member)

4. To connect two related independent clauses without a coordinating conjunction

_____

_____

_____

Quotation Marks (Use this textbook as your source for quotations.)

5. To set off a quotation (words taken from the written work or the speech of others)

_____

_____

_____

Italics, Shown by Underlining (school)

6. Word or letter referred to by its name

_____

_____

_____

7. Title of a book

_____

_____

_____

Colon (computers)

8. To introduce a list

_____

_____

_____

Apostrophe (friendship)

9. A singular possessive

_____

_____

_____

10. A plural possessive

_____

_____

_____

11. A contraction

_____

_____

_____

Hyphen (shopping)

12. Numbers

_____

_____

_____

STUDENT COMPANION SITE
For additional practice, visit www.cengage .com/devenglish/ brandon/sph6e.

13. Two-word modifiers

_____

_____

_____

MICROTHEME

To practice your skills acquired in this chapter, return to the Microtheme on page 208 and complete Exercise B.

Chapter 12

Spelling and Phrasing

FLOW OF WRITING

MICROTHEME	Writing Activity in Miniature

EXERCISE A

Before you work on this chapter, write a Microtheme on the following topic. Write small enough to leave room for marking later. **After** you have studied this chapter, return to your Microtheme and complete Exercise B to practice what you have learned.

Suggested Microtheme Topic: Write a Microtheme of 80 to 100 words about an imaginary vacation to a time and place of your choice. (Space travel is acceptable, but no space-alien abduction pieces unless approved by your instructor.)

EXERCISE B

Connecting Your Learning Objectives with Your Microtheme

Complete this exercise after you have studied this chapter.

1. Circle the questionable spelling of words and check them in a dictionary.
2. Make sure you did not use second-best words because you could not spell the best words.
3. Clear your writing of wordy phrases.

FLOW OF WRITING

Some people are born good spellers. They see a word and can spell it correctly forever; others struggle. This chapter offers you a systematic approach and several strategies for spelling correctly in a language that is inconsistent to a significant degree. Some words just do not look the way they sound; they are not phonetic, and they do not pattern in ways parallel with other words of the same spelling. This anonymous poem shows some of the problems:

> When in the English language we speak
> Why is *break* not rhymed with *freak*?
> Will you tell me why it's true
> That we *sew*, but we also saw *few*?
> And why cannot makers of verse
> Rhyme the word *horse* with *worse*?
> *Beard* sounds much different from *heard*
> *Cord* is so different from *word*
> *Cow* is *cow*, but *low* is *low*.
> *Shoe* never rhymes with *foe*,
> And think of *hose*, and *dose*, and *lose*,
> And think of *goose* and yet of *choose*,
> *Doll* and *roll*, and *home* and *some*.
> And since *pay* is rhymed with *say*,
> Why *paid* and *said*, I pray?
> *Mood* is not pronounced like *wood*
> And *done* is not like *gone* and *lone*.
> To sum it all up, it seems to me
> That sounds and letters just do not agree.

Despite these problems inherent in the English language, you can be an effective speller. Unfortunately, for those who are not, there are unhappy consequences. In a society as literate as ours, if you are a poor speller, you will find yourself with a serious handicap. The professions and trades, as well as schools, are demanding that individuals spell well and write effectively. If you write *thier* for *their* or *definately* for *definitely* in compositions, term reports, examinations, letters of application, or business reports, you will draw unfavorable attention from your audience.

Steps to Efficient Spelling

1. Make up your mind that you are going to spell well.

2. Use your Self-Evaluation Chart (on the inside front cover of this book) to keep a list of words you misspell; work on spelling them correctly.

3. Get into the habit of looking up new words in a dictionary for correct spelling as well as for meaning.

4. Look at each letter in a word carefully and pronounce each syllable; that is, *change-a-ble, con-tin-u-ous, dis-ap-pear-ance*.

5. Visualize how the word is made up.

6. Write the word correctly several times. After each writing, close your eyes and again visualize the word.

7. Set up frequent recall sessions with problem words. Become aware of the reasons for your errors.

Your Spell Checker

Your computer spell checker is an important tool with many benefits and some limitations. With about 100,000 words in a typical database, the spell checker alerts you to problem words that should be verified. If you agree that the spelling of a word should be checked, you can then select from a list of words with similar spellings. A likely substitute word will be highlighted. With a keystroke, you can correct a problem, add your own word to the database, or ignore the alert. With a few more keystrokes, you can type in your own correction. You may even be able to program your spell checker to correct automatically your most frequent spelling or typing errors. You will be amazed at how many times your computer will catch misspellings that your eye did not see.

However, the spell checker has limitations. If you intended to type *he* and instead typed *me*, the spell checker will not alert you to a possible problem because the word you typed is spelled correctly. If you use the wrong word, such as *herd* instead of *heard*, the spell checker will not detect a problem. Thus you should always proofread your writing after you have spell checked it. Do not be lulled into a false sense of spelling security simply because you have a machine on your side. As a writer, you are the final spell checker.

Spelling Tips

The following tips will help you become a better speller:

1. Do not omit letters.

Many errors occur because certain letters are omitted when the word is pronounced or spelled. Observe the omissions in the following words. Then concentrate on learning the correct spellings.

Incorrect	Correct	Incorrect	Correct
agravate	aggravate	irigation	irrigation
ajourned	adjourned	libary	library
aproved	approved	paralell	parallel
aquaintance	acquaintance	parlament	parliament
artic	arctic	paticulaly	particularly
comodity	commodity	readly	readily
efficent	efficient	sophmore	sophomore
envirnment	environment	stricly	strictly
familar	familiar	unconsious	unconscious

2. Do not add letters.

Incorrect	Correct	Incorrect	Correct
athelete	athlete	ommission	omission
comming	coming	pasttime	pastime
drownded	drowned	priviledge	privilege

Incorrect	Correct	Incorrect	Correct
folk*es*	folks	simil*i*ar	similar
occa*s*sionally	occasionally	tra*d*gedy	tragedy

3. **Do not substitute incorrect letters for correct letters.**

Incorrect	Correct	Incorrect	Correct
benefi*s*ial	benefi*c*ial	offen*c*e	offen*s*e
bull*i*tins	bull*e*tins	peculi*e*r	peculi*a*r
*s*ensus	*c*ensus	re*s*itation	re*c*itation
d*i*scription	d*e*scription	scre*a*ch	scre*e*ch
de*s*ease	d*i*sease	substan*s*ial	substan*t*ial
dissen*t*ion	dissen*s*ion	surpri*z*e	surpri*s*e
it*i*ms	it*e*ms	techn*a*cal	techn*i*cal

4. **Do not transpose letters.**

Incorrect	Correct	Incorrect	Correct
alu*nm*i	alu*mn*i	p*re*haps	p*er*haps
child*er*n	child*re*n	p*er*fer	p*re*fer
dup*il*cate	dup*li*cate	p*er*scription	p*re*scription
irre*ve*lant	irre*le*vant	princip*el*s	princip*le*s
kind*el*	kind*le*	ye*i*ld	y*ie*ld

Note: Whenever you notice other words that fall into any one of these categories, add them to the list.

5. **Apply the spelling rules for spelling *ei* and *ie* words correctly.**

Remember the poem?

Use *i* before *e*
Except after *c*
Or when sounded like *a*
As in *neighbor* and *weigh*.

i before e

achieve	chief	niece	relieve
belief	field	piece	shield
believe	grief	pierce	siege
brief	hygiene	relief	variety

Except after c

ceiling	conceive	deceive	receipt
conceit	deceit	perceive	receive

Exceptions: either, financier, height, leisure, neither, seize, species, weird

When sounded like a

deign	freight	neighbor	sleigh
eight	heinous	reign	veil
feign	heir	rein	vein
feint	neigh	skein	weigh

6. **Apply the rules for dropping the final *e* or retaining the final *e* when a suffix is added.**

Words ending in a silent *e* usually drop the *e* before a suffix beginning with a vowel; for example, *accuse* + *-ing* = *accusing*. Here are some common suffixes beginning with a vowel: *-able*, *-age*, *-al*, *-ary*, *-ation*, *-ence*, *-ing*, *-ion*, *-ous*, *-ure*.

admire + *-able* = admirable   imagine + *-ary* = imaginary
arrive + *-al* = arrival   locate + *-ion* = location
come + *-ing* = coming   please + *-ure* = pleasure
explore + *-ation* = exploration   plume + *-age* = plumage
fame + *-ous* = famous   precede + *-ence* = precedence

Exceptions: *dye* + *-ing* = *dyeing* (to distinguish it from *dying*), *acreage*, *mileage*.

Words ending in a silent *e* usually retain the *e* before a suffix beginning with a consonant; for example: *arrange* + *-ment* = *arrangement*. Here are some common suffixes beginning with a consonant: *-craft*, *-ful*, *-less*, *-ly*, *-mate*, *-ment*, *-ness*, *-ty*.

entire + *-ty* = entirety   manage + *-ment* = management
hate + *-ful* = hateful   safe + *-ly* = safely
hope + *-less* = hopeless   stale + *-mate* = stalemate
like + *-ness* = likeness   state + *-craft* = statecraft

Exceptions: Some words taking the *-ful* or *-ly* suffixes drop the final *e*:

awe + *-ful* = awful   true + *-ly* = truly
due + *-ly* = duly   whole + *-ly* = wholly

Some words taking the suffix *-ment* drop the final *e*; for example:

acknowledgment   argument   judgment

Words ending in silent *e* after *c* or *g* retain the *e* when the suffix begins with the vowel *a* or *o*. The final *e* is retained to keep the *c* or *g* soft before the suffixes.

advantageous   noticeable
courageous   peaceable

7. **Apply the rules for doubling a final consonant before a suffix beginning with a vowel.**

Words of one syllable:

blot	blotted	get	getting	rob	robbed
brag	bragging	hop	hopped	run	running
cut	cutting	hot	hottest	sit	sitting
drag	dragged	man	mannish	stop	stopped
drop	dropped	plan	planned	swim	swimming

Words accented on the last syllable:

acquit	acquitted	commit	committee
admit	admittance	concur	concurring
allot	allotted	confer	conferring
begin	beginning	defer	deferring

equip	equipped	refer	referred
occur	occurrence	submit	submitted
omit	omitting	transfer	transferred
prefer	preferred		

Words that are not accented on the last syllable and words that do not end in a single consonant preceded by a vowel do not double the final consonant (regardless of whether the suffix begins with a vowel).

Frequently Misspelled Words

a lot	eighth	likely
absence	eligible	lying
across	eliminate	marriage
actually	embarrassed	mathematics
all right	environment	meant
among	especially	medicine
analyze	etc.	neither
appearance	exaggerate	ninety
appreciate	excellent	ninth
argument	exercise	nuclear
athlete	existence	occasionally
athletics	experience	opinion
awkward	explanation	opportunity
becoming	extremely	parallel
beginning	familiar	particular
belief	February	persuade
benefit	finally	physically
buried	foreign	planned
business	government	pleasant
certain	grammar	possible
college	grateful	practical
coming	guarantee	preferred
committee	guard	prejudice
competition	guidance	privilege
complete	height	probably
consider	hoping	professor
criticism	humorous	prove
definitely	immediately	psychology
dependent	independent	pursue
develop	intelligence	receipt
development	interest	receive
difference	interfere	recommend
disastrous	involved	reference
discipline	knowledge	relieve
discussed	laboratory	religious
disease	leisure	repetition
divide	length	rhythm
dying	library	ridiculous

sacrifice	sincerely	tried
safety	sophomore	tries
scene	speech	truly
schedule	straight	unfortunately
secretary	studying	unnecessary
senior	succeed	until
sense	success	unusual
separate	suggest	using
severely	surprise	usually
shining	thoroughly	Wednesday
significant	though	writing
similar	tragedy	written

Confused Spelling and Confusing Words

The following are more words that are commonly misspelled or confused with one another. Some have similar sounds, some are often mispronounced, and some are only misunderstood.

a	An adjective (called an article) used before a word beginning with a consonant or a consonant sound, as in "I ate *a* donut."
an	An adjective (called an article) used before a word beginning with a vowel (*a*, *e*, *i*, *o*, *u*) or with a silent *h*, as in "I ate *an* artichoke."
and	A coordinating conjunction, as in "Sara *and* I like Johnny Cash."
accept	A verb meaning "to receive," as in "I *accept* your explanation."
except	A preposition meaning "to exclude," as in "I paid everyone *except* you."
advice	A noun meaning "guidance," as in "Thanks for the *advice*."
advise	A verb meaning "to give guidance," as in "Will you please *advise* me of my rights?"
all right	An adjective meaning "correct" or "acceptable," as in "It's *all right* to cry."
alright	Not used in formal writing.
all ready	An adjective that can be used interchangeably with *ready*, as in "I am *all ready* to go to town."
already	An adverb meaning "before," which cannot be used in place of *ready*, as in "I have *already* finished."
a lot	An adverb meaning "much," as in "She liked him *a lot*," or a noun meaning "several," as in "I had *a lot* of suggestions."
alot	Misspelling.
altogether	An adverb meaning "completely," as in "He is *altogether* happy."
all together	An adverb meaning "as one," which can be used interchangeably with *together*, as in "The group left *all together*."
choose	A present-tense verb meaning "to select," as in "Do whatever you *choose*."
chose	The past-tense form of the verb *choose*, as in "They *chose* to take action yesterday."
could of	A misspelled phrase caused by confusing *could've*, meaning *could have*, with *could of*.

could have	Correctly spelled phrase, as in "I *could have* danced all night."
effect	Usually a noun meaning "result," as in "That *effect* was unexpected."
affect	Usually a verb meaning "change," as in "Ideas *affect* me."
hear	A verb indicating the receiving of sound, as in "I *hear* thunder."
here	An adverb meaning "present location," as in "I live *here*."
it's	A contraction of *it is*, as in "*It's* time to dance."
its	Possessive pronoun, as in "Each dog has *its* day."
know	A verb usually meaning "to comprehend" or "to recognize," as in "I *know* the answer."
no	An adjective meaning "negative," as in "I have *no* potatoes."
lead	A present-tense verb, as in "I *lead* a stable life now," or a noun referring to a substance, such as "I sharpened the *lead* in my pencil."
led	The past-tense form of the verb *lead*, as in "I *led* a wild life in my youth."
loose	An adjective meaning "without restraint," as in "He is a *loose* cannon."
lose	A present-tense verb from the pattern *lose, lost, lost*, as in "I thought I would *lose* my senses."
paid	The past-tense form of *pay*, as in "He *paid* his dues."
payed	Misspelling.
passed	The past-tense form of the verb *pass*, meaning "went by," as in "He *passed* me on the curve."
past	An adjective meaning "former," as in "That's *past* history," or a noun, as in "He lived in the *past*."
patience	A noun meaning "willingness to wait," as in "Job was a man of much *patience*."
patients	A noun meaning "people under care," as in "The doctor had fifty *patients*."
peace	A noun meaning "a quality of calmness" or "absence of strife," as in "The guru was at *peace* with the world."
piece	A noun meaning "part," as in "I gave him a *piece* of my mind."
quiet	An adjective meaning "silent," as in "She was a *quiet* child."
quit	A verb meaning "to cease" or "to withdraw," as in "I *quit* my job."
quite	An adverb meaning "very," as in "The clam is *quite* happy."
receive	A verb meaning "to accept," as in "I will *receive* visitors now."
recieve	Misspelling.
stationary	An adjective meaning "not moving," as in "Try to avoid running into *stationary* objects."
stationery	A noun meaning "paper material to write on," as in "I bought a box of *stationery* for Sue's birthday present."
than	A conjunction, as in "He is taller *than* I am."
then	An adverb, as in "She *then* left town."
their	A possessive pronoun, as in "They read *their* books."
there	An adverb, as in "He left it *there*," or a filler word, as in "*There* is no time left."
they're	A contraction of *they are*, as in "*They're* happy."
to	A preposition, as in "I went *to* town."

too	An adverb meaning "excessively" or "very," as in "You are *too* late to qualify for the discount," or "also," as in "I have feelings, *too*."
two	An adjective of number, as in "I have *two* jobs."
thorough	An adjective meaning "complete" or "careful," as in "He did a *thorough* job."
through	A preposition, as in "She went *through* the yard."
truly	An adverb meaning "sincerely" or "completely," as in "He was *truly* happy."
truely	Misspelling.
weather	A noun meaning "condition of the atmosphere," as in "The *weather* is pleasant today."
whether	A conjunction, as in "*Whether* he would go was of no consequence."
write	A present-tense verb, as in "Watch me as I *write* this letter."
writen	Misspelling.
written	Past participle of the verb *write*, as in "I have *written* the letter."
you're	A contraction of *you are*, as in "*You're* my friend."
your	A possessive pronoun, as in "I like *your* looks."

EXERCISE 1   Spelling Confusing Words

Underline the correct word or words.

1. I cannot (hear, here) the answers.

2. She is taller (then, than) I.

3. They left town to find (their, they're, there) roots.

4. Sam went (through, thorough) the initiation.

5. I am only asking for a little (peace, piece) of the action.

6. Whatever you say is (alright, all right) with me.

7. I (passed, past) the test, and now I'm ready for action.

8. That smash was (to, too, two) hot to handle.

9. I did not ask for her (advise, advice).

10. I found (a lot, alot) of new ideas in that book.

11. She has (all ready, already) left.

12. I (chose, choose) my answer and hoped for the best.

13. I knew that I would (recieve, receive) fair treatment.

14. Juan was (quit, quite, quiet) happy with my decision.

15. Maria (could of, could have) completed the assignment.

16. Marlin knew they would (lose, loose) the game.

17. I've heard that (it's, its) a good movie.

18. June would not (accept, except) my answer.

19. I did not (know, no) what to do.

20. Sean (paid, payed) his bill and left town.

EXERCISE 2   Spelling Confusing Words

Underline the correct word or words.

1. She said that my application was (alright, all right).

2. Sheriff Dillon worked hard for (peace, piece) in the valley.

3. She was the first woman to (recieve, receive) a medal.

4. He spoke his mind; (then, than) he left.

5. The cleaners did a (through, thorough) job.

6. After the loud explosion, there was (quit, quiet, quite).

7. The nurse worked diligently with his (patience, patients).

8. They were not (altogether, all together) happy, but they (could of, could have) been.

9. Yesterday, the cowboys (led, lead) the cows to water.

10. For my hobby, I study (grammar, grammer).

11. Elvis (truly, truely) respected his mother.

12. Zeke asked for the (whether, weather) report.

13. I never (advise, advice) my friends about gambling.

14. You should (accept, except) responsibility for your actions.

15. Joan inherited (alot, a lot) of money.

16. We waited for the gorilla to (chose, choose) a mate.

17. Virginia thinks (its, it's) a good day for a party.

18. It was a tale of (to, too, two) cities.

19. I went (they're, their, there) to my childhood home.

20. It was the best letter Kevin had ever (writen, written, wrote).

Wordy Phrases

Certain phrases clutter sentences, consuming our time in writing and our readers' time in reading. Watch for wordy phrases as you revise and edit your composition.

Wordy: *Due to the fact that* he was unemployed, he had to use public transportation.

Concise:	*Because* he was unemployed, he had to use public transportation.
Wordy:	*Deep down inside* he believed that the Red Sox would win.
Concise:	He believed that the Red Sox would win.

Wordy	Concise
at the present time	now
basic essentials	essentials
blend together	blend
it is clear that	(delete)
due to the fact that	because
for the reason that	because
I felt inside	I felt
in most cases	usually
as a matter of fact	in fact
in the event that	if
until such time as	until
I personally feel	I feel
in this modern world	today
in order to	to
most of the people	most people
along the lines of	like
past experience	experience
at that point in time	then
in the final analysis	finally
in the near future	soon
have a need for	need
in this day and age	now

EXERCISE 3   Wordy Phrasing

Circle the wordy phrases and write in concise phrases.

1. I tried to recall that moment, but my memories seemed to blend together.

2. I expect to get out of this bed and go to work in the near future.

3. As a matter of fact, when I was a child, I had an imaginary playmate.

4. I feel in my heart that bees work too hard.

5. I am not surprised by this conviction due to the fact that as a child he used to torment vegetables.

6. In this modern world most of the people do not use enough shoe polish.

7. I was crowned Mr. Clean for the reason that I always wash my hands before I wash my hands.

8. At the present time I am concentrating on not thinking about warthogs.

9. Procrastination is an idea I will consider in the near future.

10. I personally feel that Cupid just shot me with a poisoned arrow.

CHAPTER REVIEW   Spelling and Phrasing

1. Do not omit letters.

   Incorrect: *libary*

   Correct: *library*

2. Do not add letters.

   Incorrect: *athalete*

   Correct: *athlete*

3. Do not substitute incorrect letters for correct letters.

   Incorrect: *technacal*

   Correct: *technical*

4. Do not transpose letters.

   Incorrect: *perfer*

   Correct: *prefer*

5. Apply the spelling rules for spelling *ei* and *ie* words correctly.

   Use *i* before *e*
   Except after *c*
   Or when sounded like *a*
   As in *neighbor* and *weigh*.

   Exceptions: *either, financier, height, leisure, neither, seize, species, weird.*

6. Apply the rules for dropping the final *e* or retaining the final *e* when a suffix is added. (See the exceptions on page 246.)

   Correct: *come   coming*

7. Apply the rules for doubling a final consonant before a suffix beginning with a vowel if the final syllable is accented.

   Correct: *transfer   transferred*

8. Study the list of frequently misspelled words (see pages 248–249).

9. Some words are sometimes misspelled because they are mispronounced or share a pronunciation with another word.

> **Incorrect:**   *alright*
>
> **Correct:**   *all right*

Two words with the same sound and different meanings: *hear   here*

10. Use your spell checker, but be aware of its limitations and always proofread your writing.

CHAPTER REVIEW   Exercises

REVIEW 1   **Adding Suffixes**

Add the indicated suffixes to the following words. If you need help, see page 247 for adding suffixes.

1. fame + *-ous* = _____

2. locate + *-ion* = _____

3. notice + *-able* = _____

4. drop + *-ed* = _____

5. like + *-ly* = _____

6. hope + *-less* = _____

7. manage + *-ment* = _____

8. hot + *-est* = _____

9. rob + *-ed* = _____

10. stop + *-ed* = _____

11. safe + *-ly* = _____

12. argue + *-ment* = _____

13. judge + *-ment* = _____

14. courage + *-ous* = _____

15. swim + *-ing* = _____

16. commit + *-ed* = _____

17. occur + *-ence* = _____

18. omit + *-ed* = _____

19. begin + *-ing* = _____

20. prefer + *-ed* = _____

| REVIEW 2 | ## Correcting Misspelling |

Underline the misspelled words and write the correct spelling above the words. Draw two lines under the words that are incorrectly spelled but would go unchallenged by your spell checker.

Professor Pufnagel was torturing his English students once again, and he relished his familar evil roll. "Today, class, we will write without the assistence of computers. In fact, never again will we use them in this class. They are a perscription for lazyness. And they make life to easy for alot of you."

The profesor lectured the students for an hour, stresing that when he was in school, there were no computers in his enviroment. He extoled the virtues of writting with little yellow pensils, fountain pens, and solid, dependible typewriters. He went on with his ranting, listing computer games, television sets, frozen foods, plastic wrap, asperin, and Velcro as similiar and familiar negative forces that had lead society to it's truely sorry state. "You are nothing but a pityful pack of party people, and you will recieve no sympathy from me," he sputtered. Grabbing a student's laptop computer, Pufnagel reared back and, like an athalete, hurled it against the wall. In the corner of the classroom lay a pile of high-tech junk, once fine, shinning machines, now just garbage—smashed in a senseless, aweful war against technology.

The students starred in embarassed amazement at there professor, who was developing a nervous twitch. His mouth began twisting and contorting as his limbs jerked with the helter-skelter motion of a tangled marionette. He clutched desparately at his throat, and smoke began to poor out of his ears and neck. Unconsious, he crashed to the floor with a clatter.

One of the students, who had just taken a CPR class, rushed forward and attempted to revive the fallen educator. As the student pounded with a catchy rap rhythem on the chest of his stricken teacher, everyone herd a loud pop and sizzle.

It was a door in Pufnagel's chest, which had poped open to reveal the complex electrical control panel of a short-circuited cyborg!

Just than a security team in white jumpsuits from student goverment entered the class, carefully deposited Pufnagel on a wheelbarrow, and roled him out to the Faculty Service Center.

A few minutes later a Professor Ramirez arrived. "Ladys and gentlemen," she said, "its time to start your search engines. Your prevous professor's mainframe is down, but I'm his substitute and mine is fine, fine, fine, fine, fine, fine, fine, fine, fine, fine...."

MICROTHEME

To practice your skills acquired in this chapter, return to the Microtheme on page 243 and complete Exercise B.

Chapter 13

Brief Guide for ESL Students

If you came to this country knowing little English, you probably acquired vocabulary first. Then you began using that vocabulary within the basic patterns of your own language. If your native language had no articles, you probably used no articles; if your language had no verb tenses, you probably used no verb tenses, and so on. Using the grammar of your own language with your new vocabulary may initially have enabled you to make longer and more complex statements in English, but eventually you learned that your native grammar and your adopted grammar were different. You may even have learned that no two grammars are the same, and that English has a bewildering set of rules and an even longer set of exceptions to those rules. Chapters 2 through 12 present grammar (the way we put words together) and rhetoric (the way we use language effectively) that can be applied to your writing. The following are some definitions, rules, and references that are of special help to writers who are learning English as a second language (ESL).

Using Articles in Relation to Nouns

ARTICLES

Articles are either indefinite (*an*, *a*) or definite (*the*). Because they point out nouns, they are often called *noun determiners*.

NOUNS

Nouns can be either singular (*book*) or plural (*books*) and are either count nouns (things that can be counted, such as "book") or noncount nouns (things that cannot be counted, such as "homework"). If you are not certain whether a noun is a count noun or a noncount noun, try placing the word *much* before the word. You can say "much homework," so *homework* is a noncount noun.

RULES

- **Use an indefinite article (*a* or *an*) before singular count nouns and not before noncount nouns**. The indefinite article means "one," so you would not use it before plural count nouns.

    Correct: I saw a book. [count noun]

    Correct: I ate an apple. [count noun]

    Incorrect: I fell in a love. [noncount noun]

    Correct: I fell in love. [noncount noun]

    Incorrect: I was in a good health. [noncount noun]

    Correct: I was in good health. [noncount noun]

- **Use the definite article (*the*) before both singular and plural count nouns that have specific reference**.

    Correct: I read the book. [a specific one]

    Correct: I read the books. [specific ones]

    Correct: I like to read a good book. [nonspecific, therefore the indefinite article]

    Correct: A student who works hard will pass. [any student, therefore nonspecific]

    Correct: The student on my left is falling asleep. [a specific student]

- **Use the definite article with noncount nouns only when they are specifically identified**.

    Correct: Honesty [as an idea] is a rare commodity.

    Correct: The honesty of my friend has inspired me. [specifically identified]

    Incorrect: I was in trouble and needed the assistance. [not specifically identified]

    Correct: The assistance offered by the paramedics was appreciated. [specifically identified]

- **Place the definite article before proper nouns (names) of**

    oceans, rivers, and deserts (for example, *the* Pacific Ocean and *the* Red River).

countries, if the first part of the name indicates a division (*the* United States of America).

regions (*the* South).

plural islands (*the* Hawaiian Islands).

museums and libraries (*the* Los Angeles County Museum).

colleges and universities when the word *college* or *university* comes before the name (*the* University of Oklahoma).

These are the main rules. For a more detailed account of rules for articles, see a comprehensive ESL book in your library.

Sentence Patterns

Chapter 4 defines and illustrates the patterns of English sentences. Some languages include sentence patterns not used in standard English. The following principles are well worth remembering:

- The conventional English sentence is based on one or more clauses, each of which must have a subject (sometimes the implied "you") and a verb.

    Incorrect: Saw the book. [subject needed even if it is obvious]

    Correct: I saw the book.

- English does not repeat a subject, even for emphasis.

    Incorrect: The book that I read it was interesting.

    Correct: The book that I read was interesting.

Verb Endings

- **English indicates time through verbs.** Learn the different forms of verb tenses and the combinations of main verbs and helping verbs.

    Incorrect: He watching the game. [A verblike word ending in *-ing* cannot be a verb all by itself.]

    Correct: He is watching the game. [Note that a helping verb such as *is*, *has*, *has been*, *will*, or *will be* always occurs before a main verb ending in *-ing*.]

- **Take special care in maintaining consistency in tense.**

    Incorrect: I went to the mall. I watch a movie there. [verb tenses inconsistent]

    Correct: I went to the mall. I watched a movie there.

All twelve verb tenses are covered with explanations, examples, and exercises in Chapter 7.

Idioms

Some of your initial problems with writing English are likely to arise from trying to adjust to a different and difficult grammar. If the English language used an entirely systematic grammar, your learning would be easier, but English has patterns that are both complex and irregular. Among them are idioms, word groups that often defy grammatical rules and mean something other than what they appear to mean.

The expression "He kicked the bucket" does not mean that someone struck a cylindrical container with his foot; instead, it means that someone has died. That example is one kind of idiom. Because the expression suggests a certain irreverence, it would not be the choice of most people who want to make a statement about death; but if it is used, it must be used with its own precise wording, not "He struck the long cylindrical container with his foot," or "He did some bucket-kicking." Like other languages, the English language has thousands of these idioms. Expressions such as "the more the merrier" and "on the outs" are ungrammatical. They are also very informal expressions and therefore seldom used in college writing, although they are an indispensable part of a flexible, effective, all-purpose vocabulary. Because of their twisted meanings and illogic, idioms are likely to be among the last parts of language that a new speaker learns well. A speaker must know the culture thoroughly to understand when, where, and how to use slang and other idiomatic expressions.

If you listen carefully and read extensively, you will learn English idioms. Your library will have dictionaries that explain them.

More Suggestions for ESL Writers

1. Read your writing aloud and try to detect inconsistencies and awkward phrasing.

2. Have others read your writing aloud for the same purposes.

3. If you have severe problems with grammatical awkwardness, try composing shorter, more direct sentences until you become more proficient in phrasing.

4. On your Self-Evaluation Chart, list the problems you have (such as articles, verb endings, clause patterns), review relevant sections of Chapters 2 through 12, and concentrate on your own problem areas as you draft, revise, and edit.

EXERCISE 1   Correcting a First Draft

Make corrections in the use of articles, verbs, and phrasing.

GEORGE WASHINGTON AT TRENTON

One of most famous battles during the War of Independence occur at Trenton, New Jersey, on Christmas Eve of the 1776. The colonists outmatched in supplies and finances and were outnumbered in troop strength. Most observers in other countries think rebellion would be put down soon. British overconfident and believe there would be no more battles until spring. But George Washington decide to fight one more time. That Christmas, while large army of Britishers having party and thinking about the holiday season, Americans set out for surprise raid. They loaded onto boats used for carrying ore and rowed across Delaware River. George Washington stood tall in lead boat. According to legend, drummer boy floated across river on his drum, pulled by rope tied to boat. Because British did not feel threatened by the ragtag colonist forces, they unprepared to do battle. The colonists stormed living quarters and the general assembly hall and achieved victory. It was good for the colonists' morale, something they needed, for they would endure long, hard winter before fighting again.

Part III

USING THE WRITING PROCESS

Most college writing occurs as paragraphs and essays in response to special assignments, tests, reports, and research papers. Chapters 14 through 17 concentrate on the paragraph, showing you how to use the stages of the writing process and giving you opportunities to experiment. A common form for short composition answers for various tasks, the well-organized paragraph is often a miniature structural version of the essay. Chapter 17 demonstrates how you can use your mastery of process writing for paragraphs in essays.

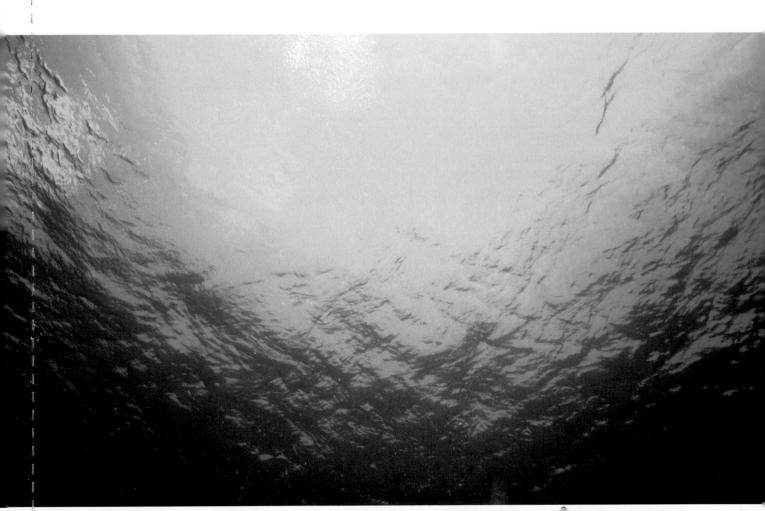

Chapter 14

The Writing Process
Stage One: Exploring / Experimenting / Gathering Information

The Paragraph Defined

Defining the word *paragraph* is no easy task because there are different kinds of paragraphs, each one having a different purpose:

Introductory: Usually the first paragraph in an essay, it gives the necessary background and indicates the main idea, called the **thesis**.

Developmental: A unit of several sentences, it expands on an idea. This book features the writing of developmental paragraphs.

Transitional: A very brief paragraph, it merely directs the reader from one point in the essay to another.

Concluding: Usually the last paragraph in an essay, it makes the final comment on the topic.

The following paragraph is both a definition and an example of the developmental paragraph.

Topic sentence

Support

Support

Support

Concluding sentence

The developmental paragraph contains three parts: the subject, the topic sentence, and the support. The **subject** is what you will write about. It is likely to be broad and must be focused or qualified for specific treatment. The **topic sentence** contains both the subject and the treatment—what you will do with the subject. It carries the central idea to which everything else in the paragraph is subordinated. For example, the first sentence of this paragraph is a topic sentence. Even when not stated, the topic sentence as an underlying idea unifies the paragraph. The **support** is the evidence or reasoning by which a topic sentence is developed. It comes in several basic patterns and serves any of the four forms of expression: narration, description, exposition, and argumentation. These forms, which are usually combined in writing, will be presented with both student and professional examples in the following chapters. The **developmental paragraph**, therefore, is a group of sentences, each with the function of supporting a controlling idea called the topic sentence.

Basic Paragraph Patterns

The most important point about a developmental paragraph is that it should state an idea and support it. The support, or development, can take several forms, all of which you already use. It can

- give an account (tell a story).
- describe people, things, or events.
- explain by analyzing, giving examples, comparing, showing how to do something, or showing causes.
- argue that something should be done or resisted, that something is true or untrue, or that something is good or bad.

(All of these forms of expression are discussed with examples in Chapters 18 through 24.) You will not find it difficult to write solid paragraphs once you understand that good writing requires that main ideas have enough support so that your reader can understand how you have arrived at your main conclusions.

Two effective patterns of conventional paragraph structure are shown in Figure 14.1. Pattern A merely states the controlling idea, the topic sentence, and develops it; Pattern B adds a concluding sentence following the development.

A paragraph, however, is not a constraining formula: it has variations. In some instances, for example, the topic sentence is not found in a single sentence. It may be the combination of two sentences, or it may be an easily understood but unwritten underlying idea that unifies the paragraph. Nevertheless, the paragraph in most college writing contains discussion that supports a stated topic sentence, and the instruction in this book is based on that fundamental idea.

A SAMPLE PARAGRAPH

The following paragraph was written by college student Cyrus Norton. The subject of the paragraph and the treatment of the paragraph have been marked. Norton's topic sentence (not the first sentence in this case), his support of the topic sentence, and his concluding sentence are also marked.

Figure 14.1
Paragraph Patterns

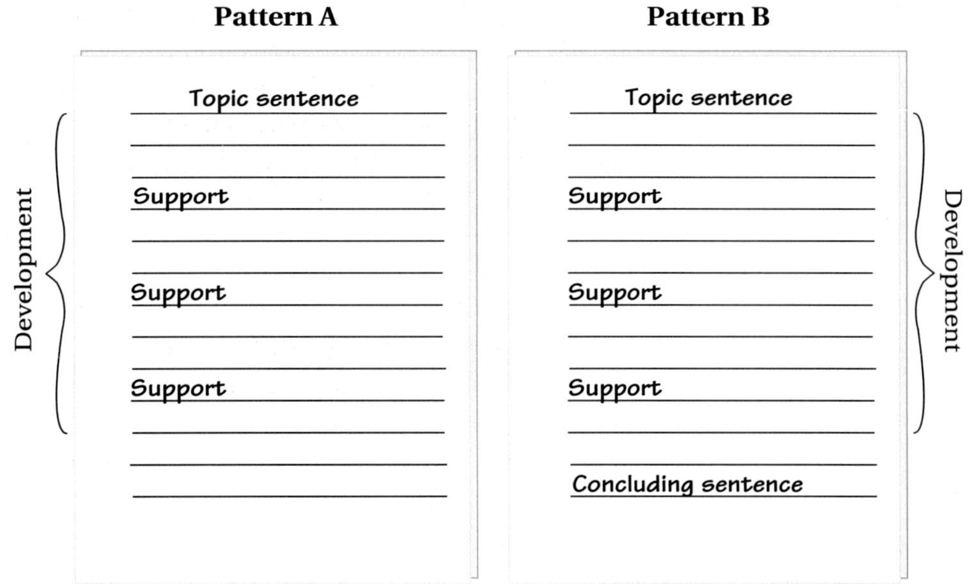

Pattern A	Pattern B

Pattern A

Topic sentence
_____
_____

Support
_____
_____

Support
_____
_____

Support
_____
_____
_____

(Development)

Pattern B

Topic sentence
_____
_____

Support
_____
_____

Support
_____
_____

Support
_____

Concluding sentence
_____

(Development)

This is the final draft. Following it, we will back up and, in this chapter and the next two, show how Norton moved during the writing process from his initial idea to this polished paragraph.

MAGIC JOHNSON, AN NBA GREAT
Cyrus Norton

Topic sentence
Support for shooting

Support for passing

Support for rebounding

Support for leading

Concluding sentence

Some NBA (National Basketball Association) players are good because they have a special talent in one area. <u>Magic Johnson was a great NBA star because he was excellent in shooting, passing, rebounding, and leading</u>. As a shooter few have ever equaled him. He could slam, shovel, hook, and fire from three-point range—all with deadly accuracy. As for free throws, he led all NBA players in shooting percentage in 1988–1989. While averaging more than twenty points per game, he helped others become stars with his passes. As the point guard (the quarterback of basketball), he was always near the top in the league in assists and was famous for his "no-look" pass, which often surprised even his teammates with its precision. When he was not shooting or passing, he was rebounding. A top rebounding guard is unusual in professional basketball, but Magic, at six feet, nine inches, could bump shoulders and leap with anyone. These three qualities made him probably the most spectacular triple-double threat of all time. "Triple-double" means reaching two digits in scoring, assists, and rebounding. Magic did not need more for greatness in the NBA, but he had more. With his everlasting smile and boundless energy, he was also an inspirational team leader. He always believed in himself and his team. When his team was down by a point and three seconds remained on the game clock, the fans looked for Magic to get the ball. They watched as he dribbled once, he faded, he leaped, he twisted, and he hooked one in from twenty feet. That was magic. <u>That was Magic</u>.

Let us consider Norton's paragraph given what we know about paragraphs in general. Magic Johnson, the subject, is what the paragraph is all about. In this example, the title also names the subject. The topic sentence, the unifying and controlling idea, makes a clear statement about what the writer will do with the subject. As usual, the topic sentence appears near the beginning of the paragraph. The support gives evidence and examples to back up the controlling idea. The last sentence, "That was Magic," echoes the topic sentence. It is usually called the concluding sentence.

The author has told you what he was going to say, he has said it, and finally he has reminded you of what he has told you. The concluding sentence is sometimes omitted. The two most common designs of paragraphs in college writing are these:

- Topic sentence ⟶ support ⟶ concluding sentence
- Topic sentence ⟶ support

"Magic Johnson, an NBA Great" is a typical paragraph: a group of sentences that present and develop an idea. In college writing, a paragraph is usually expository; that is, its purpose is to explain. In this example, you, the reader, get the point. You are informed and maybe even entertained a little by the explanation.

The Writing Process

Although the first section of this chapter defined and illustrated the paragraph as a concept, it stopped short of presenting an overall plan for paragraph writing. The reason for that omission is simple. Each assignment has its own guidelines that vary according to the kind of topic, the source of ideas, the time permitted, the conditions for writing (especially in or outside class), and the purpose. Obviously, if one is to use a system, it must be flexible, because a technique that is an asset for one assignment may be a burden for another. Therefore, a good writer should know numerous techniques, treating each as a tool that can be used when needed. All of these tools are in the same box, one labeled "The Writing Process."

The writing process consists of strategies that can help you proceed from your purpose or initial idea to a final developed paragraph. Those strategies can be divided into prewriting techniques and writing stages. Using prewriting, you explore, experiment, gather information, formulate your thesis, and develop and organize your support. Then you write a first draft, revise your draft as many times as necessary, and edit your writing. The typical college writing assignment process looks like this:

Stage One: Exploring / Experimenting / Gathering Information
Stage Two: Writing the Controlling Idea / Organizing and Developing Support
Stage Three: Writing / Revising / Editing

These stages are discussed in Chapters 14, 15, and 16, respectively. Collectively they represent what is known as the writing process.

A blank Writing Process Worksheet with brief directions for completing the three stages of the writing process appears at the end of the Student Overview (page 6). This Writing Process Worksheet is designed to be duplicated and completed with each major writing assignment. It gives you clear, consistent guidance and provides your instructor with an easy format for finding and checking information. Customarily it should be stapled to the front of your rough and final drafts. A sample worksheet completed by a student appears on pages 291–292 in Chapter 16.

Stage One Strategies

Certain strategies commonly grouped under the heading *prewriting* can help you get started and develop your ideas. These strategies—freewriting, brainstorming, clustering, note taking—are very much a part of writing. The understandable desire to skip to the finished statement is what causes the most common student-writer grief: that of not filling the blank sheet or of filling it but not significantly improving on the blankness. The prewriting strategies described in this section will help you attack the blank sheet constructively with imaginative thought, analysis, and experimentation. They can lead to clear, effective communication.

FREEWRITING

Freewriting is an exercise that its originator, Peter Elbow, has called "babbling in print." When you freewrite, you write without stopping, letting your ideas tumble forth. You do not concern yourself with the fundamentals of writing, such as punctuation and spelling. Freewriting is an adventure into your memory and imagination. It is concerned with discovery, invention, and exploration. If you are at a loss for words on your subject, write in a comment such as "I don't know what is coming next" or "blah, blah, blah" and continue when relevant words come. It is important to keep writing. Freewriting immediately eliminates the blank page and thereby helps you break through an emotional barrier, but that is not the only benefit. The words that you sort through in that idea kit will include some you can use. You can then underline or circle those words and even add notes on the side so that the freewriting continues to grow even after its initial spontaneous expression.

The way you proceed depends on the type of assignment: working with a topic of your choice, a restricted list of topics, or a prescribed topic.

The *topic of your choice* affords you the greatest freedom of exploration. You would probably select a subject that interests you and freewrite about it, allowing your mind to wander, perhaps mixing fact and fantasy, direct experience, and hearsay. A freewriting about music might uncover areas of special interest and knowledge, such as jazz or folk rock, that you would want to pursue further in freewriting or other prewriting strategies.

Working from a *restricted list* requires a more focused freewriting. With the list, you can, of course, experiment with several topics to discover what is most suitable for you. If, for example, "career choice," "career preparation," "career guidance," and "career prospects" are on the restricted list, you would probably select one and freewrite about it. If it works well for you, you would probably proceed with the next step of your prewriting. If you are not satisfied with what you uncover in freewriting, you would explore another item from the restricted list or take notes from the Internet or library sources.

When working with a *prescribed topic*, you focus on a particular topic and try to restrict your freewriting to its boundaries. If your topic specifies a division of a subject area such as "political involvement of your generation," then you would tie those key words to your own information, critical thinking, and imaginative responses. If the topic is restricted to, let us say, a particular reading selection such as a poem, then that poem would give you the framework for your free associations with your own experiences, creations, and opinions.

You should learn to use freewriting because it will often serve you well, but you need not use it every time you write. Some very short writing assignments do not call for freewriting. An in-class assignment may not allow time for freewriting.

Nevertheless, freewriting is often a useful strategy in your toolbox of techniques. It can help you get words on paper, break emotional barriers, generate topics, develop new insights, and explore ideas.

Freewriting can lead to other stages of prewriting and writing, and it can also provide content as you develop your topic.

The following example of freewriting and the writing, revising, and editing examples in Chapter 16 relate to student Cyrus Norton's paragraph titled "Magic Johnson, an NBA Great" (page 267). Norton's topic came from a restricted list; he was directed to write about the success of an individual. Had he been working with a prescribed topic, he might have been directed to concentrate on a specific aspect of Johnson's career, such as business, philanthropy, public service, or the one Norton chose: great basketball playing.

great
leader, inspiration

rich

playing
scoring
passing
rebounding

Magic Johnson was the <u>greatest</u> player I have ever seen in professional basketball. Actually not just a player but a <u>leader</u> and an <u>inspiration</u> to the team so they always gave him the ball when the game was on the line. It was too bad his career was cut short when they discovered he was HIV positive. Actually he came back but then retired again. He made <u>a lot of money</u> and I guess he invested it wisely because his name is linked to the Lakers and theaters and more. Also to programs making people aware of the danger of AIDS and helping kids grow up and stay out of trouble. But the main thing about Magic is the <u>way he played</u>. He could do everything. He even played center one time in a championship game. He always <u>scored a lot</u> and he could <u>pass</u> like nobody else. Even though he was a guard, he was tall and could <u>rebound</u>. He was great. Everyone says so.

After doing this freewriting, Norton went back through his work looking for ideas that might be developed in a paper.

Observe how he returned to his freewriting and examined it for possible ideas to develop for a writing assignment. As he recognized those ideas, he underlined important words and phrases and made a few notes in the margins. By reading only the underlined words, you can obtain a basic understanding of what is important to him. It is not necessary to underline entire sentences.

In addition to putting some words on that dreaded blank sheet of paper, Norton discovered that he had quite a lot of information about Magic Johnson and that he had selected a favorable topic to develop. The entire process took little time. Had he found few or no promising ideas, he might have freewritten about another topic. In going back through his work, he saw some errors in writing, but he did not correct them, because the purpose of freewriting is discovery, not correct grammar, punctuation, or spelling. Norton was confident that he could then continue with the process of writing a paper.

Norton's understanding of the topic came mainly from information he had collected from reading and from watching sports programs on television. He knew that if he needed to gather more information, he could do further research, which could take the form of reading, underlining, annotating, note taking, outlining, and summarizing. These techniques are explained in Chapter 1.

EXERCISE 1   Freewriting

Try freewriting on a broad topic such as one of these: the best car on the market, a popular college course, a controversial television program, a favorite retail store or mall, a good school, a neighborhood you know well, a memorable learning experience, a person who has influenced you, or a useful piece of software. Following the example on page 270, underline and annotate the phrases that may lead you to ideas to explore further.

BRAINSTORMING

Brainstorming features important words and phrases that relate in various ways to the subject area or to the specific topic you are concerned about. Brainstorming includes two basic forms: (1) asking and answering questions and (2) listing.

Big Six Questions

One effective way to get started is to ask the big six questions about your subject: *Who? What? Where? When? Why? How?* Then let your mind run free as you jot down answers in single entries or lists. Some of the big six questions may not fit, and some may be more important than others, depending on the purposes of your writing. For example, if you were writing about the causes of a situation, the *Why?* question could be more important than the others; if you were concerned with how to do something, the *How?* question would predominate. If you were writing in response to a reading selection, you would confine your thinking to questions appropriately related to the content of that reading selection.

Whatever your focus for the questions is, the result is likely to be numerous ideas that will provide information for continued exploration and development of your topic. Thus your pool of information for writing widens and deepens.

Norton continued with the topic of Magic Johnson, and his topic tightened to focus on particular areas.

Who: Magic Johnson
What: great basketball player
Where: the NBA
When: for more than ten years
Why: love of game and great talent
How: shooting, passing, rebounding, leading, coolness, inspiring

As it turned out, *How?* was the most fruitful question for Norton.

Listing

Another effective way to brainstorm, especially if you have a defined topic and a storehouse of information, is to skip the big six questions approach and simply make a list of words and phrases related to your topic.

Had Norton known at the outset that he would write about Magic Johnson's greatness as a basketball player, he might have gone directly to a list such as this:

(shooting)
intelligence
(rebounding)
coolness
quickness
(passing)
split vision
determination
(leading)
work ethic
unselfishness
attitude
ambition

From this list, Norton might have selected perhaps four ideas for his framework, circling them for future reference.

Even if you do not have a focused topic, you may find a somewhat random listing useful, merely writing or typing in phrases as they occur to you. This exploratory activity is similar to freewriting. After you have established such a list, you can sort out and group the phrases as you generate your topic and find its natural divisions. Feel free to accept, reject, or insert phrases.

EXERCISE 2   Brainstorming

Further explore the topic you worked with in Exercise 1 first by answering the big six questions and then by making a list.

Big Six Questions

Who? _____

What? _____

Where? _____

When? _____

Why? _____

How? _____

List

_____

_____

_____

_____

_____

_____

_____

_____

_____

_____

CLUSTERING

Clustering is still another prewriting technique. Start by "double-bubbling" your topic; that is, write it down in the middle of the page and draw a double circle around it. Then, responding to the question "What comes to mind?" single-bubble other ideas on spokes radiating from the hub that contains the topic. Any bubble can lead to another bubble or numerous bubbles in the same way. This strategy is sometimes used instead of or before making an outline to organize and develop ideas.

The more restricted the topic inside the double bubble, the fewer the number of spokes that will radiate with single bubbles. For example, a topic such as "high school dropouts" would have more spokes than "reasons for dropping out of high school."

Here is Norton's cluster on the subject of Magic Johnson. He has drawn broken circles around subclusters that seem to relate to a feasible unified topic.

EXERCISE 3   Clustering

Continuing with your topic, develop a cluster of related ideas. Draw broken circles around subclusters that have potential for focus and more development.

GATHERING INFORMATION

For reading-related writing—especially the kind that requires a close examination of the selection—you will gather information by reading print or electronic sources, such as the Internet; make notes; and perhaps outline or summarize (see Chapter 1) the text. Of course, you may also want to make notes for other topics to write about as they occur to you. This kind of note taking can be combined with other strategies such as brainstorming and clustering. It can even take the place of them. It can also be used in conjunction with strategies such as outlining.

WRITER'S GUIDELINES   The Writing Process: Stage One

1. A **paragraph** is a group of sentences, each with the function of stating or supporting a single controlling idea that is contained in the topic sentence.

2. A paragraph contains two parts: the topic sentence and the support.

   • The **topic sentence** expresses the controlling idea of the paragraph. It has a subject (what the paragraph is about) and indicates the treatment (what the writer will do with the subject).
   • The **support** is the evidence, such as details, examples, and explanations, that backs up the topic sentence.

3. The two most common paragraph designs in college writing are these:

   • Topic sentence ⟶ support ⟶ concluding sentence
   • Topic sentence ⟶ support

4. **Prewriting** includes activities you do before writing your first draft or whenever you need new ideas. You should use only the activities that will best help you explore, generate, limit, and develop your topic.

- *Freewriting*: writing without stopping, letting your ideas tumble forth. Freewriting helps you break emotional barriers, generate topics, and discover and explore ideas. If you need more information, consult sources on the Internet or in the library and take notes.
- *Brainstorming*: a listing procedure that helps you discover key words and phrases that relate to your subject. Begin by asking *Who? What? Where? When? Why?* and *How?* questions about your subject or by merely listing ideas concerning your subject.
- *Clustering*: a graphic way of showing connections and relationships. Start by double-bubbling your topic. Then ask "What comes to mind?" and single-bubble other ideas on spokes radiating from the double bubble.
- *Gathering information*: reading with underlining, annotating, and note taking.

Chapter 15

The Writing Process
Stage Two: Writing the Controlling Idea / Organizing and Developing Support

FLOW OF WRITING

The most important advice this book can offer you is *state your controlling idea and support it.* If you have no controlling idea—no topic sentence—your paragraph will be unfocused, and your readers may be confused or bored. If you organize your material well, so that it supports and develops your controlling idea, you can present your views to your readers with interest, clarity, and persuasion.

Stating the controlling idea and organizing support can be accomplished effectively and systematically. How? This chapter presents several uncomplicated techniques you can use in Stage Two of the writing process.

Writing the Controlling Idea as a Topic Sentence

An effective topic sentence has both a subject and a focus. The **subject** is what you intend to write about. The **focus** is what you intend to do with your subject.

Consider, for example, this topic sentence:

<u>Magic Johnson</u> <u>was a great all-around NBA player</u>.
      subject   focus

It is an effective topic sentence because it limits the subject and indicates focus that can be developed in additional sentences. Another sound version is the following, which goes further to include divisions for the focus.

<u>Magic Johnson</u> <u>was a great NBA star because he was excellent in</u>
      subject   focus

shooting, passing, rebounding, and leading.

Ineffective topic sentences are often vague, too broad, or too narrow.

Ineffective:	Magic Johnson was everything to everybody.
Too Broad or Vague:	Magic Johnson was fun.
	Magic Johnson was a success in basketball.
Ineffective:	Magic Johnson went to college in Michigan.
Too Narrow:	Magic Johnson signed with the Los Angeles Lakers.

Usually, simple statements of fact do not need or do not allow for development.

EXERCISE 1   Evaluating Topic Sentences

In the following statements, underline and label subject (S) and focus (F). Also judge each sentence as effective (E) or ineffective (I). Effective statements are those that you can easily relate to supporting evidence. Ineffective statements are vague, too broad, or too narrowly factual.

_____   **1.** Columbus is located in Ohio.

_____   **2.** Columbus is a fabulous city.

_____   **3.** Columbus has dealt thoroughly with its housing problems.

_____   **4.** A monkey is a primate.

_____   **5.** Monkeys are fun.

_____   **6.** In clinical studies monkeys have demonstrated a remarkable ability to reason.

_____   **7.** More than a million cats are born in California each year.

_____   **8.** A simple observation of a domesticated cat in the pursuit of game will show that it has not lost its instinct for survival.

_____   **9.** The two teams in the Rose Bowl have similar records.

_____   **10.** Michigan State is in the Rose Bowl.

EXERCISE 2   Writing Topic Sentences

Complete the following entries to make each one a solid topic sentence. Only a subject and part of the focus are provided. The missing part may be more than a single word.

Example: Car salespeople behave differently depending on <u>the car they are selling</u> <u>and the kind of customer they are serving.</u>

1. Television commercials are often _____

   _____

2. Word-processing features can _____

   _____

3. My part-time job taught me _____

   _____

4. I promote environmental conservation by _____

   _____

5. The clothing that a person wears often reveals _____

   _____

6. My close friend is preoccupied with _____

   _____

7. Winning a lot of money is not always _____

   _____

8. Country music appeals to our most basic _____

   _____

9. Friendship depends on _____

   _____

10. A good salesperson should _____

    _____

EXERCISE 3   Writing Topic Sentences

Convert each of the following subjects into a topic sentence by providing a focus.

1. Computer literacy   _____

_____

2. My taste in music   _____

_____

3. Bus transportation   _____

_____

4. The fear of crime   _____

_____

5. An excellent boss   _____

_____

6. Doing well in college English classes   _____

_____

7. Violence on television   _____

_____

8. Child-care centers   _____

_____

9. Good health   _____

_____

10. Teenage voters   _____

_____

Writing an Outline

An **outline** is a pattern for showing the relationship of ideas. The two main outline forms are the **sentence outline** (each entry is a complete sentence) and the **topic outline** (each entry is a key word or phrase). The topic outline is commonly used for paragraphs and short essays.

Indentation, number and letter sequences, punctuation, and the placement of words are important to clear communication. We do not read an outline expecting to be surprised by form and content, as we may read a poem. We go to the outline for information, and we expect to find ideas easily. Unconventional marks (circles, squares, half-parentheses) and items out of order are distracting and, therefore, undesirable in an outline. The standard form is as easily mastered as a nonstandard form, and it is worth your time to learn it. Outlining is not difficult: The pattern is flexible and can have any number of levels and parts.

Basically, an outline shows how a topic sentence is supported. Thus it shows the organization of the paragraph. The most important supporting material, called the **major support**, is indicated by Roman numerals. That major support is developed by less important supporting material, called the **minor support**, which in turn may be developed by details or examples. The major and minor support may be derived from one or more strategies of prewriting such as listing and clustering. Here is the outline developed by Norton:

Topic Sentence: Magic Johnson was a great NBA star because he was excellent in shooting, passing, rebounding, and leading.

I. Shooting (major support)

    A. Short shots (minor support)

        1. Shovel (detail)

        2. Slam-dunk (detail)

    B. Long shots (minor support)

    C. Free throws (minor support)

II. Passing (major support)

    A. No-look (minor support)

    B. Precise (minor support)

III. Rebounding (major support)

    A. Tall (minor support)

    B. Strong (minor support)

IV. Leading (major support)

    A. Energy (minor support)

    B. Spirit (minor support)

        1. Faith (detail)

        2. Smile (detail)

The foundation of a good outline and, hence, of a good paragraph is a strong topic sentence, which means one with a specific subject and a well-defined focus. After you have written a good topic sentence, the next step is to divide the focus into parts. Just what the parts are will depend on what you are trying to do in the focus. Consider the thought process involved. What sections of material would be appropriate in your discussion to support or explain that topic sentence? You will probably find that your listing or clustering has already addressed one or more ways of dividing your material. Therefore, reexamine your other forms of prewriting for patterns of development, as well as support.

Among the most common forms of division are the following:

- Divisions of time or incident to tell a story

    I. Situation

    II. Conflict

    III. Struggle

    IV. Outcome

    V. Meaning

- Divisions of examples

    I. First example

    II. Second example

    III. Third example (or divide one example into three or more aspects)

- Divisions of causes or effects

    I. Cause (or effect) one

    II. Cause (or effect) two

    III. Cause (or effect) three

- Divisions of a unit into parts (such as the federal government into executive, legislative, and judicial branches—or Magic Johnson's all-around skill into shooting, passing, rebounding, and leading)

    I. Part one

    II. Part two

    III. Part three

- Divisions of how to do something or how something was done

    I. Preparation

    II. Steps
        A. Step 1
        B. Step 2
        C. Step 3

EXERCISE 4   Completing Outlines

Fill in the missing parts of the following outlines. Consider whether you are dealing with time, examples, causes, effects, parts, or steps. The answers will vary, depending on your individual experiences and views.

1. Too many of us are preoccupied with material things.
    I. Clothing
    II. Cars
    III. _____

2. Television sitcoms may vary, but every successful show has certain components.

    I. Good acting

    II. _____

    III. Good situations

    IV. _____

3. A person who is trying to discourage unwanted sexual advances should take several measures.

    I. _____

    II. Set clear boundaries

    III. Avoid compromising situations

4. Concentrating during reading involves various techniques.

    I. Preview material

    II. Pose questions

    III. _____

5. Crime has some bad effects on a nearby neighborhood.

    I. People fearful

       A. Don't go out at night

       B. _____

    II. People without love for neighborhood

       A. _____

       B. Put houses up for sale

    III. People as victims

       A. Loss of possessions

       B. _____

6. Exercising can improve a person's life.

    I. Looks better

       A. Skin

       B. _____

    II. Feels better

       A. _____

       B. Body

    III. Performs better

       A. Work

       B. _____

7. Shoppers in department stores can be grouped according to needs.

    I. _____

    II. Special-needs

    III. Bargain hunters

8. There are different kinds of intelligence based on situations.

    I. Street-smart

    II. Common sense

    III. _____

9. Smoking should be discouraged.

   I. Harm to smokers

      A. _____

      B. Cancer risk

   II. Harm to those around smokers

      A. _____

      B. Fellow workers

   III. Cost

      A. Industry—production and absenteeism

      B. _____

10. An excellent police officer must have six qualities.

   I. _____

   II. Knowledge of law

   III. _____

   III. Emotional soundness

   V. Skill in using weapons

   VI. _____

EXERCISE 5 Writing a Topic Sentence and an Outline

Still working with the same topic you chose in Exercise 1, page 271, write a topic sentence and an outline. The topic sentence may suggest a particular pattern of development. Following the lead of that topic sentence, the Roman-numeral headings will often indicate divisions of time or place, examples, steps, causes, effects, or parts of a unit. For example, if you have selected your favorite retail store for your subject and your reasons for choosing it as the focus, then those reasons would be indicated with Roman-numeral headings.

WRITER'S GUIDELINES   The Writing Process: Stage Two

1. An effective **topic sentence** has both a subject and a focus. The subject is what you intend to write about. The focus is what you intend to do with your subject.

> **Example:**   Wilson High School offers a well-balanced academic program.
> subject   focus

2. An **outline** is a form for indicating the relationship of ideas. The outline shows how a topic sentence is supported. Thus it reveals the organization of the paragraph. Major support is indicated by Roman numerals. The major support is developed by minor support, which in turn may be developed by details or examples.

Topic sentence
I. Major support
   A. Minor support
   B. Minor support
      1. Details or examples
      2. Details or examples
II. Major support
   A. Minor support
   B. Minor support

STUDENT COMPANION SITE
For additional practice, visit www.cengage .com/devenglish/ brandon/spb6e.

Chapter 16

The Writing Process
Stage Three:
Writing / Revising / Editing

FLOW OF WRITING

Writing Your First Draft

Once you have written your topic sentence and completed your outline (or list or cluster), you are ready to begin writing your paragraph. The initial writing is called the **first**, or rough, **draft**. Your topic sentence is likely to be at or near the beginning of your paragraph and will be followed by your support as ordered by your outline.

Paying close attention to your outline for basic organization, you should proceed without worrying about the refinements of writing. This is not the time to concern yourself with perfect spelling, grammar, or punctuation.

Whether you write in longhand or use a computer depends on which works better for you. Some writers prefer to do a first draft by hand, mark it up, and then go to the computer. Computers save you time in all aspects of your writing, especially revision.

Do not be embarrassed by the roughness of your first draft. You should be embarrassed only if you leave it that way. You are seeing the reason why a first draft is called "rough." Famous authors have said publicly that they would not show their rough drafts to their closest, most forgiving friends.

THE RECURSIVE FACTOR

The process of writing can be called **recursive**, which means "going back and forth." In this respect, writing is like reading. If you do not understand what you have read, you back up and read it again. After you have reread a passage, you may still need to read it selectively. The same can be said of writing. If, for example, after having developed an outline and started writing your first draft, you discover that your subject is too broad, you have to back up, narrow your topic sentence, and then adjust your outline. You may even want to return to an early cluster of ideas to see how you can use a smaller grouping of them. Revision is usually the most recursive of all parts of the writing process. You will go over your material again and again until you are satisfied that you have expressed yourself as well as you possibly can.

In this textbook, the recursive factor is also called the "Flow of Writing," as captured by the icon of the waves at the beach. Waves move in cycles, going forward and doubling back and thrusting again, moving with more vigor toward a high tide. You may have to catch a lot of trial rides before you get close to that perfect wave of expression. The revising and editing of your work make up those rides.

Revising Your Writing

The term **first draft** suggests quite accurately that there will be other drafts, or versions, of your writing. Only in the most dire situations, such as an in-class examination when you have time for only one draft, should you be satisfied with a single effort.

What you do beyond the first draft is revising and editing. **Revision** concerns itself with organization, content, and language effectiveness. **Editing** involves a final correcting of mistakes in spelling, punctuation, and capitalization. In practice, editing and revising are not always separate activities, although writers usually wait until the next-to-the-last draft to edit some minor details and attend to other small points that can be easily overlooked.

Successful revision almost always involves intense, systematic rewriting. You should learn to look for certain aspects of skillful writing as you enrich and repair your first draft. To help you recall these aspects so that you can keep them in mind and examine your material in a comprehensive fashion, this textbook offers a memory device—an acronym in which each letter suggests an important feature of good writing and revision. This device enables you to memorize the features of good writing quickly. Soon you will be able to recall and refer to them automatically. These features need not be attended to individually when you revise your writing, although they may be. They need not be attended to in the order presented here. The acronym is **CLUESS** (pronounced "clues"), which provides this guide: **c**oherence, **l**anguage, **u**nity, **e**mphasis, **s**upport, **s**entences.

COHERENCE

Coherence is the flow of ideas, with each idea leading logically and smoothly to the next. It is achieved by numbering parts or otherwise indicating (*first, second, third, then, next, soon,* and so on), giving directions (according to space, as in "To the right is a map, and to the left of that map is a bulletin board"), using transitional words (*however, otherwise, therefore, similarly, hence, on the other hand, then, consequently, accordingly, thus*), using demonstrative pronouns (*this, that, those*), and moving in a clear order (from the least important to the most important or from the most important to the least important).

LANGUAGE

Language here stands for diction or word choice: using words that clearly convey your ideas and are suitable for what you are writing and for your audience. In college writing that means you will usually avoid slang and clichés such as "a barrel of laughs," "happy as a clam," and "six of one and a half dozen of another." Your writing will contain standard grammar and usage. See page 308 for a discussion of general and specific words.

If you are writing with a computer, use the thesaurus feature for careful diction, but keep in mind that no two words share exactly the same meaning.

UNITY

Unity in a paragraph begins with a good topic sentence. Then everything in your paragraph should be related and subordinated to that topic sentence. Repetition of a key word or phrase can make the unity even stronger.

EMPHASIS

Emphasize important ideas by using **position** (the most emphatic parts of a work are the beginning and the end), **repetition** (repeat key words and phrases), and **isolation** (a short, direct sentence among longer ones will usually command attention).

SUPPORT

Support is the material that backs up, justifies, or proves your topic sentence. Work carefully with the material from your outline (or list or cluster) to make sure that your ideas are well supported. If your paragraph is skimpy and your ideas seem slender, you are probably generalizing and not explaining how you arrived at your conclusions. Avoid repetition that does not add to the content; use details and examples; indicate parts and discuss relationships; and explain why your generalizations are true, logical, and accurate. Your reader cannot accept your ideas unless he or she knows by what reasoning or use of evidence you developed them.

SENTENCES

Be sure your sentences are complete (not fragments) and that you have not incorrectly combined word groups that could be sentences (comma splices and run-ons). See Chapter 4 for different types of sentences and different sentence beginnings.

Write as many drafts as necessary, revising as you go for all the aspects of effective writing. Do not confuse revising with editing (the final stage of the writing process); do not get bogged down in fixing such things as spelling and punctuation.

Editing Your Writing

Editing, the final stage of the writing process, involves a careful examination of your work. Look for problems with **c**apitalization, **o**missions, **p**unctuation, and **s**pelling (**COPS**).

Because you can find spelling errors in others' writing more easily than in your own, a computerized spell checker is extremely useful. However, a spell checker will not detect wrong words that are correctly spelled, so you should always proofread.

Before you submit your writing to your instructor, do what almost all professional writers do before sending their material along: Read it aloud, to yourself or to a willing accomplice. Reading material aloud will help you catch any awkwardness of expression, omission, and misplacement of words, and other problems that are easily overlooked by an author.

As you can see, writing is a process and is not a matter of just sitting down and producing sentences. The parts of the process from prewriting to revising to editing are connected, and your movement is ultimately forward, but this process allows you to go back and forth in the recursive manner discussed earlier. If your outline is not working, perhaps the flaw is in your topic sentence. You may need to go back and fix it. If one section of your paragraph is skimpy, perhaps you will have to go back and reconsider the pertinent material in your outline or clustering. There you might find more details or alter a statement so that you can move into more fertile areas of thought.

Norton wrote the following first draft, marked it for revision, and then completed the final draft, which you read on page 267. For simplification, only this draft is shown, although a typical paper might require several drafts, including one in which the author has done nothing but edit his or her revised writing.

Magic Johnson, an NBA Great

(National Basketball Association)   have a special talent
Some NBA players are good because they ~~are good~~ in one area ~~such as~~

                                                          a   NBA star
~~shooting, passing, or rebounding.~~ Magic Johnson was great because he

excellent   shooting, passing, rebounding, and leading.   ever equaled him.
was good in ~~all of those things and more.~~ As a shooter few have ~~been able~~

~~to do what he could.~~ He could slam, shovel, hook, and fire from three-point

          —all with deadly accuracy   As for
range. ~~When it came to~~ free throws, he led all NBA players in shooting

                                 While   ing
percentage in 1988–1989. ~~Then he~~ averaged more than twenty points per

              s   with his passes   (the quarterback of basketball),
game, he helped other become stars. As the point guard he was always near

                                                              "   "
the top in the league in asists and was famous for his no-look passes

                                           its
Which often surprised even his teammates with ~~their~~ precision.

When he was not shooting or passing, he was rebounding.   in professional basketball
A top rebounding guard is unusual, but Magic, standing at six feet nine inches

          u   leap
tall, could bump sholders and jump with anyone. These three qualities

made him probably the most spectacular triple-double threat of all time.
"Triple-double" means reaching two digits in scoring, assists, and rebounding.
Magic did not need more for greatness in the NBA, but he had more. He was

also an inspirational team leader ~~with~~ *With* his everlasting smile and boundless energy.
He Always believ~~ing~~*ed* in himself and his team. When his team was down by a

point and three seconds ~~were left, you always~~ *remained on the game clock,   the fans* looked for Magic to get

the ball. ~~Then you~~ *They* watched as he dribbled once, *he* faded, *he* leaped, *he* twisted, and

he hooked one in from twenty feet *! That was magic.* ~~That was Magic.~~

The Writing Process Worksheet

One effective and systematic way to organize your writing is by using the Writing Process Worksheet. The procedure is simple. First, copy the directions for your assignment, making certain that you know precisely what you are to do and when you are to submit your paper. Few things are more frustrating to both student and instructor than an assignment that falls outside the directions or is not turned in on time.

Next, do your prewriting, beginning on the worksheet and using extra pages if necessary. Prewriting will vary according to your assignment and according to your instructor's requirements.

Then follow your prewriting activities with writing, which includes revising and editing.

Keep in mind that the writing process is recursive and that you can go back and forth between different activities, depending on your needs. For example, if one part of your outline does not work as you write your rough draft, go back to your outline or other prewriting activities to add or subtract ideas.

The Writing Process Worksheet is useful in helping you understand the assignment, in reminding you of the best tools the writing process offers for prewriting and writing, and in providing an organized packet of material for your instructor. For some instructors that packet will include these parts stapled in this order: a completed Writing Process Worksheet, a rough draft marked for revision, and a final draft.

Norton's Writing Process Worksheet follows (on pages 291–292). You will find a full-size blank Writing Process Worksheet on page 6. It can be photocopied, filled in, and submitted with each assignment if your instructor directs you to do so.

EXERCISE 1   Revising and Editing

Treat the following paragraph as your own rough draft and mark it in the way Norton marked his rough draft. First consider coherence, language, unity, emphasis, support, and sentences (CLUESS). Then edit the paragraph, correcting fundamentals such as capitalization, omissions, punctuation, and spelling (COPS).

Young voters are not voting the way they should. The latest figures show that only

20 percent are going to the poles. The next-older generation is, the so-called baby

boomers, they are going to the poles at about twice that rate. Because I am part of the young group, I am concerned, but the answers to why we usually do not bother to vote are as obvious as the nose on your face. For one thing the younger people do not think voting changes anything. The political parties are all about the same, and the candidates look and talk alike, even though they seem angry with each other. For another a lot of young voters do not have parents that voted or even talked about politics when they were growing up, they don't either. Still another thing is that the issues going around do not move young people that much. The politicians talk about the national debt and social security and health care and we are concerned about jobs and the high cost of education. If they could get people we could believe in and they would talk about issue that matter to us, then maybe they would see more of us at the polls.

EXERCISE 2   Revising and Editing

Mark this rough draft for coherence, language, unity, emphasis, support, and sentences (CLUESS). Then edit the paragraph, correcting fundamentals such as capitalization, omissions, punctuation, and spelling (COPS).

High school dress codes do not make any sense to me. I have heard all the reasons. Too many kids wear gang clothes, and some get attacked or even killed. Parents have to put up too much money and even then the kids without parents with deep pockets can not compete. And then there are those that say kids behave bad if they dress in a free spirit way. Let's take them one at a time. As for the gang stuff, it is mainly how you act, not how you look, and if the gang stuff is still a problem, then just ban certain items of clothing. You do not have to go to the extreames of uniforms, just change the attitude, not the clothes. Then comes the money angle. Let the kid get a part-time job if they want better clothes. The behavior number is not what I can relate to. I mean, you go to class and learn, and you do it the school way, but the way you dress should have something to do with how you want to express yourself. Do they want to turn out a bunch of little robots that think the same way, behave the same way, and yes with the dress code even look the same way. Get real! If they will cut us some slack with how we dress, they will get happier campers in the classroom. Later better citizens in society.

Writing Process Worksheet
(completed through Stage Two)

Name Cyrus Norton   **Title** Magic Johnson, an NBA Great   **Due Date** Monday, October 22, 9 a.m.

Use the back of this page or separate paper if you need more space.

Assignment

In the space below, write whatever you need to know about your assignment, including information about the topic, audience, pattern of writing, length, whether to include a rough draft or revised drafts, and whether your paper must be typed.

Topic: person who has achieved excellence / about qualities that made him or her excellent / analysis by division / 200 to 300 words / paragraph / one or more rough drafts / typed final draft / audience of instructor and other students, those who have heard of the subject but don't have detailed information—

Stage One

Explore Freewrite, brainstorm (list), cluster, or take notes as directed by your instructor.

Stage Two

Organize Write a topic sentence or thesis; label the subject and focus parts.

Magic Johnson was a great NBA star because he was excellent in shooting,
<u>subject</u>   <u>focus</u>

passing, rebounding, and leading.

Write an outline or an outline alternative. For reading-based writing, include quotations and references with page numbers as support in the outline.

I. Shooting
   A. Short shots
   B. Long shots
   C. Free throws
II. Passing
   A. No-look
   B. Precise
III. Rebounding
   A. Tall
   B. Strong
IV. Leading
   A. Energy
   B. Spirit

Stage Three

Write   On separate paper, write and then revise your paragraph or essay as many times as necessary for **c**oherence, **l**anguage (usage, tone, and diction), **u**nity, **e**mphasis, **s**upport, and **s**entences (**CLUESS**). Read your work aloud to hear and correct any grammatical errors or awkward-sounding sentences.

Edit any problems in fundamentals, such as **c**apitalization, **o**missions, **p**unctuation, and **s**pelling (**COPS**). (See the revised and edited rough draft on page 267.)

EXERCISE 3   Revising and Editing

Mark this rough draft for coherence, language, unity, emphasis, support, and sentences (CLUESS). Then edit the paragraph, correcting fundamentals such as capitalization, omissions, punctuation, and spelling (COPS).

In the los Angeles Basin, people know why the Santa Anas are called the "devil winds." I know I do. At their worst they come in from the desert searing hot like the breeth of a blast furnace, tumbling over the mountain ranges and streaking down the canyons. Pitilessly destroying and disrupting. I hate them. Trees are striped of foliage, broken, and toppled. Fires that starts in the foothills may become firestorms. And bombard the downwind areas with lots of stuff. That sounds bad, doesn't it? But even without fire, the winds picks up sand, dirt, and debris and sent them toward the ocean as a hot, dry tide going out. All the time the Santa Anas are relentless, humming, howling, and whining through yards, and rattling and ripling lose shingles. Palm fronds move around. I have seen it and heard it lots of times. Dogs howl and often panic and run away, birds hunkers down in windbreaks; and human beings mostly stay inside Wiping up dust, cough-

ing, and getting grumpy. The devil winds earning their reputation. Santa Anas suck.

EXERCISE 4   Revising and Editing

Using your topic from Exercise 5 in Chapter 15, write a rough draft and a final draft. Use CLUESS and COPS for revising and editing.

Or, do the following:
Fill in the blank to complete the topic sentence: _____ [person's name] is an excellent [coach, doctor, neighbor, parent, preacher, teacher, sibling].

Then use the topic sentence to write a paragraph. Go through the complete writing process. Use one or more prewriting techniques (freewriting, brainstorming, clustering, outlining), write a first draft, revise your draft as many times as necessary, edit your work, and write a final polished paragraph.

In your drafts, you may rephrase the topic sentence as necessary. Using the paragraph on page 267 (showing Magic Johnson as a shooter, passer, rebounder, and leader) as a model, divide your topic into whatever qualities make your subject an excellent example of whichever type of person you have chosen.**

WRITER'S GUIDELINES   The Writing Process: Stage Three

1. **Writing the rough draft**: Referring to your outline for guidance and to your topic sentence for limits, write a first, or rough, draft. Do not get caught up in correcting and polishing your writing during this stage.

2. **Revising**: Mark and revise your rough draft, rewriting as many times as necessary to produce an effective paragraph. The main points of revision are contained in the acronym **CLUESS**, expressed here as questions.

   Coherence: Does the material flow smoothly, with each idea leading logically to the next?

   Language: Are the words appropriate for the message, occasion, and audience?

   Unity: Are all ideas related to and subordinate to the topic sentence?

   Emphasis: Have you used techniques such as repetition and placement of ideas to emphasize your main point(s)?

   Support: Have you presented material to back up, justify, or prove your topic sentence?

   Sentences: Have you used some variety of structure and avoided fragments, comma splices, and run-ons?

3. **Editing**: Examine your work carefully. Look for problems in **c**apitalization, **o**missions, **p**unctuation, and **s**pelling (**COPS**).

4. **Using word-processing features**: Use your thesaurus and spell checker to help you revise and edit, but note that those features have their limitations.

5. **Using the Writing Process Worksheet**: Explore your topic, organize your ideas, and write your paragraphs using the Writing Process Worksheet as your guide. Photocopy the blank form on page 6.

Chapter 17

Paragraphs and Essays

FLOW OF WRITING

Writing the Short Essay

The definition of a paragraph gives us a framework for defining an essay: A **paragraph** is a group of sentences, each with the function of supporting a single, main idea, which is contained in the topic sentence.

The main parts of a paragraph are the topic sentence (subject and focus), support (evidence and reasoning), and, often, the concluding sentence at the end. Now let's use that framework for an essay. An **essay** is a group of paragraphs, each with the function of stating or supporting a controlling idea called the **thesis**.

The main parts of an essay are as follows:

Introduction: carries the thesis, which states the controlling idea—much like the topic sentence for a paragraph but on a larger scale.
Development: introduces the evidence and reasoning—the support.
Conclusion: provides an appropriate ending—often a restatement of or reflection on the thesis.

Thus, considered structurally, a paragraph is often an essay in miniature. That does not mean that all paragraphs can grow up to be essays or that all essays can shrink to become paragraphs. For college writing, however, a good understanding of the parallel between well-organized paragraphs and well-organized essays is useful. As you learn the properties of effective paragraphs—those with a strong topic sentence and strong support—you also learn how to organize an essay, if you just magnify the procedure. The reverse can be said for the essay in relation to the paragraph. The essay form can be used across the curriculum and, with modifications, at the workplace.

Figure 17.1
Paragraph and Essay
Compared

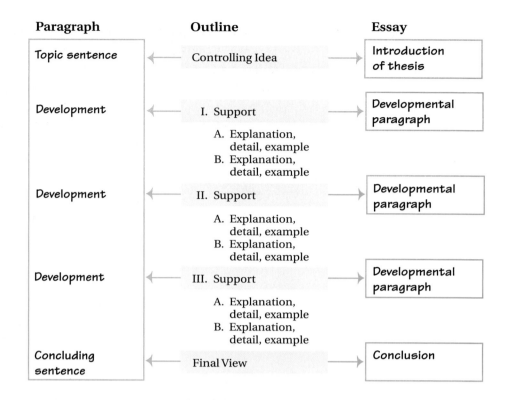

Figure 17.1 illustrates the parallel parts of outlines, paragraphs, and essays. Of course, the parallel components are not exactly the same in a paragraph and an essay. The paragraph is shorter and requires much less development, and some paragraph topics simply could not be developed much more extensively to their advantage. But let us consider the ones that can. What happens? How do we proceed?

INTRODUCTORY PARAGRAPH

The topic-sentence idea is expanded to the introductory paragraph through elaboration: explanation, historical background, anecdote, quotation, or stress on the significance of an idea. Usually the introduction is about three to six sentences long. If you say too much in your introduction, your paper will be top-heavy. If you do not say enough, your readers will be confused. A solid opening paragraph should

- introduce the subject through the thesis or controlling idea.
- gain reader interest.
- move the reader into the middle paragraphs.
- avoid any statement of apology about your topic or your writing and avoid beginning with a statement such as "I am writing an essay about. . . ."

MIDDLE PARAGRAPHS

The middle paragraphs are similar to the paragraphs you have been writing. They are developmental paragraphs used to support the thesis. Each has its own unity based on the topic sentence, moves logically and coherently, and has adequate and appropriate development. The topic sentence is usually at the beginning of the paragraph in a college essay, regardless of the form. Although some essays are an expansion of a particular form of discourse and therefore use basically the same pattern for each paragraph, almost all essays combine the forms. For example, you might have one middle paragraph that gives examples, one that defines, and one that clarifies. You may also have combinations within paragraphs. Nevertheless, developmental paragraphs are always related to the central idea and presented in a logical arrangement. The coherence of the paragraphs can often be improved by the use of the same principles that you have applied to individual paragraphs: using sequence words such as *first*, *second*, and *third*; using transitional words such as *therefore*, *moreover*, and *for example*; and arranging material in chronological order, spatial order, or order of relative importance.

CONCLUDING PARAGRAPH

Like the introductory paragraph, the concluding paragraph is a special unit with a specific function. In the concluding paragraph, usually three to six sentences long, you end on a note of finality. The way that you end depends on what you want to do. If you cannot decide on how to end, try going back to your introduction and see what you said there. If you posed a question, the answer should be in the conclusion. If you laid out the framework for an exploration of the topic, then perhaps you will want to bring your discussion together with a summary statement. Or, perhaps a quotation, an anecdote, or a restatement of the thesis in slightly different words would be effective. Do not end with a complaint, an apology, or the introduction of a new topic or new support. Do not begin your conclusion with a worn-out phrase such as "last but not least" or "in conclusion." Try for a fresh approach.

Examining a Paragraph and an Essay

The following paragraph and essay, both on the topic of drunk driving, were written by the same student. Notice how each is developed.

GET THEM OFF THE ROAD (paragraph)
Daniel Humphreys

Topic sentence

Drunk driving has become such a severe problem in California that something must be done. The best solution is to do what Sweden did long ago: Lower the blood-alcohol content level to .04 percent for drunk-driving arrests.

I. Support

Driving is not a right; it is a privilege, and that privilege should not be extended to the person who drinks to the extent that his or her physical and

II. Support

mental abilities are significantly impaired. Alcohol, working as a depressant, affects our entire nervous system, according to numerous sources cited in *The Police Officer's Source Book*. As a result of this impairment, "50 percent of all fatal traffic accidents" involve intoxicated drivers, as reported by the National Highway Traffic Safety Administration. Cavenaugh and Associates, research specialists, say that in California 8,430 people were killed in alcohol-related accidents in the four-year period from 2001 through 2005. They go on to say

III. Support

Concluding sentence

that nationally intoxicated drivers cost us somewhere between $14 billion and $16 billion each year. It is time to give drunk drivers a message: "Stay off the road. You are costing us pain, injury, and death, and no one has the right to do that."

GET THEM OFF THE ROAD (essay)
Daniel Humphreys

Introduction

Thesis of essay

The state of California, along with the rest of the nation, has a problem with society involving drinking and driving. Prohibition is not the answer, as history has demonstrated. But there is a practical answer to be found in a law. <u>I believe that the legal BAC (blood-alcohol concentration) while driving should be lowered from .08 percent to .04 percent for three strong reasons.</u>

Topic sentence of paragraph

I. Support paragraph 1

First, <u>driving in California is a privilege</u>, not a right, and <u>a person impaired by alcohol should not be allowed that privilege</u>. Statutory law states that when stopped by a police officer who suspects drunk driving, one must submit to a BAC test. The level of impairment is an individual trait because of the elapsed time of consumption, body size, and tolerance, but <u>alcohol</u> is a depressant to all of us. It <u>affects our nervous system and slows our muscular reactions</u>. As a result of extensive scientific study, Sweden determined that .04 percent BAC was the level of significant impairment, and, therefore, it passed a federal law to enforce drunk-driving penalties at that point. Penalties there are extreme.

Topic sentence of paragraph

II. Support paragraph 2

Second, <u>we</u>, like the people in Sweden, <u>are concerned about the dangers of drunk driving</u>. The National Highway Traffic Safety Administration has stated that <u>"50 percent of all fatal accidents"</u> involve intoxicated drivers <u>and that 75 percent of those drivers have a BAC of .10 percent or higher</u>. Cavenaugh and Associates, a California think tank, reports that in the four-year period between 2001 and 2005, 19,784 people were injured and 8,430 were killed in alcohol-related accidents in California.

Topic sentence of paragraph

III. Support paragraph 3

Third, even if we are among the fortunate few who are not touched directly by the problems of drunk driving, <u>there are other effects</u>. <u>One is money</u>. There are the loss of production, cost of insurance, cost of delays in traffic, cost of medical care for those who have no insurance, and many other costs. Cavenaugh and Associates say that drunk drivers cost us nationally somewhere between $14 billion and $16 billion a year.

Conclusion

Restated thesis

Police officers report that drinking people are quick to say, "I'm okay to drive," but every four years our nation loses more lives to drunk drivers than it lost in the entire Vietnam War. To lower the legal BAC limit to .04 percent would mean saving lives, property, and money.

EXERCISE 1   Expanding a Paragraph to an Essay

The following paragraph could easily be expanded into an essay because the topic sentence and its related statements can be developed into an introduction; each of the main divisions (five) can be expanded into a separate paragraph; and the restated topic sentence can, with elaboration, become the concluding paragraph. Divide the following paragraph with the symbol ¶ and annotate it in the left-hand margin with the words *Introduction*, *Support* (and numbers for the middle five paragraphs), and *Conclusion* to show the parts that would be developed further. The topic sentence has already been marked for you.

WHAT IS A GANG?
Will Cusak

The word *gang* is often used loosely to mean "a group of people who go around together," but that does not satisfy the concerns of law-enforcement

Topic sentence

people and sociologists. <u>For those professionals, the definition of gang has five parts that combine to form a unit</u>. First a gang has to have a name. Some well-known gang names are Bloods, Crips, Hell's Angels, and Mexican Mafia. The second part of the definition is clothing or other identifying items such as tattoos. The clothing may be of specific brands or colors, such as blue for Crips and red for Bloods. Members of the Aryan Brotherhood often have blue thunderbolt tattoos. A third component is rituals. They may involve such things as the use of handshakes, other body language or signing, and graffiti. A fourth is binding membership. A gang member is part of an organization, a kind of family, with obligations and codes of behavior to follow. Finally, a gang will be involved in some criminal behavior, something such as prostitution, drugs, thievery, or burglary. There are many different kinds of gangs—ethnic, regional, behavioral—but they all have these five characteristics.

EXERCISE 2   Analyzing Essay Form

Underline the thesis in the first paragraph; the topic sentences in paragraphs 2, 3, and 4; and the most forceful concluding statement in the last paragraph. In the left-hand margin, label each part you underlined. In this essay the topic sentences are not all at the beginning of paragraphs. Observe how information is used to support the topic sentences, and double underline some key phrases of that support.

MODERN WIFE
Marie Maxwell

1   The modern woman, according to dozens of magazine articles, is a super being of incredible organization, patience, wisdom, and grooming. She is never cross with loved ones and never too tired for a game with her children. She wouldn't think of throwing a frozen dinner into the oven and calling it supper. She even has the courage (and the cleaning skills) to own a white carpet. She is a being apart, and I could never quite measure up. I believed that, until I recently decided there were far more women like me than there were Wonder Women.

2   The ideal woman featured in the magazines has a lovely home, a handsome husband, and children who at all times appear to have just stepped from the pages of a clothing catalog. Her house is always clean and ready for drop-in guests, and should these guests arrive at supper time, so much the better. My reality is a single-parent home. I have a son who I suspect is color-blind, judging from some of his outfits. Often when I return home from work, I must step carefully to avoid the assortment of books, clothes, and toys strewn from one room to the next. Unexpected company better not show up! As for feeding uninvited guests—they had better have an invitation if they expect to be fed.

3   Unlike me, the women in the articles always seem to have such glamorous and exciting jobs. Most of them receive six-figure incomes and love their jobs (oops!) *careers*. They are fashion designers, doctors, or managers on their way up the corporate ladder. Every working day is another fascinating challenge to anticipate. I sigh wistfully as I read, and I think how dull my secretarial duties are by comparison. I've received two promotions in eight years—hardly a mercurial rise to

the top. I generally enjoy my job; it pays the bills and a little bit more, and it has enough variety to prevent abysmal boredom. It's just that I feel somehow shamed by the way I earn my living after reading an article about the "new woman."

4   Most magazine writers choose as a subject a woman who has also returned to school, in addition to everything else she does. It depresses me to read that she has usually earned a 3.80 grade point average, seemingly effortlessly. Her family cheers her on and never seems to mind the time that school and homework demand from her. Even more disheartening is that her family members report with pride that she was able to make those grades without depriving them of their normal family life. That certainly hasn't been my experience. Algebra, for example, demanded so much of my time and energy that bitter words and sarcasm were routine. When I was married, my husband was supportive only as long as my classes didn't disrupt his life.

5   Some modern women may indeed be just as they are described in the magazines, but I feel certain that there are many more just like me. My wish would be to have a writer showcase a woman, if not with feet of clay, at least shuffling her way artlessly through a cluttered life and, at times, barely coping. I might not admire her, but I wouldn't feel inadequate, and I'm certain I could identify with her. In fact, I think I would like her.

Topics for Short Essays

Many paragraph topics in this book can become topics for short essays. In Part IV, the writing instruction is presented according to the well-known patterns listed here. Although the writing topics suggested at the end of Chapters 18 through 24 refer to paragraph writing, almost all of the topics can be further developed into essays. You may want to refer back to the following list if you are working on an essay assignment.

Descriptive Narration: Expand each part of the narrative form (situation, conflict, struggle, outcome, meaning) into one or more paragraphs. Give the most emphasis to the struggle. Incorporate descriptive details.

Exemplification: Expand one example into an extended example or expand a group of examples into separate paragraphs. Each paragraph should support the main point.

Analysis by Division: Expand each part of the unit into a paragraph.

Process Analysis: Expand the preparation and each step in the process into a separate paragraph.

Cause and Effect: Expand each cause or effect into a separate paragraph.

Comparison and Contrast: In the point-by-point pattern, expand each point into a separate paragraph. In the subject-by-subject pattern, first expand each subject into a separate paragraph. If you have sufficient material on each point, you can also expand each point into a separate paragraph.

Argument: Expand the refutation and each main division of support into a separate paragraph.

WRITER'S GUIDELINES   Paragraphs and Essays

You do not usually set out to write an essay by first writing a paragraph. However, the organization for the paragraph and the essay is often the same, and the writing process is also the same. You still proceed from initial prewriting to topic, to outline, to draft, to revising, to editing, to final paper. The difference is often only a matter of development and indentation.

1. The well-designed paragraph and the well-designed essay often have the same form.

   a. The **introduction** of an essay carries the thesis, which states the controlling idea—much like the topic sentence for a paragraph but on a larger scale.

   b. The **development**, or middle part, supplies evidence and reasoning—the support.

   c. The **conclusion** provides an appropriate ending—often a restatement of or reflection on the thesis.

2. These are the important relationships:

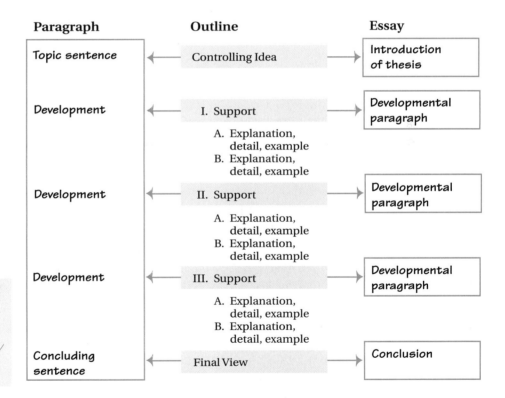

Part IV WRITING PARAGRAPHS AND ESSAYS: INSTRUCTION, WITH INTEGRATED READING SELECTIONS

Part IV discusses—and also demonstrates through reading selections—how our thoughts often occur in flexible, useful patterns. As you write in classes across the campus, notice how many regular writing assignments—especially papers and essay tests—direct you to describe, narrate, analyze (in many forms such as causes and effects, comparison and contrast, and definition), or argue a point. Following the same principles, you may be asked to use similar forms at the workplace as you write incident reports, proposals, evaluations, and recommendations. Though one form may indicate purpose and guide organization, it is important to note that writing passages are almost always a combination of forms.

Chapter 18

Descriptive Narration
Moving Through Space and Time

FLOW OF WRITING

WHEN TO USE DESCRIPTIVE NARRATION

FOR COLLEGE WRITING ASSIGNMENTS

- Descriptive narratives are written for many assignments in different college subject areas. If you intend to become a teacher, you will attend schools and make observations or perhaps sit in on a class on campus involving child care, where you will observe students and write brief case-study reports or incident reports. In police- or fire-science courses, you may write about incidents you observe when you visit stations or do a ride-along in a squad car. In science courses you may report on experiments. In marketing classes you may write about personal experiences as they relate to concepts of workplace behavior, ethics, or retail sales.

IN CAREERS AND AT THE WORKPLACE

- At the workplace you may be called upon to write descriptive narratives as incident reports, case studies, support in a proposal, comparative evaluation of products or services, text of sales advertisement, or promotional release of products or services.
- Your ability to write effective descriptive narratives will aid your company and reflect well on you as an intelligent, educated employee. Although the form of these statements will vary, the basic principles presented in this chapter can be applied to all.

DESCRIPTIVE NARRATION IN A CARTOON

THE QUIGMANS   by Buddy Hickerson

B. Hickerson, copyright Los Angeles Times Syndicate. Reprinted by permission.

Francine's virtue is saved from a reckless
advance with the deployment of her
first-date air bag.

WRITING DESCRIPTIVE NARRATION

As patterns of writing for college assignments, description and narration are
almost always associated. You would seldom describe something extensively
without relating it to something else, especially to a story, or a narrative.
Conversely, you would seldom narrate something (tell the story) without including
some description. A narrative moves through time; a description occupies and,
often, moves through space. Narrative and description run together seamlessly,
the narrative providing the structure of something happening and the description
providing details of what things seem to be. In this chapter we discuss narration
and description separately and then show how the two can very naturally and
easily be blended as descriptive narration. First let's examine their individual
principles and see how each one can be a major concern of a particular
assignment; then we'll read some paragraphs and essays to see how description
and narration can function together for mutual benefit.

The Narrative Pattern

In our everyday lives, we tell stories and invite other people to do so by asking questions such as "What happened at work today?" and "What did you do
last weekend?" We are disappointed when the answer is "Nothing much." We
may be equally disappointed when a person does not give us enough details or
gives us too many and spoils the effect. After all, we are interested in people's
stories and in the people who tell them. We like narratives.

What is a narrative? A **narrative** is an account of an incident or a series of incidents that make up a complete and significant action. A narrative can be as short as a joke, as long as a novel, or anything in between, including the essay. Each narrative has five properties: situation, conflict, struggle, outcome, and meaning.

SITUATION

Situation is the background for the action. The situation may be described only briefly, or it may even be implied. ("Tom Sawyer, a youngster living in a small town, has been directed by his Aunt Polly to whitewash the fence in front of their house.")

CONFLICT

Conflict is friction, such as a problem in the surroundings, with another person(s), or within the individual. The conflict, which is at the heart of each story, produces struggle. ("A fun-loving boy who would rather go fishing than do simple, manual chores, Tom wants to find others to do his work for him. He knows that others would not want to paint the fence, so he must persuade them.")

STRUGGLE

Struggle, which need not be physical, is the manner of dealing with the conflict. The struggle adds action or engagement and generates the plot. ("Hearing Ben Rogers nearby making huffing steamboat sounds and enjoying play, Tom pretends he is a serious artist as he brushes the sparkling white paint onto the dark fence before standing back to admire it. When Ben starts to tease Tom about having to work, Tom says, 'What do you call work?' 'Why, ain't that work?' Ben asks. Tom says it suits him, and few boys could do it. Soon Tom has Ben asking if he can paint the fence and offering an apple for the privilege. Tom relents. Then other friends drop by and fall for the same scheme.")

OUTCOME

Outcome is the result of the struggle. ("In a short time the fence has three coats of paint, and Tom has a collection of treasures, including a dead rat and a one-eyed cat.")

MEANING

Meaning is the significance of the story, which may be deeply philosophical or simple, stated or implied. ("Tom has discovered that to make a person want something it is only necessary to make that something seem difficult to obtain.")

Most narratives written as college assignments will have an expository purpose (that is, they explain a specified idea). Often the narrative will be merely an extended example. Therefore, the meaning of the narrative is exceedingly important and should be clear, whether it is stated or implied.

The Descriptive Pattern

Description is the use of words to represent the appearance or nature of something. Often called a **word picture**, description attempts to present its subject for the mind's eye. In doing so, it does not merely become an indifferent camera; instead, it selects details that will depict something well. Just what details the descriptive writer selects will depend on several factors, especially the type of description and the dominant impression in the passage.

TYPES OF DESCRIPTION

On the basis of treatment of subject material, description is customarily divided into two types: objective and subjective.

Effective **objective description** presents the subject clearly and directly as it exists outside the realm of feelings. If you are explaining the function of the heart, the characteristics of a computer chip, or the renovation of a manufacturing facility, your description would probably feature specific, impersonal details. Most technical and scientific writing is objective in that sense. It is likely to be practical and utilitarian, making little use of speculation or poetic technique while focusing on details of sight.

Effective **subjective description** is also concerned with clarity and it may be direct, but it conveys a feeling about the subject and sets a mood while making a point. Because most expression involves personal views, even when it explains by analysis, subjective description (often called **emotional description**) has a broader range of uses than objective description.

Descriptive passages can have a combination of objective and subjective description; only the larger context of the passage will reveal the main intent.

IMAGERY

To convey your main concern effectively to readers, you will have to give some sensory impressions. These sensory impressions, collectively called **imagery**, refer to that which can be experienced by the senses—what we can see, smell, taste, hear, and touch.

Subjective description is more likely to use more images and words rich in associations than is objective description. But just as a fine line cannot always be drawn between the objective and the subjective, a fine line cannot always be drawn between word choice in one and in the other. However, we can say with certainty that whatever the type of description, careful word choice will always be important.

General and Specific Words

To move from the general to the specific is to move from the whole class or body to the individual(s); for example:

General	Specific	More Specific
food	pastry	Twinkie
mess	grease	oil slicks on table
drink	soda	mug of root beer
odor	smell from grill	smell of frying onions

Abstract and Concrete Words

Words are classified as abstract or concrete depending on what they refer to. **Abstract words** refer to qualities or ideas: *good, ordinary, ultimate, truth, beauty, maturity, love*. **Concrete words** refer to substances or things; they have reality: *onions, grease, buns, tables, food*. The specific concrete words, sometimes called **concrete particulars**, often support generalizations effectively and convince the reader of the accuracy of the account.

DOMINANT IMPRESSION

Never try to give all of the details in a description. Instead, be selective, picking only those that you need to make a dominant impression, always taking into account the knowledge and attitudes of your readers. Remember, description is not photographic. If you wish to describe a person, select only those traits that will project your intended dominant impression. If you wish to describe a landscape, do not give all the details that you might find in a picture; just pick the details that support what you want to say. That extremely important dominant impression is directly linked to your purpose and is created by the choosing and arranging of images, figurative language, and revealing details.

Transitional Words

Consider using the following transitional words to improve coherence by connecting ideas with ideas, sentences with sentences, and paragraphs with paragraphs.

FOR DESCRIPTION (PLACE): above, over, under, below, nearby, near, across, beyond, among, to the right, to the left, in the background, in the foreground, further, beside, opposite, within sight, out of sight

FOR NARRATION (TIME): after, before, later, earlier, initially, soon, recently, next, today, tomorrow, yesterday, now, then, until, currently, when, finally, not long after, immediately, (at) first, (at) last, third, previously, in the meantime, meanwhile

FOR ALL PATTERNS OF WRITING: The <u>HOTSHOT CAT</u> words: <u>H</u>owever, <u>O</u>therwise, <u>T</u>herefore, <u>S</u>imilarly, <u>H</u>ence, <u>O</u>n the other hand, <u>T</u>hen, <u>C</u>onsequently, <u>A</u>lso, <u>T</u>hus (See pages 74–75 for additional transitional words.)

PROCEDURES FOR WRITING DESCRIPTIVE NARRATION

- For extensive use of description, these questions may be helpful:

  What is your subject? (a college stadium)
  What is the dominant impression? (deserted)
  What is the situation? (You are walking through the stands an hour after a game.)
  What is the order? (time and place)

What details support the dominant impression?

1. (the sight of vacant seats and an abandoned playing field)
2. (intermingled smell of stale food and spilled beer)
3. (sight of napkins, paper plates and cups, programs, and peanut shells blowing in a fierce wind)
4. (raspy sound of the wind blowing paper products and whining through the steel girders)
5. (the tacky feel and popping sound of your sneakers as they stick to and pull free from cement coated with spilled soft drinks)

Clustering may be useful.

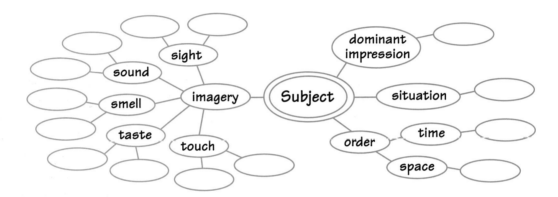

• For narration use a simple outline composed of these parts: situation, conflict, struggle (not necessarily physical), outcome, and meaning.

AN ANNOTATED DESCRIPTIVE NARRATION

My Burning Scarf

JULIE LEE

Student Julie Lee writes about a scarf that was mistakenly burned in a family ceremony. Her attention to descriptive detail highlights this vivid recollection and conveys the poignancy of her experience.

Description	Narration	
Dominant impression	Situation	During my childhood, my <u>favorite possession</u> was the yellow scarf my dad gave me when I was five. <u>It would bring me pleasure and pain</u>.
Topic sentence		Hand-sewn with care in Japan, it attracted many curious and envious eyes. Needless to say, I was the proud owner of that scarf and loved the
Objective descriptive details		attention it brought me. The scarf was <u>about two feet square and made of pure virgin wool</u>. <u>It was decorated with a fringed green edge, and in</u>
Images: sight		<u>one corner five embroidered yellow-colored chicks played against the</u> <u>background needlework of lush green grass.</u> The material was as <u>soft</u>
Images: touch		<u>as cashmere</u> and had the <u>warmth of fur</u>. It kept my cheeks warm when
	Conflict	I wrapped it loosely around my neck. But when I was six, I let my seriously ill sister wear my scarf to the doctor's office. She didn't give it back to me immediately, and because she was sick, I didn't ask for it. Sadly, she died of leukemia after months of suffering. A few days after
Images: sight	Struggle	she died, from my bedroom, I <u>saw my mother</u> in the backyard <u>burning</u> <u>personal items</u> that belonged to my dead sister. It is a Korean custom

Images: sight Images: sound		to do so. My mother was crying and so were other adults standing in a circle around the fire. Then I saw my mother pick up my <u>wadded yellow scarf</u> and shake it out. I rushed outside, <u>shrieking</u> for her to stop. Over the sounds of <u>sobbing</u> and the <u>popping</u> of the fire, I wanted
	Outcome	to shout, "That's my scarf, my precious possession." But I didn't, and my mother, thinking I was crying only for my sister, flung it into the
Images: sound	Meaning	flames of the fire that sizzled and cracked, and the green and yellow of my childhood turned to orange, then red, then gray.

Career-Related Writing

THE NARRATIVE AS INCIDENT REPORT

In most instances the incident report denotes problems. Something unforeseen has occurred—an accident, a theft, a disturbance, a dangerous condition, a lost child, an act of vandalism, an equipment failure, a health emergency other than one caused by an accident—and it must be documented. A report on one of these incidents is likely to be written up as an important record. It may be the essential information on which law enforcement acts, equipment is replaced, clients are served, safety is assured, security is established, or the physical plant is protected.

These reports are sometimes dictated, but they are more often written by the person most directly related to the incident. Your ability to write an effective report will aid your company and reflect well on you as an intelligent, educated employee. Although the procedure and the form of these incident reports will vary somewhat, there are some basic principles that can be applied to all.

Obviously, your report will be a narrative, and the techniques you use in writing both the personal and the cross-curricular statements will serve you well in writing the career-related, or workplace, incident report. The principles of writing an incident report include the following:

1. Identify the kind of problem. This may be part of a form provided by your employer.

2. Indicate when the problem occurred.

3. Provide an account of what happened.
   - Write in the first person ("I"); you are the one who is writing the report.
   - Start with the date, time, and your reason for involvement.
   - Include quotation marks if you use the words of anyone reporting on the incident.
   - Use facts, not opinions.
   - Remain objective, do not step outside your work expertise and become a psychologist, philosopher, physician, or moralist. If you do, should this report make its way to a court case, what you say will be discredited.
   - Use past tense. You are writing about something that has already happened.
   - Use mostly active voice. For example, write, "Mills made the report," not "The report was made by Mills."
   - Identify those involved. Drop the titles, such as Mr., Mrs., Dr., and so on. After the first reference to the person in the report, use only the surname or the first initial and the surname.

4. If appropriate, write a recommendation for what could be done to avoid a repeat of such an incident.

See pages 326–327 for an example of an incident report.

FINDING PATTERNS IN PHOTOS

EXERCISE 1   A Text-Based Activity for Groups or Individuals

Portrait of a coughing waitress

Paul Franklin/Image Stock Imagery/Photolibrary

Here you see the famous "Coughing Waitress" photo. Imagine you are in the Night Hawk Diner just before dawn. You are hungry, really hungry. You are headed toward a long day of job interviews, with no breaks for sit-down meals. You have ordered an Omaha Omelet as big as the waitress's apron, Texas Toast with two wedges of butter, a frothy glass of whole milk, and a cup of strong black coffee. Your mouth waters in anticipation as the fry cook slides the platter of steaming omelet across an oil-slicked counter to the waitress. Then the waitress, who sniffled daintily when she took your order, now coughs robustly into her hand just as she begins to arrange your meal on your table. You figure her hand filtered out most of her cough, but you worry that a possible germ fog descended on your food, and you notice that her hand brushed against your Texas Toast. What do you do? Here are some options. Others may occur to you. You can (a) ask for a new order, (b) leave with the intentions of getting some items from a vending machine later, (c) talk to the manager about a new order and a different waitress, or (d) eat the meal.

Pick one of those options or compose one of your own and complete these basic parts of a narrative pattern. Use one or more sentences for each heading.

Situation:

Conflict:

Struggle (weighing the options):

Outcome (your immediate decision and the long-range consequences):

Meaning (what you learned from the experience):

Before you identify too much with the role of the hungry customer, try another perspective, that of the waitress. What if she had a bad cold but was not blessed with sick leave and was way in debt? What if she was also a single mother with a sick child and bad health insurance? She is coughing at work.

If your instructor directs you to do so, write a paragraph or short essay about this incident. Include descriptive details, and write about one or both perspectives.

Practicing Patterns of Narration

Some narratives seem more structured than others, but all have the same basic patterns. The parts, especially conflict and struggle, will vary in extent, depending on the circumstances.

EXERCISE 2   Completing Narrative Patterns

Fill in the blanks to complete the pattern for the topic "Lost and Found." Add descriptive details as needed.

(Situation)   I.   Person taking store money deposit bag to bank

(Conflict)   II. Person loses bag

(Struggle)   III. _____

(Outcome)   IV. _____

(Meaning)   V.   _____

EXERCISE 3   Completing Narrative Patterns

Fill in the blanks to complete the pattern for the topic "Good Samaritan." Add descriptive details as needed.

(Situation)   I.   Driver with flat tire, dead of night

(Conflict)   II. No spare tire

(Struggle)   III. _____

(Outcome)   IV. _____

(Meaning)   V.   _____

Practicing Patterns of Description

Description, which is almost always used with other patterns, is very important and often neglected. The following exercise features descriptive writing that supports a dominant impression.

EXERCISE 4   Completing Descriptive Patterns

Fill in the blanks to complete the following outline.

A Produce Area in a Supermarket

(Dominant impression: Diversity)

I. Food displays (sight—color, shape)

    A. Pile of red radishes _____

    B. _____

    C. _____

II. Smells (from vegetables, fruits)

    A. Acidic tangerines _____

    B. _____

III. Textures (smooth or rough to touch)

    A. Rough-skinned potatoes _____

    B. _____

IV. Taste (samples of sweet/sour, ripe/unripe)

    A. _____

    B. _____

Readings for Critical Thinking, Discussion, and Writing

READING STRATEGIES AND OBJECTIVES

Underlining and annotating these reading selections will help you answer the questions that follow the selections, discuss the material in class, and prepare for reading-based writing assignments. As you underline and annotate, pay special attention to the author's writing skills, logic, and message, and consider the relevance of the material to your own experiences and values.

Most selections begin with a Mindset suggestion that can help you create a readiness for connecting with what you are about to read.

PARAGRAPH

Blue Winds Dancing

THOMAS S. WHITECLOUD

In this passage Thomas S. Whitecloud gives his reaction at Christmastime to the area where he grew up on a Chippewa reservation. He is reacquainted with much more than the environment. His thoughts move both outward and inward as he returns home after a long absence.

MINDSET

Lock It In

Close your eyes and imagine you are returning to a memorable location from your childhood. What stands out to you that might be overlooked by others?

Christmas Eve comes in on a north wind. Snow clouds hang over the pines, and the night comes early. Walking along the railroad bed, I feel the calm peace of snow-bound forests on either side of me. I take my time; I am back in a world where time does not mean so much now. I am alone; alone but not nearly so lonely as I was back on the campus at school. Those are never lonely who love the snow and the pines, never lonely when the pines are wearing white shawls and snow crunches coldly underfoot. In the woods I know there are the tracks of deer and rabbit; I know that if I leave the rails and go into the woods, I shall find them. I walk along feeling glad because my legs are light and my feet seem to know that they are home. A deer comes out of the woods just ahead of me and stands silhouetted on the rails. The North, I feel, has welcomed me home. I watch him and am glad that I do not wish for a gun. He goes into the woods quietly, leaving only the design of his tracks in the snow. I walk on. Now and then I pass a field, white under the night sky, with houses at the far end. Smoke comes from the chimneys of the houses, and I try to tell what sort of wood each is burning by the smoke; some burn pine, others aspen, others tamarack. There is one from which comes black coal smoke that rises lazily and drifts out over the tops of the trees. I like to watch houses and try to imagine what might be happening in them.

EXERCISE 5   Discussion and Critical Thinking

1. State the dominant impression in a word or phrase.

2. Circle key words that support the dominant impression.

3. What is the point of view—first or third person?

4. What is the order—time, space, emphasis, or a combination?

5. Underline the topic sentence or thesis. If one is not stated, supply a brief one here.

ESSAYS

W-A-T-E-R

HELEN KELLER

Helen Keller was a remarkable person. With the help of her teacher and companion, Anne Sullivan, she conquered the disabilities of blindness and deafness and became one of the most famous and admired people of her time. In this passage, she wrote about what was perhaps the most important, constructive event in her life.

MINDSET
Lock It In

Reach out and touch an item on your desk. If you had never heard its name or seen it, what would be your thought?

1   One day, while I was playing with my new doll, Miss Sullivan put my big rag doll into my lap also, spelled "d-o-l-l" and tried to make me understand that "d-o-l-l" applied to both. Earlier in the day we had had a tussle over the words "m-u-g" and "w-a-t-e-r." Miss Sullivan had tried to impress it upon me that "m-u-g" is *mug* and that "w-a-t-e-r" is *water*, but I persisted in confounding the two. In despair she had dropped the subject for the time, only to renew it at the first opportunity. I became impatient at her repeated attempts and, seizing the new doll, I dashed it upon the floor. I was keenly delighted when I felt the fragments of the broken doll at my feet. Neither sorrow nor regret followed my passionate outburst. I had not loved the doll. In the still, dark world in which I lived there was no strong sentiment of tenderness. I felt my teacher sweep the fragments to one side of the hearth, and I had a sense of satisfaction that the cause of my discomfort was removed. She brought me my hat, and I knew I was going out into the warm sunshine. This thought, if a wordless sensation may be called a thought, made me hop and skip with pleasure.

2   We walked down the path to the well-house, attracted by the fragrance of the honeysuckle with which it was covered. Someone was drawing water and my teacher placed my hand under the spout. As the cool stream gushed over one hand she spelled into the other the word *water*, first slowly, then rapidly. I stood still, my whole attention fixed upon the motions of her fingers. Suddenly I felt a misty consciousness as of something forgotten—a thrill of returning thought; and somehow the mystery of language was revealed to me. I knew then that "w-a-t-e-r" meant the wonderful cool something that was flowing over my hand. That living word awakened my soul, gave it light, hope, joy, set it free! There were barriers still, it is true, but barriers that could in time be swept away.

EXERCISE 6   Discussion and Critical Thinking

1. What is the situation?

2. What is the conflict?

3. What struggle occurs?

4. What is the outcome of the struggle?

5. What is the meaning of this narrative?

The Jacket

GARY SOTO

Gary Soto, born April 12, 1952, was raised in Fresno, California. He is the author of eleven poetry collections for adults, most notably New and Selected Poems, *a 1995 finalist for both the Los Angeles Times Book Award and the National Book Award. His poems have appeared in many literary magazines, including* Ploughshares, Michigan Quarterly, Poetry International, *and* Poetry.

MINDSET

Lock It In

Imagine that someone special has just given you a necktie or pair of socks so unattractive it cries out for closet space. But this time you cannot hide the item. Instead you must wear it frequently until it is worn out.

1   My clothes have failed me. I remember the green coat that I wore in fifth and sixth grades when you either danced like a champ or pressed yourself against a greasy wall, bitter as a penny toward the happy couples.

2   When I needed a new jacket and my mother asked what kind I wanted, I described something like bikers wear: black leather and silver studs with enough belts to hold down a small town. We were in the kitchen, steam on the windows from her cooking. She listened so long while stirring dinner that I thought she understood for sure the kind I wanted. The next day when I got home from school, I discovered draped on my bedpost a jacket the color of day-old guacamole. I threw my books on the bed and approached the jacket slowly, as if it were a stranger whose hand I had to shake. I touched the vinyl sleeve, the collar, and peeked at the mustard-colored lining.

3   From the kitchen Mother yelled that my jacket was in the closet. I closed the door to her voice and pulled at the rack of clothes in the closet, hoping the jacket on the bedpost wasn't for me but my mean brother. No luck. I gave up. From my bed, I stared at the jacket. I wanted to cry because it was so ugly and so big that I knew I'd have to wear it a long time. I was a small kid, thin as a young tree, and it would be years before I'd have a new one. I stared at the jacket, like an enemy, thinking bad things before I took off my old jacket whose sleeves climbed halfway to my elbow.

4   I put the big jacket on. I zipped it up and down several times, and rolled the cuffs up so they didn't cover my hands. I put my hands in the pockets and flapped the jacket like a bird's wings. I stood in front of the mirror, full face, then profile, and then looked over my shoulder as if someone had called me. I sat on the bed, stood against the bed, and combed my hair to see what I would look like doing something natural. I looked ugly. I threw it on my brother's bed and looked at it for a long time before I slipped it on and went out to the backyard, smiling a "thank you" to my mom as I passed her in the kitchen. With my hands in my pockets I kicked a ball against the fence, and then climbed it to sit looking into the alley. I hurled orange peels at the mouth of an open garbage can and when the peels were gone I watched the white puffs of my breath thin to nothing.

5   I jumped down, hands in my pockets, and in the backyard on my knees I teased my dog, Brownie, by swooping my arms while making bird calls. He jumped at me and missed. He jumped again and again, until a tooth sunk deep, ripping an L-shaped tear on my left sleeve. I pushed Brownie away to study the tear as I would a cut on my arm. There was no blood, only a few loose pieces of fuzz. Damn dog, I thought, and pushed him away hard when

he tried to bite again. I got up from my knees and went to my bedroom to sit with my jacket on my lap, with the lights out.

6   That was the first afternoon with my new jacket. The next day I wore it to sixth grade and got a D on a math quiz. During the morning recess Frankie T., the playground terrorist, pushed me to the ground and told me to stay there until recess was over. My best friend, Steve Negrete, ate an apple while looking at me, and the girls turned away to whisper on the monkey bars. The teachers were no help: They looked my way and talked about how foolish I looked in my new jacket. I saw their heads bob with laughter, their hands half-covering their mouths.

7   Even though it was cold, I took off the jacket during lunch and played kick-ball in a thin shirt, my arms feeling like braille from goose bumps. But when I returned to class I slipped the jacket on and shivered until I was warm. I sat on my hands, heating them up, while my teeth chattered like a cup of crooked dice. Finally warm, I slid out of the jacket but a few minutes later put it back on when the fire bell rang. We paraded out into the yard where we, the sixth graders, walked past all the other grades to stand against the back fence. Everybody saw me. Although they didn't say out loud, "Man, that's ugly," I heard the buzz-buzz of gossip and even laughter that I knew was meant for me.

8   And so I went, in my guacamole jacket. So embarrassed, so hurt, I couldn't even do my homework. I received Cs on quizzes, and forgot the state capitals and the rivers of South America, our friendly neighbor. Even the girls who had been friendly blew away like loose flowers to follow the boys in neat jackets.

9   I wore that thing for three years until the sleeves grew short and my fore-arms stuck out like the necks of turtles. All during that time no love came to me—no little dark girl in a Sunday dress she wore on Monday. At lunchtime I stayed with the ugly boys who leaned against the chainlink fence and looked around with propellers of grass spinning in our mouths. We saw girls walk by alone, saw couples, hand in hand, their heads like bookends pressing air together. We saw them and spun our propellers so fast our faces were blurs.

10   I blame that jacket for those bad years. I blame my mother for her bad taste and her cheap ways. It was a sad time for the heart. With a friend I spent my sixth-grade year in a tree in the alley waiting for something good to happen to me in that jacket, which had become the ugly brother who tagged along wherever I went. And it was about that time that I began to grow. My chest puffed up with muscle and, strangely, a few more ribs. Even my hands, those fleshy hammers, showed bravely through the cuffs, the fingers already hardening for the coming fights. But that L-shaped rip on the left sleeve got bigger; bits of stuffing coughed out from its wound after a hard day of play. I finally Scotch-taped it closed, but in rain or cold weather the tape peeled off like a scab and more stuffing fell out until that sleeve shriveled into a palsied arm. That winter the elbows began to crack and whole chunks of green began to fall off. I showed the cracks to my mother, who always seemed to be at the stove with steamed-up glasses, and she said that there were children in Mexico who would love that jacket. I told her that this was America and yelled that Debbie, my sister, didn't have a jacket like mine. I ran outside, ready to cry, and climbed the tree by the alley to think bad thoughts and watch my breath puff white and disappear.

11   But whole pieces still casually flew off my jacket when I played hard, read quietly, or took vicious spelling tests at school. When it became so spotted that my brother began to call me "camouflage," I flung it over the fence into the alley. Later, however, I swiped the jacket off the ground and went inside to drape it across my lap and mope.

12   I was called to dinner: Steam silvered my mother's glasses as she said grace; my brother and sister with their heads bowed made ugly faces at their glasses of powdered milk. I gagged too, but eagerly ate big rips of buttered tortilla that held scooped up beans. Finished, I went outside with my jacket across my arm. It was a cold sky. The faces of clouds were piled up, hurting. I climbed the fence, jumping down with a grunt. I started up the alley and soon slipped into my jacket, that green ugly brother who breathed over my shoulder that day and ever since.

EXERCISE 7   Discussion and Critical Thinking

1. Why is the jacket more of a disappointment than it would have been if Soto's mother had given it to him as a surprise?

2. What kind of jacket did Soto request?

3. How is the jacket like a person and an evil force?

4. What are some of the failures Soto attributes to his jacket?

5. Why doesn't he lose it or throw it away?

SHORT STORY

Apply the basic narrative pattern on pages 306–307 as you analyze the short story. The *situation* indicates setting. The *conflict* provides the dynamics for the narrative and gives insight into the characters. The *struggle* shows the action or plot. The *outcome* is the resolution or lack of it. And the *meaning* is the significance of what occurred, or the theme. Description is appropriately persuasive.

The Story of an Hour

KATE CHOPIN

The author of this famous story on love and marriage, Kate Chopin, was left a widow with six children at age thirty-two. Turning to writing seriously, she wrote stories set mainly in the Creole bayou country around New Orleans. Her independent thinking, especially about women's emotions, attracted a firestorm of critical attention to her novel The Awakening, *and two collections of short stories,* Bayou Folk *and* A Night in Acadie, *and established her reputation as a feminist.*

MINDSET

Lock It In

Consider these three words: love, marriage, freedom. Rank them for importance. If you had to give up one, which one would it be? Which one could you not live without?

1   Knowing that Mrs. Mallard was afflicted with a heart trouble, great care was taken to break to her as gently as possible the news of her husband's death.

2   It was her sister Josephine who told her, in broken sentences, veiled hints that revealed in half concealing. Her husband's friend Richards was there, too, near her. It was he who had been in the newspaper office when intelligence of the railroad disaster was received, with Brently Mallard's name leading the list of "killed." He had only taken the time to assure himself of its truth by a second telegram, and had hastened to forestall any less careful, less tender friend in bearing the sad message.

3   She did not hear the story as many women have heard the same, with a paralyzed inability to accept its significance. She wept at once, with sudden, wild abandonment, in her sister's arms. When the storm of grief had spent itself she went to her room alone. She would have no one follow her.

4   There stood, facing the open window, a comfortable, roomy armchair. Into this she sank, pressed down by a physical exhaustion that haunted her body and seemed to reach into her soul.

5   She could see in the open square before her house the tops of trees that were all aquiver with the new spring life. The delicious breath of rain was in the air. In the street below a peddler was crying his wares. The notes of a distant song which some one was singing reached her faintly, and countless sparrows were twittering in the eaves.

6   There were patches of blue sky showing here and there through the clouds that had met and piled above the other in the west facing her window.

7   She sat with her head thrown back upon the cushion of the chair quite motionless, except when a sob came up into her throat and shook her, as a child who has cried itself to sleep continues to sob in its dreams.

8   She was young, with a fair, calm face, whose lines bespoke repression and even a certain strength. But now there was a dull stare in her eyes, whose gaze was fixed away off yonder on one of those patches of blue sky. It was not a glance of reflection, but rather indicated a suspension of intelligent thought.

9   There was something coming to her and she was waiting for it, fearfully. What was it? She did not know; it was too subtle and elusive to name. But she felt it, creeping out of the sky, reaching toward her through the sounds, the scents, the color that filled the air.

10   Now her bosom rose and fell tumultuously. She was beginning to recognize this thing that was approaching to possess her, and she was striving to beat it back with her will—as powerless as her two white slender hands would have been.

11   When she abandoned herself a little whispered word escaped her slightly parted lips. She said it over and over under her breath: "Free, free, free!" The vacant stare and the look of terror that had followed it went from her eyes. They stayed keen and bright. Her pulses beat fast, and the coursing blood warmed and relaxed every inch of her body.

12   She did not stop to ask if it were not a monstrous joy that held her. A clear and exalted perception enabled her to dismiss the suggestion as trivial.

13   She knew that she would weep again when she saw the kind, tender hands folded in death; the face that had never looked save with love upon her, fixed and gray and dead. But she saw beyond that bitter moment a long procession of years to come that would belong to her absolutely. And she opened and spread her arms out to them in welcome.

14   There would be no one to live for during those coming years; she would live for herself. There would be no powerful will bending her in that blind persistence with which men and women believe they have a right to impose a

private will upon a fellow-creature. A kind intention or a cruel intention made the act seem no less a crime as she looked upon it in that brief moment of illumination.

15 And yet she had loved him—sometimes. Often she had not. What did it matter! What could love, the unsolved mystery, count for in face of this possession of self assertion which she suddenly recognized as the strongest impulse of her being!

16 "Free! Body and soul free!" she kept whispering.

17 Josephine was kneeling before the closed door with her lips to the keyhole, imploring for admission. "Louise, open the door! I beg; open the door—you will make yourself ill. What are you doing, Louise? For heaven's sake open the door."

18 "Go away. I am not making myself ill." No; she was drinking in a very elixir of life through that open window.

19 Her fancy was running riot along those days ahead of her. Spring days, and summer days, and all sorts of days that would be her own. She breathed a quick prayer that life might be long. It was only yesterday she had thought with a shudder that life might be long.

20 She arose at length and opened the door to her sister's importunities. There was a feverish triumph in her eyes, and she carried herself unwittingly like a goddess of Victory. She clasped her sister's waist, and together they descended the stairs. Richards stood waiting for them at the bottom.

21 Some one was opening the door with a latchkey. It was Brently Mallard who entered, a little travel-stained, composedly carrying his grip-sack and umbrella. He had been far from the scene of accident, and did not even know there had been one. He stood amazed at Josephine's piercing cry; at Richards's quick motion to screen him from the view of his wife.

22 But Richards was too late.

23 When the doctors came they said she had died of heart disease—of joy that kills.

EXERCISE 8   Discussion and Critical Thinking

1. What is Mrs. Mallard's first reaction in hearing of her husband's death?

2. What is her second reaction?

3. Why hasn't she considered freedom before?

4. Did her husband love her? Did she love him?

5. Did he abuse her?

6. Is this story mainly about women's rights, freedom, or some other subject?

7. Why does Mrs. Mallard die?

STUDENT PARAGRAPH AND ESSAYS

Writing Process Worksheet

Name _Joel Bailey_   **Title** _King of Klutziness_   **Due Date** _Monday, September 17, 9 a.m._

Use the back of this page or separate paper if you need more space.

Assignment

In the space below, write whatever you need to know about your assignment, including information about the topic, audience, pattern of writing, length, whether to include a rough draft or revised drafts, and whether your paper must be typed.

Write a one-page narrative about a work-related incident that was a learning experience and made a deep impression. Submit your Writing Process Worksheet and a rough draft marked for revision with the final draft. Type the final draft. Audience: other students and instructor.

Stage One

Explore Freewrite, brainstorm (list), cluster, or take notes as directed by your instructor.

Listing

first day at work	celebrity customer	he's really angry
Carl's Jr., Hollywood	take order	funnier now
no training	make mistake	than then
easy at first	he's angry	be cool the
things change	I spill Coke	next time
busy	smear catsup	
really busy		

Stage Two

Organize Write a topic sentence or thesis; label the subject and the focus parts.

<u>My first day at work</u> <u>was a truly memorable experience for me and my</u>
　　　　subject　　　　　　　　　　　　　　　　focus

<u>unfortunate customer.</u>

Write an outline or an outline alternative. For reading-based writing, include quotations and references with page numbers as support in the outline.

    I. Situation
        A. Carl's Jr.
        B. My first day at work
   II. Conflict
        A. No training
        B. Too many customers
        C. Make mistake with celebrity customer

III. Struggle
    A. Mistake follows mistake
    B. Attempted correction becomes mistake
    C. Customer really angry
IV. Outcome
    A. Customer upset
    B. Embarrassment for me
V. Meaning
    A. A learning experience
    B. Incident funnier now than then

Stage Three

Write On separate paper, write and then revise your paragraph or essay as many times as necessary for **c**oherence, **l**anguage (usage, tone, and diction), **u**nity, **e**mphasis, **s**upport, and **s**entences (**CLUESS**). Read your work aloud to hear and correct any grammatical errors or awkward-sounding sentences.

Edit any problems in fundamentals, such as **c**apitalization, **o**missions, **p**unctuation, and **s**pelling (**COPS**).

KING OF KLUTZINESS
Joel Bailey

Topic sentence

Situation

Conflict

Struggle

Outcome

Meaning

    <u>It was my first task of what would be a memorable day at work in Carl's Jr., a fast-food place by Universal Studio near Hollywood.</u> I was assigned to the front counter because another worker was late. There I was at noon, the busiest time of the day, with no training, scared, and nervous. In the beginning, things went well. Orders were routine, and I filled them and made change. As time passed, the lines got short, and I was still doing great because, after all, the job did not require the mentality of a rocket scientist. Several counter people left their registers to help out in back. Then a lot of people came in at one time. Only two of us were taking orders. I was nervous. I served three persons, hardly looking up as I punched the keys, called out orders, and made change. After barely glancing at the next person, I heard his voice ordering, a familiar voice. It was Alex Benson, a reporter for a TV channel I frequently watched. I repeated his order so that it would be perfect, and I took his money. After I gave him his change, he stared at the receipt and said with more than a touch of irritation, "You made a mistake. You charged me for two chicken burgers." I apologized and gave him a refund. "What about the tax," he growled. "You didn't refund the tax." I was really getting nervous. He always laughed and smiled on TV. I gave him the tax money. I grabbed someone else's chicken order just so I could give him quick service, but when I handed him the tray, my hand slipped and I spilled his Coke on his trousers. Quickly I grabbed a napkin and ran around the counter and wiped at the Coke stain. Unfortunately the napkin I grabbed had catsup on it. Now I had added a condiment to the Coke stain. By that time I might as well have salted and peppered him. Beyond anger, and looking at me wildly, he fled with his tray to a distant booth and sat with his back to the wall. I decided not to ask for an autograph.

EXERCISE 9   Discussion and Critical Thinking

1. Is Bailey really klutzy, or is this just first-day jitters?

2. Is Bailey's problem with understanding the restaurant's procedures or with executing the procedures?

3. Was this a funny situation at the time?

4. How does the conflict differ from the struggle?

READING-BASED WRITING

Revenge and Punishment

DONALD SHEPPARD

The assignment for student Donald Sheppard was to write an interpretation of "The Cask of Amontillado" by Edgar Allan Poe. The instructions were to select one aspect of the narrative—the situation (setting), the conflict, the struggle (the plot), the outcome, or the meaning (theme)—and to concentrate on it. The short essay should incorporate a summary of the story but would not focus on that. Sheppard chose the meaning, or theme. Then he read the story, underlining and annotating it with the writing assignment in mind; made an outline, which included references and quotations; and wrote a first and final draft, which follows.

Thesis and meaning, or theme, of the narrative

1   <u>Edgar Allan Poe's "The Cask of Amontillado" is a story about terrible revenge and a haunting recollection.</u> The narrator is Montresor, who tells of how he tricked Fortunado, led him into the catacombs, chained him to a wall, built another wall to seal him in, and then left him there to die. Montresor now wants the reader to believe he is proud and feels no guilt. But in his telling of the story, he reveals enough about himself for us to question his clear conscience.

Topic sentence

2   Montresor seems arrogant in explaining just how cold and calculating he was in committing this premeditated act. Fortunado was already drunk, and Montresor says he gave him more alcohol. Montresor tempted Fortunado to follow him into the catacombs by saying he had a cask there of what he thinks is Amontillado, a fine wine. Because it was carnival

Focused summary

season, Montresor could easily wear a mask for disguise and arrange for his servants to be away so that there would be no witnesses. He led Fortunado to the niche where he had hidden materials to build a wall and also a chain, lock, and key for fastening Fortunado in place. He now says

Direct reference

he wanted to kill his enemy in just the right way, meaning he himself would do the punishing, his enemy would know who punished him, and he, the punisher, would not be found out (274). That much all by itself would mark him as a psychopath, a cold-blooded killer.

Topic sentence

3   Several factors make him seem otherwise. One is the time. The crime occurred fifty years ago, yet Montresor remembers everything, even small details of speech, thought, and act. He must be going over the experience in his mind as if he is trying to justify his behavior or rid his mind of guilt.

Quotation

Among the details he recalls are two instances of what is obviously his conscience speaking. When Fortunado cried out pitifully to be spared a horrible death, Montresor now says, "For a brief moment I hesitated—I trembled" (276). Fear is not enough to explain his reaction. Then later, as he placed the last stone in the wall, he heard a jingling of the bells on Fortunado's costume, and he now says, "My heart grew sick...." He goes on

Quotation

to say, after a break in the sentence, "—on account of the dampness of the catacombs" (276), but these are the words of a murderer who looks back fifty years, not wanting to give his emotions away.

4   The fact is Montresor "trembled," and his "heart grew sick" (276). He

Conclusion and theme, or meaning, of the narrative

walled in his enemy, but now he cannot wall in all of his remorse. It comes back to him like the cries of a dying man and the jingling of the bells.

Work Cited

Poe, Edgar Allan. "The Cask of Amontillado." *Sentences, Paragraphs, and Beyond.* Ed. Lee Brandon and Kelly Brandon. 3rd ed. Boston: Houghton, 2001. 274–76. Print.

Not Invulnerable

CHARLES C. ORTIZ

College student and cadet police officer Charles C. Ortiz entered law enforcement with unwarranted confidence and a feeling of invulnerability. Then one calm summer night, only an hour into a routine patrol, eight gunshots put him more in touch with reality.

1   I had always considered myself invulnerable when I was riding in a police unit. I was a knight, a Rambo, a centurion. I was sure that there was nothing I couldn't handle. I had been with the sheriff's department for almost three years, and I was certain that I was ready for anything. Who would have guessed that that mentality would almost cost me my life?

2   On January 16, I was assigned to work 55 Frank, which was a South El Monte crime unit. Because it was my first time working this car, I felt nervous, but at the same time I was also excited. Strangely, although this wasn't my first time on patrol, I still felt somewhat apprehensive. I was sure this night was different, yet I didn't know why.

3   Our shift started out pretty slowly. All we did for the first three hours was write out traffic citations. Once the traffic began to slacken, we proceeded with our routine patrol checks of the homes and businesses in our area. On a check of Santa Anita Avenue, a man began to flag us down. As we approached him, I noticed he was staggering and yelling at the top of his lungs. He insisted that we take him to jail. Once I had explained his options, he agreed to be taken to our station to begin his sobering-up process. I cuffed him and put him in the back of the unit. This was routine stuff.

4   But as we headed toward the station, a distress call blared over the radio: "Attention, all units in the vicinity of South El Monte. 55 Adam is requesting backup. He has five at gunpoint. All units responding, go Code 3!" Because we were a minute away, we responded. As we took off, my adrenaline started to rise, causing me to feel anxious. Upon arriving at the scene, I grabbed the shotgun, got out of the car, and pointed the shotgun toward the vehicle in question. The first suspect was called out. As he emerged in front of us, he reached into his waistband, pulled out a gun, and pointed it in my direction. In a moment, he fired two shots at me.

I hit the ground. At the same time a fear of dying took over my body. I didn't know if I was hit, if I was dying, or what. I was in a state of shock.

5   After I discovered that the shots had missed me and the situation was under control, I rose somewhat slowly. I looked toward the suspect and saw him lying dead in a pool of blood. He had been shot six times by the deputies at the scene. The other four suspects were arrested for grand theft auto. Even though the incident was secured, I was able to see what "real" fear was. I understood that policing is not a game; it is life-and-death reality. Walking in a cop's shoes is not something that everyone can handle.

6   Facing my most horrible fear has truly shown me how important my life is. It's not something to be taken for granted. I also now know personally what deputies face when they encounter someone who is armed and possibly dangerous. I have found a new sense of respect for all police officers, for I have now experienced law enforcement from their view. Furthermore, I feel a lot older and a lot wiser now. Going into the streets thinking "I'm invulnerable" is the wrong kind of attitude.

EXERCISE 10   Discussion and Critical Thinking

1. What conflicting ideas does the author present in the first two paragraphs that attract reader interest and create suspense?

2. Dramatically what is the effect of the minor conflict in paragraph 3?

3. How does Ortiz's attitude about police work change?

4. To which other parts of the essay does the last line relate?

5. Underline the thesis and use annotation to mark the situation, conflict, struggle, outcome, and meaning in this essay.

CAREER-RELATED WRITING: INCIDENT REPORT

Incident Report of Mistaken Shoplifting

MICHAEL MENDOZA

Michael Mendoza's assignment was to write a narrative as an incident report at a workplace. Both the incident and the workplace could be fictional, although students were encouraged to write about an incident that did occur or could reasonably have occurred at a business where they had worked or are working. Michael Mendoza is a security guard at a large urban mall. In his incident report he recreated an account that he had actually written a year earlier. Although he used the same basic form, he says this time he had more guidelines for writing an effective report.

Form 117—Incident

Security Control, Inc
(555) 394-8803

☐ Accident
☒ Reported theft
☐ Disturbance
☐ Dangerous condition
☐ Lost child
☐ Vandalism
☐ Health emergency

Location: Mountain View Mall, Montebello, CA
Time: May 9, 2009, 18:12
Security Personnel Involved: <u>Michael Mendoza</u>

Situation
Conflict

Incident report: At 18:12 I received a call on my portable phone from Security Dispatch that shop owner Fernelle Jenkins had observed apparent shoplifting at the second table of the open temporary business area adjacent to escalator 7. Jenkins said she had observed a woman slip a piece of costume jewelry into her pocket. Jenkins described the woman as overweight with long black hair. She was wearing a brightly colored floral muumuu and a plastic lei. She had tattoos on her forearms. The woman was accompanied by a man, also tattooed and dressed in a purple, green, red, and yellow Hawaiian shirt and shorts. He was slightly balding and thick around the middle.

Struggle

I proceeded from the south end of the mall on the first floor and encountered a couple who met the description. I told them that I had some questions and asked them to follow me to security headquarters. They demanded to know my purpose. I repeated that I needed to ask some questions. They walked with me, continuing to ask my purpose.

In the security headquarters, I explained what had been reported to me. I asked to see their identification. They were Jennifer and Martin Moriarty, both teachers in the West Covina School District. They said they had just left a luau retirement party. The tattoos were temporary. J. Moriarty denied any wrongdoing. She pointed out that she had no pockets in her muumuu. I observed that she did not. She was also not carrying any purse or other container.

Outcome

I said they were free to go. The Moriartys said they would contact their attorney and asked me for the name of the person who reported them. Following company policy I pointed out that they had not been arrested, that they were free to go, and that I regretted any inconvenience.

They took my name and badge number and left.

Meaning

Recommendation: People who report shoplifting should be very sure of what they see and be responsible for mistakes.

EXERCISE 11   Discussion and Critical Thinking

1. As a part of the narrative pattern, what is the meaning?

2. Would you add anything to the "Recommendation" part?

3. In the incident report, does Mendoza always consistently write from the "I" point of view, maintain active verb voice, and relate events in the past verb tense?

4. Do you think this account written as a class assignment is likely to be almost identical to the one submitted officially at work?

Suggested Topics and Prompts for Writing Descriptive Narration

You will find a blank Writing Process Worksheet on page 6 of this book and on the Student Companion Site. It can be photocopied or printed out, filled in, and submitted with your assignment, if your instructor directs you to do so.

READING-BASED WRITING

Reading-based writing requires you to read critically, write a reply that shows you understand what you have read, and give credit for ideas you borrow and words you quote. The form can be a summary, a reaction, or a two-part response (with separated summary and reaction). Documentation, in which you give credit for borrowed ideas and words, can be either formal (MLA) or informal, as directed by your instructor. Both forms of reading-based writing and documentation are discussed with examples in Chapter 1. Definitions of the three forms follow.

Summary

- The summary is a statement presenting only the main points of what you have read by using different wording without altering the meaning, adding information, or showing bias.
- It is the purest form of reading-based writing.

Reaction

- In the reaction, the meaning of what you have read will be central to the topic sentence of your paragraph or to the thesis of your essay.
- Although the reaction is not a personal narrative by itself, it may include personal experience to explain elements of the text. For example, if your source is about driving styles, your own experiences as a driver or an observer of drivers could be relevant in your analysis of the text.
- The reaction may incorporate a summary to convey a broad view of what you have read, but your summary should never be the main part of your reaction.

Two-Part Response

- The two-part response separates the summary from the reaction.

- This form will give you practice in separating your objective summary in the first part from your more personal evaluation, interpretation, or application in the second part, the reaction.

READING-BASED WRITING TOPICS

"My Burning Scarf"

1. Write about the scarf from the scarf's point of view. Use references and quotations.

"Blue Winds Dancing"

2. Write a reaction explaining why Whitecloud's paragraph is about both memory and awareness of the moment. Use references and quotations.

"W-A-T-E-R"

3. Write a paragraph or an essay in which you explain how these quotations are central to the meaning of this passage: "This thought, if a wordless sensation that can be called a thought, made me hop and skip with pleasure." "That living word awakened my soul, gave it light, hope, joy, set it free."

"The Jacket"

4. Frequently reprinted, this essay is enormously popular with student readers. Discuss the likely reasons for its popularity. Refer directly to the essay and use quotations as you discuss the author's use of descriptive narration.

5. Use your imagination to write about the jacket from the mother's point of view. You might also imagine that she is providing her viewpoint just after reading this essay by her son; therefore, she can refer to what Gary Soto said. Use references and quotations.

6. Write about the jacket from the jacket's point of view. Refer to particular incidents in the essay. Use references to the essay and quotes from it.

"The Story of an Hour"

Writing about a short story can take many of the forms discussed in this book, especially descriptive narration, analysis by division (how parts make up a unit), cause and effect (reasons and results), comparison and contrast (similarities and differences), definition (meaning of terms), and argument (persuasion).

7. Write a two-part response. Concentrate on the main points in the story for the summary. In your separate reaction part, explain what killed Mrs. Mallard. Your interpretation may include some of the following points:

- She does not know how to reconcile freedom and marriage.
- Her emotional state regarding freedom is much more likely to be experienced by a woman than a man.
- Her husband would never have understood even if he had known her thoughts at the time of his return, and that is part of the problem.

8. Write your own narrative from situation to meaning. Here are some suggestions:

   • Write a diary entry about an imaginary event Mrs. Mallard experienced, one that made her long for freedom or become aware of the benevolent control (his view) her husband imposed on her life.

   • Pose as Mr. Mallard and write a eulogy that he would deliver at his wife's funeral. Through his words, have him reveal what type of husband he was. For instance, though well-intentioned, he reveals himself, and perhaps marriage itself, as controlling, but he does not know what he is revealing.

"Not Invulnerable"

9. Using this essay as model, write a descriptive narration about a time when you or someone you know did something that was dangerous but, through ignorance or preoccupation, approached the event with little or no fear. Consider a rescue or an incident at school, at work, or during recreation. Explain how Ortiz's fear and what he said about fear specifically relate to your experience. Use quotations and references.

GENERAL TOPICS

10. Write a narrative based on a topic sentence such as this: "One experience showed me what _____ [pain, fear, anger, love, sacrifice, dedication, joy, sorrow, shame, pride] was really like."

11. Write a simple narrative about a fire, a riot, an automobile accident, a rescue, shoplifting, or some other unusual happening you witnessed.

12. Write a narrative that supports (or opposes) the idea of a familiar saying such as one of the following:

    a. You never know who a friend is until you need one.

    b. A bird in the hand is worth two in the bush.

    c. Better to be alone than to be in bad company.

    d. Borrowing is the mother of trouble.

    e. A person who marries for money earns it.

    f. Never give advice to a friend.

    g. If it isn't broken, don't fix it.

    h. Nice people finish last.

    i. It isn't what you know, it's who you know.

    j. You get what you pay for.

    k. Haste makes waste.

Objective Description

13. Give your topic some kind of framework or purpose beyond simply writing a description. As you develop your purpose, consider the knowledge and attitudes of your readers. You might be describing a lung for a biology instructor, a geode for a geology instructor, a painting for an art instructor, or a comet for an astronomy instructor. Or maybe you could pose as the seller of an object, such as a desk, a table, or a bicycle. Describe one of the following topics:

    a. A simple object, such as a pencil, cup, sock, dollar bill, coin, ring, or notebook

    b. A human organ, such as a heart, liver, lung, or kidney

    c. A visible part of your body, such as a toe, a finger, an ear, a nose, or an eye

    d. A construction, such as a room, desk, chair, commode, or table

    e. A mechanism, such as a bicycle, tricycle, wagon, car, motorcycle, can opener, or stapler

Subjective Description

14. The following topics also should be developed with a purpose other than merely writing a description. Your intent can be as simple as giving a subjective reaction to your topic. However, unless you are dealing with a topic you can present reflectively or a topic as interesting in itself, you will usually need some kind of situation. The narrative framework (something happening) is especially useful in providing order and vitality to writing. Here are three possibilities for you to consider:

    a. Personalize a trip to a supermarket, a stadium, an airport, an unusual house, a mall, the beach, a court, a church, a club, a business, the library, or the police station. Describe a simple conflict in one of those places while emphasizing descriptive details.

    b. Pick a high point in any event and describe the most important few seconds. Think how a scene can be captured by a video camera and then give focus by applying the dominant impression principle, using relevant images of sight, sound, taste, touch, and smell. The event might be a ball game, a graduation ceremony, a wedding ceremony, a funeral, a dance, a concert, a family gathering, a class meeting, a rally, a riot, a robbery, a fight, a proposal, or a meal. Focus on subject material that you can cover effectively in the passage you write.

    c. Pick a moment when you were angry, sad, happy, confused, lost, rattled, afraid, courageous, meek, depressed, or elated. Describe how the total context of the situation contributed to your feeling.

CROSS-CURRICULAR TOPICS

15. Write a paragraph or an essay about a visit to, an observation of, or a field trip to a museum, a concert, an institution, or a workplace.

16. Write about a unit of time in which feverish action occurs. You could select a pivotal moment in history (the assassination of a president, a turning point

in a battle, the first encounter between two groups of people), in science (the discovery of a process or product), in music (a composer conducting his or her own musical composition), or in art appreciation (a painter finishing a famous painting). Content from other courses will provide most of the framework; your imagination can provide the details. Be inventive, but base your invention on what you know of individuals and the time period. Consult textbooks. Talk to instructors.

CAREER-RELATED TOPICS

17. Drawing on your experience at work or in job training, write an incident report that basically follows the directions on pages 311–312. For a useful model of form, review the student selection, "Incident Report of Mistaken Shoplifting" on pages 326–327.

18. Write a narrative account of an encounter between a customer and a salesperson. Explain what went right and what went wrong.

19. Write a narrative account of how a person solved a work-related problem perhaps by using technology.

20. Write a narrative account of a salesperson handling a customer's complaint. Critique the procedure.

21. Using a workplace form you are familiar with, write an incident report about an event such as an accident, a theft, or a disturbance.

22. Describe a well-furnished, well-functioning office or other work area. Be specific.

23. Describe a computer-related product; give special attention to the dominant trait that gives the product its reputation.

24. Describe a person groomed and attired for a particular job or interview. Be specific in giving details pertaining to the person and in naming the place or situation. Describe yourself from a detached point of view if you like.

WRITER'S GUIDELINES   Descriptive Narration

Narration

1. Include these points so that you will be sure you have a complete narrative:

- situation
- conflict
- struggle
- outcome
- meaning

2. Use these techniques or devices as appropriate:

- Images that appeal to the senses (sight, smell, taste, hearing, touch) and other details to advance action
- dialogue

- transitional devices (such as *next*, *soon*, *after*, *later*, *then*, *finally*, *when*, *following*) to indicate chronological order

3. Give details concerning action.

4. Be consistent with point of view and verb tense.

5. Keep in mind that most narratives written as college assignments will have an expository purpose; that is, they explain a specific idea.

6. Consider working with a short time frame for short writing assignments. The scope would usually be no more than one incident of brief duration for one paragraph. For example, writing about an entire graduation ceremony might be too complicated, but concentrating on the moment when you walked forward to receive the diploma or the moment when the relatives and friends come down on the field could work very well.

Description

In objective description, use direct, practical language appealing mainly to the sense of sight. In subjective description, appeal to the reader's feelings, especially through the use of figurative language and the use of images of sight, sound, smell, taste, and touch. Use concrete, specific words if appropriate.

7. Apply these questions to your writing:

- What is the subject?
- What is the dominant impression I am trying to convey?
- What details support the dominant impression?
- What is the situation?
- What is the order of the details?
- What is the point of view? (Is it first or third person? involved or objective?)

Incident Report

8. Identify the kind of problem and the location. This may be part of a form provided by your employer.

9. Indicate when the problem occurred.

10. Provide an account of what happened.

- Write in the first person (*I*); you are the one who is writing the report.

- Start with the date, time, and your reason for involvement.

- Include quotation marks if you use the words of anyone reporting on the incident.

- Use facts, not opinions.

- Remain objective. Do not step outside your work expertise and become a psychologist, philosopher, physician, or moralist.

- Use past tense. You are writing about something that has already happened.

- Use mostly active-voice verbs. For example, write, "Mills wrote the report," not "The report was written by Mills."

- Identify those involved. Drop the titles, such as Mr., Mrs., Dr., and so on. After the first reference to the person in the report, use only the surname or the first initial and the surname.

- If appropriate, write a recommendation for what could be done to avoid a repeat of such an incident.

11. Write and revise.

STUDENT COMPANION SITE
For additional practice, visit www.cengage .com/devenglish/ brandon/spb6e.

- Write and then revise your paragraph or essay as many times as necessary for **c**oherence, **l**anguage (usage, tone, and diction), **u**nity, **e**mphasis, **s**upport, and **s**entences (**CLUESS**).
- Read your work aloud to hear and correct any grammatical errors or awkward-sounding sentences.
- Edit any problems in fundamentals, such as **c**apitalization, **o**missions, **p**unctuation, and **s**pelling (**COPS**).

Chapter 19

Exemplification
Using Examples

FLOW OF WRITING

WHEN TO USE EXEMPLIFICATION

FOR COLLEGE WRITING ASSIGNMENTS

- When it is time to describe, narrate, explain, or argue, it is time to be specific. There is no better way of being specific than by using exemplification. Write a generalization and you convey an idea; provide an example and you make a focused connection. Moreover, by using the example(s), you demonstrate to your reader (probably your instructor) that you have some depth of information. As you study for regular assignments or prepare for tests, consider making lists of a few examples that are included in the texts you read or that come from your experiences.

IN CAREERS AND AT THE WORKPLACE

- As you take courses related to your career or intended career, you can make good use of examples in writing field-trip reports, case studies, observation reports, and—finally—letters of application. Once at the workplace, your examples can enliven, explain, and persuade in testimonials for products or services, case studies, incident reports, memos, and proposals.

EXEMPLIFICATION IN A CARTOON

THE QUIGMANS   by Buddy Hickerson

After his human mating technique fails, Bob tries the traditional, love-snaring neck bloat of the common toad.

WRITING EXEMPLIFICATION

Exemplification means using examples to explain, convince, or amuse. Lending interest and information to writing, exemplification is one of the most common and effective ways of developing ideas. Examples may be developed in a sentence or more, or they may be only phrases or even single words, as in the following sentence: "Eating fast foods, such as *hamburgers*, *pizza*, *pupusas*, *wonton*, and *tacos*, has become a shared cross-cultural experience."

CHARACTERISTICS OF GOOD EXAMPLES

As supporting information, the best examples are specific, vivid, and representative. These three qualities are closely linked; collectively, they must support the topic sentence of a paragraph and the thesis of an essay.

You use examples to inform or convince your reader. Of course, an example by itself does not necessarily prove anything. We know that examples can be found on either side of an argument, even at the extreme edges. Therefore, in addition to providing specific examples so that your reader can follow your argument precisely and vivid ones so that your reader will be interested, you should choose examples that are representative. Representative examples are examples that your reader can consider, accept as appropriate, and even match with his or her own examples. If you are writing a paragraph about cheating and you give one specific, vivid, and representative example, your reader should be able to say, "That's exactly what happens. I can imagine just how the incident occurred, and I could give some examples that are similar."

TECHNIQUES FOR FINDING EXAMPLES

Writing a good paragraph or essay of exemplification begins, as always, with prewriting. The techniques you use will depend on what you are writing about. Assuming that you begin with a topic idea, one useful technique is listing. Base your list on what you have read, heard, and experienced. Here is a list, compiled by student Maxine Johnson on the topic "women who fought in combat situations during the War of Independence." She used her textbook and a few Internet sites as sources to compile this list:

Margaret Corbin
    Fired cannons, was wounded
Mary Hayes (Molly Pitcher)
    Fired cannons, carried water, received military pension
Sybil Ludington
    Rode more successfully than Paul Revere to proclaim "British are coming"
Deborah Samson
    Dressed as man, enlisted, was wounded
Mary Hagidorn
    Held off British with a spear
Mary Morgan Hart
    Killed British soldiers in her cabin
Anna Warner, Rachel Martin, Grace Martin
    Dressed as men, fought

NUMBER AND ORDER OF EXAMPLES

After you have explored your topic and collected information, you must decide whether to use only one example with a detailed explanation, a few examples with a bit less information, or a cluster of examples. A well-stated topic sentence will guide you in making this decision. When you are writing about a personal topic, you will probably have far more examples than you can use.

Transitional Words

Consider using the following transitional words to improve coherence by connecting ideas with ideas, sentences with sentences, and paragraphs with paragraphs.

FOR EXEMPLIFICATION: for example, as an example, another example, for instance, such as, including, specifically, especially, in particular, to illustrate, as an illustration, that is, i.e. (meaning *that is*), e.g. (meaning *for example*)

FOR ALL PATTERNS OF WRITING: The <u>H</u>OTSHOT <u>CAT</u> words: <u>H</u>owever, <u>O</u>therwise, <u>T</u>herefore, <u>S</u>imilarly, <u>H</u>ence, <u>O</u>n the other hand, <u>T</u>hen, <u>C</u>onsequently, <u>A</u>lso, <u>T</u>hus (See pages 74–75 for additional transitional words.)

If your example is an incident or a series of incidents, you will probably use time order, reinforcing that arrangement with terms such as *next*, *then*, *soon*, *later*, *last*, and *finally*. If your examples exist in space (maybe in different parts of a room), then you would use space references (*up*, *down*, *left*, *right*, *east*, *west*, *north*, *south*). Arranging examples by emphasis means going from the most important example to the least important or from the least to the most important.

CONNECTING EXAMPLES WITH PURPOSE

Here is the paragraph that student Maxine Johnson wrote on the topic "women who fought in combat situations during the War of Independence." After compiling the list of examples, Johnson decided that for her purpose in this paragraph, two specific, vivid, and representative examples with explanations would make her point. Those examples are listed in the following simple outline:

Topic sentence
  I. Sybil Ludington
     A. Served as messenger
     B. Was in combat situation
 II. Mary Hayes
     A. Fired cannon
     B. Received military pension
Concluding sentence

THE FIGHTING FOUNDING MOTHERS
Maxine Johnson

Topic sentence

    People argue a lot about the prospects of women in the military fighting in combat, but in the War of Independence, several women distinguished themselves in combat situations. In 1775, Paul Revere got the main credit for riding to warn the Patriots that the British were coming in a military move on Concord and Lexington, Massachusetts. The fact is that although he did warn some Patriots, he was stopped by the British. Who did get through?

Example

Several people, including Sybil Ludington, a teenage woman who fearlessly rode her horse like the wind. Another famous woman was known as Molly

Example

Pitcher. Her real name was Mary Hayes. She went with her husband to the battlefield, where she brought the men pitchers of water (hence her nickname) and helped load the cannon her husband fired. When her husband was shot at the Battle of Monmouth in 1778, she took over the cannon and fought bravely. At the end of the battle, won by the Patriots, she carried a wounded man for two miles. For her services, she was later granted a

Concluding sentence

military pension. More than two hundred years ago, women such as these proved that their gender can be soldiers in every sense.

USEFUL PROCEDURE FOR WRITING WITH EXAMPLES

Asking yourself the following questions will help you write effective paragraphs using exemplification.

1. What am I trying to say? (Write a topic sentence or thesis.)

2. What examples might support that idea? (Use listing.)

3. How many examples and what order should I use? (Use judgment.)

4. Are my examples specific, vivid, and representative? (Reflect.)

5. Have I made a connection between my examples and my topic sentence or thesis? (Use an outline to determine the connection.)

FINDING PATTERNS IN PHOTOS

EXERCISE 1   A Text-Based Activity for Groups or Individuals

1957 Plymouth Belvedere time capsule excavated in Tulsa

© Mark Savage/Corbis

Examine the photo of mementos from a time capsule excavated after it had been buried for exactly fifty years in Tulsa, Oklahoma. Though a "futuristic" 1957 high-finned Plymouth Belvedere coupe rusted and rotted away during those five decades, much survived in an air-tight metal cylinder, including newspapers, high school yearbooks, a tube of lipstick, a pack of chewing gum, several combs, an American flag with forty-six stars, some coins and bills, some cigarettes, an unpaid parking ticket, numerous photos, vinyl recordings of popular songs, a case of Schlitz beer, a bottle of tranquilizers, maps, and postcards; each item had been selected for its cultural ties to 1957.

Imagine you are assembling items for a time capsule (or actually begin assembling one). What items would you select to represent significant parts of your culture—the fads, the styles, the expressions, the habits, the attitudes, the passions, the beliefs, the preferences, the hopes and fears, the pains and pleasures, the dreams and nightmares, the ugliness and beauty, and the cool and uncool of the world around you—that will change as the items in your time capsule remain the same, if properly sealed away?

Make a list of at least ten items and include a word or two to indicate how each reveals something about what you and your associates like or dislike. Each item is an example of what in your contemporary culture?

Items

1. _____

2. _____

3. _____

4. _____

5. _____

6. _____

7. _____

8. _____

9. _____

10. _____

Cultural Connection

1. _____

2. _____

3. _____

4. _____

5. _____

6. _____

7. _____

8. _____

9. _____

10. _____

Practicing Patterns of Exemplification

A well-designed outline can help you make clear connections between your topic sentence and your examples. Remember that in some instances you can support your point with a single example extended in detail, and in other cases you may need several examples. In Exercise 2, the topic sentences are developed by multiple examples.

EXERCISE 2   Completing Patterns of Exemplification

Fill in the blanks to add more examples that support the topic sentence.

1. Topic sentence: Just walking through my favorite mall shows me that the world is smaller than it used to be.

   I. People of different cultures (with specific examples)

   II. Foods of different cultures (with specific examples)

   III. _____

   IV. _____

2. Topic sentence: Driving to work (or school) this month and observing the behavior of other drivers have convinced me that road rage has invaded my community.

   I. A man honking his horn impatiently at an elderly driver

   II. _____

   III. _____

3. Controlling idea: Some people let television watching interfere with their social lives.

   I. Watching football games at a family gathering on holidays

   II. Watching television in a restaurant (sports bar)

   III. _____

4. Controlling idea: Most successful movies are more concerned with action than with character, and the action is violent.

   I. (Name of movie) _____

   II. (Name of movie) _____

   III. (Name of movie) _____

Readings for Critical Thinking, Discussion, and Writing

READING STRATEGIES AND OBJECTIVES

Underlining and annotating these reading selections will help you answer the questions that follow the selections, discuss the material in class, and prepare for text-based writing assignments. As you underline and annotate, pay special attention to the author's writing skills, logic, and message, and consider the relevance of the material to your own experiences and values.

Some selections begin with a Mindset suggestion that can help you create a readiness for connecting with what you are about to read.

PARAGRAPH

Colorado Springs—Every Which Way

ERIC SCHLOSSER

In his best-selling book Fast Food Nation, *Eric Schlosser exposes an ignorant and largely uncaring society dependent on fast food. At the end of unsavory supply lines are rudderless cities thickly populated by fast-food chains serving up unhealthful food. One such city is Colorado Springs.*

Colorado Springs now has the feel of a city whose identity is not yet fixed. Many longtime residents strongly oppose the extremism of the newcomers, sporting bumper stickers that say, "Don't Californicate Colorado." The city is now torn between opposing visions of what America should be. Colorado Springs has twenty-eight Charismatic Christian churches and almost twice as many pawnbrokers, a Lord's Vineyard Bookstore and a First Amendment Adult Bookstore, a Christian Medical and Dental Society and a Holey Rollers Tattoo Parlor. It has a Christian summer camp whose founder, David Noebel, outlined the dangers of rock 'n' roll in his pamphlet *Communism, Hypnotism, and the Beatles*. It has a gay entertainment complex called The Hide & Seek, where the Gay Rodeo Association meets. It has a public school principal who recently disciplined a group of sixth-grade girls for reading a book on witchcraft and allegedly casting spells. The loopiness once associated with Los Angeles has come full-blown to Colorado Springs—the strange, creative energy that crops up where the future's consciously being made, where people walk the fine line separating a visionary from a total nutcase. At the start of a new century, all sorts of things seem possible there. The cultural and the physical landscapes of Colorado Springs are up for grabs.

EXERCISE 3   Discussion and Critical Thinking

1. Underline the two sentences that focus on the author's main idea.

2. Of the two sentences, which one is directly tied to most of the examples?

3. Circle each example that supports the idea in the third sentence in the paragraph. Notice that they appear in contrasting patterns.

4. How does the last sentence function as part of the paragraph structure?

5. Do you know of other cities that are "torn between opposing visions of what America should be"? If so, what are some examples to support your contention?

ESSAYS

When Those Tattoos Really Get Under the Skin

PETER CARLSON

In writing this article, Peter Carlson consulted numerous tattoo-removal specialists, collecting anecdotes about people who regretted getting tattoos. This article was first published in the Washington Post.

MINDSET

Lock It In

When writing on your computer, you can add, delete, and revise content, and even use a spell checker, as you reflect on what is about to become permanent. Would you like the same options on tattoos?

1   Bzzzzzt!

2   The laser shoots a beam of light that looks like fire and makes a sizzling noise—Bzzzzzt!—as it moves across Melissa Morrissette's tattoo. Morrissette winces. She closes her eyes, which are covered by orange goggles, and takes long, slow breaths, fighting the pain. It hurts to get a tattoo removed.

3   "It's 10 times more painful than getting it put on," she says.

4   The tattoo is on her left arm—three ankhs connected in a circle around her biceps. An ankh is a cross topped with a loop, an ancient Egyptian symbol of eternal life. Morrissette, 37, has worn it for seven years. But now she's a real-estate agent working for an Annapolis company that doesn't permit visible tattoos. For a year, she covered it with long sleeves, but this summer she decided to get it removed. That's why she's here in the Laser Center of Maryland in Severna Park, paying $1,700 for six laser treatments that sting and burn.

5   Waiting to get zapped, her skin numbed by a cream, she remembers the day she got the tattoo, when the guy wielding the needle had a burst of artistic inspiration and decided to add flourishes. "I could feel him doing something different and I looked and saw these red lines coming out of the ankh," she recalls. "I said, 'What's that?' And he said, 'It's a mystic mist.' I said, 'What does that mean?' To me, it looked like varicose veins." She had to hire another tattoo artist to cover up those red lines with a reddish-orange cloud. Now, seven years later, the whole glorious artwork is being blasted away.

6   Bzzzzzzzt!

7   "The interesting thing about tattoo removal," says Ross Van Antwerp, the doctor who founded the Laser Center of Maryland, "is that there's always a story behind every tattoo." Over 16 years, Van Antwerp, 52, has erased thousands of tattoos and heard thousands of tattoo stories—bizarre stories, hilarious stories, stories that support the recent revelation that human beings are 98 percent genetically identical to the chimpanzee. "Years ago, I had one homemade tattoo that covered the whole cheek of a woman's buttock and it said, in very crude lettering, Property of Nicky," Van Antwerp says.

"This woman was not married to Nicky and, to add insult to injury, the word 'property' was misspelled." He smiles. "It's a fairly simple word," he says, "but apparently Nicky was a fairly simple guy." He bursts out laughing.

8   "I like to talk to my patients," he says. "When they're having a name removed, I ask them, Is this person no longer around? I had a guy some years ago who had the name Colleen on his arm. He said, 'That's my first wife's name, but I've been through three Colleens.' I said, 'Really? Is that a requirement of yours? Do they all have to be named Colleen?' He said, 'No, not at all. Colleen is not that common a name and I think I'm attracting them because I have their name on my arm. And the Colleen thing has never worked for me. That's why I'm here. I have to get this thing off. I have to try something else.'"

9   Van Antwerp laughs again. He's sitting in his office between patients, wearing dark-blue scrubs. He has removed homemade tattoos, professional tattoos, tribal tattoos, gang tattoos, even jailhouse tattoos made with a safety pin and cigarette ash. He has erased tattoos from every part of the human body surface, even parts you'd think are far too tender to be exposed to a tattoo needle. The phrase "love pump" was tattooed on one guy's . . . well, never mind. Van Antwerp once erased a naked woman from the arm of a minister of God. "He was a guy who grew up on the streets of Baltimore and went through rough times," he says, "and then he had a religious transformation and became a pastor."

10   One day, a young woman came in with a Chinese character tattooed on her neck. "She was told it meant 'desert flower,'" Van Antwerp says. "And she was getting a lot of attention from Chinese men. And finally somebody told her that it was a very crude Chinese word for prostitute. Some Chinese tattoo artist was making a joke."

11   So many tattoos, so many stories. But they all have one thing in common: Somebody made a mistake and now wants to erase it. Like divorce lawyers, revival preachers and parole officers, tattoo removers are in the business of helping people shed the past and start anew. The second chance—it's a great American tradition. But sometimes it doesn't work out as planned.

12   "I had a guy who had a tattoo on his arm and he wanted it off and he'd gone through five treatments," Van Antwerp says. "It was a big tattoo and it was costing him a significant amount of money. Then he went to a business meeting in D.C. and he got out a little early and he hit a happy hour and he's walking down the street and he goes into a tattoo parlor and he walks out with a big black-and-red yin-yang thing in the same spot on his arm.

13   "He came in the next day, distraught," Van Antwerp continues. "He said, 'It's the worst mistake I ever made.'"

14   "I said, 'Look, you're a married guy, you've got kids, you have a business. I'm sure there are worse mistakes you could have made. At least this one we can fix.'"

15   Van Antwerp pauses. His lips curl into an impish grin. "But still, every time I saw him, I'd say, 'I can't wait to see what's coming here next!'" And he bursts out laughing again.

The Colors of Money

16   Tattoo removal is a great growth industry! A fabulous business opportunity! Look around, my friends. Look at those fresh-faced young people with their backward ball caps and their droopy jeans. Notice the tattoos adorning their slender, tender flesh—the string of barbed wire around that buff guy's biceps, the little heart on that pretty gal's belly with her boyfriend's name—Dwayne—inscribed inside it. Lovely, isn't it? But some day, my friends, these young people will grow older and fatter and their bodies will sag and they'll

look in the mirror and think, Boy, that tattoo looks dumb, and besides, I haven't seen Dwayne since I caught him in bed with . . . When that day comes, my friends, you will wish you were in the tattoo removal business.

17   Consider the history: Fifty years ago, tattoos were signs of adventure—exotic markings found on the arms of sailors and bikers and guys who got them on Cellblock D in exchange for 10 packs of smokes and a homemade shiv. But in the last 20 years, tattoos have gone mainstream. Now, according to a 2004 Harris Interactive poll, 16 percent of American adults have at least one tattoo, and among 18- to 29-year-olds, the figure is 49 percent.

18   The same poll revealed that 17 percent of Americans who have tattoos regret getting them. Those folks are in luck because the science of tattoo removal has climbed out of the Stone Age. Twenty years ago, if you wanted to remove Dwayne's name before you married Harry, you had three choices, none good. You could have Dwayne surgically removed, sliced off with a scalpel. Or you could have him burned off with acid. Or you could sandpaper him off with a process called dermabrasion. "All these techniques," Van Antwerp says, "traded a scar for a tattoo."

19   But in the early '90s, dermatologists began using the new short-pulse "Nd:YAG" laser, which can remove tattoos with little or no scarring. But these lasers aren't cheap: They cost about $100,000. And the doctors, nurses and physician's assistants who perform the procedure must be trained and certified. But if you've got the laser and the license, there's plenty of business. The American Society for Dermatologic Surgery reports that tattoo removal procedures increased by 27 percent from 2001 to 2003. Statistics for 2005 are not complete, but spokeswoman Laura Davis says the society expects another big increase.

20   Zapping tattoos can be quite profitable. Prices vary, depending on size and color (black and red inks are easier to remove; green and light blue require more treatments). Your average 2-by-2-inch tattoo of "Mom" in a red heart can be erased in six 10-minute sessions for $1,000 to $2,000. That's roughly 10 times what the same tattoo costs to put on. Which is why tattoo removers tend to be richer than tattoo artists.

21   "My patients often comment on how much it costs to remove compared to how much it cost to put on," Van Antwerp says, getting that impish grin again. "I tell them that they've stumbled onto one of the truths of the universe: If you take the cost of obtaining a tattoo compared to the cost of removing it, it's almost exactly the same ratio as the cost of a marriage license compared to the cost of a divorce. So I tell them the take-home message is: Think real hard before you get a tattoo or get married."

Common Denominator

22   "They almost all use the same words," says David Green. He's a Bethesda dermatologist and he's talking about the patients who come in to get tattoos removed. "They say, It's the stupidest thing I ever did. This could be St. Patrick's Cathedral and I'm Father Green and they're confessing: Forgive me, Father, this is the stupidest thing I ever did."

23   Green, 52, is thumbing through photos of tattoos he has obliterated. Doctors who do tattoo removal keep albums of before-and-after pictures to impress prospective patients. He pauses at a tattooed black panther climbing up a white arm, its claws digging into the shoulder, leaving tattooed drops of bright red blood. "The woman who had this," Green says, "she's a kindergarten teacher." He flips to another picture. It shows five crude black lines tattooed across a woman's neck. "This is a tribal tattoo," he says. "A lot of Ethiopians and Somalis have tribal tattoos."

24   Three out of four of his clients are women, he says: "I don't know what that means, I don't know whether they have more remorse. Or maybe women are more likely to admit a mistake and get them removed." Of course, he has plenty of male clients, too. He points to a picture of a hairy male ankle tattooed with the word "bitch." "He got mad at his girlfriend, so he and his buddies said, 'We'll fix her,'" he says. "That was like 10 years ago and he's married now and he had this ridiculous thing on his foot."

25   He flips to another male ankle, this one with a bright red heart inscribed with the names Amy, Brittany and Emily. "Those are his daughters," Green says. "He goes to Myrtle Beach for a golf weekend with his buddies and he comes back and he tells his wife, 'Honey, look, I got the girls' names on—' And his wife says, 'You idiot! That's coming off! Get that off and then you can come back in the bedroom!' So when he came in here, it was barely dry."

An Endless Cycle

26   Bzzzzzt!

27   The laser beam crawls across Melissa Morrissette's ankh tattoo, making that sizzling noise. Then it stops. "Okay, now we're going to go after the red," says Jessie Mallalieu, a physician's assistant. She pushes a button that changes the color of the laser beam from a white light, which removes black ink, to a green light, which removes red ink.

28   Bzzzzzt!

29   In less than 10 minutes, Mallalieu is done. "I'm glad it's over," Morrissette says. "It kind of feels like you're on fire." Mallalieu swabs the raw, reddened tattoo with a numbing cream, then wraps it in gauze. "At work," Morrissette says, "I'm telling everybody, 'Please don't get yourself tattooed any place visible because you're gonna hate 'em and it hurts when you get 'em removed.'"

30   After Morrissette leaves, Mallalieu tidies up, preparing for the next patient. At 25, she has been removing tattoos for only a year, but she already has stories to tell. "I had a man come in and say, 'I woke up with this tattoo. I went to a party and ended up with a tattoo, and I had no idea till I woke up the next morning.'" What kind of tattoo was it? She laughs. "It was a Playboy bunny."

EXERCISE 4   Discussion and Critical Thinking

1. Which paragraph contains the main idea in the article, and what is the idea?

2. Excluding the imagined examples in paragraph 16, how many examples are used for support?

3. What do all the examples have in common, thereby connecting with the central idea?

4. What is Van Antwerp's most important message?

5. Do you think Carlson is writing primarily for a tattooed or nontattooed audience? Explain.

6. Do you think Carlson has a tattoo or might get a tattoo?

7. Which paragraph seems to convey Carlson's opinion about tattoos?

8. Carlson says that 49 percent of 18- to 29-year-olds and 16 percent of the entire American adult population have at least one tattoo and that 17 percent of tattooed Americans wish they were not. As the larger percentage of those with at least one tattoo become senior citizens, do you think they will be more likely or less likely to regret being tattooed? Explain.

My Way!

MARGO KAUFMAN

Freelance author Margo Kaufman's essays have appeared in the New York Times, Newsweek, USA Today, Cosmopolitan, *and the* Village Voice. *This essay is from her first book* 1-800-Am-I-Nuts, *published by Random House.*

MINDSET

Lock It In

If people who try to control you were to stop doing so, would you experience joy, relief, indifference, suspicion, emptiness, helplessness, or a combination of those feelings?

1   Is it my imagination, or is this the age of the control freak? I'm standing in front of the triceps machine at my gym. I've just set the weights, and I'm about to begin my exercise when a lightly muscled bully in turquoise spandex interrupts her chest presses to bark at me. "I'm using that," she growls as she leaps up from her slant board, darts over to the triceps machine, and resets the weights.

2   I'm tempted to point out that, while she may have been planning to use the machine, she was, in fact, on the opposite side of the room. And that her muscles won't atrophy if she waits for me to finish. Instead, I go work on my biceps. Life's too short to fight over a Nautilus machine. Of course, *I'm* not a control freak.

3   Control freaks will fight over anything: a parking space, the room temperature, the last pair of marked-down Maude Frizon pumps, even whether you should barbecue with the top on or off the Weber kettle. Nothing is too insignificant. Everything has to be just so.

4   Just so *they* like it. "These people compulsively have to have their own way," says Los Angeles psychologist Gary Emery. "Their egos are based on being right," Emery says, "on proving they're the boss." (And it isn't enough for the control freak to win. Others have to lose.)

5   "Control freaks are overconcerned with the means, rather than the end," Emery says. "So it's more important that the string beans are the right kind than it is to just enjoy the meal."

6   "What do you mean just enjoy the meal?" scoffs my friend Marc. "There's a right way to do things and then there's everything else." It goes without saying that he, and only he, has access to that Big Right Way in the Sky. And that Marc lives alone.

7   "I really hate to be in any situation where my control over what I'm doing is compromised," he admits. "Like if somebody says, 'I'll handle the cooking and you can shuck the corn or slice the zucchini,' I tell them to do it without me."

8   A control freak's kitchen can be his or her castle. "Let me show you the right way to make rice," said my husband the first time I made the mistake of fixing dinner. By the time Duke had sharpened the knives, rechopped the vegetables into two-inch squares, and chided me for using the wrong size pan, I had decided to surrender all control of the stove. (For the record, this wasn't a big sacrifice. I don't like to cook.)

9   "It's easier in a marriage when you both don't care about the same things," says Milton Wolpin, a psychology professor at the University of Southern California. "Otherwise, everything would be a battle."

10   And every automobile would be a battleground. There's nothing worse than having two control freaks in the same car. "I prefer to drive," my friend Claire says. "But no sooner do I pull out of the driveway than Fred starts telling me what to do. He thinks that I'm an idiot behind the wheel and that I make a lot of stupid mistakes."

11   She doesn't think he drives any better. "I think he goes really, really fast, and I'm sure that someday he's going to kill us both," she says. "And I complain about it constantly. But it's still a little easier for me to take a back seat. I'd rather get to pick him apart than get picked on."

12   My friend Katie would withstand the abuse. "I like to control everything," she says. "From where we're going to eat to what we're going to eat to what movie we're going to see, what time we're going to see it, where we're going to see it, where we're going to park. Everything!"

13   But you can't control everything. So much of life is beyond our control. And to me, that's what makes it interesting. But not to Katie. "I don't like having my fate in someone else's hands," she says firmly. "If I take charge, I know that whatever it is will get done and it will get done well."

14   I shuffle my feet guiltily. Not too long ago I invited Katie and a bunch of friends out to dinner to celebrate my birthday. It was a control freak's nightmare. Not only did I pick the restaurant and arrange to pick up the check, but Duke also called in advance and ordered an elaborate Chinese banquet. I thought Katie was going to lose her mind.

15   "What did you order? I have to know," she cried, seizing a menu. "I'm a vegetarian. There are things I won't eat." Duke assured her that he had accounted for everybody's taste. Still, Katie didn't stop hyperventilating until the food arrived. "I was very pleasantly surprised," she confesses. "And I would trust Duke again."

16   "I'm sure there are areas where you're the control freak," says Professor Wolpin, "areas where you're more concerned about things than your husband." *Me?* The champion of laissez-faire? "You get very upset if you find something visible to the naked eye on the kitchen counter," Duke reminds me. "And you think you know much better than me what the right shirt for me to wear is."

17   But I'm just particular. I'm not a control freak.

18   "A control freak is just someone who cares about something more than you do," Wolpin says.

19   So what's wrong with being a control freak?

EXERCISE 5   Discussion and Critical Thinking

1. Kaufman defines "control freak" by quoting two psychologists. In paragraph 4, psychologist Gary Emery says control freaks "have to have their own way" and prove "they're the boss." In paragraph 18, psychology professor Milton Wolpin says: "A control freak is just someone who cares about something more than you do." After using numerous examples to illustrate her definitions, Kaufman ends her essay by seeming to admit she is also a control freak as she says in the last paragraph, "So what's wrong with being a control freak?"

   Apply those views to the following examples by Kaufman and explain if they fit. What is wrong, if anything, with the behavior shown in each of these instances?

   Example 1 (paragraphs 1 and 2): The person who "controls" the exercise machine in the gym.

   Example 2 (paragraphs 6 and 7): Her friend Marc, who proclaims, "There is a right way to do things and then there's everything else."

   Example 3 (paragraph 8): Her husband Duke, who showed her "the right way to make rice."

   Example 4 (paragraphs 10 and 11): Kaufman's friend Claire, who would rather be a backseat driver than drive the vehicle.

   Example 5 (paragraphs 12 through 15): Her friend Katie, who wanted to review the food choices before attending a dinner at which she was a guest.

   Example 6 (paragraph 16): Kaufman herself, who polices the kitchen counter for food droppings and wants to dictate which shirts her husband should wear.

2. Considering the range of behavior in the examples from mild to antisocial, would you say that the degree of being controlling is significant? If so, how would you modify Wolpin's statement?

3. In the last paragraph, does Kaufman contradict what she says elsewhere, or does she just finally become profoundly honest and open-minded?

Underground Dads

WIL HAYGOOD

As a child, Wil Haygood did not have an actual dad around the house. But he was fortunate. He had men around who gave him the love and guidance he needed. Three men in particular were his surrogate fathers, and he learned important lessons from each. This essay was first published in the New York Times Magazine.

1   For years, while growing up, I shamelessly told my playmates that I didn't have a father. In my neighborhood, where men went to work with lunch pails, my friends thought there was a gaping hole in my household. My father never came to the park with me to toss a softball, never came to see me in any of my school plays. I'd explain to friends, with the simplicity of explaining to someone that there are, in some woods, no deer, that I just had no father. My friends looked at me and squinted. My mother and father had divorced shortly after my birth. As the years rolled by, however, I did not have the chance to turn into the pitiful little black boy who had been abandoned by his father. There was a reason: other men showed up. They were warm, honest (at least as far as my eyes could see) and big-hearted. They were the good black men in the shadows, the men who taught me right from wrong, who taught me how to behave, who told me, by their very actions, that they expected me to do good things in life.

2   There are heartbreaking statistics tossed about regarding single-parent black households these days, about children growing up fatherless. Those statistics must be considered. But how do you count the other men, the ones who show up—with perfect timing, with a kind of soft-stepping loveliness—to give a hand, to take a boy to watch airplanes lift off, to show a young boy the beauty of planting tomatoes in the ground and to tell a child that all of life is not misery?

3   In my life, there was Jerry, who hauled junk. He had a lean body and a sweet smile. He walked like a cowboy, all bowlegged, swinging his shoulders. It was almost a strut. The sound of his pickup truck rumbling down our alley in Columbus, Ohio, could raise me from sleep.

4   When he wasn't hauling junk, Jerry fixed things. More than once, he fixed my red bicycle. The gears were always slipping; the chain could turn into a tangled mess. Hearing pain in my voice, Jerry would instruct me to leave my bike on our front porch. In our neighborhood, in the 60's, no one would steal your bike from your porch. Jerry promised me he'd pick it up, and he always did. He never lied to me, and he cautioned me not to tell lies. He was, off and on, my mother's boyfriend. At raucous family gatherings, he'd pull me aside and explain to me the importance of honesty, of doing what one promised to do.

5   And there was Jimmy, my grandfather, who all his life paid his bills the day they arrived: that was a mighty lesson in itself—it taught me a work ethic. He held two jobs, and there were times when he allowed me to accompany him on his night job, when he cleaned a Greek restaurant on the north side of Columbus. Often he'd mop the place twice, as if trying to win some award. He frightened me too. It was not because he was mean. It was because he had exacting standards, and there were times when I didn't measure up to those standards. He didn't like shortcutters. His instructions, on anything, were to be carried out to the letter. He believed in independence, doing as much for yourself as you possibly could. It should not have surprised me when, one morning while having stomach pains, he chose not to wait for a taxi and instead walked the mile to the local hospital, where he died a week later of stomach cancer.

6   My uncles provided plenty of good background music when I was coming of age. Uncle Henry took me fishing. He'd phone the night before. "Be ready. Seven o'clock." I'd trail him through woods—as a son does a father—until we found our fishing hole. We'd sit for hours. He taught me a patience and an appreciation of the outdoors, of nature. He talked, incessantly, of family—his family, my family, the family of friends. The man had a reverence for family. I knew to listen.

7   I think these underground fathers simply appear, decade to decade, flowing through the generations. Hardly everywhere, and hardly, to be sure, in enough places, but there. As mystical, sometimes, as fate when fate is sweet.

8   Sometimes I think that all these men who have swept in and out of my life still couldn't replace a good, warm father. But inasmuch as I've never known a good, warm father, the men who entered my life, who taught me right from wrong, who did things they were not asked to do, have become unforgettable, I know of the cold statistics out there. And yet, the mountain of father-son literature does not haunt me. I've known good black men.

EXERCISE 6   Discussion and Critical Thinking

1. Copy here the sentence that focuses on the main idea of the essay.

2. Paraphrase the thesis.

3. Name the three examples used to support Haygood's main idea.

4. What did Haygood learn from each man?

5. How does Haygood relate his experiences shown in the examples to statistics?

STUDENT PARAGRAPH AND ESSAY

Writing Process Worksheet

Name _Sarah Betrue_   **Title** _Sweet and Sour Workplace_   **Due Date** _Friday, October 19, 11 a.m._

Use the back of this page or separate paper if you need more space.

Assignment   In the space below, write whatever you need to know about your assignment, including information about the topic, audience, pattern of writing, length, whether to include a rough draft or revised drafts, and whether your paper must be typed.

Paragraph of about 300 words on irritations that produce stress and anger. Use specific examples for support. Take the examples from experiences at work, home, school, or any place in my life. Audience: people similar to me, who will be familiar with stress, although maybe not with my examples. Submit this completed sheet, a rough draft marked for revision, and a typed final draft.

Stage One

Explore Freewrite, brainstorm (list), cluster, or take notes as directed by your instructor.

Listing

School	*Home + personal*	*Work*
Parking	Keeping	Complaining boss
Registration	balance	Fellow employees
for classes	Boyfriend	immature
Confusing,	Shopping	self-centered
difficult		lazy
assignments		Customers
Annoying students		freeloaders
Food		name callers

Stage Two

Organize Write a topic sentence or thesis; label the subject and the focus parts.

<u>Stressful and frustrating situations</u> <u>occur daily behind the scenes at my</u>
          subject   focus

<u>workplace, making it almost impossible for me to maintain a positive</u>

<u>attitude</u>.

Write an outline or an outline alternative. For reading-based writing, include references and short quotations with page numbers as support in the outline.

   I. Boss
     A. Strict
     B. Unappreciative
       1. Usually
       2. This morning
  II. Fellow employees
     A. Cooks
     B. Cashiers
     C. Waitresses
       1. Self-centered
       2. Behaving typically yesterday
 III. Customers
     A. Complaining generally
     B. One in particular
       1. Demanding
       2. Insulting

Stage Three

Write   On separate paper, write and then revise your paragraph or essay as many times as necessary for **c**oherence, **l**anguage (usage, tone, and diction), **u**nity, **e**mphasis, **s**upport, and **s**entences (**CLUESS**). Read your work aloud to hear and correct any grammatical errors or awkward-sounding sentences.

Edit any problems in fundamentals, such as **c**apitalization, **o**missions, **p**unctuation, and **s**pelling (**COPS**).

SWEET AND SOUR WORKPLACE
Sarah Betrue

Every morning as I enter my workplace, I admire the vibrant colors of both the tropical fish in the aquarium and the ancient silk Chinese robes hung from the wall. But as I take the dreaded step from the dining area to the kitchen, the scenery drastically changes. <u>Stressful and frustrating situations occur daily behind the scenes at the restaurant, making it almost impossible for me to maintain a positive attitude.</u> Yesterday is a typical shift. <u>The first voices I hear are the owners complaining about how filthy the restaurant looks,</u> although the night before the other employees and I worked with Ajax for three hours scrubbing shelves and floor sinks. As the day progresses, I try to squeeze in some extra cleaning between busy times, but I find myself doing all the extra work myself. The young girls I work with think having this job is just an extension of their social lives. During lunch hour, the dining area is packed, the line for takeout has reached a ridiculous length, and two phone calls are on hold. <u>That is when Morgan decides to call her boyfriend on her cell phone.</u> Naturally I become frustrated and proceed to speak with her. She glares at me with fire in her eyes and screams, "I've got more important things to deal with at this time!" Getting nowhere with politeness, I grab the phone from her hand and turn it off. No sooner has this crisis ended than the house phone rings again. <u>On the line is a very unhappy woman.</u> After listening to a few colorfully disparaging descriptions of a meal she ordered, I tell her I cannot give refunds or food exchanges if her order is not returned first. She threatens to report our restaurant to newspapers and authorities, and then tells me to do something I am physically incapable of doing and hangs up in my ear. At the end of the day I am so angry and frustrated with having to put up with such occurrences that I want to grab hold of one of the woks and hit someone upside the head. But just as I reach for the handle, I get a vision, an image of my paycheck, and I begin to relax. <u>I leave the restaurant with no blood on my hands, wishing everyone a wonderful evening.</u>

Margin labels:
Topic sentence
Example
Example
Example
Concluding sentence

EXERCISE 7   Discussion and Critical Thinking

1. What evidence is there that Betrue is not essentially a negative thinker?

2. What kind of order does Betrue use for her three specific supporting examples?

3. If you were one of the owners of the restaurant, how would you react to Betrue's paragraph?

READING-BASED WRITING

....

Hungering for Sounds of Silence

EILEEN BAYLOR

The assignment for student Eileen Baylor was to select an article from a list and write a brief essay of reaction to it. She was to convey the important ideas of her subject piece with direct references and quotations, but she was not to feature a summary of it. She was required to photocopy the article, mark it with underlines and annotations, and submit it along with a brief outline, a rough draft, and a typed final draft of her brief essay of reaction.

Text identification Thesis	1	"Cell Phone Backlash" by Margaret Loftus is full of good examples. They are good because they support her main point and remind me of similar examples. Like many people, Loftus is sick and tired of loud secondhand cell phone talking.
Topic sentence Quotation Statistics Quotation Statistics	2	The worst part is that the offensive, loud talking is getting worse. She says, "Nearly 75 percent of those surveyed in our poll think mobile phone etiquette has declined over the past five years" (26). One may be inclined to distrust an "our poll," but Loftus backs hers up by referring to a *National Geographic Traveler*/Yahoo! poll concluding that 75 percent of travelers are "sometimes or frequently annoyed" (26). For airline travelers, that percentage may go up because the Federal Communications Commission may allow companies to remove its ban on cell phone use during flights.
Topic sentence Example Example	3	Some of those who are already annoyed are very annoyed. Loftus gives several colorful examples. One is about a loudmouth traveler calling numerous friends to brag about where he was staying, where he was dining, and which limousine service he had booked. For revenge, an annoyed fellow traveler slipped outside and used his own cell phone to cancel all the reservations. In another example, a man on a commuter train finally had had enough of a long secondhand conversation about a fellow passenger's divorce, including custody of the dog. Finally he walked across the aisle, grabbed the phone, and smashed it on the floor of the train. In still another example, a person confessed he carries an illegal "jammer that kills cell phone conversations within a 20-foot radius" (26).
Topic sentence	4	Stories like that may be satisfying to those of us who are irritated by the noise, but those solutions are not good ideas for the general public. Canceling the reservations may be just punishment, but it is the kind of punishment that can lead to retaliation. Smashing the cell phone invites a violent response. And not only is jamming the phone illegal, as mentioned, but it might prevent a call coming through about a medical emergency.
Topic sentence Extended example	5	Those reservations do not mean I am pure of thought. I have concocted my own unwholesome schemes during loud cell phone conversations at restaurants, in shopping lines, and even one in a church at a funeral. Last week in a restaurant a nearby loudmouth had a cell phone conversation with his wife about her purchasing a tablecloth. He told her the one she was considering was too expensive and that she should shop for a cheaper one on the Web. He even told his wife he was dining alone, though a sweet young thing sat smiling across from him. I will admit I thought up a plot of how I could blow his cover, but instead I just left without ordering dessert.
Topic sentence Extended example	6	In another incident I witnessed in a middle-scale restaurant, a man came in alone and sat in a booth across from me. Almost immediately

I heard static, electric ratchet wrench sounds, and booming voices. He had brought a walkie-talkie with him and was monitoring calls from his nearby place of work in a large tire store. He was a huge man, mean-looking and sweaty. He could carry a tire in either hand—above his head. I stared at him. He glared back. I thought of suggesting he use his cell phone. Politely.

Conclusion   7   Right then I concluded that Loftus was right in her article about cell phone etiquette. Things are bad and getting worse, but maybe she does not know what *worse* is. Maybe cell phones are just a threshold weapon in rudeness. I ordered a dessert to go.

Work Cited

Loftus, Margaret. "Cell Phone Backlash." *National Geographic Traveler* July/Aug. 2005: 26. Print.

Suggested Topics and Prompts for Writing Exemplification

STUDENT COMPANION SITE
For additional practice, visit www.cengage .com/devenglish/ brandon/spb6e.

You will find a blank Writing Process Worksheet on page 6 of this book and on your Student Companion Site. It can be photocopied or printed out, filled in, and submitted with your assignment, if your instructor directs you to do so.

READING-BASED WRITING

Reading-based writing requires you to read critically, write a reply that shows you understand what you have read, and give credit for ideas you borrow and words you quote. The form can be a summary, a reaction, or a two-part response (with separated summary and reaction). Documentation, in which you give credit for borrowed ideas and words, can be either formal (MLA) or informal, as directed by your instructor. Both the forms of reading-based writing and documentation are discussed with examples in Chapter 1. Definitions of the three forms follow.

Summary

- The summary is a statement presenting only the main points of what you have read by using different wording without altering the meaning, adding information, or showing bias.
- It is the purest form of reading-based writing.

Reaction

- In the reaction, the meaning of what you have read will be central to the topic sentence of your paragraph or to the thesis of your essay.
- Although the reaction is not a personal narrative by itself, it may include personal experience to explain elements of the text. For example, if your source is about driving styles, your own experiences as a driver or an observer of drivers could be relevant in your analysis of the text.
- The reaction may incorporate a summary to convey a broad view of what you have read, but your summary should never be the main part of your reaction.

Two-Part Response

- The two-part response separates the summary from the reaction.
- This form will give you practice in separating your objective summary in the first part from your more personal evaluation, interpretation, or application in the second part, the reaction.

READING-BASED WRITING TOPICS

"When Those Tattoos Really Get Under the Skin"

1. Write a summary of this essay, or a summary of just one of two ideas: the regret people have about having gotten tattooed or the fact that tattoo removal is a good business with great potential.

2. Write a reaction to this essay. Consider discussing the author's view that as people grow older and their bodies have less elasticity, they will regret having the tattoos put on. Use examples from personal experience or observation to agree or disagree. Is the reporter apparently biased or not? Would the conclusion be different if more of the examples came from tattoo enthusiasts? Consider interviewing a few people proud of their tattoos, a few senior citizens with tattoos, and some individuals who are just past middle age. Keep in mind that examples illustrate a point but do not prove it. One can find supporters for almost any view, including some that are extremely unusual or even bizarre. Use references and quotations.

"My Way!"

3. In a paragraph or an essay, explain the title, "My Way!" One possibility is that it relates to the song of the same name sung by Frank Sinatra, which is about the singer being a unique individual who follows his own inclinations instead of being directed by outside pressures. Another possibility is that it is related to the slogan "My Way or the Highway," which suggests that the person expects all associates to follow his or her directions and views, or just leave the scene. Of the two interpretations, which one better fits the author's intention? Use references to and quotations from the essay to explain your understanding.

4. Study the following two views from Kaufman's essay. Then in a paragraph or an essay of reaction, paraphrase the meaning of each and explain which view Kaufman seems to favor. Either agree or disagree with her. Use references and quotations. Include some of your own examples of controlling persons if that helps you make your points. (These conflicting views were also covered in detail in item 1 from Exercise 5 on page 348.)

"These people compulsively have to have their own way," says Los Angeles psychologist Gary Emery. "Their egos are based on being right," Emery says, "on proving they're the boss." (And it isn't enough for the control freak to win. Others have to lose.) [Paragraph 4]

"A control freak is just someone who cares about something more than you do," [Professor] Wolpin says. [Paragraph 18]

5. Write a reaction in which you discuss Kaufman's conclusion about control freaks in relation to the examples she gives. Is she consistent? She seems to excuse herself at the end for the ways she controls. But is all of the controlling in examples to be excused in the same way? Discuss the range of controlling behavior from the endearing to the oppressive. Use references and quotations.

"Underground Dads"

6. Write a summary of this essay.

7. Write a two-part response in which you summarize the essay and then in a separate section explain how you can relate to the author's examples or how individuals with cultural backgrounds other than African-American have had similar experiences. Use personal examples or examples from friends or relatives. Include references and quotations.

"Hungering for Sounds of Silence"

8. Write a paragraph or an essay of reaction in which you disagree or agree with the main view expressed in this essay. Use some of your own examples from personal experience. Include references and quotations.

GENERAL TOPICS

9. Write a paragraph or an essay about a town that seems to project different sets of values as it exhibits contradictory features of products, services, and individual behavior. For a helpful model of form on a similar topic, review "Colorado Springs—Every Which Way" on page 341.

10. Use examples to write about irritations in a neighborhood; in restaurants; in theaters during a movie; on airplanes, buses, or trains; on streets, highways, or freeways; or in your home. For a helpful model of form on a similar topic, review "Sweet and Sour Workplace" on page 352.

11. Make a judgmental statement about an issue you believe in strongly and then use one or more examples to illustrate your point. These are some possible topics:

    a. The price of groceries is too high.

    b. Professional athletes are paid too much.

    c. A person buying a new car may get a lemon.

    d. Drivers sometimes openly ignore the laws on a selective basis.

    e. Politicians should be watched.

    f. Working and going to school is tough.

    g. Working, parenting, and going to school is tough.

    h. All computer viruses have common features.

    i. Many people under the age of eighteen spend too much time playing computer games.

    j. Some computer games teach children useful skills.

CROSS-CURRICULAR TOPIC

12. Use examples as supporting information in discussing a person, an event, or an issue pertaining to another class you have taken or are taking. Your explanation might focus on why someone or something was successful or unsuccessful. As a report on a field trip, examples might support a dominant impression of, say, a museum exhibit in an art-history class or an observation for a case study in an education or a psychology class.

CAREER-RELATED TOPIC

13. Use specific examples to support one of the following statements as applied to business or work:

    a. Don't burn your bridges.

    b. Like Lego®, business is a matter of connections.

    c. Tact is the lubricant that oils the wheels of industry.

    d. The customer is always right.

    e. Money is honey, my little sonny, and a rich man's joke is always funny.

    f. If you take care of the pennies, the dollars will take care of themselves.

    g. A kind word turns away wrath.

WRITER'S GUIDELINES   Exemplification

1. Use examples to explain, convince, or amuse.

2. Use examples that are vivid, specific, and representative.

- Vivid examples attract attention.
- Specific examples are identifiable.
- Representative examples are typical and therefore the basis for generalizations.

3. Tie your examples clearly to your topic sentence or thesis.

4. Draw your examples from what you have read, heard, and experienced.

5. Brainstorm a list of possible examples before you write.

6. Order your examples by time, space, or level of importance.

7. Ask yourself the following questions as you proceed:

- What am I trying to say?
- What examples might support that idea? (Use listing.)
- How many examples and what order should I use?
- Are my examples specific, vivid, and representative?
- Have I made a connection between my examples and my topic sentence or thesis?

8. Write and revise.

STUDENT COMPANION SITE
For additional practice, visit www.cengage .com/devenglish/ brandon/spb6e.

- Write and then revise your paragraph or essay as many times as neces-sary for **c**oherence, **l**anguage (usage, tone, and diction), **u**nity, **e**mphasis, **s**upport, and **s**entences (**CLUESS**). Read your work aloud to hear and correct any grammatical errors or awkward-sounding sentences.
- Edit any problems in fundamentals, such as **c**apitalization, **o**missions, **p**unctuation, and **s**pelling (**COPS**).

Chapter 20

Analysis by Division
Examining the Parts

FLOW OF WRITING

WHEN TO USE ANALYSIS BY DIVISION

FOR COLLEGE WRITING ASSIGNMENTS

- If a writing assignment in any class requires that you divide your subject into parts and discuss how the parts relate to make up a unit, then you will turn to analysis by division. The principle is essentially the same regardless of the unit: a short story, a person, an organism, a rock, a painting, or a piece of music.

IN CAREERS AND AT THE WORKPLACE

- Whether you are preparing for a career or engaged in a career, analysis by division will serve you well as you deal with any unit: requirements to complete your degree (how each one is part of the unit and relates to the other parts); the chain of command at work (each part, or level, with responsibilities and rewards); the job description at the workplace (each aspect separate and all related to a work assignment); the performance review (made up of categories of how you will be [are] evaluated and, perhaps, how you [will] evaluate others).

ANALYSIS BY DIVISION IN A CARTOON

THE QUIGMANS   by Buddy Hickerson

"Woo! Check out the third and seventh segments on THAT babe. YEAH!"

WRITING ANALYSIS BY DIVISION

Being able to analyze is the key to learning, performing, and teaching. If you need to explain how something works or exists as a unit, you will write an analysis by division. You will break down a unit (your subject) into its parts and explain how each part functions in relation to the operation or existence of the whole. The most important word here is *unit*. You begin with something that can stand alone or can be regarded separately. Here are some examples of units that can be divided into traits, characteristics, or other parts in different contexts:

Personal
- a relationship
- love
- a role, such as parent, neighbor, friend (traits)
- an activity, such as a hobby

Cross-Curricular
- a musical composition
- a prepared food
- an organism
- a government
- a poem or short story

Career-Related

- a job description
- an evaluation of an individual, a product, a service, an institution, or a company
- management style
- management

PROCEDURE

The following procedure will guide you in writing an analysis by division. Move from subject to principle, to division, to relationship:

1. Begin with something that is a unit.

2. State one principle by which the unit can function.

3. Divide the unit into parts according to that principle.

4. Discuss each of the parts in relation to the unit.

You might apply that procedure to evaluating a restaurant in the following way:

1. Unit	A particular restaurant
2. Principle of function	Overall quality
3. Parts based on the principle	Ambiance, food, service
4. Discussion	Consider each part in relation to the quality of a dining experience

ORGANIZATION

In a paragraph or an essay of analysis by division, the main parts are likely to be the main points of your outline or main extensions of your cluster. If they are anything else, reconsider your organization.

A basic outline of analysis by division might look like this:

Thesis: In judging this restaurant, one should consider these aspects.
  I. Ambiance
  II. Food
  III. Service

See pages 376–377 for an example of a restaurant review by a student.

SEQUENCE OF PARTS

The order in which you discuss the parts will vary according to the nature of the unit and the way in which you view it. Here are some possible sequences for organizing the parts of a unit:

- **Time**: The sequence of the parts can be mainly chronological, or time-based (if you are dealing with something that functions on its own, such as a heart, with the parts presented in relation to stages of the function).
- **Space**: If your unit is a visual object, especially if, like a pencil, it does nothing by itself, you may discuss the parts in relation to space. In the example of the pencil, the parts of the pencil begin at the top with the eraser and end at the bottom with the pencil point.

- **Emphasis**: Because the most emphatic location of any piece of writing is the end (the second most emphatic point is the beginning), consider placing the most significant part of the unit at the end.

Transitional Words

Consider using the following transitional words to improve coherence by connecting ideas with ideas, sentences with sentences, and paragraphs with paragraphs.

FOR ANALYSIS BY DIVISION:
Time or Numbering: first, second, third, another, last, finally, soon, later, currently, before, along with, another part (section, component)

Space: above, below, to the left, to the right, near, beyond, under, next to, in the background, split, divide

Emphasis: most important, equally important, central to the, to this end, as a result, taken collectively, with this purpose in mind, working with the, in fact, of course, above all, most of all, especially, primarily, without question

FOR ALL PATTERNS OF WRITING: The <u>HOTSHOT CAT</u> words: <u>H</u>owever, <u>O</u>therwise, <u>T</u>herefore, <u>S</u>imilarly, <u>H</u>ence, <u>O</u>n the other hand, <u>T</u>hen, <u>C</u>onsequently, <u>A</u>lso, <u>T</u>hus (See pages 74–75 for additional transitional words.)

Restaurant Review as Analysis by Division

In the wide range of uses of analysis by division, one use is featured in this chapter: the restaurant review.

Definition

The **restaurant review** is an article of one or more paragraphs that contains three elements: ambiance, service, and food.

- **Ambiance** is the atmosphere, mood, or feeling of a place. For restaurants, it may begin with landscaping and architecture (building style). Ambiance is certainly produced by what is inside, such as the furnishings, seating, style, upkeep, sounds, sights, smells, behavior of other customers, and management style—whatever produces that mood or the feeling, even if it is franchise plastic and elevator music.
- **Service** is mainly concerned with food delivery and those who do it: their attitude, manners, helpfulness, promptness, accuracy, and availability. Self-service or pick-up establishments would be judged by similar standards.
- **Food** is the emphasis—its variety, quality, quantity, price, and presentation.

Writing the Review

- Use first person (*I*) as you relate your experience in a particular restaurant or chain.
- If possible, base your evaluation on more than one food item. Here is a low-cost way to do that: Dine with others and ask your companions to order

different foods. Then ask them if you can taste (two small bites will suffice) what they are served, thus increasing your experience. Offering to pay a portion of their check may make others more receptive to sharing their food.

- While you are dining, use a simple outline or listing to make sure you have information on ambiance, service, and food. Copy names of foods and prices from the menu. Use quotation marks around any descriptive phrases for items you copy.
- You need not separate comments on ambiance, service, and food or present them in a particular order, but be specific in your details and examples. Use quotation marks for any descriptive phrases you borrow from the menu.
- For a really special review, choose an independent restaurant, one that is not part of a national chain.
- Consider writing a review about your campus cafeteria.

For an example of a skillfully written restaurant review, read "Johnny's Wiener Wagon on a Roll" on pages 376–377.

Career Review as Analysis by Division

The career review is a summary of a career, which you can personalize by relating it to your background, interests, aptitude, and other relevant vocational matters.

The organization and development of your career review follow the basic procedure for writing an analysis by division as you move from unit to division to development. It is logical, systematic, and highly manageable.

- The unit for an essay is the career field, and your quest of that career.
- The parts of that unit are the parts of the career field and your quest. Those parts can be further subdivided.
- The extent of the dividing may vary, depending on your particular purpose (assignment), the expected audience, and, if applicable, your current involvement in the career field.
- Your college library has an abundance of material that will inform you with career information you can summarize in your review. Your best overall source is probably the *Occupational Outlook Handbook* by the U.S. Department of Labor. It is available in print and online, and is ideal for you to summarize selectively for your career review. Updated and published every two years, the handbook covers hundreds of career fields, providing information about earnings, prerequisites of training and education, expected job prospects, job duties, and working conditions. Of course, you should give credit to your source(s) in your "Work(s) Cited" at the end of your review. This is the online address, which can be used for locating the source online or in the library or for giving credit in your "Work(s) Cited."

> United States. Dept. of Labor. *Occupational Outlook Handbook.* 2008–09 Web. 19 Dec. 2009.

- The following main-part outline shows some useful divisions for an essay as a career review. For a shorter essay, you can just select the main parts that fit the assignment you have in mind. For an even shorter assignment of a paragraph, you can subdivide one of these Roman-numeral parts for basic organization of your career review, or analysis by division.

Unit: (the career itself)

Divisions: (parts of the unit, the career itself)

I. My background, interests, and aptitude

II. My desired field—an overview

III. Working conditions, pay, benefits

IV. Requirements for employment

V. My step-by-step plan to enter this field

See pages 381–383 for an example of a student career review in the form of an analysis by division.

FINDING PATTERNS IN PHOTOS

EXERCISE 1 A Text-Based Activity for Groups or Individuals

Elvis Presley performing on stage

Imagine you are a pop-culture critic for a leading magazine. You are assigned to write about an innovator of rock 'n' roll and arguably the top musical performer of the twentieth century: Elvis Presley. For prewriting of your analysis by division, start with Elvis as your unit (Step 1), proceed to "the excellence of Elvis" as your principle of function (Step 2), and move to Elvis's characteristics as the parts (Step 3). For parts, use the Roman-numeral headings in the form shown below and mention some or all of these: *I. Costume* (young Elvis, old Elvis, or both), *II. Appearance* (especially sex appeal), *III. Style of performance* (moving on the stage and connecting with the audience), *IV. Songs* ("You Ain't Nothin' But a Hound Dog," "Heartbreak Hotel," "Love Me Tender," "Blue Christmas," "My Teddy Bear"), and *V. Trademark behavior* (throwing the scarf to the audience, bestowing extravagant gifts, such as cars).

If your instructor directs, use your outline to write a paragraph or an essay showing how the parts all relate (Step 4) to "the excellence of Elvis." Alter and rearrange points in the outline to reflect the design of the article you are writing.

Possible alternative assignment for students unfamiliar with Elvis: Paste in an action photo of a performer you regard as "great," and apply the four steps indicated above.

I. _____

   A. _____

   B. _____

II. _____

   A. _____

   B. _____

III. _____

    A. _____

    B. _____

IV. _____

    A. _____

    B. _____

V. _____

    A. _____

    B. _____

Practicing Patterns of Analysis by Division

In analysis by division, Roman-numeral headings are almost always parts of the unit you are discussing as your subject. Learning to divide the unit into parts will help you move through your assignment quickly and efficiently.

EXERCISE 2   Completing Patterns

Fill in the blanks in the following outlines to complete each analysis by division. The Roman-numeral items represent major divisions of the unit and consequently would indicate the major parts of a paragraph or an essay.

A. Unit: Federal government

    Principle: Division of power

    Parts based on the principle:

     I. Executive

     II. _____

     III. _____

B. Unit: Newspaper

    Principle: Sections for readers

    Parts based on the principle:

     I. News

     II. Sports

     III. _____

     IV. _____

     V. _____

C. Unit: Doctor

Principle: Effective as a general practitioner

Parts based on the principle:

I. Ability to _____

II. Knowledge of _____

III. Knowledge of computers and other equipment

EXERCISE 3   Writing Patterns

Fill in the blanks in the following outlines as if you were organizing material for a paragraph or an essay. Have a specific person, job, service, institution, or product in mind.

A. Unit: Evaluation of a person (one who is on the job or applying for a job)

Principle: Traits that would make a person praiseworthy (as a worker or an applicant)

The name of the person (may be fictitious): _____

I. _____

II. _____

III. _____

IV. _____

(Add other headings if necessary.)

B. Unit: Product, institution, or service

Principle: Qualities that would make the unit excellent

Specific name of the unit: _____

I. _____

II. _____

III. _____

IV. _____

(Add other headings if necessary.)

Readings for Critical Thinking, Discussion, and Writing

READING STRATEGIES AND OBJECTIVES

Underlining and annotating these reading selections will help you answer the questions that follow the selections, discuss the material in class, and prepare for reading-based writing assignments. As you underline and annotate, pay special attention to the author's writing skills, logic, and message, and consider the relevance of the material to your own experiences and values.

One selection begins with a Mindset suggestion that can help you create a readiness for connecting with what you are about to read.

PARAGRAPHS

Who Are Our Heroes?

PONCHITTA PIERCE

Taken from an essay of the same name by journalist Ponchitta Pierce, this paragraph defines a personal hero by using analysis by division and supporting it with specific examples.

The poet Maya Angelou, 67—whose works include the autobiography *I Know Why the Caged Bird Sings* and "On the Pulse of Morning," the poem she read at President Clinton's inauguration—also doesn't use the word "hero." She prefers the term "hero/shero," because "hero" too often is thought of as male. "Young women and young men need to know that there are women who give encouragement and succor, nourishment and insight," explained Angelou. "A hero/shero encourages people to see the good inside themselves and to expand it." Angelou lists Eleanor Roosevelt, the author Pearl S. Buck and the abolitionist Frederick Douglass among her heroes. "They confronted societies that did not believe in their ideas and faced hostile adversaries," she said. "At times they were angry. Anger is very good—but I have not seen any case where any of them became bitter." We can develop the heroic in ourselves, Angelou continued, by seeking to do right by others. "Are you concerned about the poor, the lonely and the ill?" she asked. "Do you follow your concern with action? I try to act as I would want my hero/shero to act. I want to display courtesy, courage, patience and strength all the time. Now, I blow it 84 times a day. But I'm trying."

EXERCISE 4   Discussion and Critical Thinking

1. Why does Maya Angelou use the term *hero/shero*?

2. On the first line below, write the name of a hero/shero, either an ordinary person you know or have known or a famous person from history or current times. Then, for the Roman-numeral headings, write the four qualities listed by Maya Angelou.

Unit (as person):

_____

Parts (as qualities):

I. _____

II. _____

III. _____

IV. _____

Qualities of Good Bosses

PAUL B. HERTNEKY

When we are shopping or receiving service at a business, we will probably never see the manager—the individual whom employees call the "boss"—but almost certainly the nature of our care will be affected significantly by the qualities of that person. In this paragraph from "You and Your Boss," Paul B. Hertneky discusses those qualities.

Good bosses? They know who they are. If you wonder about the qualities most valued in bosses, they are opposite the faults of bad bosses, and you've probably heard about and known a few. Their egos fit through doorways. They listen to everyone and treat everyone the way they would like to be treated. They extend themselves in an effort to appreciate those who are new and different. They set a good example. They take interest in the lives of their employees. They possess what it took Scrooge a couple of horrifying nights to acquire—eyes that are open wide, and hearts and minds that follow.

EXERCISE 5   Discussion and Critical Thinking

1. What does Hertneky mean by saying, "They know who they are."

2. What is the unit being discussed by Hertneky?

3. What is the principle used in the analysis by division?

4. Specifically what are those qualities?

ESSAYS
. . . .

Female Mea Culpa

LIN ROLENS

Freelance author Lin Rolens has a proposal to end all this animosity between the sexes. It is based on openness, and it starts and finishes with a list of needs and considerations, which are thinly veiled grievances. Ideally, this solution would be an exchange of lists. This essay was first printed in the Santa Barbara News Press Magazine.

1   For years now I've wanted a man who comes with a list: how he likes his coffee, what he won't eat, how he really feels about the remote control, how he likes his socks folded. I don't want the complete list, that would take volumes, but a starter list would be nice. And I don't want it presented with great ceremony; I want it slipped quietly into my pocket at just the right moment to make both our lives easier.

2   Of course, there should be a reciprocal list of all my little quirks, foibles, needs, pleasures and the like. Some of this is particular to me (I take my coffee with milk, will eat anything but okra, believe the remote should enjoy shared custody and will take my socks folded any way he cares to fold them), but certainly there are some general things about women that men would do well to know, some things that seem to escape them.

3   I offer a generalized starter list:

4   In our female hearts, we know, if there were any justice in the world, courtship would not be a phase in a relationship: It would be a way of life. Never mind dating, which is generally exhausting, but we really love, and even feel we deserve, all the little touches and enthusiasms, all those wonderful surprises and attentions that helped convince us you were the right one in the first place.

5   We love flowers: It isn't by accident that one of the features of our local farmers' market is masses of women leaving with great armfuls of flowers. We are, simply, suckers for flowers, and they often move us as words can't; men of sensibility know that women of sensibility never have too many flowers. The size of the bouquet decidedly is not the issue: We would rather receive a hand-selected nosegay than a floral display ordered through a secretary. And, this is important, flowers given for no apparent reason are flowers given for the best reason.

6   In the complicated logic of women, it is generally accepted that the only flowers not worth receiving are guilt flowers, those flowers proffered as moral groin cover or in lieu of a real apology. I have shoved more than one rose bouquet in the trash compactor because the sender mistakenly believed I would have a total brain lapse about some recent transgression when I received them.

7   While we usually know what we want, we don't want to tell you what we want. Yes, we'll provide hints, murmured suggestions, but we don't want to have to lay it on the line. We want you to know; it's no mystery to us, and it's difficult to understand why it seems to be such a mystery to you. This goes for everything from where we want to vacation to what we would give if you just don't wear that particular pair of pants to the family reunion. Don't ask me to explain.

8   Talk is often balm, and truly being listened to is one of life's great luxuries. When the day or our lives overwhelm us, it is the wine of talk that proves settling. As we air whatever it is that disturbs us, the problem doesn't go away, but it deflates to a point where we see it in context.

9   Our rituals count; they are important and often meditative indulgences that help us center ourselves. Whether it's painting our toenails yet again in the color that horrifies you or taking long steamy baths or, as one of my friends recently did, spending an entire evening re-ironing all the cloth napkins in her linen closet, these endeavors prove healing. When we return to the fray, we will be better versions of ourselves.

10   When we buy new clothes, we want you to like them—a lot. We want to be adored, validated, or, if you can manage it, occasionally worshipped. (See "fat" for further clarification.)

11   Although it is all right, even inevitable, that we believe, whatever our current weight, that we are fat, it is never all right if you believe we are fat. We need and expect that you will find us just right, whatever our weight. While we are free to loathe extra dimples, bumps, lumps and curves, we trust that you will adore them with the same vigor that you adored our original youthful and girlish figures.

12   Food is not just food. When we cook for you, it is a way of loving you, and we'd appreciate it if you received it in the spirit in which it is given. This is

particularly true when we make not only your favorite dinner or our own stellar specialty, but something, say, like your mother's secret spaghetti sauce recipe.

13   There is a widely held belief that we want to change you, that we see men as delicious raw material and that, by careful and patient encouragement or insistence, a good man can be molded into an excellent one. This is actually a problem of semantics: As we see it, we are simply providing you the opportunity to become your best self.

14   Finally, we like chick flicks, that's how they got the name. Action films are fine, but we bring hankies to the movies for a reason.

15   So that's it, a starter list. I'm sure every woman will have her own additions and variations, but it might be worth a try simply to slip this into his pocket.

EXERCISE 6   Discussion and Critical Thinking

1. Why does Rolens use flowers to explain "the complicated logic of women" (paragraph 6)?

2. What does she mean when she compares "talk" to "balm" (paragraph 8)?

3. What does Rolens mean when she says, "While we usually know what we want, we don't want to tell you what we want" (paragraph 7)?

4. Is Rolens really serious about making lists? After all, she did say, "We don't want to tell you what we want" (paragraph 7).

5. In making her list, is Rolens mainly concerned with herself or the man?

6. Explain what she means by referring to courtship as a "way of life" (paragraph 4).

7. Does Rolens believe that women are superior to men in showing respect and consideration? Is she right?

EXERCISE 7   Vocabulary Highlights

Write a short definition of each word as it is used in the essay. (Paragraph numbers are given in parentheses.) Be prepared to use these words in your own sentences.

reciprocal (2)	transgression (6)
quirks (2)	balm (8)
foibles (2)	meditative (9)
sensibility (5)	stellar (12)
proffered (6)	semantics (13)

Low Wages, High Skills

KATHERINE S. NEWMAN

As an anthropologist, Katherine S. Newman specializes in urban life and the working poor. This excerpt is from her well-researched, celebrated book No Shame in My Game *(1999). As the title suggests, the workers have reasons for taking pride in what they do.*

MINDSET

Lock It In

Imagine you are being interviewed for an entry-level job at a large company. You are asked what skills you learned in your only other job: cashier and manager in the local, nonfranchised Speedy Burgers. What is your answer? Quickly!

1   Elise has worked the "drive-through" window at Burger Barn for the better part of three years. She is a virtuoso in a role that totally defeated one of my brightest doctoral students, who tried to work alongside her for a week or two. Her job pays only twenty-five cents above the minimum wage (after five years), but it requires that she listen to orders coming in through a speaker, send out a stream of instructions to co-workers who are preparing the food, pick up and check orders for customers already at the window, and receive money and make change, all more or less simultaneously. She has to make sure she keeps the sequence of orders straight so that the Big Burger goes to the man in the blue Mustang and not the woman right behind him in the red Camaro who has now revised her order for the third time. The memory and information-processing skills required to perform this job at a minimally acceptable level are considerable. Elise makes the operation look easy, but it clearly is a skilled job, as demanding as any of the dozen better-paid positions in the Post Office or the Gap stores where she has tried in vain to find higher-status employment.

2   This is not to suggest that working at Burger Barn is as complex as brain surgery. It is true that the component parts of the ballet, the multiple stations behind the counter, have been broken down into the simplest operations. Yet to make them work together under time pressure while minimizing wastage requires higher-order skills. We can think of these jobs as lowly, repetitive, routinized, and demeaning, or we can recognize that doing them right requires their incumbents to process information, coordinate with others, and track inventory. These valuable competencies are tucked away inside jobs that are popularly characterized as utterly lacking in skill.

3   If coordination were the only task required of these employees, then experience would probably eliminate the difficulty after a while. But there are many unpredictable events in the course of a workday that require some finesse to manage. Chief among them are abrasive encounters with customers, who . . . often have nothing better to do than rake a poor working stiff over the coals for a missing catsup packet or a batch of french fries that aren't quite hot enough. One afternoon at a Burger Barn cash register is enough to send most sane people into psychological counseling. It takes patience, forbearance, and an eye for the long-range goal (of holding on to your job, of impressing management with your fortitude) to get through some of these encounters. If ever there was an illustration of "people skills," this would be it.

4   Coping with rude customers and coordinating the many components of the production process are made all the more complex by the fact that in most Harlem Burger Barns, the workers hail from a multitude of countries and speak in a variety of languages. Monolingual Spanish speakers fresh from the Dominican Republic have to figure out orders spoken in Jamaican English. Puerto Ricans, who are generally bilingual, at least in the second generation, have to cope with the English dialects of African Americans. All of these people have to figure out how to serve customers who may be fresh off the boat from Guyana, West Africa, Honduras. The workplace melting pot bubbles along because people from these divergent groups are able to come together and learn bits and snatches of each other's languages—"workplace Spanish" or street English. They can communicate at a very rudimentary level in several dialects, and they know enough about each other's cultural traditions to be able to interpret actions, practices, dress styles, and gender norms in ways that smooth over what can become major conflicts on the street.

5   In a world where residential segregation is sharp and racial antagonism no laughing matter, it is striking how well workers get along with one another. Friendships develop across lines that have hardened in the streets. Romances are born between African Americans and Puerto Ricans, legendary antagonists in the neighborhoods beyond the workplace. This is even more remarkable when one considers the competition that these groups are locked into in a declining labor market. They know very well that employers are using race- and class-based preferences to decide who gets a job, and that their ability to foster the employment chances of friends and family members may well be compromised by a manager's racial biases. One can hear in their conversations behind the counter complaints about how they cannot get their friends jobs because—they believe—the manager wants to pick immigrants first and leave the native-born jobless. In this context, resentment builds against unfair barriers. Even so, workers of different ethnic backgrounds are able to reach across the walls of competition and cultural difference.

6   We are often admonished to remember that the United States is a multicultural society and that the workforce of the future will be increasingly composed of minorities and foreigners. Consultants make thousands of dollars advising companies in "diversity training" in order to manage the process of amalgamation. Burger Barn is a living laboratory of diversity, the ultimate melting pot for the working poor. They live in segregated spaces, but they work side by side with people whom they would rarely encounter on the block. If we regard the ability to work in a multiethnic, multilingual environment as a skill, as the consulting industry argues we should, then there is much to recommend the cultural capital acquired in the low-wage workplaces of the inner city.

7   Restaurant owners are loath to cut their profits by calling in expensive repair services when their equipment breaks down, the plumbing goes out, or the electrical wiring blows. Indeed, general managers are required to spend time in training centers maintained by Burger Barn's corporate headquarters learning how to disassemble the machinery and rebuild it from scratch. The philosophers in the training centers say this is done to teach managers a "ground-up" appreciation for the equipment they are working with. Any store owner will confess, however, that this knowledge is mainly good for holding labor costs down by making it unnecessary to call a repairman every time a milk shake machine malfunctions. What this means in practice is that managers must teach entry-level workers, especially the men (but the women as well), the art of mechanical repair and press them into service when the need strikes. Indeed, in one Harlem restaurant, workers had learned how to replace floor-to-ceiling windows (needed because of some bullet holes), a task they performed for well below the prevailing rates of a skilled glazier.

8   Then, of course, there is the matter of money. Burger Barn cash registers have been reengineered to make it possible for people with limited math abilities to operate them. Buttons on the face of the machine display the names of the items on the menu, and an internal program belts out the prices, adds them up, and figures out how much change is due a customer, all with no more than the push of a finger on the right "pad." Still, the workers who man the registers have to be careful to account for all the money that is in the till. Anything amiss and they are in deep trouble: they must replace any missing cash out of their wages. If money goes missing more than once, they are routinely fired. And money can disappear for a variety of reasons: someone makes a mistake in making change, an unexpected interloper uses the machine when the main register worker has gone into the back for some extra mustard packets, a customer changes her mind and wants to return an item (a transaction that isn't programmed into the machine). Even though much of the calculation involved in handling funds is done by computer chips, modest management skills are still required to keep everything in order.

9   While this is not computer programming, the demands of the job are nonetheless quite real. This becomes all too clear, even to managers who are of the opinion that these are "no-skill" jobs, when key people are missing. Workers who know the secrets of the trade—how to cut corners with the official procedures mandated by the company on food preparation, how to "trick" the cash register into giving the right amount of change when a mistake has been made, how to keep the orders straight when there are twenty people backed up in the drive-through line, how to teach new employees the real methods of food production (as opposed to the official script), and what to do when a customer throws a screaming fit and disrupts the whole restaurant—keep the complicated ballet of fast food operation moving smoothly. When "experts" disappear from the shift, nothing works the way it should. When they quit, the whole crew is thrown into a state of near-chaos, a situation that can take weeks to remedy as new people come "on line." If these jobs were truly as denuded of skill as they are popularly believed to be, none of this would matter. In fact, however, they are richer in cognitive complexity and individual responsibility than we acknowledge.

10   This is particularly evident when one watches closely over time how new people are trained. Burger Barn, like most of its competitors, has prepared training tapes designed to show new workers with limited literacy skills how to operate the equipment, assemble the raw materials, and serve customers courteously. Managers are told to use these tapes to instruct all new crew members. In the real world, though, the tapes go missing, the VCR machine doesn't work, and new workers come on board in the middle of the

hamburger rush hour when no one has time to sit them down in front of a TV set for a lesson. They have to be taught the old-fashioned way—person to person—with the more experienced and capable workers serving as teachers.

11   One of my graduate students learned this lesson the hard way. A native of Puerto Rico, Ana Ramos-Zayas made her way to a restaurant in the Dominican neighborhood of upper Harlem and put on an apron in the middle of the peak midday demand. Nobody could find the tapes, so she made do by trying to mimic the workers around her. People were screaming at her that she was doing it all wrong, but they were also moving like greased lightning in the kitchen. Ana couldn't figure out how to place the cheese on the hamburger patty so that it fit properly. She tried it one way and then another—nothing came out right. The experienced workers around her, who were all Spanish-speakers, were not initially inclined to help her out, in part because they mistook her for a white girl—something they had not seen behind the counter before. But when they discovered, quite by accident, that Ana was a Latina (she muttered a Spanish curse upon dropping the fifth bun in a row), they embraced her as a fellow migrant and quickly set about making sure she understood the right way to position the cheese.

12   From that day forward, these workers taught Ana all there was to know about the french fry machine, about how to get a milk shake to come out right, about the difference between cooking a fish sandwich and a chicken sandwich, and about how to forecast demand for each so that the bins do not overfill and force wastage. Without their help, provided entirely along informal lines, Ana would have been at sea. Her experience is typical in the way it reveals the hidden knowledge locked up inside what appears to surface observers (and to many employees themselves) as a job that requires no thinking, no planning, and no skill.

13   As entry-level employment, fast food jobs provide the worker with experience and knowledge that ought to be useful as a platform for advancement in the work world. After all, many white-collar positions require similar talents: memory skills, inventory management, the ability to work with a diverse crowd of employees, and versatility in covering for fellow workers when the demand increases. Most jobs require "soft skills" in people management, and those that involve customer contact almost always require the ability to placate angry clients. With experience of this kind, Burger Barn workers ought to be able to parlay their "human capital" into jobs that will boost their incomes and advance them up the status ladder.

14   The fact that this happens so rarely is only partially a function of the diplomas they lack or the mediocre test scores they have to offer employers who use these screening devices. They are equally limited by the popular impression that the jobs they hold now are devoid of value. The fast food industry's reputation for de-skilling its work combines with the low social standing of these inner-city employees to make their skills invisible. Employers with better jobs to offer do recognize that Burger Barn veterans are disciplined: they show up for work on time, they know how to serve the public. Yet if the jobs they are trying to fill require more advanced skills (inventory, the ability to learn new technologies, communication skills), Burger Barn is just about the last place that comes to mind as an appropriate proving ground. A week behind the counter of the average fast food restaurant might convince them otherwise, but employers are not anthropologists out looking for a fresh view of entry-level employment. They operate on the basis of assumptions that are widely shared and have neither the time nor the inclination to seek out the hidden skills that Burger Barn employees have developed.

15   Perhaps fast food veterans would do better in the search for good jobs
if they could reveal that hidden reservoir of human capital. But they are as
much the victims of the poor reputation of their jobs as the employers they
now seek to impress. When we asked them to explain the skills involved in
their work, they invariably looked at us in surprise: "Any fool could do this
job. Are you kidding?" They saw themselves as sitting at the bottom of the
job chain and the negative valence of their jobs as more or less justified.
A lot of energy goes into living with that "truth" and retaining some sense of
dignity, but that effort does not involve rethinking the reputation of their work
as skillfree. Hence they are the last people to try to overturn a stereotype
and sell themselves to other employers as workers who qualify for better
jobs.

16   I have suggested here that neither the employers nor the job-seekers have
got it right. There are competencies involved in these jobs that should be
more widely known and more easily built upon as the basis for advancement
in the labor market. Yet even if we could work some magic along these lines,
the limitations built into the social networks of most low-wage workers in the
inner city could make it hard to parlay that new reputation into success.

EXERCISE 8   Vocabulary Highlights

**Write a short definition of each word as it is used in the essay. (Paragraph
numbers are given in parentheses.) Be prepared to use these words in your own
sentences.**

virtuoso (1)   amalgamation (6)

abrasive (3)   amiss (8)

forbearance (3)   interloper (8)

rudimentary (4)   denuded (9)

antagonism (5)   cognitive (9)

EXERCISE 9   Discussion and Critical Thinking

1. Newman maintains that low-wage workers in this ordinary fast-food establishment perform tasks that require exceptional skills. To reach her conclusion,
   she uses analysis by division. Fill in the blanks to indicate how she proceeded.

   Unit (What is she concerned with?):

   Principle of function (What aspect does she focus on?):

   Parts based on the principle (What are those potentially transferable skills?)

   •

   •

   •

•

•

•

2. Could the transferable skills discussed in this essay be included effectively on a résumé for a person seeking a higher-paying job?

3. Have you held a low-paying job that requires or required important transferable skills? Discuss.

4. Do you agree with the author's conclusions? Why or why not?

5. How do you interpret the last sentence in the essay: "Yet even if we could work some magic along these lines, the limitations built into the social networks of most low-wage workers in the inner city could make it hard to parlay that new reputation into success"?

RESTAURANT REVIEW
. . . .

Johnny's Wiener Wagon on a Roll

FLOYD GARRISON

Community college student and budding freelance writer Floyd Garrison was not interested in exotic cuisine, a waiter in tuxedo, and Bohemian crystal. Instead, he turned to his favorite place for eats. It had tasty food, friendly service, and down-home atmosphere.

1   More than a food stand and less than a diner, Johnny's Wiener Wagon is shaped like a giant hotdog with wheels, though it has rested on blocks for years. It once belonged to its designer, a man named Johnny, who needed a job after World War II. Since he had been an army mess sergeant, he decided that maybe he had enough on-the-job experience to run his own hotdog stand. And run it he did for decades until about fifteen years ago when he died, and the place was bought by a Korean woman who goes by the name of Sunny. Even though the owner has changed, the menu and recipes remain with the wagon, and the food is reportedly still the same—mouth-watering hotdogs with every topping imaginable served from a giant towable hotdog!

2   At Johnny's, diners stand in the open air or sit outside under an awning at a counter that extends right out of the middle of the hotdog trailer, which was moved to the current location in 1958 when the new baseball stadium was built. Eight original vinyl-topped barstools are lined up next to the ancient stainless steel counter that Sunny folds out of the framework every morning at 8 a.m. after she hoses down the sidewalk.

3   Most regular customers are guys in work clothes, but increasingly some young women and men in suits have been coming in, and there's uneasy talk among the regulars that the place could become trendy. As it is, Sunny's regulars don't have much time or money for lunch; they want food that tastes good and fills them up. The crowd is often noisy with banter, and much of the talk is about sports or work, but when Sunny delivers an order of food, conversation lags momentarily as if out of envy for the lucky recipient, who is about to chow down.

4   And I do mean *chow down*. The food at Johnny's is simple and delicious—hotdogs, chips, soda, and coffee. Sunny has kept the original menu invented by Johnny, and that means hot dogs and toppings—almost every conceivable combination of toppings that I could ever think of is available. But before I get to these, let's start with the dog. Sunny uses only Vienna Beef hotdogs, and that's important because they have the natural casing that gives the hotdog that all-important snap when bitten into. Sunny always grills the dogs and burns them just a little to increase that snap on the first bite. Resting comfortably in an oversized grilled sesame roll, the dog awaits the finishing touch, and this is where the artistry comes in; this is where the cook carefully dresses the dog, not the bun, except for the combined toppings when things go all over.

5   When Johnny started planning the menu of his place, he was still thinking of the hungry soldiers' complaints about the often unvaried, bland food he had prepared out of necessity. In his new diner, he would offer every possible combination of toppings to his single menu item, thus creating variety and the illusion of even greater variety, while keeping things simple for the cook, namely, Johnny. The result is that customers can enjoy everything from a dog in napkin for the carb-conscious, to a no-nonsense New York–style dog, to the more elaborate and eclectic Chicago style, or to the fancy and hearty Canuck served with maple syrup and Canadian bacon piled on top of the wiener. Then at the bottom of the menu board lurks the big one: the Gutbuster. You have to be serious about your eating to consume a hotdog topped with pastrami, sauerkraut, chili, cheese, and a fried egg. There are at least twenty-five different dogs available, and people love to eat them. After the eating, maybe the second best feature is the price. A hotdog, soda, and bag of chips combo is never more than six dollars.

6   The ambience is unique and the food is great, but it's Sunny who really pulls everything together, the way old-timers say Johnny did. To Sunny, the customer is family. She knows the regulars by name, and remembers little facts about their lives. "Hey, Bill, how's the truck? Got those brakes fixed, yet?" she says as she delivers a mouth-stretching Gutbuster to a young construction worker, who looks hungry enough to eat the stool he's sitting on. Sunny laughs and shouts another order back to her helper, who toils at the grill with at least ten dogs and buns down.

7   Finally I take my place at the counter, admiring the plywood menu hanging down above the grill. Within thirty seconds, Sunny has arrived, grinning as if I were a long-lost friend. "Hey, I haven't seen you for a while. Welcome back to Johnny's. What toppings do you like?" Reflecting on my more than twenty trips to Johnny's, I know which ones I like—all of them, but only one at a time, please. One fills me up every time.

EXERCISE 10   Discussion and Critical Thinking

1. Of the three parts to this restaurant review, which happens to be an analysis by division, which part is emphasized, if any?

2. How helpful would this review be to someone wanting to try this restaurant?

3. Would you have preferred more details for any section(s)? If so, which one(s)?

READING-BASED WRITING

Summary of "A Big Wheel" by Louis Grossberger

JESSICA RUIZ

Student Jessica Ruiz was assigned to write a summary of one of several essays that had previously been used in her English program. She came across "A Big Wheel." It was more than ten years old, but it was still relevant. The essay was an analysis by division explaining why a game show was successful then. As one who occasionally watches game shows, Ruiz observed that the show, The Wheel of Fortune, *was still successful, and for essentially the same reasons. In her summary it was her task to use mostly her own words to convey the main ideas of the author.*

Text identification
Topic sentence

Quotation

Main parts of analysis by division

        In his essay "A Big Wheel," Louis Grossberger explains that *The Wheel of Fortune* game show has prospered for years because it has the right ingredients. He says the idea that holds the parts together is "vicariousness. Viewers don't exactly identify with the contestants; they become the contestants" (151). The parts are the players, the game, the payoff, and the cast. The players are ordinary people. They reveal only a few seconds of information about themselves and then turn to the wheel. Viewers can identify with them. The game is a combination of skill and luck. The skill is in solving a word puzzle based on the old hangman's game. Viewers are not told the answer in advance, and they can play the game at home. They may even win and feel superior. In the game there is a payoff. The contestants call out a letter and spin the wheel. Dollar amounts and prizes are given for correct letter answers. If contestants miss, they lose their turn at the wheel. Bad luck occurs when the wheel stops on "Bankrupt" or "Lose a Turn." Good luck occurs when they hit special prize slots. All the while the cast plays its parts. The good-natured

Quotation

Pat Sajak is the host. He is like "everyone's son-in-law" (152). He is supported by Vanna White. She is the glitzy sidekick. She does not talk. She reveals letters in the word puzzles. She claps her hands. She is the

Concluding sentence

cheerleader. These four parts work together to make the show successful.

Work Cited

Grossberger, Louis. "A Big Wheel." *Paragraphs and Essays: With Culturally Diverse Readings.* Ed. Lee Brandon. 7th ed. Boston: Houghton, 1998. 151–52. Print.

STUDENT ESSAY
· ·

Writing Process Worksheet

Name Jerry Price   **Title** More Than Book 'Em   **Due Date** Monday, May 7, 11 a.m.

Use the back of this page or separate paper if you need more space.

Assignment

In the space below, write whatever you need to know about your assignment, including information about the topic, audience, pattern of writing, length, whether to include a rough draft or revised drafts, and whether your paper must be typed.

Write a short essay of analysis by division about the different parts of your work. Assume that your audience is not working in your field but is familiar with it. Submit this completed worksheet, a rough draft, and a typed final draft.

Stage One

Explore Freewrite, brainstorm (list), cluster, or take notes as directed by your instructor.

Counselor	*Referee*	*Law enforcer*
listen	separate them	stop the fight
talk	let each one talk	determine the extent of
give my opinion	evaluate progress	injuries
suggest professional	maybe send one away	inform fighters of the law
counseling	maybe I leave and return	maybe make arrest

Stage Two

Organize Write a topic sentence or thesis; label the subject and the focus parts.

As a <u>police officer</u>, I wear different hats during a family dispute: <u>counselor,</u>
       subject   focus

<u>referee, law enforcer</u>.

Write an outline or an outline alternative. For reading-based writing, include quotations and references with page numbers as support in the outline.

I. Counselor
  A. Listen to each
  B. Talk with each
  C. Offer practical
     advice

II. Referee
  A. Separate
     combatants
  B. Let them talk
  C. Sometimes send
     one away

III. Law enforcer
  A. Stop the fight
  B. Determine its
     seriousness
  C. Make an arrest
     or inform fighters
     about the law

Stage Three

Write On separate paper, write and then revise your paragraph or essay as many times as necessary for **c**oherence, **l**anguage (usage, tone, and diction), **u**nity, **e**mphasis, **s**upport, and **s**entences (**CLUESS**). Read your work aloud to hear and correct any grammatical errors or awkward-sounding sentences.

Edit any problems in fundamentals, such as **c**apitalization, **o**missions, **p**unctuation, and **s**pelling (**COPS**).

MORE THAN BOOK 'EM
Jerry Price

As a police officer, when I am on patrol I have a wide variety of duties. I respond to several different types of calls. One of the most common calls involves a family dispute between a husband and wife. When I respond to that kind of problem, I have to play one or more quite different roles. The main roles for family disputes are counselor, referee, and law enforcer.

The most common family dispute involves a husband and wife arguing. Usually the argument is almost over when I arrive. I need to talk to both sides. Depending on how intense they are, I either separate them or talk to them together. Both the husband and wife will tell me they are right and the other spouse is wrong. I then become a counselor. In this role I must be a good listener to both parties, and when they are done talking, it is my turn to talk. In the worst situation I may tell them it looks as if they are headed for a separation or divorce. However, most of the time I tell them to act like adults and talk to their spouse as they talked to me. I may suggest that they seek professional counseling. With the husband and wife now having everything off their chests, and after their having received my small lecture, they may be able to go back to living relatively peaceful lives together.

In a different scenario, if the yelling and screaming is still going on when I arrive, I may want to just stand back and be a referee. I usually allow the wife to talk first. She typically tells her husband off. Not forgetting my role as referee, I step in only if the argument gets extremely ugly. When this happens, I send the wife to a neutral corner to cool off. Then I allow her to continue her verbal assault. When I feel the husband has had enough, I stop the wife and give the husband a turn. All the time, I am watching and listening. My main task is to keep the fight clean. If I think progress is being made with the couple, I let it continue. If the argument is going in circles, I may stop the fight. At this time I may send one of the fighters out for a drive or to a friend's house to cool off. This diversion is, however, only a temporary solution to the problem, for when the couple gets back together I will probably be needed for round two.

When the family dispute turns into a fistfight, it is usually the husband hitting his wife. Wives do hit their husbands, but the male ego usually will not let the men call the police. When the husband has hit his wife, and she has only a very minor injury, it will be up to her to have her husband arrested. If the wife is bleeding or has several bruises, then I make the decision. In these cases I become the enforcer of the law. I always place the husband under arrest even if the wife does not want it. As the enforcer I then take the husband to jail. The severity of the wife's injuries will determine how long the husband will stay in jail. He may be released in a couple of hours with a ticket and a court date, or he may be in jail until he can be seen by a judge. Prior convictions and restraining orders are considerations.

As a typical police officer on patrol, I make many decisions and play many roles in domestic disturbance cases. The circumstances of these cases dictate the way each is handled. As an experienced officer, I should be able to make the right decision, and I should know when to be a counselor, a referee, or a law enforcer.

EXERCISE 11   Discussion and Critical Thinking

1. The subject of this piece is "police officer," which is the larger unit for analysis. How did Price apply a principle to limit his subject for analysis by division? In other words, with which aspect of being a police officer is he concerned?

2. What are the different roles Price may assume (as indicated in the last sentence of the introductory paragraph)? These roles become the parts for the functional analysis.

3. Of the three roles, which one requires the least judgment?

4. Of these roles, which are seldom thought of in connection with police work?

CAREER-RELATED WRITING: THE CAREER QUEST

My Chosen Career: Respiratory Therapy

JOLENE HAWKINS

Student Jolene Hawkins was instructed to write an essay combining an analysis of her chosen career field with her suitability for work in that field. Hawkins's only workplace experiences were in food service, but growing up in a household with an ill grandmother had given her some insights into both a career field and herself. A recent freshman orientation program that included an aptitude test gave her more useful information for her consideration.

1   All my young life I've heard about vocational burnout—and I've seen the results with numerous people in various careers, including some that others would, almost literally, kill for. So when I started college and went about choosing my career, I knew I should choose a field I could work in for life and not be bored. In respiratory therapy I believe I have found that field.

Passions and Interests

2   It's not by chance that I explored the career of respiratory therapy. When I was ten years old, my grandmother came to live with us. She suffered from emphysema, as a result of smoking cigarettes for years. She'd quit smoking years before she moved in, but the damage was already done. Her lungs were slowly filling with fluid, and she was losing her ability to breathe. I watched her go from coughing and a need for rest to wheezing and a need for an oxygen bottle. I was her attendant, not just because she was my favorite person but because I was the best person in our family to do it. Although my favorite subjects in high school included biology, math, and chemistry, I certainly did not know enough on my own to do anything but follow the directions of physicians, nurses, and respiratory therapists. Naturally my interest in medical science was much less than my concern for my grandmother. People called me a born caregiver, both compassionate and efficient. Recently, aptitude tests have confirmed that I am fitted for working with and helping others.

3   Being somewhat familiar with respiratory therapy as a result of my helping Grandma and having numerous conversations with therapists, I decided to follow my aptitude test with some research of the field. I found the best survey on the Internet in the *Occupational Outlook Handbook*, 2008–2009 edition, published by the U.S. Bureau of Labor Statistics (http://www.bls.gov/ocd). It covers job duties, education, training, working conditions, employment, and the likely job outlook.

Job Duties

4   The job duties of the respiratory therapist are various. Treating persons from infancy to old age, therapists help people who are having problems breathing, from victims of accidents to those who have heart and lung diseases. They analyze breath capacity and blood content and deliver that information to physicians, who will perform the diagnoses and prescribe therapy and medication, which in turn will be administered by the therapists. Therapy often includes the use of an oxygen mask or a ventilator, a machine that delivers pressurized oxygen to the lungs. Therapists also instruct and monitor the work of lay people who are providing home care. Performed around the clock in shifts, this work requires sound, informed judgment and concentration while the therapist maintains sincere, reassuring human contact.

Education and Training

5   Education and training are offered by colleges, universities, trade schools, vocational schools, and the Armed Services. One common approach is through a community college such as the one I am attending. In two years one can complete a program that includes core courses in anatomy, mathematics, chemistry, physics, microbiology, and physiology. Additional courses in supervised training are taught at local hospitals. At the same time one is completing general education courses that lead to an Associate of Science degree. The program represents the first two years of college, and some students will transfer to a four-year institution to complete a Bachelor of Science degree in a field of medical science.

Employment and Job Outlook

6   Regardless of the source of one's training, each respiratory therapist must pass a test or tests for certification and registration in order to practice. Some states permit entry-level employment to those who have the experience and education necessary to take the test(s). Students with a Bachelor of Science degree and some experience may move immediately into a supervisory position. According to the *Occupational Outlook Handbook*, the median salary for respiratory therapists in 2007 was $39,780.

7   The long-range outlook is favorable for this field. With people living longer, the incidence of cardiopulmonary disease will increase. Respiratory therapy also plays a key part in supporting the advances in medicine by aiding distressed people from premature infants to ailing adults.

8   Respiratory therapy fits my interests and passions. The required, ongoing education is challenging but not unrealistic. The nature of the work seems satisfying and interesting. As for the future of the field, it will grow, and I will grow with it.

Work Cited
United States. Dept. of Labor. *Occupational Outlook Handbook*. 2008–09.
Web. 19 Dec. 2009.

EXERCISE 12   Discussion and Critical Thinking

1. Write in the steps:

Step 1: What is the unit (in this case, involving a relationship of two concerns)?

Step 2: What is the principle on which the unit will be divided into parts?

Step 3: What are the parts of the unit?

Step 4: How does the discussion proceed? (What relates to what?)

2. Circle the thesis.

3. Underline the topic sentence in each paragraph.

Suggested Topics and Prompts for Writing Analysis by Division

STUDENT COMPANION SITE
For additional practice, visit www.cengage .com/devenglish/ brandon/spb6e.

You will find a blank Writing Process Worksheet on page 6 of this book and on the Student Companion Site. It can be photocopied or printed out, filled in, and submitted with your assignment, if your instructor directs you to do so.

READING-BASED WRITING

Reading-based writing requires you to read critically, write a reply that shows you understand what you have read, and give credit for ideas you borrow and words you quote. The form can be a summary, a reaction, or a two-part response (with separated summary and reaction). Documentation, in which you give credit for borrowed ideas and words, can be either formal (MLA) or informal, as directed by your instructor. Both the forms of reading-based writing and documentation are discussed with examples in Chapter 1. Definitions of the three forms follow.

Summary

- The summary is a statement presenting only the main points of what you have read by using different wording without altering the meaning, adding information, or showing bias.
- It is the purest form of reading-based writing.

Reaction

- In the reaction, the meaning of what you have read will be central to the topic sentence of your paragraph or to the thesis of your essay.
- Although the reaction is not a personal narrative by itself, it may include personal experience to explain elements of the text. For example, if your source is about driving styles, your own experiences as a driver or an observer of drivers could be relevant in your analysis of the text.
- The reaction may incorporate a summary to convey a broad view of what you have read, but your summary should never be the main part of your reaction.

Two-Part Response

- The two-part response separates the summary from the reaction.
- This form will give you practice in separating your objective summary in the first part from your more personal evaluation, interpretation, or application in the second part, the reaction.

READING-BASED WRITING TOPICS

"Who Are Our Heroes?"

1. Using Maya Angelou's definition with its parts or a slight modification of its parts as a framework, write a paragraph or an essay of reaction about a well-known person from history or current times you regard as a hero. Use references and quotations.

2. Adapt Angelou's definition so that it can be applied to an ordinary person who struggles and distinguishes himself or herself, perhaps only within the family. Then use that definition in a reaction discussing an example from your experience. Use references and quotations.

"Qualities of Good Bosses"

3. As the title suggests, this paragraph by Hertneky is an analysis by division of good bosses. He provides the general subject and the parts. Now, in a paragraph or short essay develop some of the parts by applying them to a good boss you have worked with and for. Include some specific examples of that boss' behavior and character, but retain the pattern of analysis by division. Refer to the paragraph directly and use quotations.

"Female Mea Culpa"

4. Rolens seems to be apologizing for her weaknesses, while actually pointing out what males should understand and do naturally and lovingly. In a personal list and a general list, she is attempting to answer the age-old question "What do women really want?" The answer, if realized in the several parts of an analysis by division, should be equal to the subject of "happy and satisfied" females. In a paragraph or an essay of reading-based writing, evaluate her list—agreeing or disagreeing with her list and adding to or subtracting from that list as you go. Following Rolens's example, exclude examples of physical behavior. For a variation, your writing can be either narrowly personal with yourself and a companion in mind or broadly general as it applies to genders. Use references and quotations.

5. Now consider the topic from the male perspective. Provide a list for the concerns of males that would make them satisfied and happy. What should females understand and do naturally and lovingly (without your list) to make males "happy and satisfied"? Following Rolens's example, exclude examples of physical behavior. For a variation, your writing can be either narrowly personal with yourself and a companion in mind or broadly general as it applies to genders. Use references and quotations.

"Low Wages, High Skills"

6. Write a summary of this essay.

7. Write a two-part response to the essay. Concentrate your critical thinking on Newman's idea that those who work at Burger Barn have transferable skills. Relate those skills to what you have experienced in a low-paying service job. Agree or disagree with Newman.

8. Write a paragraph or an essay about a low-wage job you once held. Explain how you learned and practiced transferable skills that helped you in other jobs or other life situations. The skills will be the parts of your analysis by division. Some of these skills may be the same as or similar to the ones discussed by Newman, so use references and quotations.

"More Than Book 'Em"

9. In police officer Jerry Price's role in family disputes, he is a counselor, a referee, and a law enforcer. Using modifications of his analysis, write about the different divisions of one of your roles, such as parent, spouse, employee, employer, student, or neighbor. Point out how your divisions are similar to or different from his. Use some references and quotations.

GENERAL TOPICS

10. Write your own restaurant review about a specific establishment. Consider your campus cafeteria as a subject. As an exercise in analysis by division, which it naturally is, discuss the ambiance, food, and service. If the service is minimal, then discuss the qualities of those who take your order, clear tables, open doors, answer your questions about something not in sight (salt and pepper, napkins, and so on), and work the cash register. Be specific. For a useful model of form and topic, review "Johnny's Wiener Wagon on a Roll" on pages 376–377.

11. Write a paragraph or an essay about one of the following:

   a. An offensive team in football (or any team in any game)

   b. A family, a relationship, a gang, a club, a sorority, or a fraternity

   c. A CD, a performance, a song, an actor, a musical group, or a musical instrument

   d. A movie, a television program, or a video game

   e. Any well-known person—an athlete, a politician, a criminal, or a writer

CROSS-CURRICULAR TOPIC

12. For a paragraph or an essay topic pertaining to a current or former class other than English, select a unit that can be divided into parts. Consult your textbook(s) for ideas on that subject. Talk with your instructor(s) in other fields, especially those that relate to your major field of study. Your writing instructor may require you to photocopy a page or more of your source material if your work is largely summary. Following are a few examples from various disciplines:

    a. Art History: Points for analyzing a painting or another work of art

    b. Music History: Points for analyzing a musical composition or the performance of a musical composition

    c. Agriculture: Points for judging livestock

    d. History: Characteristics that made a historical figure great

    e. Government: Basic organization of the United Nations

    f. Biology: Working parts of an organ or organism

    g. Physical Education: Parts of a football team in a particular offensive or defensive formation

    h. Business: Structure of management for a particular business

    i. Law Enforcement: Organization of a specific precinct

CAREER-RELATED TOPICS

13. Write a career review. Instructions on pages 362–363 will provide you with the form and specify an easily accessed collection of career information. The Career Quest "My Chosen Career: Respiratory Therapy" on pages 381–383 will provide you with a model review of form and similar content. The basic career quest has five parts: background, desired field, working conditions and pay, requirements for employment, and a personal plan for entering the field. One of those will work well as a paragraph. A combination of parts or all five parts can be covered in an essay.

14. Explain how each of several qualities of a specific person—such as his or her intelligence, sincerity, knowledgeability, ability to communicate, manner, attitude, and appearance—makes that individual an effective salesperson, manager, or employee. Looking at copies of workplace evaluation (performance) sheets can help you decide on the points you will use.

15. Write a self-evaluation of you as a worker or as a student. Keep in mind that most self-evaluations are more generous than evaluations coming from supervisors.

16. Write an evaluation of a product or service that can be analyzed according to its parts. Name the product or service. Use the Internet or library services as source material.

WRITER'S GUIDELINES   Analysis by Division

Almost any unit can be analyzed by division—for example, how the parts of the ear function in hearing; how the parts of an idea represent the whole idea; how the parts of a machine function; how the parts of a committee, department, or company function at the workplace. You can also use analysis by division to evaluate programs, products, and persons. Subjects such as these are all approached with the same systematic procedure.

1. This is the procedure.

   - *Step 1.* Begin with something that is a unit.
   - *Step 2.* State the principle by which that unit functions.
   - *Step 3.* Divide the unit into parts according to the principle.
   - *Step 4.* Discuss each of the parts in relation to the unit.

2. This is the way you might apply that procedure to a good boss.

   - Unit   Manager
   - Principle of function   Effective as a leader
   - Parts based on the principle   Fair, intelligent, stable, competent
                                     in the field
   - Discussion   Consider each part in relation to the
                                     person's effectiveness as a manager.

3. This is how a basic outline of analysis by division might look.

   Thesis: To be effective as a leader, a manager needs specific qualities.

   I. Fairness
   II. Intelligence
   III. Stability
   IV. Competence in the field

   This procedure can be modified for assignments in different disciplines. At the workplace you are likely to have forms for evaluations.

4. For a restaurant review, use ambiance, food, and service as parts.

5. The career review has five parts:

   Unit: (the career itself)
   Divisions: (parts of the unit, the career itself)

   I. My background, interests, and aptitude
   II. My desired field—an overview
   III. Working conditions, pay, benefits
   IV. Requirements for employment
   V. My step-by-step plan to enter this field

6. Write and revise.

   - Write and then revise your paragraph or essay as many times as necessary for **c**oherence, **l**anguage (usage, tone, and diction), **u**nity, **e**mphasis, **s**upport, and **s**entences (**CLUESS**). Read your work aloud to hear and correct any grammatical errors or awkward-sounding sentences.
   - Edit any problems in fundamentals, such as **c**apitalization, **o**missions, **p**unctuation, and **s**pelling (**COPS**).

STUDENT COMPANION SITE

For additional practice, visit www.cengage .com/devenglish/ brandon/spb6e.

Chapter 21

Process Analysis
Writing About Doing

FLOW OF WRITING

WHEN TO USE PROCESS ANALYSIS

FOR COLLEGE WRITING ASSIGNMENTS

Much of your college work appears as process analysis. Instructors and instructional materials, such as this textbook, are explaining how things are done or how things occurred.

- In labs you experiment with processes and learn to perform tasks. To demonstrate your knowledge of what you have learned and your ability to perform tasks, you write paragraphs, essays, and reports, and you take tests.

- Having a systematic pattern for organization for writing these process analyses will enable you to write with efficiency.

IN CAREERS AND AT THE WORKPLACE

Process analysis is central to both career preparation and workplace activities. You learn what to do and how to perform.

- As you work with others, as a member of a team or as a supervisor of new employees, you will need to write memos and directives as process analysis to explain what to do and how something is done.

- Regardless of whether you do the technical writing and advertising, you will need to explain, often in writing, how your products and services are used and how they are beneficial.

PROCESS ANALYSIS IN A CARTOON

THE QUIGMANS   by Buddy Hickerson

The Babysitter Channel.

WRITING PROCESS ANALYSIS

If you have any doubt about how frequently we use process analysis, just think about how many times you have heard people say, "How do you do it?" or "How is [was] it done?" Even when you are not hearing those questions, you are posing them yourself when you need to make something, cook a meal, assemble an item, take some medicine, repair something, or figure out what happened.

Defining Directive and Informative Process Analysis

Directive process analysis explains how to do something. As the name suggests, it gives directions and instructs the reader. It says, for example, "Read me, and you can tune up your car [analyze a book, write an essay, take some medicine, assemble a bicycle]." Because it is presented directly to the reader, it usually addresses the reader as "you," or it implies "you" by saying something such as "First [you] purchase a large turnip, and then [you]. . . ." In the same way, this textbook addresses "you" or implies "you" because it is a long how-to-do-it (directive process analysis) statement.

Informative process analysis explains how something is (was) done by giving data, or information. Therefore, it is not primarily a how-to-do-it statement. It is primarily a how-it-was-done (I got a job), how-it-happened (a battle was won), or how-it-is-happening (the polar caps are melting) statement. Whereas the directive process analysis tells you what to do in the future, the informative process analysis tells you what has occurred or what is occurring. Because you are not mainly concerned with direction in the informative process analysis, you usually do not refer to the reader as *you* or *your*.

Working with Directive Process Analysis

PREPARATION

In the first stage of directive process analysis, list the materials or equipment needed for the process and discuss the necessary setup arrangements. For some topics, this stage will also provide technical terms and definitions. The degree to which this stage is detailed will depend on both the subject itself and the expected knowledge and experience of the projected audience.

STEPS

Each step must be presented in word choice and detail in a way appropriate for the intended audience. In directive process analysis the language is likely to be simple and concise; however, process analysis written in sentences as paragraph and essay assignments should avoid the dropping of words such as *and*, *a*, *an*, *the*, and *of* and thereby lapsing into "recipe language." The steps may be accompanied by explanations about why certain procedures are necessary and how not following directions carefully can cause problems.

Directive process analysis is a common form for career-related writing and is used to serve both academic and workplace needs. See page 407 for a student example about her workplace experience.

BASIC FORM FOR DIRECTIVE PROCESS ANALYSIS

Consider using this form for the directive process (with topics such as how to cook something or how to fix something).

How to Fry Green Tomatoes

   I. Preparation
      A. Stove and utensils
      B. Cast-iron skillet
      C. Ingredients
         1. Sliced green tomatoes
         2. Cornmeal
         3. Buttermilk
         4. Bacon grease (or oil)
         5. Seasoning (salt, pepper, and so on)
  II. Steps
      A. Heat skillet on high flame
      B. Add bacon grease to coat skillet
      C. Dip sliced green tomatoes in buttermilk
      D. Dip sliced green tomatoes in cornmeal
      E. Drop sliced green tomatoes into hot skillet

F. Reduce flame under skillet
G. Brown and turn sliced green tomatoes once
H. Drain golden brown green tomatoes on paper towel
I. Serve

Working with Informative Process Analysis

BACKGROUND

Informative process analysis may begin with background or context rather than with preparation. If you are explaining how you repaired your computer, you would describe the problem. If you were explaining the Battle of Gettysburg, you would begin with some historical perspective. If you were explaining how some mountains were formed, you might begin with a discussion of how the earth is made up of plates that are arranged like a jigsaw puzzle with molten rock below.

SEQUENCE

To continue with the last example, the sequence of informative analysis would involve the progression by which the plates move constantly against each other, causing undercuts, overruns, and blocks that can result in huge raised earth formations and can release fountains and explosions of molten rock.

Consider using this form for the informative process (with topics such as how a volcano functions or how a battle was won).

How a Tornado Occurs

I. Background
A. Cool, dry air from the north
B. Warm, humid air from the south
C. Usually afternoon or early evening

Transitional Words

Consider using the following transitional words to improve coherence by connecting ideas with ideas, sentences with sentences, and paragraphs with paragraphs.

FOR PROCESS ANALYSIS:

Preparation and Background: at the outset, before stages develop, before steps occur, before work begins, as preparation for, in anticipation of, in laying the groundwork

Steps and Stages: first, second, third, another step, next, now, then, at this point, at this stage, at this step, after, at last, finally, subsequently, to begin with, initially, after that, afterward, at the same time, concurrently, meanwhile, soon, during the process, during . . . , in order to, for a minute, for a . . . .

FOR ALL PATTERNS OF WRITING: The <u>HOTSHOT CAT</u> words: <u>H</u>owever, <u>O</u>therwise, <u>T</u>herefore, <u>S</u>imilarly, <u>H</u>ence, <u>O</u>n the other hand, <u>T</u>hen, <u>C</u>onsequently, <u>A</u>lso, <u>T</u>hus (See pages 74–75 for additional transitional words.)

    II. Sequence

        A. Narrow zone of thunderstorms forms

        B. Warm, humid air rises

        C. More warm air rushes in to replace it

        D. In-rushing air rotates

        E. Pressure drops

        F. Wind velocity increases

        G. Twisting, snaking funnel-shaped cloud extends down from larger cloud formation

Combined Forms

Combination process analysis occurs when directive process analysis and informative process analysis are blended, usually when the writer personalizes the account. Take this scenario:

> Two people with the log-on names Captain Ahab and Ishmael are texting.
>
> *Ishmael*: "I'm really intrigued with your idea of raising your own catfish, but I don't know how to make a pond."
>
> *Captain Ahab*: "Let me tell you how I made mine. First I shoveled out a 20′ × 5′ × 5′ hole in my back lawn. Then I turned on the hose and . . ."

This process analysis begins as if it is only informative, but the main intent and the main need are clearly directive.

Often the personalized account is more interesting, and many assignments are done in that fashion. A paper about making a pecan pie may be informative—but uninspiring. A paper about the time you helped your grandfather make a pecan pie (giving all the details) may be informative, directive, and entertaining. It is often the cultural framework provided by personal experience that transforms a pedestrian directive account into something memorable.

All the strategies of freewriting, brainstorming, and clustering can be useful in writing a process analysis. However, if you already know your subject well, you can simply make two lists, one headed *Preparation* or *Background* and the other *Steps* or *Sequence*. Then jot down ideas for each. After you have finished with your listing, you can delete parts, combine parts, and rearrange parts for better order. That editing of your lists will lead directly to a formal outline you can use in Stage Two of the writing process.

Patty Serrano used the following lists as her initial prewriting activity for "*Pupusas*: Salvadoran Delight."

Preparation	*Steps*
get vegetables	cook meat
meat, fresh	cook tomatoes and spices
cheese, stringy white Jalisco	shape tortilla
spices	put meat, cheese, vegetables into tortilla
masa	fold and seal tortilla
skillet	place pupusa into skillet

hot stove   make more pupusas

                                   turn pupusas

                                   remove pupusas

                                   eat pupusas

Student Demonstration of Combined Forms

In this example of combined forms, student Patty Serrano explains how her mother makes pupusas, and in doing so she shows how others can make pupusas, step by step. Serrano's writing also demonstrates the use of prewriting in organizing process analysis.

Some selections begin with a Mindset suggestion that can help you create a readiness for connecting with what you are about to read.

Pupusas: Salvadoran Delight

PATTY SERRANO

We all have at least one kind of food that reminds us of childhood, something that has filled our bellies in times of hunger and perhaps comforted our minds in times of stress. For Patty Serrano, a community college student living at home, that special dish is pupusas. In El Salvador these are a favorite item in homes and restaurants and at roadside stands. In Southern California, they are available in little restaurants called pupusarias.

Topic sentence	Every time my mom decides to make pupusas, we jump for joy. <u>A pupusa contains only a few ingredients, and it may sound easy to make, but really good ones must be made by experienced hands</u>. My mom is an
Preparation	expert, having learned as a child from her mother in El Salvador. All the <u>ingredients</u> are <u>chosen fresh</u>. The <u>meat</u>, either pork or beef, can be bought
Step 1	prepared, but my <u>mom chooses to prepare it herself</u>. The <u>meat</u>, which is called "carnitas," <u>is ground and cooked with tomatoes and spices</u>. The cheese—she uses a white Jalisco—has to be stringy because that kind gives pupusas a very good taste, appearance, and texture. Then comes the
Steps 2	<u>preparation of the "masa," or cornmeal</u>. It has to be soft but not so soft that it falls apart in the making and handling. All of this is done while the "comal," or skillet, is being heated. She then grabs a chunk of <u>masa</u> and
3	<u>forms it into a tortilla</u> like a magician turning a ball into a thin pancake.
4	Next she grabs small chunks of <u>meat</u> and <u>cheese</u> and <u>places them in the</u>
5	<u>middle of the tortilla</u>. The <u>tortilla</u> is <u>folded in half and formed again</u>.
6	After <u>placing the pupusa into the sizzling skillet</u> with one hand, she is already starting another pupusa. It is amazing how she does two things at the same time. She <u>turns</u> the <u>pupusas over and over</u> again <u>until</u> she
7	is sure that <u>they are done</u>. We watch, mouths open, plates empty. In my family it is a tradition that I get the first pupusa because I like them so much. I love opening the hot pupusas, smelling the aroma, and seeing the stringy cheese stretching in the middle. I am as discriminating as a wine taster. But I never eat a pupusa without "curtido," chopped cabbage with
Concluding sentences	jalapeño. Those items balance the richness of the other ingredients. <u>I could eat Mom's pupusas forever</u>. <u>I guess it has something to do with the way she makes them, with experienced, magical, loving hands</u>.

CAREER-RELATED WRITING AS PROCESS ANALYSIS

Process Analysis as a Common Form at the Workplace

Arguably, no form is more common for career-related writing than process analysis. Almost all tasks at the workplace involve an understanding of how things work and about how one performs tasks. Both the understanding and the performance pertains to procedure. Many of those procedures, in turn, involve much learning and training, meaning a lot of how-to-do-it and how-it-was-done. There will be training sessions after training sessions as companies restructure and workers change employment and even change career fields. Skills in thinking and writing can be applied to different situations. You will be more versatile and adaptable.

Learning to Learn at the Workplace, Learning to Teach at the Workplace

When you are new on the job, you will be expected first to learn. Knowing the techniques for process analysis will help you master the subject material more easily. Then at some point, you will probably be expected to train others. The training you do may require you both to talk and to write. Even if you are expected only to talk about a process, you will probably write it out first, at least in rough form. Regardless of the occasion or the method of communication, the organizational pattern, with some modification for your audience and subject, will be either Preparation and Steps or Background and Steps.

Knowing how to write a clear, logical, correct process analysis will be an asset for you as you look for employment or workplace advancement. Fortunately for you, the twin organizations of process analysis provide structures in this chapter as basic outlines. Remembering these outline patterns will serve you well in writing the process analysis. It will also serve you equally well in your oral presentation. If you use PowerPoint, imagine your outline as an overview and then as chronological development. Keep in mind that these techniques for writing process analysis in your current class differ little from what you will be doing at work. The paragraph "Making Faces" on page 407 is a how-to-do-it task. The essay "The Skinny on Working for a Dermatologist" on pages 409–410 is an explanation of one procedure of the writer's job. Either one in outline form could be used to indicate the main and supporting points in a PowerPoint presentation.

FINDING PATTERNS IN PHOTOS

EXERCISE 1   A Text-Based Activity for Groups or Individuals

Examine the image carefully. Like messages in bottles, the paper airplanes are being designed and launched. Some fly and some do not. Your task now is simple—or it may seem that way. You are to draw up a plan for a paper airplane that will fly. Imagine that actual production (known hereafter as *Production*) has been outsourced to a small village in Mongolia where somehow the people

Bored businesswoman with paper airplanes

have never seen a paper airplane. These production people, who fortunately have been studying English, will do exactly what you write, but they will be instructed not to improvise or to supply any steps you leave out. They will not talk with you, and they will not see any drawings. Your instructions are for Production to begin with an 8½-by-11-inch sheet of paper. You will explain each step—with each crease, fold, and bend. If you like, you may provide measurements for the shaping of the paper and instruct Production to place marks on the paper for the shaping.

The following outline gives you the basic pattern. Complete it, adding or subtracting lines or adding subdivisions as necessary. The success of your instructions can be determined by the appearance and especially the performance of your airplane. Your instructor may ask you to write a simple process-analysis paragraph or essay as either a collaborative activity of exchanging directions with other students or an individual assignment.

I. Preparation

    A. One 8½-by-11-inch sheet of paper

    B. Pencil or pen

II. Steps

    A. _____

    B. _____

    C. _____

    D. _____

    E. _____

    F. _____

    G. _____

    H. _____

Practicing Patterns of Process Analysis

Underlying a process analysis is a definite pattern. In some presentations, such as directions with merchandise to be assembled, the content reads as mechanically as an outline, and no reader objects. The same can be said of most recipes. In other presentations, such as your typical college assignments, the pattern is submerged in flowing discussion. The directions or information must be included, but the writing should be well developed and interesting. Regardless of the form you use or the audience you anticipate, keep in mind that in process analysis the pattern provides a foundation for the content.

EXERCISE 2   Completing Patterns of Process Analysis

A. Using directive process analysis, fill in the blanks to complete this pattern for replacing a flat tire with a spare. Work in a group if possible.

I. Preparation

    A. Park car.

    B. _____

    C. Obtain car jack.

    D. _____

    E. _____

II. Steps

    A. Remove hub cap (if applicable).

    B. Loosen lug nuts a bit.

    C. _____

    D. _____

    E. Remove wheel with flat tire.

    F. _____

    G. _____

    H. Release jack pressure.

    I. _____

B. Using informative process analysis, fill in the blanks to complete this pattern for an explanation of how a watermelon seed grows into a plant and produces a watermelon. Work in a group if possible.

I. Background (what happens before the sprouting)

    A. Seed planted in cultivated land

    B. _____

    C. Receives heat (from sun)

II. Sequence (becomes plant and produces fruit)

    A. Sprouts

    B. _____

    C. Responds to sunlight and air

    D. _____

    E. _____

    F. Flower pollinated

    G. _____

EXERCISE 3   Writing Patterns of Process Analysis

A. Using directive process analysis, fill in the blanks to complete this pattern for directions on how to cook a specific food or to fix an item.

I. Preparation

    A. _____

    B. _____

    C. _____

    D. _____

    E. _____

II. Steps

    A. _____

    B. _____

    C. _____

    D. _____

    E. _____

    F. _____

    G. _____

    H. _____

B. Using informative process analysis, fill in the blanks to complete this pattern for an explanation of how a person can be hired, trained, and promoted at a specific job.

I. Background (hiring)

    A. _____

    B. _____

    C. _____

II. Sequence (training, promotion)

    A. _____

    B. _____

    C. _____

    D. _____

    E. _____

    F. _____

    G. _____

Readings for Critical Thinking, Discussion, and Writing

READING STRATEGIES AND OBJECTIVES
. . . .

Underlining and annotating these reading selections will help you answer the questions that follow the selections, discuss the material in class, and prepare for text-based writing assignments. As you underline and annotate, pay special attention to the author's writing skills, logic, and message, and consider the relevance of the material to your own experiences and values.

PARAGRAPH
. . . .

Nature on the Rampage

ANN SUTTON AND MYRON SUTTON

If you are about to die under tons of snow, ice, and debris and you have, say, one chance in thousands to live, what do you do? The Suttons offer steps that will at least increase your odds for survival.

If you're caught: get moving! Ski or snowshoe as fast as you possibly can to the edge of the avalanche. Get rid of all of your accessories, or as many as you can, and do it at once—ski poles, pack, snowshoes, whatever you have. When the avalanche overtakes you, swim! This sounds ridiculous, but it's the best thing you can do to avoid being sucked under. Swim for your life, lying on your back if possible and with your feet downhill. Of course, you may have no choice, and the avalanche may tumble you whither it wishes, but do what you can to stay on the surface. Cover your mouth and nose—suffocation is easy in dry-snow avalanches. If you do get pulled under, make a supreme effort to widen a little airspace around you just as you come to a stop, and do it instantly! The snow may harden, pack and freeze almost at once. Then pray for help, and remember that the great Houdini made a living proving how long man could survive in tight and nearly airless spaces if he remained calm and confident and didn't panic. How to avoid panic in an avalanche is your problem.

EXERCISE 4   Discussion and Critical Thinking

1. What type of process analysis (informative or directive) is used?

2. To what type of audience (well informed, moderately informed, or poorly informed on the topic) does the writer direct this selection?

3. What is the prevailing tone (objective, humorous, reverent, argumentative, cautionary, playful, ironic, ridiculing) of this selection?

4. At which point do the preparation (materials, setup, explaining words, and so on) end and the steps begin? Underline the words where the steps begin.

5. Write numbers in the margin to indicate the steps or stages in the process.

6. Circle any transitional words indicating time or other progression (*first*, *second*, *then*, *soon*, *now*, *next*, *after*, *before*, *when*, *finally*, *at last*, *therefore*, *consequently*, and—especially for the informative process analysis—words used to show the passage of time, such as hours, days of the week, and so on).

ESSAYS

Binding Decisions

JOAN GOULD

With a reputation for penetrating insight and almost detached honesty, Joan Gould is a freelance author of numerous essays and books with major publishers. In reviewing her acclaimed book Spirals: A Woman's Journey Through Family Life *(Random House, 1988),* Publishers Weekly *referred to her style as "exquisitely simple, unsentimental and powerfully moving." Here we have an account of how a respectable young woman of the early 1950s dressed for a date and why she did so.*

MINDSET

Lock It In

Imagine you (a young, middle-class male or female) were born sixty years ago. How would you dress and make yourself look your best for a blind date?

1   I'm out of the bathtub. I'm ready to get dressed for my date tonight, which is a blind date, serious business in this year of 1950 for any girl who's over 20 and still single. I'm 22. No matter how much money I may earn in my job, I'll never be allowed to have an apartment of my own; I'll never pay an electric bill or buy a bedspread or spend a night away from home without my parents; in fact, I'll never be a grown-up as long as I remain single.

2   How shall I dress? I want to look sexy enough to attract this unknown man, so that he'll call and ask me for another date next week. (Needless to say, I won't call him, even if my life depends on it.) On the other hand, I don't want to hide the fact that I'm what's known as a Nice Girl, addicted to Peter Pan collars and velvet hats and white gloves, which means that I'm good wife material, and also makes it clear that he'll get nothing more than a goodnight kiss from me tonight.

3   And so I dress carefully. Every single item that I put on not only is complicated in itself but carries an even more complicated message.

4   My girdle comes first. Here's the badge, the bind, the bondage of womanhood. Here's the itch of it. This is the garment that tells me I'm not a little girl anymore, who wears only underpants, but neither am I middle-aged like my mother, who wears a real corset with bones that dig into her diaphragm and leave cruel sores there. I can get away with either a panty girdle or a two-way stretch, both of which are made of Lastex with a panel of stiff satin over the abdomen. The basic difference is that a panty girdle, unlike a two-way stretch, covers the crotch, which was considered a shocking—indeed obscene—idea when first introduced. Victorian women were obliged to wear half a dozen petticoats at a time to be respectable, but never, never would they put on anything that slipped between their thighs, like a pair of pants.

5   But why should I be bothering with this sausage casing when I weighed a grand total of a hundred and two pounds?

6   I bother because being thin has nothing to do with it. A girdle is a symbolic garment, and unless I wanted to be regarded as a child or a slut I have to put it on. When I go out with girlfriends in the daytime I may choose to be more comfortable in only a garter belt, a device with four long, wiggly elastics that dangle down my thighs like hungry snakes lunging at my stockings. When I'm with a boy, however, it would be unthinkable—it would be downright indecent—to let him see my rear end jiggle or let him notice it has two halves. (All males are called "boys," no matter what their age, so long as they're single.) My backside is supposed to be molded in a rigid piece that divides into two legs, like a walking clothespin.

7   Besides, if I don't wear a girdle every day, the older girls warn me, I'm going to "spread." Spreading is somehow related to letting my flesh hang loose, which is in turn related to the idea of the "loose" woman, and none of us wants to be considered loose. A man doesn't buy a cow if he can get milk for free, our mothers tell us in dire tones. We don't point out that we're not cows, and we don't fight against girdles, which apparently do a good job of discouraging wandering hands, since most of the single girls I know are virgins.

8   But which girdle should I wear? If I pick the panty girdle, I'll need 10 minutes' advance notice before going to the toilet. If I wear the two-way stretch, it will ride up and form a sausage around my waist. Either way, my flesh will be marked with welts and stripes when, at that delirious moment in my bedroom, I can strip off my clothes and scratch and scratch.

9   I pick the two-way stretch but, born compromiser that I am, put underpants over it.

10   Next comes the bra. I don't dare look at myself in the mirror as I put it on. This is the era of the pinup girl, the heyday of Lana Turner and Betty Grable, when breasts bubble and froth over the rims of C-cups and a flat chest is considered about as exciting as flat champagne. Not until Twiggy appears on the scene in the 1960s will thinness become acceptable in a girl, much less desirable—but how am I supposed to survive until then? The answer is the garment I've just put on, the confession of my disgrace—a padded bra. If I wear a strapless gown, I pin foamrubber bust pads, which are known as "falsies," in place. Occasionally one of these breaks loose during a particularly ardent conga or mambo and rises above my dress like the rim of the sun peering over a hilltop.

11   At least the bra won't show under my silk slip. Silk is expensive, of course, and no male will see my underwear unless he marries me or I'm carried off to a hospital emergency room—but then, as all the mothers warn us, accidents do happen.

12   Stockings next. During World War II, just as I became old enough to wear them, our wonderful new nylons were snatched away from us in order to make parachutes for what was known as the "war effort." What were we girls supposed to do—go out on a date in socks, like little children? If there weren't any stockings around, we'd have to create them. And so we bought bottles of makeup base and painted stockings on our legs and drew seams up the back with eyebrow pencils, which was undoubtedly the last time my seams were ever straight.

13   My dress, oddly enough, is easy to choose. For a woman of my years, a skirt-and-sweater is out of the question on a date. The dress mustn't be too high-style or expensive, however, or else the young man will think that I'm spoiled, a fatal defect in a girl who might otherwise qualify as good wife material. Never mind that I earned the money to buy my own clothes; I still

have to show that it won't cost much to support me once we marry and I quit my job. For the same reason, wherever we go—which is always at his expense, of course—I'll insist that we travel by bus or subway, never by taxi. If he invites me out to dinner (which doesn't happen often, because of cost, and never on a first date), I'll eat a sandwich at home before I leave, to make sure I won't be tempted to order an appetizer or dessert in the restaurant.

14   Shoes. I'd like to wear my fashionable new ones, with their ankle straps criss-crossing in back and fastening above the ankle bone, but they have 3½-inch heels, and I have no idea if I'll tower over this unknown man. If I choose low heels, on the other hand, he may think that I'm condescending. I pick the high heels but hide a low-heeled pair in the hall closet, just in case. Blind dates have their special hazards.

15   I still have to put on my makeup, which includes lots of lipstick, loose face powder and an eyebrow pencil to extend my brow line, but no eye shadow, much less liner. I also have to do my hair, which is set with heavy lotion and rollers in the beauty parlor every week. (At night I sleep in a cotton mesh hairnet that I tie around my head, in order to preserve the set for at least a week.)

16   Speeding up the pace, I rush to equip my pocketbook with a monogrammed handkerchief and some "mad money," including several nickels for phone calls or a bus, obligatory for a blind date. I run to my glove drawer and hunt up a pair in white kid, since he's invited me to a concert. I won't need a hat. He'll wear one, of course.

17   The doorbell rings. I dab Shalimar on a tuft of cotton, which I tuck inside my bra; I check my stocking seams and move toward the door. For an instant, my hand rests on the knob, while I wonder what sort of person is breathing out there, only inches away from me but still unrevealed, unexplored. And then I open the door, and I see his face and hear his voice, because he's already in mid-sentence. As a matter of fact, he's in mid-story, as if it's inconceivable that anyone could be less than fascinated with what he's saying, which happens to be true, or as if he's my husband already and has waited all day, or maybe all his life, to tell me what happened to him that afternoon.

18   A box of Kleenex is tucked under his arm, because he has a cold, and he lays the box down on the hall table with the assurance of the rightful prince stepping into his kingdom at last. This one I'll marry or I'll marry no one, I say to myself an hour later.

19   Three dates—which means three weeks—later, he proposes. "Wait I have to tell you something first," I declare in distress. He waits. I'm in turmoil. I'm risking everything on candor, and candor isn't a virtue in which I've much practice. I've never said anything like this out loud before. "You have a right to know," I announced. "I wear a padded bra."

20   He says he imagines he can handle that.

21   We were married three months later. I wonder, if he hadn't proposed so promptly, how much longer it would have been before he discovered my secret for himself.

EXERCISE 5   Vocabulary Highlights

Write a short definition of each word as it is used in the essay. (Paragraph numbers are given in parentheses.) Be prepared to use these words in your own sentences.

diaphragm (4)   condescending (14)

symbolic (6)   monogrammed (16)

dire (7)   obligatory (16)

delirious (8)   assurance (18)

ardent (10)   candor (19)

EXERCISE 6   Discussion and Critical Thinking

1. Is this essay directive (telling the reader how to do something) or informative (telling the reader how something occurred or is occurring)?

2. This essay is written in the present tense ("And so I dress carefully. . . ."; paragraph 3) except for the last paragraph, which is in the past tense ("We were. . . ."). What does the author accomplish by using the present tense for what she has to say here?

3. Does Gould see particular "rules" of dressing for a date in 1950 as a matter of wrong attitudes or just cultural differences?

4. Which paragraphs occupy the background (the situation that will be discussed in stages) part of this process analysis?

5. List the paragraph numbers and the words that mark the beginning of the first three stages of Gould's dressing.

6. Looking back on 1950, we are likely to see quaintness, foolishness, and unfairness, mixed with innocence and sweetness. Do you think any aspects of current behavior—especially regarding dating and dressing in relation to values, intentions, and mating strategy—that might be regarded in, say, sixty years, as quaint or even misguided?

Fast, Sleek, and Shiny: Using the Internet to Help Buy New Cars

PRESTON GRALLA

In this essay adapted from The Complete Idiot's Guide to Online Shopping, *Preston Gralla presents down-to-earth advice on how to shop for a car on the Internet and how to avoid getting taken. Cars are only one of the many products featured in this book. This essay includes a discussion on how to buy a car and finance it, all through using your computer.*

1   Whether or not you plan to buy your new car over the Internet, make sure to do your prepurchase research online. Use the Internet to help decide which car to buy and to get the best deal possible from the dealer—or even to buy online. You'll get pleasure not only out of saving money, but also out of seeing car dealers gnash their teeth over the thought of how you were able to bargain them down to very little profit. There goes their trip to Cancun this year!

Step 1: Go Online to Research and Find Your Dream Machine

2   Your clunker has finally spit the last bit of black exhaust out of its tail pipe, and it's time to get a new dream machine. But what should you get? Should it be a supermacho, ego-enhancing sports utility vehicle? A trusty family station wagon? A hell-bent-for-leather sports car? Or just a plain old sedan? And which is the best model for your needs and pocketbook?

3   You'll find many sites to help you narrow down what you should buy. If you're not quite sure what you want, immediately head to the GTE Superpages Consumer Guide at www.consumerguide.com. Use the Interactive Car Finder—think of it as the "Complete Idiot's Guide to Choosing a Car." You select the kind of car (compact, sports utility vehicle, and so on), the price range, fuel economy, and features such as air-conditioning, and voilà—you'll get a list of cars that match your pocketbook and the features you want.

4   Car aficionados who want to know what the insiders think about cars should head to the online site of *Car and Driver* magazine at www.caranddriver.com. As you might guess, many, many more car sites online can help you decide which car to buy, and many also offer car reviews. I'd suggest that after you use the Consumer Guide and the *Car and Driver* site to narrow down your choices, you check in with as many sites as possible to get their takes on the cars of your dreams. One excellent site is Edmund's at www.edmunds.com.

Step 2: Get Ready to Bargain—Find Out the True Dealer Invoice Price

5   Sure, the last time you bought a car, you probably thought you got a pretty good deal. The dealer may even have said something like, "You got the best of me that time, Buddy." Guess what? The dealer was lying. (What a shock!) You got taken for a ride. The dealer got the best of you. And it's not because you're not smart enough to drive a good bargain. It's because the dealer knows exactly how much the car cost, and you don't have a clue. Sticker price, retail price, rebates, MSRP (what in the world does that stand for, anyway?—oh, yeah, Manufacturer's Suggested Retail Price), the costs of all the "extras" (such as doors and an engine, it seems)—trying to put it all together makes your head start to spin. The whole pricing scheme for new cars is designed to confuse you. So what's a poor car buyer to do?

6   It's simple. Head to the Internet and find out exactly how much the dealer paid for the car (the dealer cost) to the dollar—including all the extras. When you're armed with that information, you can force the dealer to meet your price—or you can walk out the door and find a dealer who *will* meet it.

7   You can find the dealer invoice price at a number of sites on the Internet. But head to www.edmunds.com to get the best lowdown. It not only provides the most comprehensive information but also explains the ins and outs of car pricing, which is arcane enough to have confused a medieval philosopher. This site offers excellent how-to-buy articles as well.

8   The MSRP is the car's base price that the dealer will quote to you. Never, ever, ever pay that price for a car. If you do, the dealer and salesperson will be breaking out the champagne after you leave.

9   Find the invoice price. That's the most important number on the page. It's the price that the dealer pays the manufacturer for the base model of the car, without any extras. That's the number you're going to use when you start to bargain. Do you notice something interesting about the MSRP price and the invoice price? I thought you did; you have sharp eyes. The MSRP (sticker) price is several thousand dollars higher than the invoice price. So if a dealer knocks off $1,000 from the sticker price, you might think you're getting a good deal, but you're not—the dealer is still making out like a bandit.

10   Next, check out the invoice prices of the options you want—things like automatic transmission, a luggage rack, and a stereo. As you can see, each item has an MSRP as well as an invoice price, which means that the dealer is making money by marking up all your extras as well. The dealer also has to pay a destination charge, which can be $500 or more. Edmund's reports that charge as well.

11   To figure out the true cost to the dealer of the car you're interested in buying, do this math:

Invoice Price + Invoice Price of Extras + Destination Charge = Dealer's Costs

Now here's a strange fact: Even if you pay only the dealer's invoice costs for a car, in most instances the dealer *still* makes a profit. That's because of a little-known program called the "Dealer Hold Back." The dealer hold back is a percentage of the MSRP of the vehicle, including all extras. When a dealer sells a vehicle, the manufacturer sends the dealer a check based on the hold back percentage and the MSRP of the vehicle. Domestic carmakers typically pay a 3 percent dealer hold back, and foreign makers often pay 2 percent. But the amount varies from manufacturer to manufacturer. Edmund's tells you the dealer hold back for the car you're buying.

12   Let's take an example. Say the MSRP of the car and extras you've bought is $25,000, and the dealer hold back is 3 percent. According to this formula, after you buy the car, the manufacturer sends the dealer a check for $750. Therefore, even if the dealer sells the car at invoice price, he or she is still making money. Note, though, that the money doesn't go to your salesperson—it goes straight to the dealer. So, no salesperson is going to agree to give you a car at invoice price.

13   Another way to save hundreds or even thousands of dollars when buying your next car is to find out what kinds of rebates and dealer incentives are available; on the www.edmunds.com site, just click on Incentives and Rebates.

Step 3: Psyching Out Your Dealer with Information You Got Online

14   So now you know the invoice cost of the car you want to buy, the destination charge, the dealer hold back, and any kinds of rebates and incentives available on the car you're interested in buying. What next? Let's say you want to buy a car from a dealer, not through the Web.

15   First, print everything out directly from the Web so that you have a sheaf of papers you can refer to. When you walk in with the printouts, the dealer will

16   realize you know your business and won't try to pull a fast one on you. (Well, the dealer may *try* to pull a fast one, but won't be able to succeed.)

Also, figure out on a sheet of paper how much you're willing to pay for the car. Base it on the invoice price of the car. You should hold the line at 3 percent over invoice cost if you can—and if the car isn't very popular or new models are about to come out, try to get it at 2 percent or less over invoice cost. If you're looking to buy a hot-selling car, you might not be able to drive such a hard bargain, but it's worth a try. For cars that aren't moving fast, you should be able to bargain down to your 2 percent or 3 percent figure. Also, when figuring the price you should pay for a car, be sure to consider any rebates or incentives.

EXERCISE 7   Discussion and Critical Thinking

1. Is this essay informative or directive?

2. Sometimes the preparation stage is implied or assumed. To shop on the Internet, of course, a person needs a computer with Internet access. Does Gralla specify the preparation stage, or does he simply make an assumption about the computer and Internet access?

3. Gralla gives much information, but he also is writing with a particular audience in mind. Just what does he expect the reader to know about computers?

4. How many steps does Gralla use?

5. In tone (the way the author regards the subject and the reader), what distinguishes this essay from many directive process-analysis statements?

STUDENT PARAGRAPHS AND ESSAY

· ·

Writing Process Worksheet

Name Seham Hammat   **Title** Making Faces   **Due Date** Thursday, November 15, 8 a.m.

Use the back of this page or separate paper if you need more space.

Assignment   In the space below, write whatever you need to know about your assignment, including information about the topic, audience, pattern of writing, length, whether to include a rough draft or revised drafts, and whether your paper must be typed.

Write a directive process analysis. Personalize it by using a narrative framework. If possible, write about one procedure you do at work. Audience: general readers outside the field of work. One paragraph of about 250 words. Include this sheet completed, one or more rough drafts, and a typed final draft.

Stage One

Explore Freewrite, brainstorm (list), cluster, or take notes as directed by your instructor.

Listing

Preparation	*Steps*
Check out customer	Take off old makeup
Get right products	Wash face
Discuss price	Toner on
Discuss time	Moisturizer
	Foundation
	Powder
	Fix eyebrows and lashes
	Put on blush
	Add liner and lipstick

Stage Two

Organize Write a topic sentence or thesis; label the subject and the focus parts.

<u>If you would like to do what I do</u>, <u>just follow these directions</u>.
           subject   focus

Write an outline or an outline alternative. For reading-based writing, include quotations and references with page numbers as support in the outline.

I. Preparation
  A. Evaluate client
  B. Select supplies
    1. Cleanser
    2. Toner
    3. Others
  C. Check tray of tools
II. Steps
  A. Strip off old makeup
  B. Scrub face
  C. Put on toner
  D. Add moisturizer
  E. Rub on foundation
  F. Dust on powder
  G. Gel eyebrows
    1. Trim
    2. Shape
    3. Pencil
  H. Curl lashes
  I. Dab on blush
  J. Paint lips

Stage Three

Write On separate paper, write and then revise your paragraph or essay as many times as necessary for **c**oherence, **l**anguage (usage, tone, and diction), **u**nity, **e**mphasis, **s**upport, and **s**entences (**CLUESS**). Read your work aloud to hear and correct any grammatical errors or awkward-sounding sentences.

Edit any problems in fundamentals, such as **c**apitalization, **o**missions, **p**unctuation, and **s**pelling (**COPS**).

MAKING FACES
Seham Hammat

Topic sentence

Preparation

Steps 1

2

3
4
5

6

7

8
9

10

Concluding sentence

The Face Place, a trendy mall store, is where I work. Making faces is what I do. I do not mean sticking out my tongue; I mean reworking the faces of women who want a new or fresh look. When I get through, if I have done a good job, you can not tell if my subject is wearing makeup or not. <u>If you would like to do what I do, just follow these directions</u>. Imagine you have a client. Her name is Donna. <u>Check her out</u> for skin complexion, skin condition, size of eyes, kind of eyebrows, and lip shape. Then <u>go to the supply room and select</u> the <u>items</u> you need for the faceover, including a cleanser and toner with added moisturizers. <u>Put them on a tray by your brushes and other tools and basic supplies</u>. <u>Begin by stripping off her old makeup</u> with a few cotton balls and cleanser. Donna's skin is a combination of conditions. Her forehead, nose, and chin are oily, and her cheeks are dry. <u>Scrub her down</u> with Tea Tree, my favorite facial cleanser from a product line that is not tested on animals. Scour the oil slicks extra. Then <u>slather on</u> some <u>Tea Tree toner</u> to close her pores so that the dirt does not go back in. <u>Add</u> a <u>very light moisturizer</u> such as one called Elderflower Gel. Donna has a pale complexion. <u>Put on a coat of 01 foundation</u>, the fairest in the shop, which evens out her skin tone. Next, with a big face brush, <u>dust on a layer of 01 powder</u> to give her a smooth, dry look. Now Donna, who is watching in a mirror, speaks up to say she wants her eyebrows brushed and lightened just a bit. She has dark eyebrows and eyelashes that will not require much mascara or eyebrow pencil. <u>So use gel to fix the eyebrows</u> in place while you <u>trim, shape, and pencil them</u>. Move downward on the face, going next to her eyes. Use brown mascara to <u>curl her already dark lashes</u>. With your blusher brush, <u>dab</u> some peach rose <u>blush on</u> her <u>cheeks</u> and <u>blend it in</u>. <u>Line her lips</u> with bronze sand lip liner pencil and <u>fill in the rest</u> with rouge mauve lipstick. Swing Donna around to the big lighted mirror. Watch her pucker her lips, squint her eyes, flirt with herself. See her smile. Now you pocket the tip. Feel good. <u>You have just given a woman a new face, and she is out to conquer the world</u>.

EXERCISE 8   Discussion and Critical Thinking

1. Is this paragraph of process analysis mainly directive or informative?

2. How does Hammat take her paragraph beyond a list of mechanical directions?

3. In addition to using chronological (time) order, what other order does she use briefly?

4. In writing this essay, Hammat conferred with her collaborative learning group. The male members said she was using some word choices that would appeal only to women. They even offered suggestions, and in her final draft, she included seven of their phrases. List the phrases you think were provided by the guys.

5. Do the terms suggested by the males enliven the writing, or do they detract from the message? Explain.

READING-BASED WRITING

Summary of "McDonald's—We Do It All for You"

LABRON BRITTON

The reading and writing assignment for student Labron Britton was to write a summary of one of several reading selections. He chose "McDonald's—We Do It All for You" by Barbara Garson. His summary was to be objective and to use his own words unless otherwise noted; it would stress the main points of the essay.

Quotation

"McDonald's—We Do It All for You" by Barbara Garson is presented as an essay, but it is actually an interview of Jason Pratt, a teenager who had worked at McDonald's three times but said he would never return because "there's a procedure for everything and you just follow the procedure" (325). He explained that the kitchen is regulated by bells and buzzers. Everything is timed. When an order comes in for burgers, the grill person goes into a routine that has been taught to employees by a video. With beepers giving signals for sequence and timing, the meat is cooked while the buns are warmed. Then the onions go on the meat after the patties are turned, and the crowns are taken from the oven and lined up. Next the crowns are loaded with mustard, ketchup, pickles, lettuce, and cheese (if requested) in that order. Finally, the meat is placed on top of the lettuce and the heel of the bun on top of that. All portions are prescribed, even to the measured squirts of ketchup and mustard, the number of pickle slices (2 large or 3 small), and the pieces of reconstituted onions. Pratt says he could not stand the procedure that left nothing to the imagination of the individual. He said workers at McDonald's do not need a brain because they are required to be robots.

Work Cited

Garson, Barbara. "McDonald's—We Do It All for You." *Sentences, Paragraphs, and Beyond.* Ed. Lee Brandon and Kelly Brandon. 3rd ed. Boston: Houghton, 2001. 325–27. Print.

CAREER-RELATED WRITING

The Skinny on Working for a Dermatologist

KIM BIRDINE

After having traveled a long way, from a Korean orphanage to the United States, J. Kim Birdine is still on the move. In writing this essay of process analysis, she demonstrates the same intellectual qualities she uses so well in her role as an assistant to a doctor, both in the office and in the operating room.

1   As a medical assistant for a dermatologist, I am actively involved in every aspect of the practice, recommending products, doing laser treatments for veins, and administering skin peels. The younger patients generally see the doctor to correct their skin problems, whether they're suffering from a persistent dry patch, uneven skin tone, or a bout with acne. A good number of the patients come in for cosmetic reasons, wanting their wrinkles smoothed out or their dark blotches lasered off. The most important part of my job, though, is to prepare surgical trays for the patients with skin cancer and to assist the doctor through the procedure.

2   My initial concern when setting up a surgical tray is that everything is sterile. This means that all the metal instruments, gauze, and applicators (Q-Tips) are put through an Autoclave (steam sterilizer), to ensure sterilization. Once everything is processed, I begin setting up my surgical tray by placing a sterile field on a tray, which has long legs and wheels at the base so it can be rolled. The tray should stand about waist high so the physician can reach the instruments easily. The sterile field is a large white tissue that I carefully take out of a sealed pack, touching it only at the corners to unfold it to its full size. It serves as a base on which to place all the instruments.

3   Next all of the metal instruments are placed on the tray with a long-handled "pick-up." The necessary instruments are a scalpel, a skin hook, large forceps, small forceps, straight scissors, curved scissors, a large needle holder, and a small needle holder. All are placed with handles facing toward me, except the small needle holder and the straight scissors. These two should be positioned at a corner away from me with the handles facing out. The position of all of the instruments is important so that the doctor can reach them with ease. The ones placed in the corner are for me to use while assisting with suturing. A surgical tray is not complete without a small stack of gauze (large) and about twenty applicators. The entire tray is covered with another sterile field exactly like the one placed initially on the tray.

4   Just prior to surgery, I set up extras. I place on the counter anesthesia—a 3cc syringe of lidocaine with epinephrine—and a disinfectant skin cleanser, along with two pair of surgical gloves, one for the doctor and one for me. I turn on the hyfrecator, which is a cauterizer used to stop bleeding by burning the tissue. I prepare a specimen bottle indicating on its label the patient's name, the date, the doctor's name, and the area of the body from which the specimen is taken. I remove the sterile field on top of the instruments and place the sutures requested by the doctor and a different kind of sterile field, which has a hole in the middle of it, on the tray. This field enables the doctor to place the hole directly over the surgery site, exposing only the area to be worked on and covering the surrounding areas.

5   During surgery, once the doctor removes the section that needs to be tested, I place it in the specimen jar, seal the lid on it, and place it on the counter. I have to be attentive to the surgery at this point to assist in reducing the bleeding. My job is to apply gauze or applicators wherever bleeding occurs and to ready the hyfrecator in case the doctor needs it. When

bleeding is minimized, the doctor begins suturing. At this point I have the small needle holder in hand as well as the straight scissors. I use the small needle holder to grab the tip of the needle after the doctor inserts it through the skin, to pull it through for her. This makes her job easier. I use the straight scissors to cut the suture once she is finished with knotting. Sometimes she does some internal suturing for the tissue under the skin, with dissolvable thread, and knots each turn. This is when I cut directly on top of the knot. The surface suturing is usually knotted at the beginning and at the end of the line of sutures and needs cutting down to one-quarter of an inch.

6   After surgery, I use peroxide to clean the patient's surgical site. I apply either a pressure bandage or a plain Band-Aid with antibiotic ointment. The pressure bandage is applied usually when there is a concern of more bleeding post surgery. I explain to the patient how to take care of the surgical area and when to come back to have the sutures removed. This makes my job complete, until it is time for another set-up, when I will repeat the same process of ensuring a sterile environment for the patient.

EXERCISE 9   Discussion and Critical Thinking

1. Underline and label the thesis (in the first paragraph).

2. Annotate the essay for the preparation and the steps of this process analysis. Number the parts of each stage. Underline key words corresponding with your annotations.

3. Why is the preparation stage longer than the steps stage for Birdine?

4. On what principle is Birdine's order of presentation based—time or space?

Suggested Topics and Prompts for Writing Process Analysis

STUDENT COMPANION SITE
For additional practice, visit www.cengage .com/devenglish/ brandon/spb6e.

You will find a blank Writing Process Worksheet on page 6 of this book and on the Student Companion Site. It can be photocopied or printed out, filled in, and submitted with your assignment, if your instructor directs you to do so.

READING-BASED WRITING

Reading-based writing requires you to read critically, write a reply that shows you understand what you have read, and give credit for ideas you borrow and words you quote. The form can be a summary, a reaction, or a two-part response (with separated summary and reaction). Documentation, in which you give credit for borrowed ideas and words, can be either formal (MLA) or informal, as directed by your instructor. Both the forms of reading-based writing and documentation are discussed with examples in Chapter 1. Definitions of the three forms follow.

Summary

- The summary is a statement presenting only the main points of what you have read by using different wording without altering the meaning, adding information, or showing bias.
- It is the purest form of reading-based writing.

Reaction

- In the reaction, the meaning of what you have read will be central to the topic sentence of your paragraph or to the thesis of your essay.
- Although the reaction is not a personal narrative by itself, it may include personal experience to explain elements of the text. For example, if your source is about driving styles, your own experiences as a driver or an observer of drivers could be relevant in your analysis of the text.
- The reaction may incorporate a summary to convey a broad view of what you have read, but your summary should never be the main part of your reaction.

Two-Part Response

- The two-part response separates the summary from the reaction.
- This form will give you practice in separating your objective summary in the first part from your more personal evaluation, interpretation, or application in the second part, the reaction.

READING-BASED WRITING TOPICS

"Binding Decisions"

1. Write a two-part response (separate summary and reaction) to this essay. In your reaction, evaluate the author's personal views on how she now regards what it was necessary for her to do with her "binding decisions." Refer to and quote from the essay.

2. Write a two-part response (separate summary and reaction) to this essay. In your reaction, relate Gould's decisions to the ones that might be made by either a female or a male of your generation in dressing for a date. Remember that each decision is made for a reason, and the reasons are sometimes more interesting than the choices.

"Fast, Sleek, and Shiny: Using the Internet to Help Buy New Cars"

3. Use the information in this essay to write a reaction in which you evaluate the last time you or someone you know purchased a car. Go point by point from the decision to buy a particular car to the actual purchase. Refer to and quote from the essay as you explain what went right and what could have gone better if the buyer had done some Internet homework.

4. Following the directions in this essay, conduct an actual search for a desirable car. Explain what happened as you performed the process explained by Gralla. Refer directly to and quote from the essay.

"Making Faces"

5. In a reaction, explain how "Making Faces" compares with "Binding Decisions" (page 399) as a process of self-decoration. Use references and quotations.

6. Write an evaluation of Hammat's paragraph and rank it on a scale of 1 to 10, with 10 being the highest score. Consider coherence (especially the ordering of parts), language (especially word choice), unity, emphasis, support (especially the stated and implied reasons for performing each step), and sentences. Be specific. Refer to and use quotations from her essay.

GENERAL TOPICS

7. Write about a special food prepared for your family now or during your childhood. The food could be your favorite dish or it might be a treat prepared for a special holiday. Personalize it by providing a group context. For a helpful model of form on a similar topic, review "*Pupusas*: Salvadoran Delight" on pages 392–393.

8. Explain how to increase your chances for survival in a tornado, a hurricane, an earthquake, a fire in a high-rise building, or a flood. For a helpful model of form on a similar topic, review "Nature on the Rampage" on page 398.

9. Write about any grooming or personal service that you either perform or use or understand very well and can perform. Suggestions: hair, nails, facials, skin art, skin alteration, or massage. For a helpful model of form on a similar topic, review "Making Faces" on page 407.

10. Most of the following topics are directive as they are phrased. However, each can be transformed into a how-it-was-done informative topic by personalizing it and explaining stage by stage how you, someone else, or a group did something. For example, you could write either a directive process analysis about how to deal with an obnoxious person or an informative process analysis about how you or someone else dealt with an obnoxious person. Keep in mind that the two types of process analysis are often blended, especially in personal writing. Many of the following topics will be more interesting to you and your readers if the process is personalized.

    Most of the topics require some narrowing to be treated in a paragraph or a short essay. For example, writing about playing baseball is too broad; writing about how to throw a curve ball may be manageable.

    a. How to pass a test for a driver's license.

    b. How to get a job at _____

    c. How to repair _____

    d. Imagine you will have a houseguest from a country that does not have our household conveniences. You will be away on the day the person arrives, and you need to write some instructions on how to operate something (and perhaps a few warnings about the consequences of not following directions).

CROSS-CURRICULAR TOPIC

11. Write about a process related to another class in which you use equipment for a small unit of work. Include drawings, diagrams, or photocopies of images marked with numbers or letters to correspond with your directions. Consider the following processes:

- viewing a slide of a specific item in a biology lab
- identifying a rock in a geology class
- testing soil in an agriculture class
- preflighting an aircraft

CAREER-RELATED TOPICS

12. Imagine that you are about to leave a job after giving only a one-day notice to your employer. That employer kindly asks you to write a paragraph or short essay (actually as a process analysis) about how you fulfill your job description for a certain task. This information will be studied by your successor tomorrow. Do not attempt to explain what you do for all your job description, just the task. For useful models of form and workplace content, review "Making Faces" on pages 405–407 and "The Skinny on Working for a Dermatologist" on pages 409–410.

13. Explain how to perform a service or to repair or install a product.

14. Explain the procedure for operating a machine, a computer, a piece of equipment, or another device at the workplace.

15. Explain how to manufacture, construct, or cook something at the workplace.

WRITER'S GUIDELINES   Process Analysis

1. Decide whether your process analysis is mainly directive or informative, and be appropriately consistent in using pronouns and other designations.

   - For directive process analysis, use the second person, addressing the reader as *you*. The *you* may be understood, even if it is not written.
   - For informative process analysis, use the first person, speaking as *I* or *we*, or the third person, speaking about the subject as *he, she, it,* or *they*, or by name.

2. Consider using these basic forms.

Directive	Informative
I. Preparation	I. Background
A.	A.
B.	B.
II. Steps	II. Sequence
A.	A.
B.	B.
C.	C.

3. Listing is a useful prewriting activity for process analysis. Begin with the Roman-numeral headings indicated in number 2.

4. The order of a process analysis will usually be chronological (time based) in some sense. Certain transitional words are commonly used to promote coherence: *first, second, third, then, soon, now, next, finally, at last, therefore,* and *consequently.*

5. Process analysis may be the most common form of career-related writing.

   • You learn much on the job by reading process analysis, both how to do something and how something works or is done.
   • As you advance at the workplace, you will teach others how to do something and how something works or is done.
   • Knowing the techniques of writing process analysis will provide you with structure for learning and teaching.
   • The preparation or background followed by the steps are organizational patterns that can be points for PowerPoint presentations.

6. Write and revise.

   • Write and then revise your paragraph or essay as many times as necessary for **c**oherence, **l**anguage (usage, tone, and diction), **u**nity, **e**mphasis, **s**upport, and **s**entences (**CLUESS**). Read your work aloud to hear and correct any grammatical errors or awkward-sounding sentences.
   • Edit any problems in fundamentals, such as **c**apitalization, **o**missions, **p**unctuation, and **s**pelling (**COPS**).

STUDENT COMPANION SITE
For additional practice, visit www.cengage .com/devenglish/ brandon/spb6e.

Chapter 22

Cause and Effect
Determining Reasons and Outcomes

FLOW OF WRITING

WHEN TO USE CAUSE AND EFFECT

FOR COLLEGE WRITING ASSIGNMENTS

- Cause-and-effect questions are the center of scientific investigation. They are also commonplace in reading assignments, class discussion, reports, research papers, and tests. If you want to study for an examination or just to be prepared for class discussion, highlight any situation, event, or trend and list relevant causes and effects. Try that approach with these general topics: gang activity, high blood pressure, obesity, divorce rate, drug addiction, inflation, economic depression, drought, flood, political change, racism, foreign policy, earthquake, volcanic eruption, and tax increase. In your college classes, topics like those have a way of getting attached to the words *causes* and *effects*. Being able to use cause-and-effect analysis will help you to learn and to get credit for what you know.

IN CAREERS AND AT THE WORKPLACE

- Businesses and other institutions deal constantly with reasons and results. For the individual, the rise and fall of careers are usually tied to causes and effects. Businesses need to make money. Institutions need to function well. Helping them do so requires the use of cause-and-effect analysis in almost every measurable respect. Cause-and-effect issues are subjects of progress reports, performance reviews, memos, and proposals. Accountability, a key word in measuring effectiveness, is based on causes and effects. Being able to understand and explain cause and effect will make you indispensable in any vocational field. You are studying and practicing the principles of cause and effect in college. You will continue to study and practice the principles of cause and effect as you use them at your workplace.

CAUSE AND EFFECT IN A CARTOON

THE QUIGMANS   by Buddy Hickerson

B. Hickerson, copyright Los Angeles Times Syndicate. Reprinted by permission.

"Francine! Have you seen my flare gun?"

WRITING CAUSE AND EFFECT

DEFINING CAUSE AND EFFECT

Cause-and-effect relationships are common in our daily lives. A single situation may raise questions about both causes and effects:

> My computer crashed. Why? (cause)
> What now? (effect)

In a paragraph or short essay, you will probably emphasize either causes or effects, although you may mention both of them. Because you cannot write about all causes or all effects, you should try to identify and develop the most important ones. Consider that some causes are immediate, others remote; some visible, others hidden. Any one or a group of causes can be the most important. The effects of an event can also be complicated. Some may be immediate, others long-range. The sequence of events is not necessarily related to causation. For example, *B* (inflation) may follow *A* (the election of a president), but that sequence does not mean that *A* caused *B*.

EXPLORING

One useful approach in exploring a cause-and-effect analysis is *listing*. Write down the event, situation, or trend you are concerned about. Then on the left side list the causes and on the right side list the effects. Looking at the two lists, determine the better side (causes or effects) for your study.

Here is a pair of lists on the topic of alcoholism.

Causes	Event, Situation, or Trend	Effects
Inherited	My dad's	Fights
Work	alcoholism	Arguments
Social drinking out		Bad driving
of control		Embarrassed us
Lack of self-control		Looked bad
Worry about money		Stomach problems
		Lost job
		Broke
		Robbed piggy bank
		DUI
		Accidents
		Died

ORGANIZING

After you have evaluated the items in your lists, choose three or so of the most important causes or effects and proceed.

The effects could be incorporated into a *topic sentence* and then developed in an *outline*.

Topic Sentence: <u>Drinking</u> <u>took its toll in many ways</u>.
subject   focus

I. Social
   A. Neighborhood
      1. Argued
      2. Embarrassed us
   B. Home
      1. With Mom
      2. With us
II. Physical
   A. Appearance
   B. Health
III. Work
   A. Absences
   B. Fired
IV. Loses control
   A. Piggy-bank theft
   B. Accident

You can read the final paragraph based on this outline, complete in the Writer's Process Worksheet form, on pages 430–432.

Your paragraph will derive its structure from either causes or effects, although both causes and effects may be mentioned. Give emphasis and continuity to your writing by repeating key words, such as *cause, reason, effect, result, consequence*, and *outcome*.

If your pattern of causes or effects occurred in a sequence, then maintain that chronological order. Otherwise, arrange your points according to emphasis, from least to most important or from most to least important. The most likely pattern for your work is one of those shown in Figure 22.1. These patterns may look familiar to you. We discussed similar patterns in Chapter 14.

Figure 22.1
Patterns for Paragraph
and Essay

For Paragraph

| Subject and Topic Sentence |
| Cause or Effect 1 |
| Cause or Effect 2 |
| Cause or Effect 3 |
| Reflection on Topic Sentence |

For Essay

| Subject and Thesis |
| Topic Sentence |
| Cause or Effect 1 |
| Topic Sentence |
| Cause or Effect 2 |
| Topic Sentence |
| Cause or Effect 3 |
| Conclusion |

Transitional Words

Consider using the following transitional words to improve coherence by connecting ideas with ideas, sentences with sentences, and paragraphs with paragraphs.

FOR CAUSE AND EFFECT:

Cause: as, because, because of, due to, for, for the reason that, since, bring about, another cause, for this reason, one cause, a second cause, another cause, a final cause

Effect: accordingly, finally, consequently, hence, so, therefore, thus, as a consequence, as a result, resulting

FOR ALL PATTERNS OF WRITING: The <u>HOTSHOT CAT</u> words: <u>H</u>owever, <u>O</u>therwise, <u>T</u>herefore, <u>S</u>imilarly, <u>H</u>ence, <u>O</u>n the other hand, <u>T</u>hen, <u>C</u>onsequently, <u>A</u>lso, <u>T</u>hus (See pages 74–75 for additional transitional words.)

FINDING PATTERNS IN PHOTOS

EXERCISE 1   A Text-Based Activity for Groups or Individuals

Drunk driving

This photo depicts a police officer testing a driver for DUI (driving under the influence). The test is easy for one who is not intoxicated, but it is difficult for a person who has had, say, more than two drinks of alcohol in an hour (immediate cause). The officer will ask the suspect to perform mental and physical tasks that will reveal the effect of excessive drinking.

© Doug Menuez/Photodisc/Getty Images

An inebriated person will have trouble (effect) with

1. _____
2. _____
3. _____
4. _____
5. _____

If the DUI suspect does not pass the test, a second round of effects will occur in the suspect's life. What might they be? These will vary somewhat from person to person.

1. _____
2. _____
3. _____
4. _____
5. _____

If your instructor directs you to do so, write a paragaph or an essay on the immediate effects of a DUI situation, the long-range effects, or both.

Practicing Patterns of Cause and Effect

A detailed outline and your subsequent writing may include a combination of causes and effects, but almost always one of these, either causes *or* effects, will be emphasized and will provide the main structure of your paper. Whether you are writing a basic outline for an assignment outside of class without a significant time constraint or you are writing in class under the pressure of time, you will always have a chance to jot down prewriting lists in the form shown in Exercise 2.

EXERCISE 2   Completing Patterns of Cause and Effect

Select one event, situation, or trend, and circle it. Fill in the blanks to complete the list of causes and the list of effects.

Causes	Event, Situation, or Trend	Effects
1. _____	Emigrating to the United States	1. _____
2. _____	or	2. _____
3. _____	Fulfilling my educational goal (specify the goal)	3. _____
4. _____		4. _____

EXERCISE 3   Completing Patterns of Cause and Effect

Select either the "Causes" or the "Effects" column in Exercise 2 and complete the following basic outline as you would in an early phase of writing a paragraph or an essay assignment based on the three most important causes or effects. The basic outline would be the same; the essay would carry more development.

Topic sentence (for paragraph) or thesis (for essay):

_____   _____
         subject   focus

I. Cause (or Effect): _____

II. Cause (or Effect): _____

III. Cause (or Effect): _____

Readings for Critical Thinking, Discussion, and Writing

READING STRATEGIES AND OBJECTIVES

Underlining and annotating these reading selections will help you answer the questions that follow the selections, discuss the material in class, and prepare for reading-based writing assignments. As you underline and annotate, pay special attention to the author's writing skills, logic, and message, and consider the relevance of the material to your own experiences and values.

Some selections begin with a Mindset suggestion that can help you create a readiness for connecting with what you are about to read.

PARAGRAPH

Neighbors from Hell

LES CHRISTIE

This paragraph is taken from an essay of the same title, first published on the Internet by Cable News Network in 2005.

MINDSET

Lock It In

Imagine you have finally acquired that apartment, condo, house, or other abode you have wanted for so long. Then, a few minutes after you move in, the noise—a really bad noise—from next door begins and then goes on and on as the permanent auditory environment.

When Keili Gapski and her husband bought a house north of Detroit, they thought they had found paradise. Then, new neighbors moved in next door and soon acquired a Doberman-Rottweiler mix. The Gapskis bore the brunt of the animal's incessant barking. Prevailing upon the dog's owners accomplished little. Neither did bringing in the authorities. The neighbors bought another dog. The Gapskis spent $1,000 to put up a fence. They paid $40 for an anti-barking device, which emits an ultrasonic tone meant to quiet a dog. The neighbors even equipped their pooch with a battery-charged collar, which issued a shock when the dog barked. Nothing worked. So the Gapskis gave up. "We don't deal with situations, we just move," says Keili. When they tried to sell, the Gapskis learned that difficult neighbors aren't just a nuisance—they can even drive down property values. Some states require sellers to disclose neighborhood nuisances (noise, smoke, odors), if they exist. That can discourage some homebuyers and give negotiating leverage. "Every time a buyer came to look at our house, the dog would go ballistic," Keili says. "We started the house at $195,000 and had to drop it to $170,000." She couldn't blame the buyers. When she and her husband home-shopped, if they heard a dog bark, they would turn on their heels and get back in the car.

EXERCISE 4   Discussion and Critical Thinking

1. Is this paragraph mainly one of cause or effect?

2. How many effects are discussed, and what are they?

3. How many causes are there? Explain.

4. What other pattern (or patterns) of writing is used here? Discuss.

5. Does your experience tell you that this account is true to life in many instances? Could there be other factors unmentioned? Explain.

ESSAYS

The Roots of Happiness: An Empirical Analysis

WAYNE WEITEN AND MARGARET LLOYD

Wayne Weiten and Margaret Lloyd are professors of psychology and the authors of the acclaimed college textbook Psychology Applied to Modern Life: Adjustment in the 21st Century, *which is now in its 8th edition. Although they have written on a great variety of topics in applied psychology, they have taken a special interest in how attitudes affect behavior and vice versa. This study on the causes of happiness is taken from their textbook.*

MINDSET

Lock It In

What makes you happy? List five things in the order of their importance and then see if people from a special study agree with you. Be prepared for a few surprises.

1   What exactly makes a person happy? This question has been the subject of much speculation. Commonsense theories about the roots of happiness abound. For example, you have no doubt heard that money cannot buy happiness. But do you believe it? A television commercial says, "If you've got your health, you've got just about everything." Is health indeed the key? What if you're healthy but poor, unemployed, and lonely? We often hear about the joys of parenthood, the joys of youth, and the joys of the simple, rural life. Are these the factors that promote happiness?

2   In recent years, social scientists have begun putting these and other theories to empirical test. Quite a number of survey studies have been conducted to explore the determinants of happiness. The findings of these studies are quite interesting. As you will see, many commonsense notions about happiness appear to be inaccurate.

3   The first of these is the apparently widespread assumption that most people are relatively unhappy. Writers, social scientists, and the general public seem to believe that people around the world are predominantly dissatisfied, yet surveys consistently find that the vast majority of respondents characterize themselves as fairly happy. When people are asked to rate their happiness, only a small minority place themselves below the neutral point on the various scales used. The overall picture seems rosier than anticipated.

What Isn't Very Important?

Money

4   There is a positive correlation between income and feelings of happiness, but the association is surprisingly weak. Admittedly, being very poor can make people unhappy, but once people ascend above the poverty level, there is little relation between income and happiness. On the average, even wealthy people are only slightly happier than those in the middle classes. The problem with money is that in this era of voracious consumption, most people find a way to spend all their money and come out short, no matter how much they make. Complaints about not having enough money are routine even among affluent people who earn six-figure incomes.

Age

5   Age and happiness are consistently found to be unrelated. Age accounts for less than 1 percent of the variation in people's happiness. The key factors influencing people's thoughts about their own well-being may shift some as people grow

older—work becomes less important, health more so—but people's average level of happiness tends to remain remarkably stable over the life span.

Gender

6   Women are treated for depressive disorders about twice as often as men, so one might expect that women are less happy on the average. However, like age, gender accounts for less than 1 percent of the variation in people's happiness.

Parenthood

7   Children can be a tremendous source of joy and fulfillment, but they also can be a tremendous source of headaches and hassles. Compared to childless couples, parents worry more and experience more marital problems. Apparently the good and bad aspects of parenthood balance each other out, because the evidence indicates that people who have children are neither more nor less happy than people without children.

Intelligence

8   Intelligence is a highly valued trait in modern society, but researchers have not found an association between IQ scores and happiness. Educational attainment also appears to be unrelated to life satisfaction.

Physical Attractiveness

9   Good-looking people enjoy a variety of advantages in comparison to unattractive people. Given that physical attractiveness is an important resource in Western society, we might expect attractive people to be happier than others, but the available data indicate that the correlation between attractiveness and happiness is negligible.

What Is Somewhat Important?

10   Research has identified three facets of life that appear to have a moderate impact on subjective well-being: health, social activity, and religious belief.

Health

11   Good physical health would seem to be an essential requirement for happiness, but people adapt to health problems. Research reveals that individuals who develop serious, disabling health conditions aren't as unhappy as one might guess. Furthermore, good health does not, by itself, produce happiness, because people tend to take good health for granted. Researchers found only a moderate positive correlation between health status and subjective well-being.

Social Activity

12   Humans are social beings, and people's interpersonal relations do appear to contribute to their happiness. People who are satisfied with their friendship networks and who are socially active report above-average levels of happiness. At the other end of the spectrum, people troubled by loneliness tend to be very unhappy.

Religion

13   A number of large-scale surveys suggest that people with heartfelt religious convictions are more likely to be happy than people who characterize themselves as nonreligious.

What Is Very Important?

14 The list of factors that turn out to be very important ingredients of happiness is surprisingly short. Only a few variables are strongly related to overall happiness.

Love and Marriage

15 Romantic relationships can be stressful, but people consistently rate being in love as one of the most critical ingredients of happiness. Furthermore, although people complain a lot about their marriages, the evidence indicates that marital status is a key correlate of happiness. Among both men and women, married people are happier than people who are single or divorced.

Work

16 Given the way people often complain about their jobs, we might not expect work to be a key source of happiness, but it is. Although less critical than love and marriage, job satisfaction is strongly related to general happiness. Studies also show that unemployment has devastating effects on subjective well-being.

Personality

17 The best predictor of individuals' future happiness is their past happiness. Some people seem destined to be happy and others unhappy, regardless of their triumphs or setbacks. Several studies suggest that happiness does not depend on external circumstances—having a nice house, good friends, and an enjoyable job—as much as internal factors, such as one's outlook on life. With this reality in mind, researchers have begun to look for links between personality and subjective well-being, and they have found some relatively strong connections. For example, self-esteem is one of the best predictors of happiness. Not surprisingly, people who like themselves tend to be happier than those who do not. Other personality correlates of happiness include extraversion, optimism, and a sense of personal control over one's life.

EXERCISE 5   Discussion and Critical Thinking

1. In this essay, what are the causes and what is the effect?

2. The results presented in this essay come from empirical analysis. What does that mean?

3. In the grouped rankings, which root has the most surprising ranking?

4. Which root in the "What Is Very Important?" category probably has the most overlapping with one or more of the other roots?

5. Based on your own experiences and self-understanding, how would you rank these roots? To be specific, list four that you would move in the ranking.

Seeking Justice After a Fatal Spin of the Cylinder

WILLIAM GLABERSON

William Glaberson, a staff writer with the New York Times, *specializes in crime and other legal issues. He has written on military tribunals, gun control, death penalty cases, sexual harassment, youth crime, and other matters of national and international law and justice.*

1   INDIANA, Pa.—There was one round in the cylinder.

2   It was prom night at Marion Center High School in rural western Pennsylvania. Sean Miller was a senior, but he was not going to the dance. He and Carl Kellar, a ninth grader, were with Leila Dudek, another freshman; the three were listening to one CD over and over again in Carl's tiny basement bedroom. They were the only ones in the house. Early in the evening Carl went upstairs, grabbed the keys from where they were hidden on top of the family's gun cabinet and took out his father's .357 Magnum.

3   It was Sean who first spun the cylinder of the revolver, put the eight-inch barrel to his head and pulled the trigger. Much later he would admit he took no chances because he could see where the cartridge with the bullet landed in the cylinder after each spin.

4   That spring night came alive at a civil trial here last month that told an unusually detailed story of guns and teenage bluster. The trial came and went with little notice in this small town 60 miles east of Pittsburgh. But in a simply furnished courtroom here it raised the kinds of moral questions with no easy answers that are often on the dockets of courts across America.

5   The Russian roulette was a performance of sorts for the benefit of Leila. "I was just trying to impress her," Sean testified.

6   She testified, too. "It went click," she said. She was terrified, she said.

7   Sean spun the cylinder and put the gun to his head again.

8   Click.

9   He spun it again. This time he handed the revolver to Carl, who, Leila testified, could not see the back of the cylinder. It was a dare, she said. "It looked," she told the jurors, "like he was gesturing for him to do the same thing." Then she heard the blast.

10   Every day in courtrooms across the country, people grapple with the endless variety of human evil, nobility, error, stupidity and bravery. Because the oath to tell the truth is taken seriously by some people in courtrooms, from the biggest cities to the smallest towns, courtroom battles can offer unusually clear snapshots of American life—even the parts that stubbornly defy explanation.

11   For four days in March in the Court of Common Pleas of Indiana County, a jury heard the civil suit of Carl's mother, Patricia A. Kellar, against Sean T. Miller, who is now 23. In Judge Gregory A. Olson's courtroom, the crack of that revolver was described so many times it seemed almost to break the silence of the two families facing off. The suit claimed Sean was negligent in prodding Carl to his death on May 26, 1995. In court, the Kellars' lawyer, Victor H. Pribanic of White Oak, Pa., said Sean "took the life of Carl Kellar as surely as if he had pulled the trigger himself."

12   But Sean's lawyer, W. Alan Torrance Jr. of Pittsburgh, said the case hinged on "personal responsibility." Sean did a "dumb thing" that night, he said, but it was Carl who had pulled the trigger that final time. The suit asked for millions of dollars in damages. But a few days before the trial began, Mrs. Kellar, who is 39, said she wanted as much as anything to unravel the mysteries of that night. Sean and Leila lied at first about the events leading up to Carl's death, so she was left struggling with confusion as well as loss.

13   "I'd like to know what happened that night," Mrs. Kellar said a few days before the trial, sitting next to her husband, John, in their modest ranch house where their son had died. During questioning by the state police the night of the shooting, Sean and Leila left out any mention of Russian roulette. After they had all looked at the gun, they said, Carl had suddenly and inexplicably shot himself. Sean Miller was never charged with a crime. So when the trial began on March 19, it became something of an inquest into the teenage world that is hidden from parents. It also shed light on corners of a story that for six years had remained dark.

14   As the older of the two, Mr. Pribanic argued, Sean had power over Carl. Ms. Dudek testified, "Sometimes he got real bossy with him." Mr. Pribanic called Mr. Miller to the stand. Now a square-jawed young man with darting blue eyes, he simmered as Mr. Pribanic led him through a series of admissions. Yes, he had lied to the police that night. "I was afraid of what people were going to think" if they concluded he had provoked Carl to point the gun at his head. Yes, he had asked Leila to lie, too.

15   The police had received anonymous phone calls after Carl's death saying that Mr. Miller had played Russian roulette before. They had called him in for another interview a month later. Then he admitted that he had spun the cylinder and pulled the trigger too that night; that he had begun the game. Mr. Miller told the jurors he had watched where the round was before he had pulled the trigger. "I assumed he would catch onto what I was doing," he said of Carl. But "it didn't cross my mind that he was going to do that."

16   Then Mr. Pribanic asked Mr. Miller to recall for the jurors what he had said about Carl in pretrial testimony. He had called him "the kid" and had suggested he would "follow me around like a dog." There were a lot of things he had said that he wished he could change, Mr. Miller told the jurors. As the central witness in the case, Sean Miller was an enigma. He was clearly furious to be defending a lawsuit but inexplicably cool as a witness. His fingers never trembled and his voice was always firm. "Somewhat cocky," one of the jurors, Wendell Marsh, would say later in an interview.

17   Mr. Miller never said he was sorry his friend had died. "I don't think he has a lot of conscience involved," another juror, Marian Urish, would say. When he was not on the stand, Mr. Miller sat in the front row, often with his mother. While seated in front of the jurors, the two clasped hands almost every minute. Sometimes they were joined by his father, who owns a construction company, and his brother, Josh, a college student.

18   Behind the Millers sat a gray-haired man from their homeowners insurance company, which would have to pay any verdict up to the policy's limit of $100,000. In a courtroom with few strangers, his presence was never explained to the jurors.

19   On the other side of the courtroom, in the front row, Mrs. Kellar sat. Usually, she was with her husband, a machine operator at a coal mine, who had adopted her two children from an earlier marriage. Carl's sister, now 23, and her husband, were with them, and behind them, sometimes as many as a dozen family members. In the hallways of the quiet courthouse, the Millers and the Kellars shunned each other.

20   Inside the courtroom, Mr. Pribanic, a former Pittsburgh prosecutor, sketched the Sean of six years ago as a sinister 17-year-old who used a dangerous image to manipulate younger friends. He called two wiry young men, now 21 and 22; who had been Carl's classmates. They testified that shortly before the night Carl died, Sean had cajoled them to play Russian roulette with his father's revolver. When they refused, one of the young men, Richard L. Smith, testified, Sean made a macabre counteroffer, saying, "Why don't we point it out toward the field and act as if it were us in front of the bullet."

21   Mr. Miller told the jurors that conversation had never happened. But he admitted he had slipped the pins out of the hinges of his father's gun cabinet, removed a revolver and shot into the field that afternoon. As described by witnesses, Carl was a young man with ambition: a high school football player who was in R.O.T.C. He was interested in the Air Force. Though he was almost six feet tall, he had written in a school essay just before he died that he wished to be bigger so that he could have had a chance of playing football at Penn State. "For a car," he wrote, "I want a Corvette."

22   But the dead boy, like the one who lived, did not escape the attacks that are part of a legal battle. Mr. Torrance dwelled on the fact that Carl had his own guns and a hunting rifle, as many boys around here do, as well as a bow and arrow and a collection of knives. Sean's younger brother Josh testified that Carl was a daredevil dirtbike rider and said he had once seen him courting danger by "car surfing," riding on the roof of a moving vehicle.

23   Mr. Torrance brought in an adolescent psychiatrist, David R. Burns of Philadelphia, to say that Carl might have been a certain type of high-risk adolescent boy who believes "that the dangers they know about don't apply to them."

24   Just after noon on Thursday, March 22, the case went to the jury—seven men and five women from this county where coal mining dominated for decades. Guns here, as in much of America, are not a political issue, they are a part of life. When Judge Olson asked 34 potential jurors whether they or family members had firearms at home, only one did not raise her hand.

25   Four hours after they began deliberations, the jurors sent a note inquiring about a question on the verdict form that asked whether Carl "knowingly and voluntarily accepted the specific risk that caused his death." If they answered "yes," Carl's family would lose. Later, jurors would say they had been divided six to six on that threshold question. At that moment, each side could still have won.

26   Mr. Pribanic said the jurors unnerved him partly because they did not glance over at Mrs. Kellar. After they had left the courtroom, he went in search of Mr. Torrance and the gray-haired man from the insurance company. When he found them in the court's law library, he said later, they seemed as rattled as he was by the jurors' question. The gray-haired man, he said, was already on the phone to the insurance company asking for authorization to settle the case. Court fillings show that before the trial the company had offered $100,000. Both sides agreed to keep the new settlement offer secret. But other lawyers said that under the circumstances of the case it was probably only modestly more than 100,000.

27   After six years of waiting, the settlement was reached in an instant. But it happened so fast that the jurors completed their deliberations first, three of them said in interviews. Sean was negligent, their verdict would have said. He had helped cause Carl's death. But Carl was more at fault, 70 percent responsible for his own death, the jurors found, for pulling the trigger. Had the jurors delivered their verdict, the Kellars would not have collected damages. "They were both responsible for what happened," said Nolan Blystone, a juror.

28   When it was over, the Millers sat in the hall. In obvious relief, Sean and his brother shared some private joke. Sean smiled widely, looking boyish for the first time in a week in court.

29   Mrs. Kellar was subdued about the settlement her lawyer had advised her to accept. "I learned more than what I knew" about what happened that night, she said.

30   Out in the hall after six years, the two families still did not speak to each other.

EXERCISE 6   Discussion and Critical Thinking

1. In paragraph 4, Glaberson says this case "raised the kinds of moral questions with no easy answers that are often on the dockets of courts across America." Having read his essay and considered the evidence, do you agree with or do you have a strong answer to the question of guilt? Explain your answer.

2. What is significant about the age and school grade differential between Carl Kellar and Sean Miller? Explain.

3. During the initial investigation of the death of Kellar, Miller lied several times. In the context of the entire situation, do you believe his explanation of why he lied?

4. What does the reported behavior of Sean Miller during the trial suggest about his guilt, if anything?

5. Is there any suspicion that Kellar may have been strongly under the influence of Miller?

6. How was Kellar portrayed as one who could be largely responsible for what happened?

7. Do you feel that Glaberson was unbiased or biased? Explain.

8. The jurors believed that Kellar was more than 70 percent responsible for his own death. How do you think you would have voted had you been on the jury? What would be your assignment of percentage for responsibility, or guilt?

Study Says Flirtatious Women Get Fewer Raises

DEL JONES

Del Jones is a staff writer for USA Today.

MINDSET

Lock It In

Imagine that you have a management job in the headquarters office of a large company. One day an attractive new employee arrives in a short skirt and low-cut blouse. You know she will be competing against you for upcoming promotions. Should you be concerned?

1   Women who send flirtatious e-mail, wear short skirts or massage a man's shoulders at work win few pay raises and promotions, according to a Tulane University study to be presented Monday at the Academy of Management annual meeting in Honolulu.

2   In the first study to make plain the negative consequences of such behavior, 49 percent of 164 female MBA graduates said in a survey that they have tried to advance in their careers by sometimes engaging in at least one of 10 sexual behaviors, including crossing their legs provocatively or leaning over a table to let men look down their shirts. The other half said they never engaged in such activity, and those women have earned an average of three promotions, versus two for the group that had employed sexuality. Those who said they never used sexuality were, on average, in the $75,000 to $100,000 income range; the others fell, on average, in the next-lowest range, $50,000 to $75,000. The women in the study ranged in age from their mid-20s to 60. The average woman was 43 and had received an MBA 12 years ago.

3   Academic experts have not studied the use of sexual behavior in the workplace. After searching managerial literature, Tulane professor Arthur Brief and colleagues Suzanne Chan-Serafin, Jill Bradley, and Maria Watkins found no evidence showing such behavior to be effective or ineffective. Brief said the research has been limited in scope to sexual harassment. This study is groundbreaking, he said, probably because the topic of workplace sexuality is considered taboo or too lurid for some and too politically incorrect for others.

4   That has created a vacuum filled by those such as Donald Trump, who has advised women to "use those God-given assets" and be sexy, at least to a point. Such statements are not unchallenged, and Dianne Durkin, president of the management company firm Loyalty Factor, says any unprofessional behavior is detrimental to a career. "Cleavage display is not a plus," she says.

5   The Tulane study's findings are statistically significant to professional women looking for advancement, Brief said. The 10 questions, including, "I allow men to linger at certain places of my body while hugging them," were developed from a focus group of women in pharmaceutical sales who said they either employed or witnessed such behavior. Brief said the study goes so far as to suggest that women should even be careful about letting men open doors and lift boxes that aren't particularly heavy, because chivalry is "benevolent sexism" that advances the stereotype that women are vulnerable and weak. "Our story is really a feminist story, because we argue there are negative consequences for women who use sexuality in the workplace," Brief says. But Durkin says the pendulum can swing too far, and praises men for opening doors, says hugs between business friends are OK, and is happy that more feminine attire has replaced the female suit and tie.

6   Almost all the women in the Tulane study who said they used sexual behavior said they did so infrequently. But executive coach Debra Benton, who has long asked business leaders about pros and cons of sexuality in the workplace, said that if a similar survey were given to men, they would say that women use sexuality "all the time." Women need to be aware that when they say, "It's a nice day," men will often conclude "She wants me," Benton says.

EXERCISE 7   Discussion and Critical Thinking

1. Which sentence carries the thesis of this essay?

2. What is the topic, and is the essay mainly one of cause or effect?

3. What kinds of evidence (statistics, examples, testimonials, statements by authorities, reasoning) are used by the author in discussing the effects of using sexuality at the workplace for career advancement?

4. Debra Benton says that "if a similar survey were given to men, they would say that women use sexuality 'all the time'" (paragraph 6). Do you agree that men would respond that way? Why or why not?

5. Do you think men sometimes use sexuality at the workplace? If so, how? If not, what do they use? Do they use macho or intimidating behavior?

6. The subjects of this study had degrees in business management. If the same study were made of those of lesser education and salary, would the results be the same? For example, what if the employees were working at Sears in sales or in a supermarket as a clerk? Discuss.

STUDENT PARAGRAPH AND ESSAY

Writing Process Worksheet

Name Louis Crissman   **Title** My Dad, the Bank Robber   **Due Date** Friday, April 20, 1 p.m.

Use the back of this page or separate paper if you need more space.

Assignment   In the space below, write whatever you need to know about your assignment, including information about the topic, audience, pattern of writing, length, whether to include a rough draft or revised drafts, and whether your paper must be typed.

Write a paragraph of 200 to 300 words about someone you know or know of who has an addiction. It can be chemical or it can be an extreme preoccupation that has caused him or her to lose a sense of balance in relation to values and to others. Submit this completed worksheet, a rough draft, and a final typed draft. Audience: general.

Stage One

Explore Freewrite, brainstorm (list), cluster, or take notes as directed by your instructor.

Causes	*Situation*	*Effects*
inherited	my dad's	fights
work	alcoholism	arguments
social drinking out of control		bad driving
lack of self-control		embarrassed us
worry about money		looked bad
		stomach problems
		lost job
		broke
		robbed piggy bank
		DUI
		accidents
		died

Stage Two

Organize Write a topic sentence or thesis; label the subject and the focus parts.

<u>Drinking</u> <u>took its toll in many ways.</u>
     subject   focus

Write an outline or an outline alternative. For reading-based writing, include references and short quotations with page numbers as support in the outline.

  I. Social
    A. Neighborhood
      1. Argued
      2. Embarrassed us
    B. Home
      1. With Mom
      2. With us
 II. Physical
    A. Appearance
    B. Health
III. Work
    A. Absences
    B. Fired
IV. Loses control
    A. Piggy-bank theft
    B. Accident

Stage Three

Write On separate paper, write and then revise your paragraph or essay as many times as necessary for **c**oherence, **l**anguage (usage, tone, and diction), **u**nity, **e**mphasis, **s**upport, and **s**entences (**CLUESS**). Read your work aloud to hear and correct any grammatical errors or awkward-sounding sentences.

Edit any problems in fundamentals, such as **c**apitalization, **o**missions, **p**unctuation, and **s**pelling (**COPS**).

MY DAD, THE BANK ROBBER
Louis Crissman

Topic sentence
Effect (social)

    Kids of alcoholics almost never think of drunks as funny. Actually I did when my father first became an alcoholic, back when he did not know he was one, and we did not either. Because he could go to work and he could dance without falling down and he could hold conversations without getting angry, he was just a guy who drank too much at times. Then when we learned he was an alcoholic, we kept his secret. At least we thought it was a secret because we did not talk about it. <u>But drinking overtook his life in stages.</u> <u>His dignity went first.</u> He embarrassed us by being drunk at night when he came home and parked crooked on the driveway, fought with neighbors about little things, and argued with Mom about everything. He wanted to help coach my Little League baseball team, but I told him I did not want him to because I knew he would show up drunk and yell at everyone. <u>Then his sickness took over his body.</u> He lost weight, his nose got red with little veins, and his flesh turned puffy. <u>Next he "got laid off" as he put it, but we all knew he was fired for drinking on the job.</u> <u>Finally there was *the* night.</u> I was lying in my bed about midnight when Dad came in. He was carrying a knife, just a kitchen butter knife. I pretended I was not peeking at him. He went to my piggy bank that was loaded mostly with quarters and picked it up as quietly as he could and turned it upside down. Then he stuck the knife in the slot in the piggy's back and shook the bank so quarters slid down the knife blade. He extracted maybe half of them, more than twenty dollars' worth, and heaped them on my baseball glove lying there on the dresser. Then he crammed them into his pocket and slipped away in the night. That was a week before <u>the accident.</u> <u>He killed himself in a smashed car.</u> He hit a tree, not someone else. Mom said it was a blessing. At the funeral we all tried to remember how he was before his compulsion took over. We knew when it started. It started when his drinks became more important than we were or even he was. <u>To kids of alcoholics even those funny little amphibians in the commercials about beer are not really funny.</u>

Effect (physical)

Effect (work)
Effect (personal to author)

Effect (on himself)

Concluding sentence

EXERCISE 8   Discussion and Critical Thinking

1. Does Crissman refer at all to causes?

2. What example does he use?

3. What is the order of presentation?

4. How do you judge the title? Would it have been better or worse if Crissman's father had robbed a commercial bank instead of a piggy bank? Discuss.

READING-BASED WRITING

. . . .

Summary of "Girls Form Backbone of Gangs"

DONNA RAMONE

The assignment for student Donna Ramone was to write a summary of one of the essays assigned for her class. She read the essay by Holly Gilbert, underlined important ideas, and marked passages she might include as short quotations. Her annotations included comments on causes and effects. In summarizing, she identified the passage by title and author, presented the important ideas from the essay, avoided relating her personal experiences or giving her opinions, and used her own wording except for two quotations, which were marked.

Title and author of target piece Thesis	1 "Girls Form Backbone of Gangs" is a report by Holly Gilbert about gangs in Portland, Oregon. It is based primarily on interviews with police officers and youth counselors. Gilbert emphasizes the causes and the effects of girl [the term used throughout the article] gang membership.
Main points as effects Important quotation	2 The males receive most of the benefits. Police officer Dorothy Elmore says, "Girls give the males a place to lay their heads. Girls shelter them. Girls feed them. They protect them. They nurture them. Girls carry their guns and their dope. They are the key" (202). Girls also provide companionship and sex. Their initiation may involve gang rape or having sex with other members. The girls have the babies of the members, dress their children in gang colors, and teach them hand signals and traditions. Sometimes girl gang members actually use the guns they carry and are involved in group crimes.
Main points as effects Short quotation	3 For their services, the girls get boyfriends and a sense of belonging. Even though the girls are sometimes raped and slapped around, they generally seem to expect the abuse as part of the gang culture and accept it as a price to pay for what they believe is "love and emotional fulfillment" (203). They also are left alone with babies when their companion male members go off to jail or prison.
Main point as cause	4 Police officers and counselors agree that girl gang members are enablers and that if they would only refuse to associate with gangs, the gangs would collapse. Nevertheless, there is no organized program in Portland to approach the gang problem by helping girls build their esteem and self-sufficiency so that they can become independent.

Work Cited

Gilbert, Holly. "Girls Form the Backbone of Gangs." *Sentences, Paragraphs, and Beyond.* Ed. Lee Brandon and Kelly Brandon. 2nd ed. Boston: Houghton, 1997. 201–05. Print.

Suggested Topics and Prompts for Writing Cause and Effect

You will find a blank Writing Process Worksheet on page 6 of this book and on your Student Companion Site. It can be photocopied or printed out, filled in, and submitted with your assignment, if your instructor directs you to do so.

READING-BASED WRITING

Reading-based writing requires you to read critically, write a reply that shows you understand what you have read, and give credit for ideas you borrow and words you quote. The form can be a summary, a reaction, or a two-part response (with separated summary and reaction). Documentation, in which you give credit for borrowed ideas and words, can be either formal (MLA) or informal, as directed by your instructor. Both the forms of reading-based writing and documentation are discussed with examples in Chapter 1. Definitions of the three forms follow.

Summary

- The summary is a statement presenting only the main points of what you have read by using different wording without altering the meaning, adding information, or showing bias.
- It is the purest form of reading-based writing.

Reaction

- In the reaction, the meaning of what you have read will be central to the topic sentence of your paragraph or to the thesis of your essay.
- Although the reaction is not a personal narrative by itself, it may include personal experience to explain elements of the text. For example, if your source is about driving styles, your own experiences as a driver or an observer of drivers could be relevant in your analysis of the text.
- The reaction may incorporate a summary to convey a broad view of what you have read, but your summary should never be the main part of your reaction.

Two-Part Response

- The two-part response separates the summary from the reaction.
- This form will give you practice in separating your objective summary in the first part from your more personal evaluation, interpretation, or application in the second part, the reaction.

READING-BASED WRITING TOPICS

"Neighbors from Hell"

1. In a paragraph or an essay of reaction to Christie's account, discuss encounters you have had or have witnessed involving difficult neighbors. Refer to this paragraph and use quotations as you point out differences or similarities in causes and effects.

"The Roots of Happiness: An Empirical Analysis"

2. Write a two-part response to this essay. In the reaction part, discuss the grouping of causes for happiness and then discuss the placement of specific causes and the ranking of those causes. Be specific. Use references and quotations.

3. Write a reaction to the study with special emphasis on three or four causes you would rank differently because of how you feel and what you have observed. Use references and quotations.

"Seeking Justice After a Fatal Spin of the Cylinder"

4. Glaberson says in paragraph 4 that the case raises "the kinds of moral questions with no easy answers." In a focused reaction to this essay explain what the author means by referring specifically to the testimony at the trial. Then discuss whether you agree or disagree with the author on this point. Use references and quotations.

5. Write a summary of this essay. The main points will naturally point to causes and effects.

6. Imagine that you are on the jury and explain in a reaction why you would have voted a particular way. Refer specifically to statements about the trial, mainly the testimony.

"Study Says Flirtatious Women Get Fewer Raises"

7. Write a two-part response. In your reaction, evaluate the essay for logic and thoroughness of investigation. If you are unsatisfied with the quality of the study, explain how you would have proceeded with the study by expanding it, by sharpening the questions, by changing the study group, and so on. Use references and quotations.

8. In a reaction, do your own study of how men use body language for work promotion. Tie it to Jones's study by using references and quotations.

9. In a paragraph of reaction, discuss your view on Donald Trump's observation that women should use their "God-given assets" (perhaps meaning that doing so would provide almost a religious experience for everyone involved?).

"Summary of 'Girls Form Backbone of Gangs'"

10. This essay is a student-written summary. If you have direct or indirect information about this issue, pretend that you have just written the summary and now, in a separate paragraph or short essay, write a reaction, relating it to what you have read, heard, or witnessed regarding females in male gang culture.

GENERAL TOPIC

11. Regard each of the items in the following list as a subject (situation, circumstance, or trend) that has causes and effects. Then determine whether you will concentrate on causes, effects, or a combination. You can probably write a more interesting, well-developed, and therefore successful essay on a topic you can personalize. For example, a discussion about a specific young person who contemplated, attempted, or committed suicide is probably a better topic idea than a general discussion of suicide. If you do not personalize the topic, you will probably have to do some basic research to supply details for development.

a. Attending or completing college

b. Having or getting a job

c. Change in coaches, teachers, officeholder(s)

d. Gambling

e. Moving to another country, state, or home

f. Passing or failing a test or course

g. Early marriage

h. Teenage parenthood

CROSS-CURRICULAR TOPIC

12. From a class that you are taking or have taken, select a subject that is especially concerned with causes and effects and develop a topic. Begin by selecting an event, a situation, or a trend in the class content and make a list of the causes and effects; that procedure will almost immediately show you whether you have a topic you can discuss effectively. Class notes and textbooks can provide you with more specific information. If you use textbooks or other materials, give credit or make copies of the sources. Instructors across the campus may have suggestions for studies of cause and effect. Some areas for your search include history, political science, geology, astronomy, psychology, philosophy, sociology, business, real estate, child development, education, fashion merchandising and design, psychiatric technician program, nursing, police science, fire science, nutrition and food, physical education, and restaurant and food-service management.

CAREER-RELATED TOPICS

13. Discuss the effects (benefits) of a particular product or service on the business community, family life, society generally, a specific group (age, income, interest), or an individual.

14. Discuss the needs (thus the cause of development) by individuals, families, or institutions for a particular product or type of product.

15. Discuss the effects of using a certain approach or philosophy in sales, human resources, or customer service.

WRITER'S GUIDELINES   Cause and Effect

1. Determine whether your topic should mainly inform or mainly persuade, and use the right tone for your purpose and audience.

2. Use listing to brainstorm cause-and-effect ideas. This is a useful form:

Causes	Event, Situation, or Trend	Effects

3. Decide whether to concentrate on causes, effects, or a combination of causes and effects. Many short essays will discuss causes and effects but use one as the framework for the piece. A typical basic outline might look like this:

Thesis:

   I. Cause (or Effect) 1
  II. Cause (or Effect) 2
 III. Cause (or Effect) 3

4. Do not conclude that something is an effect merely because it follows something else.

5. Lend emphasis to your main concern(s), causes, effects, or a combination, by repeating key words, such as *cause*, *reason*, *effect*, *result*, *consequence*, and *outcome*.

6. Causes and effects can be primary or secondary, immediate or remote.

7. The order of causes and effects in your paper may be based on time, space, emphasis, or a combination.

8. Write and revise.

- Write and then revise your paragraph or essay as many times as necessary for **c**oherence, **l**anguage (usage, tone, and diction), **u**nity, **e**mphasis, **s**upport, and **s**entences (**CLUESS**).
- Read your work aloud to hear and correct any grammatical errors or awkward-sounding sentences.
- Edit any problems in fundamentals, such as **c**apitalization, **o**missions, **p**unctuation, and **s**pelling (**COPS**).

STUDENT COMPANION SITE
For additional practice, visit www.cengage .com/devenglish/ brandon/spb6e.

Chapter 23

Comparison and Contrast
Showing Similarities and Differences

FLOW OF WRITING

WHEN TO USE COMPARISON AND CONTRAST

FOR COLLEGE WRITING ASSIGNMENTS

- For good reasons, comparison-and-contrast topics for tests and special assignments are commonplace across the curriculum. They require the student to acquire, organize, and evaluate ideas. The sources on either side of a comparison and contrast may be abundant in the library and especially on the Internet, but usually the precise relationship of ideas must be established by the student writer.

- A comparison-and-contrast statement for a test or special assignment can be a paragraph or an essay.

IN CAREERS AND AT THE WORKPLACE

- At the workplace, employees prepare comparison-and-contrast studies in anticipation of modifying, acquiring, inventing, or discontinuing products, services, or procedures. The forms for such studies are likely to be standardized and computer-generated, but they use many of the same principles presented in this chapter.

- In determining career direction while still in college or on the job you may use comparison and contrast to assess job descriptions, employment opportunities, and personal satisfaction in different fields.

COMPARISON AND CONTRAST IN A CARTOON

THE QUIGMANS   by Buddy Hickerson

BEFORE I ORDER, ARE THERE SUBSTITUTES?

YES, MA'AM.

THEN I'D LIKE HIM!

B. Hickerson, copyright Los Angeles Times Syndicate. Reprinted by permission.

WRITING COMPARISON AND CONTRAST

Comparison and contrast is a method of showing similarities and dissimilarities between subjects. Comparison is concerned with organizing and developing points of similarity; contrast has the same function for dissimilarity. Sometimes a writing assignment may require that you cover only similarities or only dissimilarities. Occasionally, an instructor may ask you to separate one from the other. Usually, you will combine them within the larger design of your paragraph or essay. For convenience, the term *comparison* is sometimes applied to both comparison and contrast, because both use the same techniques and are usually combined into one operation.

This chapter will help you find topics and choose strategies in writing comparison and contrast.

Generating Topics and Working with the 4 *P*'s

Comparison and contrast is basic to your thinking. In your daily activities, you consider similarities and dissimilarities between persons, things, concepts, political leaders, doctors, friends, instructors, schools, nations, classes, movies, and so on. You naturally turn to comparison and contrast to solve problems and to make decisions in your actions and in your writing. Because you have had so many comparative experiences, finding a topic to write about is likely to be only a matter of choosing from a great number of appealing ideas. Freewriting, brainstorming, and clustering will help you generate topics that are especially workable and appropriate for particular assignments.

Many college writing assignments will specify a topic or ask you to choose one from a list. Regardless of the source of your topic, the procedure for developing your ideas by comparison and contrast is the same as the procedure for developing topics of your own choosing. That procedure can be appropriately called the "4 *P's*": *purpose*, *points*, *pattern*, and *presentation*.

PURPOSE

*Cessna 172**

Piper Cherokee†

Purpose indicates what you want to accomplish. Are you trying just to give information about the two parts of your subject, showing how they are similar and dissimilar; or are you trying to argue that one side is better than the other, therefore, ranking the two?

For this unit of instruction, the demonstration paragraph and essay were written by Brittany Markovic when she was a student pilot in the Aeronautics Department at Mt. San Antonio College. Her English instructor provided her with a topic of comparison and contrast about two aspects of something within her intended career field. Markovic selected two training aircraft she had flown: the Piper Cherokee and the Cessna 172. Her purpose was to show that one was better than the other for the beginning pilot.

POINTS

After you determine your purpose, you might brainstorm by listing the points, or ideas, that can be applied somewhat equally to the two parts of your subject. From such a list, you would then select the points that would be most relevant for your purpose.

Here is Brittany Markovic's list for her topic of ranking the Piper Cherokee and the Cessna 172. Notice that she first lists possible points and then selects the ones that relate most directly to her central idea of safety inherent in the features of the two airplanes.

(power)	(design)	landing gear
cabin space	affordability	(fuel system)
air frame	communication devices	steering controls

PATTERN

You will now decide on the better way to organize the points as you apply them somewhat equally to the twin parts of your topic: subject by subject (Figure 23.1) or point by point (Figure 23.2). You will use the same information in each pattern, but the pattern, or organization, will be different. Brittany Markovic chose to use the point-by-point pattern.

See pages 447–448 for an example of a paragraph using a subject-by-subject pattern.

*Cessna 172 image copyright Istvan Csak 2009/Used under license from Shutterstock.com
†Piper Cherokee image copyright Ivan Cholakov Gostock-dot-net 2009/Used under license from Shutterstock.com

Figure 23.1
Subject-by-Subject Pattern

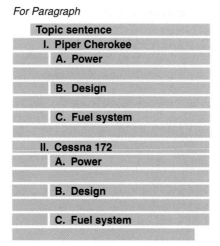

Figure 23.2
Point-by-Point Pattern

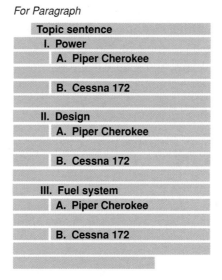

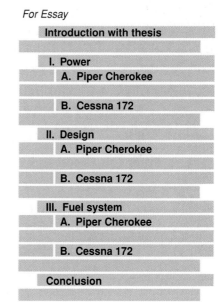

PRESENTATION

For the presentation, you will use your outline (or a list with details) to begin writing your paragraph or essay. For the essay, the Roman numerals in the outline usually indicate topic sentences, and, therefore, paragraphs. The Arabic numerals (details, examples, explanations) indicate more specific support.

The first assignment for Brittany Markovic was a paragraph. Toward the end of the semester she accepted the opportunity to amplify her paragraph into an essay. Both are given here. You will see that the essay allowed her the space to explain her topic in much more detail, but both the paragraph and the essay follow the same basic outline. Annotation in the margins indicate the use of the 4 *P*'s, topic sentences, and transitional devices. Each assignment is **career-related**.

POINT-BY-POINT PATTERN: PARAGRAPH

EVALUATING THE PIPER CHEROKEE AND THE CESSNA 172
Brittany Markovic

Purpose (and topic sentence)
Points

I. Power
  A. Piper Cherokee
  B. Cessna 172

Transition
II. Design
  A. Piper Cherokee
  B. Cessna 172

Transition
III. Fuel system
  A. Piper Cherokee
  B. Cessna 172

Concluding sentence

Pilots, especially new pilots, are divided on their ranking of small training airplanes. Most say the two at the top are the Piper Cherokee and the Cessna 172. As a new pilot who has flown in both, I believe the Cessna 172 is significantly better. All three reasons for my decision—power, design, and fuel system—are tied to safety. Of the three, power is the least decisive point. The Piper has 150 horsepower, and the Cessna has 160. That's not much difference, but in some situations it's crucial, and any pilot would be happy to have that extra 10 if things become "challenging." Next, as for design, some pilots would prefer the sleek Piper with its wing under the fuselage, offering a fine view of the sky above. For me, I like the Cessna, with the wing over the fuselage, allowing me to see the ground easily when I'm landing or taking off. The final point is the fuel delivery system. A pilot wants fuel in the tank and fuel in the carburetor. The Piper Cherokee has a highly rated fuel pump, and for some pilots that may be enough for comfort. But the Cessna 172 has the fuel tank in the wing over the fuselage. The fuel delivery system is "powered" by gravity, something that doesn't malfunction. So I like both the Piper Cherokee and the Cessna 172, but as someone still learning to fly, I feel more secure in the Cessna, and it gets my vote.

POINT-BY-POINT PATTERN: ESSAY

The Piper Cherokee and the Cessna 172

BRITTANY MARKOVIC

As a student pilot and a student in a community college, Brittany Markovic leads a life rich in variety and excitement. She rides to school in an automobile, but her mind is in the skies where she flies training aircraft. This comparison-and-contrast assignment provided her with an opportunity to compare and contrast two aircraft often used in training student pilots.

Subject 1
Subject 2
Thesis and purpose

Topic sentence
  I. Power (Point 1)
    A. Piper Cherokee

    B. Cessna 172

1   When most people think of an airplane, the picture that comes to mind is likely that of a large aircraft such as a Boeing 747. Commercial airlines are what the public is most familiar with, for that is what travelers ordinarily use for long-distance transportation. However, most business handled by airplanes—in fact, about 80 percent of all flights—is done by small planes in what is called general aviation. When a student pilot thinks of an airplane, it is probably a small training plane, the Cessna 172. Later, the student's attention may turn to another small aircraft, the Piper Cherokee. Although either can be used for training, I believe that certain features make the Cessna 172 the better aircraft for the student.

2   For the student at the controls, two key characteristics probably come to mind, all related to movement, namely the power for thrust and the landing speed. In all those respects, the two aircraft are similar. The Piper Cherokee must have enough thrust to lift a maximum of 2,350 pounds at takeoff, for which it has 150 horsepower. Then in landing, the Cherokee should come in at 63 knots. The Cessna 172 has similar ratings: it can

lift 2,400 pounds, has 160 horsepower, and lands at a speed between 60 and 70 knots. All of those factors should be considered in relation to the particular flight. The maximum weight matters little in training flights because they are made without extra passengers and baggage. The landing speeds for the two are also about the same and nonconsequential. The only significant matter is found in the power plant, which favors the Cessna 172 by 10 horsepower, small but in some situations crucial.

Topic sentence   3
  II. Design (Point 2)
    A. Piper Cherokee

    B. Cessna 172

That power and speed, of course, must be seen in relation to the design, of the aircraft, especially the wing placement. For the Piper Cherokee, the wing is mounted below the cockpit. That design allows for great visibility above the aircraft, which, in turn, is better for observing other aircraft and certain weather conditions. The big problem for the student pilot is that the wing-under arrangement partially blocks the pilot's view of the runway. On the contrary, the Cessna 172 features a wing over the fuselage, providing the new pilot with a much appreciated better view of the runway. That design allows the student pilot to more easily master the two most difficult maneuvers: taking off and landing.

Topic sentence   4
  III. Fuel system (Point 3)
    A. Piper Cherokee

    B. Cessna 172

Another point to consider seriously is the fuel system, for the new pilot has enough things to take care of without having to worry about getting gas to the carburetor. In the wing-under Piper Cherokee, the tanks are in the wing, but because the wings are lower than the engine, the fuel must be pushed to the engine by a fuel pump, and a fuel pump may not work. But that possible problem does not exist in the high-wing Cessna 172. It also has its gas tank in the wing; however, because the wing is above the engine, gravity delivers fuel to the carburetor without need of a pump. When it comes to airplanes, less may be more. We all know that gravity is more reliable than a fuel pump.

Cessna 172 better than   5
Piper Cherokee

The first features, the power for thrust and the landing speed, give the Cessna 172 only a slight edge over the Piper Cherokee. But the other two factors are decisive. Better visibility for takeoffs and landings afforded by the high wing and gas delivered by gravity make the Cessna 172 the better aircraft for student pilots.

CAREER-RELATED WRITING AS COMPARISON AND CONTRAST

When "Either-Or" Matters

Imagine you are on a career quest and you have narrowed vocational fields to two. What is your next step? Naturally you will turn to comparing and contrasting. Or imagine you are at your workplace and you have to decide between two products, two services, two management styles, two labor issues, or two employees for advancement. What pattern of thought does your mind shift to? Of course, again it is comparison and contrast.

Using the 4 *P*'s System for Speaking and Writing

If your mind sometimes drifts around—going back and forth, up and down, sideways and other ways—as you compare and contrast, then the ideas that come out of your mouth or your computer printer will be jumbled. If, however, you have a system—say, the 4 *P*'s, with purpose, points, pattern, and presentation—you will have order, and you can avoid needless repetition, overlooked ideas, and wandering thoughts. In both the written and the oral presentation, the 4 *P*'s will provide order and a logical arrangement of ideas. The kind of outline you use in writing serves you equally well in speaking, especially as a framework for PowerPoint presentations. You need only consider your audience, organize your thoughts according to your system, and proceed to communicate. Should this be a competitive situation, you will not be the one left coughing in the winner's trail dust.

The 4 *P*'s as an Academic Gift That Is Portable

In the example shown in the demonstration paragraph and essay on pages 442–443, in which she evaluates the Piper Cherokee and the Cessna 172, student Brittany Markovic writes about aircraft she has flown in a community college aeronautics program. She may continue to fly those models when she moves into her career as a pilot. Her writing is a product comparison. It is a good model for an employee writing a comparative study for the lease or purchase of any vehicle—such as a truck, a pickup, or a forklift. But with little modification it could be a comparison and contrast of two products that are sold or used at a workplace. Markovic was in school when she wrote her essay, but she could just as easily have been already working in aeronautics and studying the same thing concurrently in her college class.

Moreover, the 4 *P*'s system that Markovic employs can be used both in college career-related areas of study and at the workplace, because it fits so many different situations and needs. This flexible, systematic way for organizing ideas is an academic gift that just keeps on giving as you use it in the classroom, use it at your job, and perhaps use it repeatedly for training and retraining, maybe even at the same college.

Transitional Words

Consider using the following transitional words to improve coherence by connecting ideas with ideas, sentences with sentences, and paragraphs with paragraphs.

FOR COMPARISON AND CONTRAST:

Comparison: in the same way, similarly, likewise, also, by comparison, in a like manner, as, with, as though, both, like, just as

Contrast: but, by contrast, in contrast, despite, however, instead, nevertheless, on [to] the contrary, in spite of, still, yet, unlike, even so, rather than, otherwise

FOR ALL PATTERNS OF WRITING: The HOTSHOT CAT words: However, Otherwise, Therefore, Similarly, Hence, On the other hand, Then, Consequently, Also, Thus (See pages 74–75 for additional transitional words.)

FINDING PATTERNS IN PHOTOS

EXERCISE 1   A Text-Based Activity for Groups or Individuals

Smart Car parked beside Hummer

This photo of a Smart Car and a Hummer naturally invites an exercise in using the 4 *P*'s for a comparative study. Keeping your transportation needs and value system in mind and ignoring the purchase price, imagine you are about to buy one of the two vehicles (thereby imposing ranking, or *purpose*). Then proceed to list possible *points*, choosing features you could apply for your evaluation. If your instructor requires, continue with *pattern* and *presentation* as you select three or more of the points and write a paragraph or an essay.

Points, or Features, for Comparative Study

1. _____
2. _____
3. _____
4. _____
5. _____
6. _____

Practicing Patterns of Comparison and Contrast

Shorter compositions such as paragraphs are likely to be arranged subject by subject, and longer compositions such as essays are likely to be arranged point by point, although either pattern can work in either length. In longer works, especially in published writing, the two patterns may be mixed. Being able to organize your material quickly and effectively according to the pattern that is best for your material is important to your success as a writer. Even in a timed assignment, make a simple scratch outline that will guide you in writing a piece that is unified and coherent.

© David Cooper/Toronto Star/ZUMA/Corbis

EXERCISE 2   Completing Patterns of Comparison and Contrast

Fill in the blanks to complete the following outlines.

A. Subject-by-subject pattern

Friends: Marla and Justine

   I. Marla   (subject)

     A. Appearance   (point)

     B. _____   (point)

     C. _____   (point)

   II. Justine   (subject)

     A. _____   (point)

     B. Personality   (point)

     C. _____   (point)

B. Point-by-point pattern

Two bosses: Mr. Santo and Ms. Elliott

   I. Disposition   (point)

     A. Mr. Santo   (subject)

     B. Ms. Elliott   (subject)

   II. Knowledge of _____   (point)

     A. _____   (subject)

     B. Ms. Elliott   (subject)

  III. _____   (point)

     A. Mr. Santo   (subject)

     B. _____   (subject)

C. Subject-by-subject pattern

Two schools you have attended (or another approved topic)

   I. _____   (subject)

     A. _____   (point)

     B. _____   (point)

     C. _____   (point)

   II. _____   (subject)

     A. _____   (point)

     B. _____   (point)

     C. _____   (point)

D. Point-by-point pattern

Two jobs you have had (or another approved topic)

I. _____   (point)

   A. _____   (subject)

   B. _____   (subject)

II. _____   (point)

   A. _____   (subject)

   B. _____   (subject)

III. _____   (point)

   A. _____   (subject)

   B. _____   (subject)

Readings for Critical Thinking, Discussion, and Writing

READING STRATEGIES AND OBJECTIVES

Underlining and annotating these reading selections will help you answer the questions that follow the selections, discuss the material in class, and prepare for reading-based writing assignments. As you underline and annotate, pay special attention to the author's writing skills, logic, and message, and consider the relevance of the material to your own experiences and values.

Some selections begin with a Mindset suggestion that can help you create a readiness for connecting with what you are about to read.

PARAGRAPH

The Temple and the Cathedral

LOUISE DUDLEY AND AUSTIN FARICY

Buildings do more than serve as shelter and objects of beauty. They also reflect a society's values and aspirations. Louise Dudley and Austin Faricy show that it is not a matter of chance that the Greek temple and the medieval cathedral have certain characteristics.

The Greek temple is classic and the medieval cathedral is romantic. Both are religious edifices, but they show a difference in the attitudes that created them, a difference far deeper than the dissimilarities of construction and mechanics. The Greek temple is hard, bright, exact, calm and complete; the walls and the columns are no higher than will stand of their own strength; the lintels and the roof are simple, sane, and sensible. Nothing more is attempted than can be accomplished and the result is a perfect building, finished and finite. Anyone can understand its main construction at a glance. The Gothic cathedral, on the other hand, is built on the principle of balance. The openings are not made with lintels but are arched. One stone is held in place only by its relation to the other stones. The walls will not stand alone; they must be buttressed. As the walls go higher the arches become more pointed, the roof becomes steeper, and the buttresses are strengthened with pinnacles and flying buttresses, the whole so carefully and cleverly balanced that a fault in one stone might cause a wall or even the entire building to collapse. The whole cannot be grasped at a glance; one is conscious only of its great complexity, its infinite variety, its striving upward and beyond.

EXERCISE 3   Discussion and Critical Thinking

1. Does this selection stress comparison or contrast?

2. Is the purpose mainly to inform or to persuade?

3. What are the points (there may be only one) in this study?

4. Is the pattern mainly subject by subject or point by point? Make a simple outline of the pattern here.

ESSAYS
. . . .

From B'wood to the 'Hood

RYAN J. SMITH

A Los Angeles Times *researcher, Ryan J. Smith writes about living on the different sides of town: South Los Angeles and the Westside. His relocation is more than geography. This article was published in the* Los Angeles Times *on February 19, 2006.*

MINDSET

Lock It In

Imagine you have had a change in fortune and are now about to return to your roots. How do you expect to feel there?

1   When I broke the news to my mother that I was moving from Brentwood to the 'hood, she immediately began praying for my protection. When I told friends and colleagues at work of my planned move toward South L.A., they would pause and whisper, "Oh." Not just any "Oh," mind you, but one freighted with "Good luck, hope you don't get shot." Strangers thought I was living out the pilgrimage of a young black man who, after a stint on the "outside," was returning to his roots.

2   That couldn't be further from the truth. I was raised by my mother in Culver City before it became "on the Westside." I attended UCLA and settled in

Brentwood after graduation. But I needed to escape a bad roommate situation, and my father, separated from my mom, offered me his vacant apartment near Jefferson Park in the Crenshaw district.

3   At first I thought I couldn't survive a move south. I'd tried the 'hood in the early 1990s, when the movie "Malcolm X" came out and my mother decided I needed to know "my people." So I bypassed my usual summer YMCA experience for a camp close to Baldwin Village known as "the Jungles" because of the rampant gang activity nearby. I was called everything in the book. "Why do you talk so white, white boy?" was a frequent question as I was being punched. At night, I cried, but I never told Mom about my camp experiences. One day, though, she coyly smiled and asked, "Black folks sure can be mean, can't they?"

4   Older, more culturally aware and growing ever more desperate to leave Brentwood, I decided to face my childhood demons and take my father up on his offer. The area seemed no different than other urban landscapes in Los Angeles. But adjustments needed to be made. I soon got used to the nighttime "ghettobirds" (helicopters) that plagued the community, and the annoying chime of ice cream trucks that made their neighborhood rounds at midnight. To better fit in, I walked around with a no-nonsense 'hood face— which only made it more obvious that I was not from the neighborhood.

5   "Why did you do that, baby? You have to make sure all your doors are locked!" Aunt Cathy playfully chided me when I told her I didn't regularly lock my car. Note to self: Lock everything! My parents also reminded me of the do's and don'ts when (not if) the police pulled me over. Their advice came in handy one Halloween night when two officers cuffed me and put me in the back of a squad car while they scanned my nonexistent record. Only my embarrassing temptation to blurt out that I grew up on the Westside contained my rage.

6   More discomfiting than the dangers I have to be wary of are the conveniences I miss. I yearn for Jamba Juice and La Salsa—anything but Jack in the Box or McDonald's. A privilege I took for granted—anytime access to an ATM—ends after 10 p.m. on Crenshaw Boulevard. Nighttime jogging is also out in my new neighborhood. But the Magic Johnson theater at Baldwin Hills Crenshaw Plaza is as good as the Century City cineplex. The smothered chicken and greens at Chef Marilyn's 99-Cents-and-Up Soul Food Express makes me quickly forget the lack of sushi eateries nearby. My neighbors ask how my family and I are doing, a social custom rare on the Westside.

7   I also have become reacquainted with my younger half-brother, who lives nearby. After being shot in a gang altercation, he speaks of his struggle to stay off the streets. His dreams are often tarnished by his quest to avoid jail, drugs and death—a story I hear from too many young men his age.

8   Far more consequential, my color is not what defines me. I'm not seen as a tall black guy, lanky black man or the loud black dude. No woman clutches her purse when she sees me approaching. No walker quickens his step when I am spotted behind him. No one rushes to open a door when I walk down a hall. In my mostly black and Latino neighborhood, my race is no longer a prelude to my being.

9   I don't ache for the conveniences and glamour of my former "home." I drink coffee in Leimert Park. I cruise Crenshaw Boulevard instead of Pacific Coast Highway, enjoying the comforts of my newfound home—doors locked, of course.

EXERCISE 4   Discussion and Critical Thinking

1. What is Smith's subject of this comparison and contrast?

2. What is his purpose?

3. Does Smith use a point-by-point or a subject-by-subject pattern?

4. What points does he use for his comparison and contrast?

   I.
     A.
     B.
   II.
     A.
     B.
   III.
     A.
     B.
   IV.
     A.
     B.
   V.
     A.
     B.

5. In his conclusion (last paragraph), does Smith seem to prefer the Westside or South Los Angeles for a home neighborhood? Discuss.

A Mixed Tex-Cal Marriage

JOSÉ ANTONIO BURCIAGA

A distinguished publisher and writer, José Antonio Burciaga died in 1996, leaving his readers a rich legacy of poems, short stories, and essays. He was a Chicano cultural activist, muralist, humorist, and founding member of the comedy group Culture Clash. His Undocumented Love *won the Before Columbus American Book Award for poetry in 1992. This essay, about him and his wife, is included in his book* Drink Cultura *(1993).*

MINDSET

Lock It In

We all carry around a bag of stereotypes that we often open up for our first reactions to whatever we encounter. For example, what do you think of first when you hear the term *mixed marriage*?

1   According to Cecilia, my wife, we have a mixed marriage. She's from California, I'm from Texas. Though we have no regrets, this truly proves that love is blind.

2   When Cecilia and I first met, we thought we had a lot in common. As young, professional Chicanos in Washington, D.C., we both supported the United Farm Workers' grape and lettuce boycotts, the Coors boycott, the Gallo Wine

boycott, the Farah Pants boycott, and the Frito Bandido boycott. We still boycott some of those items, for many reasons: health, habit, nostalgia or plain, ordinary guilt if we indulged in any of these.

3   As first-generation Mexican-Americans, we both spoke *Español*, graduated from Catholic schools, and had similar politics.

4   But, as we were soon to discover, the vast desert that separates Texas and California also differentiates the culture and style of Chicanos. Because we met far from Texas and California, we had no idea at first of the severity of our differences.

5   We both liked enchiladas—the same enchiladas, I thought, until the first time Cecilia prepared them. They looked like enchiladas, and they smelled like enchiladas. And then I bit into one.

6   "These are good, *corazón*," I said. "But these are *entomatadas*. They have more tomato than chile. *Mí Mamá* used to make them all the time."

7   She threw me a piquant stare as I chewed away. "Hmmm, they're great!" I stressed through a mouthful.

8   Californians, like her parents who immigrated from the coastal state of Jalisco, Mexico, use more tomatoes than Texans like my parents, who came from the central states of Durango and Zacatecas and use more chiles.

9   Cecilia grew up with white *menudo*, tripe soup. White menudo? How could anyone eat colorless menudo? And not put hominy in it? Ours was red-hot and loaded with hominy. In Texas, we ate our menudo with bread. In California, it's with tortillas. Texas flour tortillas are thick and tasty, California flour tortillas are so thin you can see through them.

10   She didn't particularly like my Tony Lama boots or my country-western and Tex-Mex musical taste. I wasn't that crazy about Beach Boys music or her progressive, California-style country-western.

11   In California, the beach was relatively close for Cecilia. On our first date she asked how often I went to the beach from El Paso. Apparently, geography has never been a hot subject in California schools. That's understandable considering the sad state of education, especially geography, in this country. But in Texas, at one time the biggest state in the union, sizes and distances are most important.

12   In answer to Cecilia's question, I explained that to get to the closest beach from El Paso, I had to cross New Mexico, Arizona and California to reach San Diego. That's 791 freeway miles. The closest Texas beach is 841 freeway miles to the Gulf of Mexico.

13   Back when we were courting, California Chicanos saw *Texanos* as a little too *Mexicano*, still wet behind the ears, not assimilated enough, and speaking with either thick Spanish accents or "Taxes acksaints."

14   Generally speaking, Texanos saw their *Califas* counterparts as too weird, knowing too little if any Spanish and with speech that was too Anglicized.

15   After our marriage we settled in neutral Alexandria, Virginia, right across the Potomac from the nation's capital. We lived there a couple of years, and when our firstborn came, we decided to settle closer to home. But which home, Califas or Texas? In El Paso we wouldn't be close to the beach, but I thought there was an ocean of opportunity in that desert town. There was some Texas pride and machismo, to be sure. It was a tug-of-war that escalated to the point of seeking advice, and eventually I had to be realistic and agree that California had better opportunities. In El Paso, the opportunities in my field were nonexistent.

16   The rest is relative bliss. Married since 1972, I'm totally spoiled and laid-back in Northern Califas, but I still miss many of those things we took for granted in Texas, or Washington, D.C.—the seasonal changes, the snow, the heat, heating systems, autumn colors, and monsoon rains; the smell of the desert after a rain, the silence and serenity of the desert, the magnified

17   sounds of a fly or cricket, distant horizons uncluttered by trees, and the ability to find the four directions without any problem. I do miss the desert and, even more, the food. El Paso *is* the Mexican-food capital of this country.

Today, I like artichokes and appreciate a wide variety of vegetables and fruits. I even like white, colorless menudo and hardly ever drink beer. I drink wine, but it has to be a dry Chardonnay or Fume Blanc although a Pinot Noir or Cabernet Sauvignon goes great with meals. Although I still yearn for an ice cold Perla or Lone Star beer from Texas once in a while, Califas is my home now—mixed marriage and all.

EXERCISE 5   Discussion and Critical Thinking

1. Which sentence states the thesis most emphatically (see paragraph 1)? Copy it here.

2. In paragraphs 6 through 15, what are the three points used for comparison and contrast?

3. In paragraphs 16 and 17, Burciaga discusses how he has changed. In what ways does that imply comparison and contrast?

4. Because all of us are culturally complex, being the products of many cultures, we frequently blend and clash with others in matters of age, ethnicity, gender, sexual preferences, religion, and so on. As for the broad concept of "mixed marriage," were Cecilia and José fairly typical compared with other marriage partners you know? Do you have some examples of those more extreme and less extreme? You might also discuss this topic in connection with friendships you have or know about.

STUDENT PARAGRAPH AND ESSAY
. . . .

FLOW OF WRITING

Writing Process Worksheet

Name _Charles Yang_   **Title** _Chinese Parents and American Parents_   **Due Date** _Tuesday, March 27, 1 p.m._

Use the back of this page or separate paper if you need more space.

Assignment   In the space below, write whatever you need to know about your assignment, including information about the topic, audience, pattern of writing, length, whether to include a rough draft or revised drafts, and whether your paper must be typed.

Compare and contrast two kinds of families according to parenting styles. The styles may come from cultural backgrounds or individual philosophies. Submit this completed worksheet, a rough draft marked for revision, and a typed final draft of about 250 words.

Stage One

Explore Freewrite, brainstorm (list), cluster, or take notes as directed by your instructor.

Chinese
—showing love
—saying "I'm sorry"
—attitude toward school
—teaching right from wrong

American
—showing love
—saying "I'm sorry"
—attitude toward school
—teaching right from wrong

Stage Two

Organize Write a topic sentence or thesis; label the subject and the focus parts.

<u>Parents from different cultures</u> <u>have different ways of expressing love</u>.
　　　　　subject　　　　　　　　　　　　　　　　　focus

Write an outline or an outline alternative. For reading-based writing, include references and short quotations with page numbers as support in the outline.

I. Chinese
　　A. Way of relating to children
　　B. Way of guiding children
II. American
　　A. Way of relating to children
　　B. Way of guiding children

Stage Three

Write On separate paper, write and then revise your paragraph or essay as many times as necessary for **c**oherence, **l**anguage (usage, tone, and diction), **u**nity, **e**mphasis, **s**upport, and **s**entences (**CLUESS**). Read your work aloud to hear and correct any grammatical errors or awkward-sounding sentences.

Edit any problems in fundamentals, such as **c**apitalization, **o**missions, **p**unctuation, and **s**pelling (**COPS**).

CHINESE PARENTS AND AMERICAN PARENTS
Charles Yang

Topic sentence

I. Chinese

　　We Chinese are brought up with the idea that all parents are good. Therefore, I never doubt the love my parents feel for me. <u>However, now that I am in the United States, I can see that parents from different cultures have different ways of expressing love</u>. The Chinese way is protective and directive. Chinese parents express their love by caring about what their children are becoming. They seldom say "I love you" to their children because within our traditional culture it would be undignified to do so. They also do not want to say they are sorry because that might imply that they have been bad parents. They want their children to be well educated so that they will be successful as adults. They are strict in teaching right from wrong, and they dictate the highest standards of achievement in school, often even selecting career paths

II. American

for their children. The American parents, on the other hand, treat their children differently. They are more open with them and more democratic. They say "I love you" and even "I'm sorry." They give their children many choices about studying and choosing careers. They try to teach their children how to make good choices and how to be personally responsible. Thus, in many cases, the American children have greater opportunities than Chinese to be what they wish. American pressure is especially from within, and Americans delight in "finding" themselves. Chinese children respond well to the pressure from their families and statistically do better on tests and in

Concluding sentence — qualifying for top universities. Both Chinese and American parents love their children, but each culture provides its own expression.

EXERCISE 6   Discussion and Critical Thinking

1. Is the purpose of this comparison and contrast to inform or to convince?

2. Is this paragraph organized as point by point or subject by subject?

3. What are the main points in Yang's study?

4. Does Yang seem to express a preference for one type of family? Explain.

5. Do you think Yang will embrace the traditional Chinese family attitudes or the typical American ones when he has his own family? Explain.

6. As a point of logic, when Yang refers to "Chinese parents," "Chinese children," "American parents," and "American children," does he overgeneralize? If he does overgeneralize, how does that flaw in logic damage his paragraph?

7. Who are the Americans?

READING-BASED WRITING
. . . .

The Orderly, the Disorderly, and the Illogical: A Two-Part Response to "The Messy Are in Denial"

BILL WALKER

Bill Walker's assignment was to read "The Messy Are in Denial" by Joyce Gallagher and to write a two-part response. The summary part would show Walker's understanding of the main ideas. The reaction part would present his evaluation of the ideas. The topic was a good one for him because he could easily relate to the subject material. Note that he follows a simple progression: What does the text mean? How logical is it? How does it relate to my experience? The last paragraph includes Walker's comparison and contrast.

Summary

Text identification
Thesis

1   In "The Messy Are in Denial" Joyce Gallagher explains that there are two kinds of people, the orderly and the disorderly. She discusses them according to their state of mind, behavior, and group history.

Topic sentence

Quotation

2   As for state of mind, the disorganized people live for tomorrow. They are the daydreamers and seers. They can be creative, sometimes as "artists" and "musicians," but also "flakes" (285). The orderly, on the other hand, are practical people who put things and keep things in order.

Topic sentence

Quotation

3   Their behavior is consistent with their state of mind. The disorderly collect all kinds of items and do not throw them away. They "run the risk of inundating themselves with their own junk" (285). The orderly are the opposite. They throw things away, clean up, and organize. They make life possible for the disorganized. The author is married to a disorganized person. She understands his nature and her purpose.

Topic sentence

4   Gallagher says that historically these two groups have evolved according to natural selection. She reasons that Neanderthals were too disorganized and were replaced by the better-organized *homo sapiens*, who are comparatively neat. She says artists' drawings show the Neanderthals to be messy and poorly dressed. She imagines that throughout history the organized have helped the disorganized in their daily lives.

Reaction

Text identification
Thesis

5   In "The Messy Are in Denial," Joyce Gallagher has written a mostly thoughtful and often-funny essay. The main flaw in her reasoning is that she gives the impression that people can be grouped as "either/or." One group is organized and neat; the other is disorganized and messy. Those groups do exist, but they are at the extremes. People can tend toward being messy without being really sloppy and disorganized. The people who cannot throw anything away are sometimes called pack rats. They actually have a
Author's experience for explanation
psychological problem, and some receive treatment for the condition. They may have a room full of newspapers and another full of candy wrappers. Other people are at the other end of the spectrum. They cannot stand anything out of order. They will walk across the room of another person's house and straighten a napkin. I have a neighbor who actually vacuums her driveway to free it of dust. Those people are the germaphobes and other obsessive-compulsives of the world. They are so concerned about order that they can hardly function in society. Between those two groups on the fringes are those of us who just have a tendency toward messiness or neatness. Even then, some people are neat about one thing—their dress or car—and messy about something else—their yard or home.

Brief summary

Quotation

Quotation

6   If we are close to the disorganized fringe group on the scale, we may very well need help from someone from the organized fringe group. Gallagher says her husband brings home mass quantities of junk from yard sales and she donates it to charitable institutions. Her job is "to offset every shopping binge of the sloppy" (285). Yet one may balance the other. She even mentions that the disorganized may be "lovable flakes" (285).

Author's brief comparison and contrast

7   Gallagher is wrong in not considering the huge middle group of people, but she has made me laugh at and think about things in my home life. My wife tends toward the organized, and I tend toward the disorganized. She makes our home livable, and I provide variety and keep away the monotony. After reading "The Messy Are in Denial," I have become more

aware that both my wife and I do not give each other enough credit for our differences. In appreciation of her neatness, this weekend I will go out to a yard sale and buy her some fine presents.

Work Cited

Gallagher, Joyce. "The Messy Are in Denial." *Paragraphs and Essays: A Worktext with Readings.* Ed. Lee Brandon. 9th ed. Boston: Houghton, 2005. 284–86. Print.

Suggested Topics and Prompts for Writing Comparison and Contrast

STUDENT COMPANION SITE
For additional practice, visit www.cengage .com/devenglish/ brandon/spb6e.

You will find a blank Writing Process Worksheet on page 6 of this book and on your Student Companion Site. It can be photocopied or printed out, filled in, and submitted with your assignment, if your instructor directs you to do so.

READING-BASED WRITING

Reading-based writing requires you to read critically, write a reply that shows you understand what you have read, and give credit for ideas you borrow and words you quote. The form can be a summary, a reaction, or a two-part response (with separated summary and reaction). Documentation, in which you give credit for borrowed ideas and words, can be either formal (MLA) or informal, as directed by your instructor. Both the forms of reading-based writing and documentation are discussed with examples in Chapter 1. Definitions of the three forms follow.

Summary

- The summary is a statement presenting only the main points of what you have read by using different wording without altering the meaning, adding information, or showing bias.
- It is the purest form of reading-based writing.

Reaction

- In the reaction, the meaning of what you have read will be central to the topic sentence of your paragraph or to the thesis of your essay.
- Although the reaction is not a personal narrative by itself, it may include personal experience to explain elements of the text. For example, if your source is about driving styles, your own experiences as a driver or an observer of drivers could be relevant in your analysis of the text.
- The reaction may incorporate a summary to convey a broad view of what you have read, but your summary should never be the main part of your reaction.

Two-Part Response

- The two-part response separates the summary from the reaction.
- This form will give you practice in separating your objective summary in the first part from your more personal evaluation, interpretation, or application in the second part, the reaction.

READING-BASED WRITING TOPICS

"From B'wood to the 'Hood"

1. If you have lived in two different (culturally, economically, socially) parts of a city and struggled with your own adjustments, write about those experiences. Consider trailer-park units and townhouses, company houses and private neighborhoods, barrios and places like Smith's Westside, apartment buildings and private homes, car or camper living and house living, and homeless living and home (of any kind) living. Refer to and quote from the article by Smith to connect his insights with yours, in either agreement or disagreement.

2. Write a two-part response to Smith's essay. Separate your summary from your reaction in which you evaluate his views or relate them to your own experiences. Use quotations and direct references.

"A Mixed Tex-Cal Marriage"

3. Using the structural points and insights of this essay for direction, write about a marriage or relationship between two individuals who are significantly different from each other. Consider making a list of their possible differences (such as religion; education; country, regional, city, or suburban background; politics; ethnicity; and preferences for food, activities, or behavior). In your discussion, do not overlook the common characteristics that have brought and kept them together, and briefly discuss how each person has compromised. Explain how your subject couple is different from and similar to Burciaga and his wife. Use references and quotations.

4. Write a two-part response to Burciaga's essay. In your reaction, explain how Burciaga makes a powerful and colorful statement that does much to counteract the stereotyping of ethnic groups, saying in effect, "He's just like the rest of us." Document it.

"Chinese Parents and American Parents"

5. Write a reaction to Yang's paragraph in which you examine it for logic. He writes about "Chinese parents" and "Chinese children" and about "American parents" and "American children." Does he overgeneralize? What are the differences among Chinese parents and among children living in America, especially those from different generations and from different social and economic groups? Are the differences among Americans, parents and children, also likely to be significant? Moreover, how do you think Yang defines "American"? To what extent does his failure to qualify words damage his paragraph, which happens to provide some good insights and is related with remarkable balance of preference?

"The Orderly, the Disorderly, and the Illogical"

6. Use ideas about orderly and disorderly people found in Walker's two-part response to write a comparison-and-contrast paragraph or essay about a neat person and a messy person. Refer to and quote from Walker's response.

GENERAL TOPICS

7. Write a paragraph or an essay of comparison and contrast about two churches or temples as you explain how their structures reflect different religious views of what human beings are and what they should be. For a useful model of form on a similar subject, review "The Temple and the Cathedral" on pages 447–448.

8. Write a paragraph or an essay of comparison and contrast about how the design and structure of a particular mall versus randomly spaced or a cluster of neighborhood stores in terms of how they represent different attitudes toward what society wants and needs. Include your views on what you think is best. For a useful model of form on a similar subject, review "The Temple and the Cathedral" on pages 447–448.

9. Narrow one of the following topics for a paragraph or short essay. For example, "Methods of Disciplining Children" may be too broad, but "Two Parents, Two Styles of Discipline," with names given, might work well.

   a. Romantic attachments

   b. Methods of disciplining children

   c. Courage and recklessness

   d. Hope and expectations

   e. Relatives

   f. Passive student and active student

   g. Two dates

   h. Two bosses

   i. Married and living together

   j. Two malls

CROSS-CURRICULAR TOPICS

10. In the field of your interest or involvement, compare and contrast two theories, two prominent people, two practices, two products, or two services.

11. In the fields of nutritional science and health, compare and contrast two diets, two exercise programs, or two pieces of exercise equipment.

12. Compare and contrast your field of study (or one aspect of it) as it existed some time ago (specify the years) and as it is now. Refer to new developments and discoveries, such as scientific breakthroughs and technological advances.

CAREER-RELATED TOPICS

13. Select two competing businesses, such as Home Depot and Lowes, and write a paragraph or an essay to show that one is better. Support should come from your experience, independent judgment, and, perhaps, from the

Internet or library sources. Use points that apply somewhat equally to both businesses. You will see that those are the same kinds of points that would be used as talking points for a PowerPoint presentation at the workplace. For a helpful model for form, review the paragraph and the essay on the Piper Cherokee and the Cessna 172 on pages 442–443.

14. Write a paragraph or an essay on two cars, two pickups, or two motorcycles to show that one is better than the other for particular needs or purposes (such as everyday driving or certain kinds of work or recreation). Use the Internet or library sources to collect specific information. Give credit to your source(s). For a helpful model for form and similar subject material, review the paragraph and the essay on the Piper Cherokee and the Cessna 172 on pages 442–443.

15. Compare and contrast two products or services, with the purpose of showing that one is better.

16. Compare and contrast two management styles or two working styles.

17. Compare and contrast the operations of a public school and a business.

18. Compare and contrast the operations of an athletic team and a business.

WRITER'S GUIDELINES   Comparison and Contrast

1. Work with the 4 *P*'s:
   - *Purpose*: Decide whether you want to inform (show relationships) or to persuade (show that one side is better).
   - *Points*: Decide which ideas you will apply to each side. Consider beginning by making a list to select from. Order can be based on time, space, or emphasis.
   - *Pattern*: Decide whether to use subject-by-subject or point-by-point organization.
   - *Presentation*: Decide to what extent you should develop your ideas. Use references to the other side to make connections and use examples and details to support your views.

2. Your basic subject-by-subject outline will probably look like this:

   I. Subject 1
      A. Point 1
      B. Point 2
      C. Point 3
   II. Subject 2
      A. Point 1
      B. Point 2
      C. Point 3

3. Your basic point-by-point outline will probably look like this:

   I. Point 1
      A. Subject 1
      B. Subject 2

II. Point 2
    A. Subject 1
    B. Subject 2
III. Point 3
    A. Subject 1
    B. Subject 2

4. Use the *4 P*'s for cross-curricular and career-related writing.

- Adapt it for different topics.
- Use the outline entries for points in PowerPoint.

5. Write and revise.

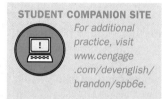

- Write and then revise your paragraph or essay as many times as necessary for **c**oherence, **l**anguage (usage, tone, and diction), **u**nity, **e**mphasis, **s**upport, and **s**entences (**CLUESS**). Read your work aloud to hear and correct any grammatical errors or awkward-sounding sentences.
- Edit any problems in fundamentals, such as **c**apitalization, **o**missions, **p**unctuation, and **s**pelling (**COPS**).

Chapter 24

Argument
Writing to Persuade

FLOW OF WRITING

WHEN TO USE ARGUMENT

FOR COLLEGE WRITING ASSIGNMENTS

- You will use argument and persuasion in all college writing—paragraphs, essays, tests, reports, and research papers—that require you to discuss and support your views on topics about which others may disagree or reluctantly follow.
- You may argue that a theory in biology is sound, that a system in philosophy is inadequate, or that a short story in literature is flawed.
- You may persuade in nursing that a particular diet or exercise program is desirable.

IN CAREERS AND AT THE WORKPLACE

- Business and other institutions require persuasive and argumentative writing in memos to employers and fellow employees about team standards, in proposals to clients about projects, in promotional material about selling items and services, and in application letters about getting hired.

THE QUIGMANS   by Buddy Hickerson

B. Hickerson, copyright Los Angeles Times Syndicate. Reprinted by permission.

PERSUASION AND ARGUMENT DEFINED

Persuasion is a broad term. When we persuade, we try to influence people to think in a certain way or to do something. **Argument** is persuasion on a topic about which reasonable people disagree. Argument involves controversy. Whereas exercising appropriately is probably not controversial because reasonable people do not dispute the idea, an issue such as gun control is. In this chapter we will be concerned mainly with the kind of persuasion that involves argument.

COMPONENTS OF ARGUMENT

Statements of argument are informal or formal. An opinion column in a newspaper is likely to have little set structure, whereas an argument in college writing is likely to be tightly organized. Nevertheless, the opinion column and the college paper have much in common. Both provide a proposition, which is the main point of the argument, and both provide support, which is the evidence or the reasons that back up the proposition.

For a well-structured paragraph or essay, an organizational plan is desirable. Consider these elements when you write, and ask yourself the following questions as you develop your ideas.

Background: What is the historical or social context for this controversial issue?

Proposition (the topic sentence of a paragraph of argument and the thesis of an essay): What do I want my audience to believe or to do?

Qualification of proposition: Can I limit my proposition so that those who disagree cannot easily challenge me with exceptions? If, for example, I am in favor of using animals for scientific experimentation, am I concerned only with medical experiments or with any use, including that pertaining to the cosmetic industry?

Refutation (taking the opposing view into account, mainly to point out its fundamental weakness): What is the view on the other side, and why is it flawed in reasoning or evidence?

Support: In addition to sound reasoning, can I use appropriate facts, examples, statistics, and opinions of authorities?

The basic form for a paragraph or an essay of argument includes the proposition (the topic sentence) and support. The support sentences are, in effect, *because* statements; that is, the proposition is valid *because* of the support. Your organization should look something like this:

Proposition (topic sentence): It is time to pass a national law restricting smoking in all public places.

   I. Discomfort of the nonsmoker (support 1)

   II. Health of the nonsmoker (support 2)

   III. Cost to the nation (support 3)

KINDS OF EVIDENCE

In addition to sound reasoning generally, you can use these kinds of evidence: facts, examples, statistics, and authorities.

First, you can offer facts. Martin Luther King Jr. was killed in Memphis, Tennessee, on April 4, 1968. Because an event that has happened is true and can be verified, this statement about King is a fact. But that James Earl Ray acted alone in killing King is, to some, questionable. That King was the greatest of all civil rights leaders is also opinion because it cannot be verified.

Some facts are readily accepted because they are general knowledge—you and your reader know them to be true, because they can be or have been verified. Other "facts" are based on personal observation and are reported in various publications but may be false or questionable. You should always be concerned about the reliability of the source for both the information you use and the information used by those with other viewpoints. Still other so-called facts are genuinely debatable because of their complexity or the incompleteness of the knowledge available.

Second, you can cite examples. Keep in mind that you must present a sufficient number of examples and that the examples must be relevant.

Third, you can present statistics. Statistics are numerical facts and data that are classified and tabulated to present significant information about a given subject.

Avoid presenting a long list of figures; select statistics carefully and relate them to things familiar to your reader. The millions of dollars spent on a war in a single week, for example, become more comprehensible when expressed in terms of what the money would purchase in education, highways, or urban renewal.

To test the validity of statistics, either yours or your opponent's, ask: Who gathered them? Under what conditions? For what purpose? How are they used?

Fourth, you can cite evidence from, and opinions of, authorities. Most readers accept facts from recognized, reliable sources—governmental publications, standard reference works, and books and periodicals published by established firms. In addition, they will accept evidence and opinions from individuals who, because of their knowledge and experience, are recognized as experts.

Transitional Words

Consider using the following transitional words to improve coherence by connecting ideas with ideas, sentences with sentences, and paragraphs with paragraphs.

FOR ARGUMENT: it follows that, as a result, causes taken collectively, as a concession, even though, of course, in the context of, in the light of, in the final analysis, following this, further, as additional support, moreover, consequently, according to, in support of, contrary to

FOR ALL PATTERNS OF WRITING: The H̲OT̲S̲H̲OT̲ C̲AT̲ words: H̲owever, O̲therwise, T̲herefore, S̲imilarly, H̲ence, O̲n the other hand, T̲hen, C̲onsequently, A̲lso, T̲hus (See pages 74–75 for additional transitional words.)

LOGICAL FALLACIES

Certain flawed patterns in thought, commonly called **logical fallacies**, are of primary concern in critical thinking.

These are among the most common logical fallacies:

1. ***Post hoc, ergo propter hoc*** (After this, therefore because of this): When one event precedes another in time, the first is assumed to cause the other.

   "I knew I'd have a day like this when I saw that black cat run across the driveway this morning."

   "See what I told you. We elected him president, and now we have high inflation."

2. **False analogy**: False analogies ignore differences and stress similarities, often in an attempt to prove something.

   "A person has to get a driver's license because unqualified drivers could have bad effects on society. Therefore, couples should also have to get a license to bear children because unqualified parents can produce delinquent children."

   "The leader of that country is a mad dog dictator, and you know what you do with a mad dog. You get a club and kill it."

3. **Hasty generalization**: This is a conclusion based on too few reliable instances.

"Everyone I've met this morning is going to vote for the incumbent. The incumbent is going to win."

"How many people did you meet?"

"Three."

4. **False dilemma**: This fallacy presents the reader with only two alternatives from which to choose. The solution may lie elsewhere.

"Now, only two things can be done with the school district. You either shut it down now or let it go bankrupt."

"The way I see it, you either bomb them back into the Stone Age or let them keep on pushing us around."

5. *Argumentum ad hominem* (Arguing against the person): This is the practice of abusing and discrediting your opponent instead of keeping to the main issues of the argument.

"Who cares what he has to say? After all, he's a wild-eyed liberal who has been divorced twice."

"Let's put aside the legislative issue for one moment and talk about the person who proposed it. For one thing he's a southerner. For another he's Catholic. Enough said."

EXERCISE 1   Critical Thinking

Each of the following sentences is based on a logical fallacy. Identify the logical fallacies with these labels: post hoc (PH), false analogy (FA), hasty generalization (HG), false dilemma (FD), or ad hominem (AH).

_____ 1. I trained my dog not to wet on the carpet by rubbing his nose in the "mess" he created; therefore, I will potty train my children by rubbing their noses in the "messes" they make.

_____ 2. The continued use of nuclear energy will lead to either nuclear war or catastrophic nuclear accidents.

_____ 3. Everyone in the front office is dipping Lippy Snuff. I figure it's the hottest item on the market.

_____ 4. Our dog eats only once a day, and look how healthy he is. I don't know why you kids keep yellin' for three meals a day.

_____ 5. No wonder she's been going around crying all day. Yesterday the government slapped a tax on Lippy Snuff.

_____ 6. I refuse to listen to his musical interpretation of the Yalta Conference because he's a card-carrying member of the ACLU.

_____ 7. Either we cave in to the terrorist demands, or we strike back with nuclear weapons.

_____ **8.** After watching the high school kids on the bus today, I would say that the whole education system could use a required course in manners.

_____ **9.** It's no wonder my Winnebago exploded today. Yesterday I bought a tank of cheap gasoline.

_____ **10.** I wouldn't trust him as far as I can throw a heifer. He rides a Harley and drinks Rebel Yell.

CAREER-RELATED WRITING AS ARGUMENT

Proposals for the Workplace

In the workplace, the proposal is the purest expression of persuasion. Yet it does not have a precise form, for there are different kinds of proposals and different situations from which proposals arise. In this chapter, we will attempt to summarize the main forms and purposes of the proposal, but we will not try to teach how to write a long, complicated one that requires extensive research. Learning to work with the basic form will give you useful practice in this kind of writing. On the job you will experience the many ways of framing proposals.

Notice the remarkable similarities between conventional college writing assignments and workplace proposals.

Paragraph or Essay of Persuasion (or Argument)	**Proposal**
Background (placing the issue into a social or historical perspective)	Background (indicating the problem or the need, emphasizing the urgency)
Proposition, with possible qualification	Solution to the problem, or need, stated concisely
Possible refutation	Possible explanation of why other solutions are inadequate
Support (reasoning and evidence)	In detail, what you can do
Support (reasoning and evidence)	How you can do it
Support (reasoning and evidence)	When you can do it
Support (reasoning and evidence)	What it will cost
Conclusion (clinching statement)	Conclusion (emphasizing the problem and solution)

The body of your proposal will usually have the parts shown in the proposal list. You will be able to determine what is necessary. For example, if you are proposing a change in procedure for an internal solution to a problem such as miscommunication, the cost may not be mentioned. As for order, the sequence shown in the list is common, but you can easily change the sequence to fit your needs.

Longer and highly technical proposals often begin with an executive summary, a statement that carries the major ideas but not the explanations. Such a component would be read by executives, who would depend on others to evaluate and report on the remaining parts of the extensively detailed proposal.

An example of an annotated student proposal, "Abolish Homework in Elementary School," appears on page 484.

FINDING PATTERNS IN PHOTOS

EXERCISE 2   A Text-Based Activity for Groups or Individuals

Security cameras watching workstation

Examine the photo carefully. Imagine you are standing in a hallway that looks into the depicted work area covered by six surveillance cameras. Your role is that of a shop steward, a person on the collective bargaining unit. Tomorrow you will meet with the management bargaining team to discuss the upcoming contract. The cameras were installed yesterday. Your fellow worker, who sits under those cameras, has asked you to have them removed. You have checked the contract and found that there are no clauses mentioning the placement of workplace cameras. You hastily call a meeting after work. You are on good terms with management, so you ask several members of their team to meet with your group for an unofficial, informal discussion. You need to discover why management thinks the surveillance cameras are necessary and why your fellow workers want them removed. You bring a flip chart to the conference room so you can write down reasons for and reasons against the use of surveillance cameras in what has been semi-private work space. Then, still using your imagination, you make a list of reasons (in the space below) for using the cameras and another for not using the cameras. (This can become a role-playing activity with members of the two sides engaging in a spirited debate.)

Reasons for Using the Cameras

1. _____
2. _____
   _____
3. _____
4. _____
   _____
   _____
5. _____
   _____

Reasons Against Using the Cameras

1. _____
2. _____
3. _____
   _____
4. _____
   _____
5. _____
6. _____

After you have finished your lists and the individuals from management have gone away, your colleagues will decide either to accept the cameras or to demand that they be removed. You should then write a proposition with the reasons for your position. Your evidence will come from a list of the reasons for or reasons against the presence of cameras. You may include a refutation. It will include one or more of the points of opposition from the other list. (If your instructor directs you to do so, you will write a paragraph or a short essay of argument on these proceedings. The final position may instead be presented in class orally.)

Practicing Patterns of Argument

The formal pattern of argument is not always followed in a set sequence, but the main components—the proposition and support—are always included. As your own argument evolves, you should also consider whether to qualify your proposition and whether to include a refutation.

EXERCISE 3 Completing Patterns of Argument

Fill in the blanks with supporting statements for each proposition. Each outline uses the following pattern:

Proposition

    I. Support 1

    II. Support 2

    III. Support 3

A. Proposition: College athletes should be paid.

    I. _____

    II. They work long hours in practice and competition.

    III. They have less time than many other students for study.

B. Proposition: Zoos are beneficial institutions.

    I. _____

    II. They preserve endangered species by captive breeding.

    III. They study animal diseases and find cures.

EXERCISE 4 Completing Patterns of Argument

Complete the following outline. Use your own topic or write on the topic "There should be no curfew for teenagers" or "There should be a curfew for teenagers."

Proposition: _____

    I. _____ (Support 1)

    II. _____ (Support 2)

    III. _____ (Support 3)

EXERCISE 5   Completing Patterns of Argument

Complete the following outline. Use your own topic or write on the topic "Known gang members should be prohibited from using public parks" or "Known gang members should not be prohibited from using public parks."

Proposition: _____

I. _____   (Support 1)

II. _____   (Support 2)

III. _____   (Support 3)

Readings for Critical Thinking, Discussion, and Writing

READING STRATEGIES AND OBJECTIVES

Underlining and annotating these reading selections will help you answer the questions that follow the selections, discuss the material in class, and prepare for text-based writing assignments. As you underline and annotate, pay special attention to the author's writing skills, logic, and message, and consider the relevance of the material to your own experiences and values.

Some selections begin with a Mindset suggestion that can help you create a readiness for connecting with what you are about to read.

PARAGRAPH

The Most Underrated Candy Bar

PATRICIA VOLK

This long paragraph by essayist and novelist Patricia Volk is one unit in a series titled "Overrated and Underrated." It was published in American Heritage, *October 2004. Volk is the author of the memoir* Stuffed: Adventures of a Restaurant Family.

MINDSET

Lock It In

Imagine this is Halloween and you are holding your trick-or-treat bag open, wishing for your favorite candy bar—a _____!

Underrated   In 1923 the Curtiss Candy Company invented Butterfinger. Dropped from airplanes over major U.S. cities, it quickly became Curtiss's number two candy bar, a bite behind Baby Ruth. I buy mine at Lotto & Photo, 1391 Madison Avenue, 70 cents a pop. Weighing in at 2.1 ounces, that's a lot of candy for the money. When I was a kid, I opted for longevity over taste, hence filling-plucker Jujubes on Saturday at the movies and Bonomo's Turkish Taffy at the playground. Sucked correctly, it turned into a lethal weapon, same as a Sugar Daddy. I once kept a Tootsie Roll hidden in my shoe bag for a year and licked it every morning before school. Now I can afford a Butterfinger whenever I want one, but its lasting a long time still matters. A Butterfinger is a leisure-eating bar. It forces you to savor. No other candy bar is striated like shale. Its core shatters on your tongue. This makes a Butterfinger dissolve unevenly and mysteriously, leaving you with interesting hard bits to roll around in your mouth. The butter in Butterfinger refers to peanut butter, ground-roasted peanuts being its third ingredient after sugar and corn syrup. Everybody tastes things differently, and what I taste most strongly is molasses, the sixth ingredient, worked to the texture of high-end halvah, only brittler. I don't particularly like peanut butter except on fresh rye with Hellmann's mayo (don't knock it till you've tried it). There's a hint of caramelization in a Butterfinger too, not chewy caramel but the glassy kind that forms when sugar is heated to 310 degrees. The chocolate dip is important, but only for contrast, smooth versus shardy. Nestlé owns Butterfinger now, but Butterfinger chocolate is better than the chocolate in a Nestlé Crunch. For some horrible reason, Crunch has been tasting fruity lately. Butterfinger is one of the only candy bars that taste the same as they did when I was a kid. It never lets me down. I don't know why I'm not frightened by its preternatural orange Day-Glo color. A Butterfinger is only 270 calories, about the same as a fruit yogurt. Bart Simpson loves them too. He considers Butterfingers a food group.

EXERCISE 6   Discussion and Critical Thinking

1. What does Volk say are the qualities that make Butterfinger the most underrated candy bar?

2. Of the qualities discussed by Volk, which can be argued on the basis of evidence other than opinion?

3. How compelling is Volk's argument?

4. What is your favorite candy bar? How would you make a case that it is better than Butterfinger?

PAIRED ESSAYS: SHOULD GRANDPARENTS HAVE VISITATION RIGHTS?

In anticipation of a U.S. Supreme Court ruling on grandparents' visitation rights, two essays with opposing views were published in *USA Today*. One was written by the *USA Today* editorial board, the other by Richard S. Victor, an attorney and the founder of Grandparents' Rights Organization. Read the two essays carefully and reach your own conclusion. Your instructor will reveal to you what the U.S. Supreme Court decided, in what was named the *Troxel* case.

Stop Violating Parents' Rights

USA TODAY'S EDITORIAL BOARD

This essay is annotated to show how some of the principles for writing argument are used.

1   The heart-rending story is one any grandparent can identify with: After their son's suicide in 1993, grandparents Jenifer and Gary Troxel of Anacortes, Washington, longed to stay close to his two young daughters, Natalie and Isabelle.

Background

2   But the girls' mother, who'd never been married to young Troxel, was building a new life for herself and her children, including three from a previous marriage. She wanted to limit the girls' visits with their grandparents to once a month. So the Troxels did the American thing: They went to court.

3   Now they're in the U.S. Supreme Court, which hears arguments today on whether parents can be forced to permit their children to visit estranged grandparents, other relatives or, in some cases, acquaintances who can convince a judge they had some kind of past relationship with the kids.

Issue

4   The issue arises because legislators in all 50 states have responded to heart-wrenching tales of Nana and Gramps denied their "rights" to dote on their grandchildren. They've adopted laws authorizing such court-ordered visits over the objections of parents.

Refutation

5   The laws are a well-intentional effort to deal with the dissolution of the idealized nuclear family. But by trying to accommodate divorce, family feuds and nontraditional family arrangements, they open the door to interference with parents' right to raise their children without undue intrusion, even by grandparents. The Troxels' case is not unique:

Evidence: Example

- In Edwardsville, Illinois, a mother is in jail for refusing to comply with a court order won by her 7-year-old daughter's grandmother; she feels she has good reason to keep the two apart.

Evidence: Example

- And in another Washington case, after a man and his ex-wife's mother killed each other in a shootout, a judge granted his parents, brother, and sister the right to visit a daughter—who'd been conceived not by the dead man but through the mother's artificial insemination by another man.

Evidence: Authority

6   Some of the more bizarre awards have been overturned on appeal. More could be thrown out if the Supreme Court upholds its own previous rulings in favor of parents' rights.

7   In the Troxels' case, the mother of their granddaughters has married a man who adopted the children. But a judge, applying Washington's generous visitation law, ordered that the girls be handed over to the dead natural father's parents on a regular schedule. The state Supreme Court threw out

Evidence: Authority

the law, saying that barring a truly compelling state interest such as the health and safety of the child, parents have a fundamental right to control the rearing of their children.

8   The bruised feelings of wounded grandparents, while a family tragedy, aren't good-enough reason for legislatures and judges to interfere. And forced visits in such a poisoned atmosphere scarcely would seem to be in the best interest of a child.

Proposition (implied) with reasoned support

9   In an ideal world, family mediation services would be able to overcome the wounds that drive generations apart; the rights of parents and the understandable emotions of grandparents would be respected. But in this less-than-ideal world, when a family feud goes to court and nobody will compromise, parents' rights generally must be respected, even if it causes pain to others.

"Family" Includes Grandparents

RICHARD S. VICTOR

1   Bloodline and heritage are unbreakable links to kids. Properly written grandparent-visitation laws do not intrude into any protected interest or right of parents. In fact, if we were to eliminate the limited right these laws provide for nonparents to seek visitation with children, there would be cruel and far-reaching effects on loving relatives, particularly grandparents, depriving them of any contact with their grandchildren.

2   The reality of "family" has changed significantly in recent decades. The concept of parental autonomy, grounded in the assumption that parents raise their own children in nuclear families, is no longer to be taken for granted. According almost absolute deference to parental rights is now less compelling because the traditional nuclear family has eroded.

3   Grandparent-visitation laws did not create that erosion. More varied and complicated family structures have arisen because of divorce, decisions not to marry, single-parent families, remarriages and step-families, parents who abandon their children to temporary caretakers and children being raised by third parties because parents are deemed unfit.

4   It would be a significant disservice to the children of this country, who look at their families through their own eyes, to ignore their reality of what family is to them. We must recognize that in some families the parents are not necessarily legally related to the same people as their children. A woman who divorces her husband or a mother of children whose father has died may no longer be related to the grandparents of her children, but the children still have a connection through bloodline and heritage to their grandparents. They are family to that child.

5   Grandparent-visitation laws conditioned on visitation being in the child's best interest are expressing a fundamental liberty interest of both grandparent and grandchild. Should a parent, only one in the chain of three generations, be given constitutional sanction to amputate the family unit of the child?

6   If death takes a grandparent away from a grandchild, that is a tragedy. But if family bickering or vindictiveness denies a child the unconditional love of a grandparent, that is a shame. The Supreme Court and the Constitution should not condone a shame.

EXERCISE 7   Discussion and Critical Thinking

1. Setting aside your view of the issue, which essay is written more effectively?

2. What are the two positions on the existing state laws and why is the U.S. Supreme Court decision so important to this issue?

3. Victor's argument is largely based on what he sees as a necessity especially caused by the restructuring of families—the demise of the traditional nuclear family. He says, "Grandparent-visitation laws did not create that erosion [of the traditional nuclear family]" (paragraph 3). Assuming that divorce is the major cause of division in that family, then what if the grandparents and the great-grandparents were also divorced? That could make as many as twelve individuals altogether who should have rights. If we are not to "amputate the family unit" (paragraph 5), should that aspect also have been discussed? Why or why not?

4. Based on your experience, do you think that a U.S. Supreme Court ruling giving the power to parents would greatly decrease the visitation rate nationally by grandparents?

5. Does the word *tragedy* in the *USA Today* essay (paragraph 8) mean the same as *tragedy* in Victor's essay (paragraph 6), or is it more similar to Victor's word *shame* (paragraph 6)?

6. In this case full of complications, what is your position, what are your reasons, and finally what is your prediction for the decision by the U.S. Supreme Court?

ESSAYS

Letting Teachers Pack Guns Will Make America's Schools Safer

JOHN R. LOTT JR.

John R. Lott Jr., a resident scholar at the American Enterprise Institute, is the author of The Bias Against Guns *(Regnery, 2003). This article was first published in the* Los Angeles Times *in 2004.*

MINDSET

Lock It In

Imagined words from a soon-to-be-released major motion picture: "Around campus, there is only one way to stop the killers and the spoilers, and that is with an English professor and the smell of gun smoke!"

1   Banning guns from schools seems the obvious way to keep children safe. Utah, though, is doing the opposite, and is stirring up debate across the nation.

2   Acting under a new state law, school districts across Utah have started drawing up regulations allowing teachers and other public employees to carry

concealed guns on school property. Opponents are still trying to fight the law, and at first glance their concern about firearms in schools is understandable. Last Sunday in New Jersey, an attack by armed teenagers against three fellow students and randomly chosen townspeople was narrowly averted.

3   But that's not the whole picture. Consider an analogy: Suppose a criminal is stalking you or your family. Would you feel safe putting a sign in front of your home saying, "This Home Is a Gun-Free-Zone"? Law-abiding citizens might be pleased by such a sign, but to criminals it would be an invitation.

4   In 1985, just eight states had right-to-carry laws—laws that automatically grant permits for concealed weapons once applicants pass a criminal background check, pay their fees and when required, complete a training class. Today, 35 states do.

5   Examining all the multiple-victim public shootings in the United States from 1977 to 1999 shows that on average, states that adopt right-to-carry laws experience a 60% drop in the rates at which the attacks occur, and a 78% drop in the rates at which people are killed or injured from such attacks.

6   To the extent such attacks still occurred in right-to-carry states, they overwhelmingly take place in so-called "gun-free zones." Indeed, the attack last week in Meridian, Mississippi, in which five people were killed took place in a Lockheed Martin plant where employees were forbidden to have guns.

7   The effect of right-to-carry laws is greater on multiple-victim public shootings than on other crimes for a simple reason: Increasing the probability that someone will be able to protect himself improves deterrence. Though it may be statistically unlikely that any single person in a crowd is carrying a concealed handgun, the probability that at least one person is armed is high.

8   Contrary to many people's impressions, before the federal law was enacted in 1995 it was possible for teachers and other adults with concealed-handgun permits to carry guns on school property in many states.

9   Many of the concerns about accidents and other problems are unwarranted. The real problems at schools occurred only after the ban. The rash of student shootings at schools began in October 1997 in Pearl, Mississippi.

10   Public reaction against guns is understandable, given the horrific events shown on TV. But the more than 2 million times each year that Americans use guns defensively are never discussed. In more than 90% of those cases, simply brandishing a weapon is sufficient to cause a criminal to break off an attack. My research also shows that citizens with guns helped stop about a third of the post-1997 public school shootings, stepping in before uniformed police could arrive.

11   Last year, news broadcasts on the three main TV networks carried about 190,000 words on gun crime stories. Not one segment featured a civilian using a gun to stop a crime. Newspapers are not much better.

12   Police are extremely important in deterring crime, but they almost always arrive after the crime has been committed. Annual surveys of crime victims in the United States by the Justice Department show that when confronted by a criminal, people are safest if they have a gun.

13   Just as the threat of arrest and prison can deter criminals, so can the fact that victims can defend themselves.

14   For multiple-victim shootings, the biggest factor determining the amount of harm is the length of time between when an attack starts and when someone with a gun can stop the attack. The longer the delay, the more are harmed.

15   Good intentions do not necessarily make good laws. What counts is whether the laws ultimately save lives. Unfortunately, too many gun laws primarily disarm law-abiding citizens, not criminals.

EXERCISE 8   Discussion and Critical Thinking

1. In paragraph 3, Lott presents an analogy about a house posted as a gun-free zone. The opposite would be a gun-holding zone. Do you think Lott would prefer that schools be posted to indicate that educators are carrying firearms to deter potential troublemakers? How would you feel about that posting?

2. Lott mentions that the victims at the Meridian, Mississippi, firm were forbidden to have guns. Would you feel more secure or less secure if you knew that your fellow workers, or perhaps your adult fellow students at college, were carrying concealed firearms?

3. In paragraphs 8 and 9, Lott says the national law banning the carrying of concealed handguns on school property was passed in 1995 and then "the rash of student shootings at schools began" (paragraph 9). Is that statement logically sound or unsound?

4. In paragraphs 5 through 11, Lott offers much statistical support for his view. As a critical thinker, what questions should you ask about his use of statistics and reasoning?

A Modest Proposal: Guys Shouldn't Drive Till 25

JOYCE GALLAGHER

Freelance writer Joyce Gallagher says we should look at the national problem of motor vehicle accidents and take a "drastic" step. To Gallagher, statistics tell the story, and the solution is as inevitable to her as it may be unthinkable to you.

MINDSET

Lock It In

Imagine you are driving on a two-lane highway and you see a car with a male driver barreling toward you, riding the yellow line. Statistically, would you be better off if the driver were 18 or 80? Hint: "Age before beauty."

1   In the year 2001, 57,480 people were killed in motor vehicle accidents.* That figure is within a few hundred of being the same number as those killed in the Vietnam War. We took drastic measures back in the early 1970s and ended that war in a way shocking to some: we left. The time has come for another drastic scheme. We need to recognize the main causes of this highway carnage and take action. According to the U.S. Department of Transportation, 25.1 percent of the roadway fatalities involve an age group constituting only 14.5 percent of the driving public. That group is the age range from 15 to 25. Within that group, one half are males. They are three times more likely to be involved in roadway fatalities, meaning that about 7 percent of the males are responsible for more than 16 percent of roadway fatalities. This proposal

*All statistics in this article are from the U.S. Bureau of Transportation Statistics: www.bts.gov.

2   may be a hard sell for politicians, but it is time for us to step forward boldly and raise the legal driving age for males nationally to 25.

2   Some may protest that it is unfair to punish the good young male drivers for the sins of their irresponsible peers. But we're already discriminating by group. Surely we all agree that drivers of a certain age should not be allowed to drive. That age varies from state to state, but it is around 15. We have concluded that those younger than 15 are too immature. We don't say those under 15 should be treated individually, not even on the basis of gender. Instead, we exclude the offending group. With my proposal, we would simply move the legal age of male drivers to 25, lumping those of similar age and sex together for the good of society.

3   For you who would like to point out that some oldsters are also menaces on the roadways, I would say that those over 88 are equal only to those between 15 and 25 for being involved in fatal crashes. Moreover, the crashes by super-seniors are likely to be caused by physical and mental impairments, which can be detected by periodic tests and remedied by pulled licenses, whereas the young, often irresponsible and impatient, are more likely to be guided by thrill-seeking impulses, tantrums, and other byproducts of testosterone, all of which are hopelessly glandular.

4   Although one salient reason—that this group of young males is responsible for the deaths of so many fellow citizens—is enough support for the proposed law, there are many side benefits for society.

- While the male 15–25 age group is waiting to drive motor vehicles, they would have time to improve their cultural lives and to lay groundwork for better driving skills and improved mental and physical health.

- Many youngsters would customarily ride with statistically superior female or elder drivers and could learn from the relatively good examples they witness.

- Being no more dependent on driving almost everywhere, the male youngsters would walk more or ride bikes or skateboards, providing them wholesome exercise so often neglected in our paunchy, weight-challenged society.

- As a group they would also use more public transportation, relieving traffic congestion on our roadways and reducing congestion in the air we breathe.

- Support for public transportation projects would soar, and cars might cease to be near the center of our lives.

- Car payment money now impoverishing so many young males might go toward savings, education, home improvement, self-improvement, and family activities.

- Gratitude from young male drivers for the rides provided by female spouses and other loved ones could promote affectionate and appreciative relationships and diminish road rage.

5   The only exceptions to this new national law would be for the military and for public security and emergency agencies. Within the armed services, male personnel under 25 would be allowed to drive on foreign soil or on military property at any time. Male drivers working for police, fire, rescue, and ambulance services would drive only when on duty and their permits would be terminated for any serious traffic infraction. No doubt, some male youngsters, obsessed with driving motor vehicles, would join our public service sectors, making our national security and infrastructural services stronger so we could all sleep more peacefully.

6   Probably some males would protest this law and would try to circumvent it with devious strategies. Such resistance could be easily combated. For example, those who attempt to cross-dress or dye their hair gray for the purpose of obtaining a drivers' license could be charged with a felony.

7   Several people who have read my modest proposal have suggested that young men are victims of their own bodies and could plead a "testosterone dementia defense." Therefore, they should be allowed to take injections of estrogen to neutralize the male hormones raging like tiny bulls within their systems. However, even these critics would surely concede that there could be a feminizing reaction to estrogen, one both psychological and physiological. Because of those possible side effects, wives of young men might find estrogen therapy unacceptable. A youthful bride might willingly bear the burden of transporting her husband to work and back, whereas she would almost certainly recoil at the thought of his wearing her bra.

8   Some might argue that improved drivers' education programs in our school system, better public transportation, the production of vehicles that are no more powerful and threatening than they need be, a reduced speed limit, counseling and restrictions for repeat offenders, and a stricter enforcement of existing laws represent a wiser approach to our national problem. However, because those ideas have failed to resonate, and young males have continued to put the pedal to the metal in a flood of blood, it is time for a simple statement that will fit on your bumper sticker:

> # Guys Shouldn't
> # Drive Till 25

EXERCISE 9   Vocabulary Highlights

Write a short definition of each word as it is used in the essay. (Paragraph numbers are given in parentheses.) Be prepared to use these words in your own sentences.

carnage (1)	salient (4)
constituting (1)	terminated (5)
impairments (3)	sectors (5)
testosterone (3)	circumvent (6)
glandular (3)	estrogen (7)

EXERCISE 10   Discussion and Critical Thinking

1. Underline the proposition.

2. How is the proposition introduced in the first paragraph?

3. How is the proposition qualified?

4. Which paragraph covers the main rebuttal (addressing the main anticipated point[s] of the opposition)?

5. What is Gallagher's main support?

6. In what way are the bulleted items related to support?

7. Would this law create some problems not discussed by the author? If so, what kind?

8. Which of the bulleted items would you disagree with and why?

9. Do you think the author is entirely serious about this argument? What author comments might suggest that she is not?

10. What is the meaning and purpose of paragraph 8?

11. Does it make any difference that the author is female? Why or why not?

Should Teachers Let Failing Students Pass by Doing an "Extra Credit" Assignment?

JULIE BARLOW

Julie Barlow is an English teacher and a yearbook adviser in Layton, Utah. This brief essay was first published in NEA Today *as one part of a Yes or No feature on the topic of extra credit.*

1   As teachers, we're stuck between a rock and a hard place at the end of each term when students, parents, and even our colleagues are all sending us the message that we should just let students pass. And high-stakes testing is making it harder and harder for teachers to pass a student who obviously does not have the required skills.

2   But the other side of high-stakes testing is that it makes our students feel even more like they are just numbers, not individuals. Sometimes, to "leave no child behind" means we must look carefully into each student's life to find the best way to educate that student.

3   Several days ago a senior in one of my AP classes came in to thank me. Last term, I allowed her to make up a number of late assignments and receive some extra credit in order to pass. She had been absent a lot

because she had to find a second job when she was kicked out of her house. I pushed back every deadline and gave her more chances than I normally offer. She finished, barely.

4   It is true that I was not as accommodating for a student whose main excuse for absences was a snooze button, but even that student began getting calls from me at 6:30 a.m. You do what you can, when you can.

5   I rarely take late work. I push hard for kids to learn that deadlines are part of a real job, and most bosses won't care if you're having a bad day. My father owns a business and employs a number of high school students. Being a good student usually translates into being a good employee, whether it's showing up on time ready to work or following through with orders even when that takes extra time. I always feel responsible for teaching students those skills through deadlines and due dates.

6   But I also know that a student's well-being and individual needs must come first. In life, we must hope that someone will cut us some slack, not all the time, but once in a while when we are really desperate.

EXERCISE 11   Discussion and Critical Thinking

1. What is Barlow's proposition?

2. How does Barlow qualify her proposition?

3. What is the main function of the example?

READING-BASED WRITING

Just Say No to Extra Credit for Rescuing Failing Students

CARLA ESTRADA

Carla Estrada was required to write a short essay response to one of several essays that were being considered for the current edition of this textbook. As a prospective teacher herself, she was especially interested in "Should Teachers Let Failing Students Pass by Doing an 'Extra Credit' Assignment?" She had mixed feelings on the topic, and this reading-based essay would give her the opportunity to sort out her own thoughts as she evaluated the view of a veteran teacher.

Text identification   1   In "Should Teachers Let Failing Students Pass by Doing an 'Extra
Thesis   Credit' Assignment?" Professor Julie Barlow gives a lot of thought to a difficult question, but I believe she comes up with the wrong answer.

Quotation   2   Barlow "rarely take[s] late work" (40), and, in the example she pro-
Quotation   vides, she says she gave the student "more chances than [she would] normally offer" (40). She grants such exceptions because she believes "we
Quotation   must look carefully into each student's life to find the best way to educate that student" (40). That is where the problem lies in her argument. Just

how does a teacher with about 120 students learn enough about the lives of each one to make understanding exceptions across the classroom?

Topic sentence
Quotation

3   If two students have severe problems and one wants to keep his or her problem private, that person would get none of the "slack" (40) Barlow might be willing to offer. And what if two students have almost identical stories, and one student is lying? Some students have a lot of dying grandmas. Does the teacher look into the students' eyes and decide what is truth? Does the teacher investigate? Barlow says she did not accom-

Quotation

modate the student whose excuse was hitting the "snooze button" (40) too many times, but what if that student had a severe case of insomnia because of a family problem? Some instructors just say no to making exceptions because they cannot draw all those lines. If a troubled student is in the class of an instructor who makes no exceptions, that student may be resentful (rightfully) when an acquaintance in Barlow's class is given an extra credit escape.

4   Actually I am impressed by what Barlow says about helping people who are desperate. But I wish she had said something such as, "I do not like the idea of giving extra credit to let failing students pass. I have done it three times in my long career, but as a principle, I do not believe in it." She seems to be a good person who is dedicated to helping stu-

Restatement of thesis

dents. I think I would like to be in her class, but I do not believe that her idea of each instructor's allowing students to pass with the aid of extra credit is practical or fair.

Work Cited

Barlow, Julie. "Should Teachers Let Failing Students Pass by Doing an 'Extra Credit' Assignment?" *NEA Today* Apr. 2005: 40. Print.

STUDENT ESSAY

Writing Process Worksheet

Name Michael Holguin   **Title** Someone Is Listening   **Due Date** Monday, September 10, 10 a.m.

Use the back of this page or separate paper if you need more space.

Assignment

In the space below, write whatever you need to know about your assignment, including information about the topic, audience, pattern of writing, length, whether to include a rough draft or revised drafts, and whether your paper must be typed.

Write an essay of persuasion about a form of discrimination. Include three or more points of support. Write for an audience of those who have probably not experienced this discrimination. Submit this completed worksheet, one or more drafts, and a typed final draft.

Stage One

Explore Freewrite, brainstorm (list), cluster, or take notes as directed by your instructor.

Church	School	Home	Friends	Society
—Pastor	—Teachers	—Parents	—Daniel	—Effects
—Parents	—Coaches	—Siblings	—Terry	
—Victims' prayers	—Students		—Billy	

Stage Two   **Organize** Write a topic sentence or thesis; label the subject and focus parts.

<u>Gay youth</u> <u>suffer from treatment by those who should be helping</u>.
   subject   focus

Write an outline or an outline alternative. For reading-based writing, include quotations and references with page numbers as support in the outline.

   I. Church
      A. Pastors' condemnation
      B. Parents' agreement
      C. Gay children's prayers
  II. School system
      A. Ridicule by teachers
      B. Hatred by coaches
 III. Home
      A. Parents' insensitivity
      B. Siblings' embarrassment
  IV. Friends
      A. Daniel with AIDS in prison
      B. Terry bullied
   V. Results of pressure by society
      A. Unstable relationships
      B. Disease
      C. Suicide

Stage Three   **Write** On separate paper, write and then revise your paragraph or essay as many times as necessary for **c**oherence, **l**anguage (usage, tone, and diction), **u**nity, **e**mphasis, **s**upport, and **s**entences (**CLUESS**). Read your work aloud to hear and correct any grammatical errors or awkward-sounding sentences.

Edit any problems in fundamentals, such as **c**apitalization, **o**missions, **p**unctuation, and **s**pelling (**COPS**).

SOMEONE IS LISTENING
Michael Holguin

   In today's society there is a form of child abuse that not even Oprah talks about. Unlike some other forms of abuse, it knows no limitations—no ethnic, no religious, no educational, and no socioeconomic boundaries. Lives are destroyed by parents who act in fear and ignorance. Dreams are shattered by the cruel and hurtful words of friends. Every day, hundreds of gay youths hide in their rooms and cry from pain caused by the mean and careless behavior of those who claim to love them.

In a Judeo-Christian society it is common for families to attend church with their children. The pastor in some of these churches stands at the podium and announces, "Homosexuals are an abomination unto the Lord." The church walls shake from the resounding "Amen" from the congregation. The pastor continues, "Homosexuals are sick. Perverted. They are a danger to our children." In agreement the congregation once more says, "Amen." I know how this feels. As a gay person, I recall the pain of many Sundays during my childhood. I prayed extra hard for God's cure before someone would find out my secret and embarrass me and my family, because I remembered what had happened to Jason the year before. So I kept answering the altar call every Sunday when the unwanted feeling would not go away. The fear of rejection and eternal damnation made me too terrified to confide in anyone or to ask for help. After all, my parents seemed to tell me I deserved such a fate every time they said, "Amen."

Every day at school became more difficult to endure. I faced the jokes in the locker room. Even my best friend told some, and sometimes, to keep from being discovered, I told some. At this point, how much self-esteem could I have had? I cringed when my coach urged us to "kick those faggots' asses" but I still kicked. Yet every day my feelings were denied. My health teacher told us, "Someday you will all grow up and get married and have children." I could not understand why I had no such desire. I would turn on the television, and there would be a cop show on. This week's criminal was a gay child molester . . . again. I think *Baretta* had the same story the week before. I changed the station to *Barney Miller*, where there was an old man wearing a polyester jumpsuit and a silk scarf around his neck, and talking with a lisp. Couldn't they drop the lisp just once. I wonder. I cringe, thinking this is my inevitable fate, my curse.

By the time I reached my teen years, I had heard and seen so much negativity toward my "condition" that my life at home became plagued with constant fears. I became afraid of rejection. I knew my Christian family would think I was sick, perverted, and dangerous to children. Dad would be disappointed, even though I had six brothers to carry on the family name. Mom would not want me around because she would worry about what to tell Grandma and Grandpa. My brother would pretend he did not know me at school.

My fears were reinforced by close-up examples. Once I had a friend named Daniel, who was the son of a local preacher. I do not know where Daniel got the nerve at the age of twelve to tell his parents he was gay, but that is what he did. It was also at the age of twelve that his father put him out on the street after all the beatings failed to cure him. Daniel managed to stay alive on the streets as a prostitute. He is in prison now, dying of AIDS. The fear of rejection was real.

I learned how to fit in out of fear of humiliation but especially out of fear of physical abuse. I had seen Daniel's father and brothers beat him up almost daily. An even earlier memory from when I was very young involved a boy named Terry, who everyone knew was different. Some kids had figured Terry out. One day behind the school, way out in the field, four kids beat Terry up. Kicking and slugging him as he fell to the ground, they called out "Sissy" and "Queer" as they swung at him. We had only heard the word *queer* from the older boys, and no one was sure what it meant exactly. We had not encountered the word *faggot* yet. I suppose I did not like Terry much either, but I felt bad as I watched in terror, knowing that the next time it could be me that they considered "different."

After years of living with low self-esteem, a battered self-image, and a secret life, one's psyche tends to give out. The highest rate of teen suicide is among gay youths. In a recent five-year study, it was determined that fear of rejection was the number one cause of suicide among gay teenagers. After losing the loving environment of friends and families, many gays turn to other means for comfort. Drug and alcohol abuse is high among gays. Many turn to multiple lovers, looking for acceptance and emotional support. The result of this has been the devastating spread of AIDS. With nowhere to go, suicide often seems to be the only option. My friend Billy, when visiting his younger sister at his mother's home, would have to stay on the front porch and talk through the screen door at his mother's request. Last February, at the age of 19, Billy drove up to the mountains and there took his own life. Before he died he wrote on the hood of his car, "God, help me." I recall my own suicide attempt, which was the result of my inability to deal with a lifestyle everyone close to me was unable to accept. It was only my self-acceptance that eventually saved me from being a statistic.

When planning a family, people should ask themselves, "Will I love my children for who they are, or will I love them only if they are what I want them to be?" If people answer the latter, they should not be parents. The same kind of thing might be said for others who are responsible for helping children develop. Abuse comes in many forms, and ignorance and self-centeredness are usually its foundation. Parents, preachers, teachers, clergy, friends—please be cautious of what you say. The children are listening.

EXERCISE 12   Discussion and Critical Thinking

1. What are the sources of abuse of gay youth?

2. Why does this kind of abuse go largely unreported?

3. What is Holguin's main support? Underline and annotate the assertion (proposition) and the supporting points.

4. How did Holguin survive?

CAREER-RELATED WRITING: STUDENT PROPOSAL

Abolish Homework in Elementary School

EMILY LUCERO

While attending college part-time, Emily Lucero is already working in the field in which she intends to advance: She is a paid teacher's aide. She also has two children in junior high school and one in elementary school. This assignment had special appeal to her:

> *Write a proposal to the manager or managers of an organization or establishment for whom you are working or have worked, or for an organization or establishment with whom you have done business. Explain the problem, discuss its increasing urgency, and propose a solution. Your solution may be the modification, replacement, or removal of a practice or procedure that is having a bad effect on the clients it is intended to serve.*

> *Lucero knew just what she wanted to propose. For her class, she wrote a proposal about her work situation. It was a proposal she wanted to send to officials in the school district where she was employed. For now, she would submit it to her English instructor. It would give her practice in developing her writing skills and in crafting a formal proposal.*

> *Lucero's essay is annotated to indicate these aspects of a proposal: proposal statement, background, solution, inadequate solution, how to do it, when it can be done, what it will cost, and conclusion.*

Proposal/solution

Inadequate solution

Background

How

When

Cost

1   As a former room mother on five occasions, a lifetime PTA member, a paid teacher's assistant, and a student on my way to becoming a teacher, I have come to a conclusion that heretofore would have been shocking to me. <u>It is time to abolish homework in elementary school</u>. Suggestions by parents and teachers to cut back on assignments have failed because an unchallenged pressure for increasing homework comes from people who do not see the bad effects of it.

2   I have reached this position because all my experiences tell me that the current situation is bad and getting worse. Even in kindergarten, students do homework, and expectations are unrealistically high. I have seen children actually wet their pants upon receiving their homework assignments. Parents will tell you that their children routinely lose sleep time and are deprived of a relaxed family relationship because of homework assignments that all too frequently are lengthy and unclear. Seeing their children struggle with projects, these parents try to teach and often do the work themselves. Teachers and aides struggle to evaluate huge stacks of material each day and to explain to the students and parents what went right and wrong. Academic competition within schools and between schools turns assignments into an escalating homework war. Everywhere we see students getting burned out, dropping out of other activities, and becoming sluggish and overweight.

3   Therefore, I propose that homework be abolished. Instead of doing homework, students would be encouraged to read, visit museums, participate in community youth activities, and enjoy their families. Relieved of evaluating homework, instructors would teach an additional approximately thirty minutes each day, with the exact time to be agreed to by district management and the teacher's union. The extra time each day could be class work directed by teachers and supported by teachers' aides and parents volunteering as tutors. This program could be drawn up during summer workshops, piloted during the fall semester, and introduced campus-wide during the spring semester. The cost to the school district would be the pay for teachers in workshops and whatever salary adjust-

		ments might be necessary, as agreed to by management and faculty negotiators.
Conclusion	4	Abolishing homework would return formal education to the schools, relieve pressures at home, and restore childhood to our children.

EXERCISE 13   Discussion and Critical Thinking

1. Do you generally agree or disagree with Lucero's proposal? Explain.

2. What would you add to or delete from her proposal?

3. Do you think Lucero should or should not submit this to the school principal where she works? Why or why not?

Suggested Topics and Prompts for Writing Argument

STUDENT COMPANION SITE

For additional practice, visit www.cengage .com/devenglish/ brandon/spb6e.

You will find a blank Writing Process Worksheet on page 6 of this book and on your Student Companion Site. It can be photocopied or printed out, filled in, and submitted with your assignment, if your instructor directs you to do so.

READING-BASED WRITING

Reading-based writing requires you to read critically, write a reply that shows you understand what you have read, and give credit for ideas you borrow and words you quote. The form can be a summary, a reaction, or a two-part response (with separated summary and reaction). Documentation, in which you give credit for borrowed ideas and words, can be either formal (MLA) or informal, as directed by your instructor. Both the forms of reading-based writing and documentation are discussed with examples in Chapter 1. Definitions of the three forms follow.

Summary

* The summary is a statement presenting only the main points of what you have read by using different wording without altering the meaning, adding information, or showing bias.
* It is the purest form of reading-based writing.

Reaction

* In the reaction, the meaning of what you have read will be central to the topic sentence of your paragraph or to the thesis of your essay.
* Although the reaction is not a personal narrative by itself, it may include personal experience to explain elements of the text. For example, if your source is

about driving styles, your own experiences as a driver or an observer of drivers could be relevant in your analysis of the text.

- The reaction may incorporate a summary to convey a broad view of what you have read, but your summary should never be the main part of your reaction.

Two-Part Response

- The two-part response separates the summary from the reaction.
- This form will give you practice in separating your objective summary in the first part from your more personal evaluation, interpretation, or application in the second part, the reaction.

READING-BASED WRITING TOPICS

"Stop Violating Parents' Rights"

1. Write a two-part response to this essay. Separate your summary from your reaction. In your reaction, evaluate the argument by the *USA Today* editorial board and either agree or disagree with it as you comment on what the author says and should have said. Use references to and quotations from the essay.

"'Family' Includes Grandparents"

2. Write a two-part response to this essay. Separate your summary from your reaction. In your reaction, evaluate the argument by Victor and either agree or disagree with him as you comment on what he says and what he should have said. Use references to and quotations from the essay.

Paired Essays: "Should Grandparents Have Visitation Rights?"

3. Write an essay in which you argue that grandparents should or should not have visitation rights; include quotations and references from both essays. Be sure to include your stated proposition, refutation, and at least two points of support.

"Letting Teachers Pack Guns Will Make America's Schools Safer"

4. Write a paragraph or an essay of reaction in which you generally agree or disagree with Lott. Be specific. Evaluate Lott's logic and use of evidence. Refer to and quote from the essay.

5. Write a two-part response with separate summary and reaction parts to Lott's essay. Keep in mind that the summary gives only the main points and the reaction is your view of the work. Be specific. Use references and quotations.

"A Modest Proposal: Guys Shouldn't Drive Till 25"

6. Write an argument in which you either agree or disagree with Gallagher's views. Refer to and quote from the essay. Make it a critique of specifically what she said and what she means. Consider using examples from your own experience and observations.

7. Write a paragraph or an essay in which you discuss Gallagher's purpose and technique. Is Gallagher serious in what she is saying, or does she exaggerate

to make her point? What phrases or ideas suggest her tone? Be specific and document your work. The title is based on a famous work by Jonathan Swift: "A Modest Proposal." You can find a copy on the Internet by keying in "Jonathan Swift" and "A Modest Proposal" on a search engine such as Google. Explain how being familiar with Swift's essay helps you understand Gallagher's message.

"Just Say No to Extra Credit for Rescuing Failing Students"

8. Write a paragraph or a short essay of argument in which you agree with Barlow, the teacher, or one in which you side with Estrada, the student. Consider using examples from your own experience or from personal knowledge. Refer to and use quotations from one or both essays.

"Someone Is Listening"

9. Write a paragraph or an essay in which you advocate some specific kind of program in schools that would alleviate the problem of homophobia in schools. Refer to and use quotations from this essay.

GENERAL TOPICS

10. Write a paragraph or an essay about something else that is underrated or overrated, such as a car, a movie, an actor, a type of food, a fast-food establishment, a drink, a politician, a performer, a teacher, a market, a game, or a sport. Write with the intention of persuading your readers to accept your view. For a useful example of form, review "The Most Underrated Candy Bar" on pages 469–470.

11. The following are broad subject areas. You will have to limit your focus for a paragraph or an essay of argument. Modify the subject to correspond with your experiences and interests. Some of these subjects will benefit from research in the library or on the Internet. Some will overlap with subject material from classes you have taken and with studies you have made.

    a. School drug tests

    b. School metal detectors

    c. Sex education

    d. Defining sexual harassment

    e. Changing the juvenile justice system

    f. Endangered species legislation

    g. Advertising tobacco

    h. Combating homelessness

    i. State-run lotteries

    j. Jury reform

    k. Legalizing prostitution

    l. Cost of illegal immigration

m. Installation of local traffic signs

n. Foot patrols by local police

o. Change in (your) college registration procedure

p. Surveillance by video (on campus, in neighborhoods, or in shopping areas)

q. Zone changes for stores selling liquor

r. Curfew for teenagers

s. Laws keeping known gang members out of parks

CROSS-CURRICULAR TOPIC

12. From a class you are taking or have taken or from your major area of study, select an issue on which thoughtful people may disagree and write an essay of persuasion or argument.

    a. An interpretation of an ambiguous piece of literature for an English class

    b. A position on global warming, public land management, or the Endangered Species Act for a class in ecology

    c. An argument about the effectiveness of a government program in a political science class

    d. A view on a certain kind of diet in a food-science class

    e. A preference for a particular worldview in a class on philosophy

    f. An assertion on the proper role of chiropractors as health care practitioners in a health-science class.

CAREER-RELATED TOPICS

Write a proposal to solve a problem in your family, neighborhood, school, or workplace. The problem is likely to be the purchase or modification of something, the introduction or modification of a procedure, or the introduction of a service. For this assignment, use basically the same form regardless of the location or circumstances of the problem. You can use a basic pattern, background, solution (as a proposition), support (how it can be done, when it can be done, what it will cost, if anything). The problem that you are proposing to alleviate or eliminate can be based on your experiences or it can be purely fictional. If you are suggesting the purchase of an item or items to solve a problem, the Internet can provide you with prices and specifications. Those data could be integrated into your proposal or photocopied and attached, with references.

For a useful model of form for a brief proposal, review "Abolish Homework in Elementary School" on page 484.

Following are a few specific topic suggestions:

13. Home

    a. Contracting with a gardener or a housekeeper

    b. Dividing the chores

    c. Respecting the privacy and space of others

14. Neighborhood

   a. Limiting noise

   b. Dealing with dogs—vicious, wandering, barking

   c. Parking recreational vehicles out front

15. College

   a. Parking

   b. Enrollment and registration

   c. Classroom procedure

   d. Safety

16. Workplace

   a. Time-saving equipment

   b. Doing your job (or part of it) at home rather than at the workplace

   c. Fringe benefits

   d. Evaluation procedures

   e. Staggering lunch hours and work breaks

   f. Communication between workers on different shifts

WRITER'S GUIDELINES   Argument

1. Ask yourself the following questions; then consider which parts of the persuasive statement or argument you should include in your essay.

   - *Background*: What is the historical or social context for this controversial issue?
   - *Proposition* (the topic sentence of the paragraph or the thesis of the essay): What do I want my audience to believe or to do?
   - *Qualification of proposition*: Can I limit my assertion so that those who disagree cannot easily challenge me with exceptions?
   - *Refutation* (taking the opposing view into account, mainly to point out its fundamental weakness): What is the view on the other side, and why is it flawed in reasoning or evidence?
   - *Support*: In addition to sound reasoning, can I use appropriate facts, examples, statistics, and opinions of authorities?

2. The basic pattern of a paragraph or an essay of persuasion or argument is likely to be in this form:

   Assertion (the topic sentence of the paragraph or the thesis of the essay)

   I. Support 1

   II. Support 2

   III. Support 3

3. The proposal has the following parts, which can be adjusted to a particular need:

- Background (indicating the problem or the need, emphasizing the urgency)
- Solution to the problem, or need, stated concisely
- Possible explanation of why other solutions are inadequate
- In detail what you can do
- How you can do it
- When you can do it
- What it will cost
- Conclusion (emphasizing the problem and the solution)

4. Write and revise.

STUDENT COMPANION SITE

For additional practice, visit www.cengage .com/devenglish/ brandon/spb6e.

- Write and then revise your paragraph or essay as many times as necessary for **c**oherence, **l**anguage (usage, tone, and diction), **u**nity, **e**mphasis, **s**upport, and **s**entences (**CLUESS**). Read your work aloud to hear and correct any grammatical errors or awkward-sounding sentences.
- Edit any problems in fundamentals, such as **c**apitalization, **o**missions, **p**unctuation, and **s**pelling (**COPS**).

Text Credits

Author/Title Index

Subject Index